I0061541

Immigration and National Identities in Latin America

UNIVERSITY PRESS OF FLORIDA

Florida A&M University, Tallahassee
Florida Atlantic University, Boca Raton
Florida Gulf Coast University, Ft. Myers
Florida International University, Miami
Florida State University, Tallahassee
New College of Florida, Sarasota
University of Central Florida, Orlando
University of Florida, Gainesville
University of North Florida, Jacksonville
University of South Florida, Tampa
University of West Florida, Pensacola

IMMIGRATION AND NATIONAL IDENTITIES IN LATIN AMERICA

EDITED BY NICOLA FOOTE
AND MICHAEL GOEBEL

University Press of Florida

Gainesville · Tallahassee · Tampa · Boca Raton

Pensacola · Orlando · Miami · Jacksonville · Ft. Myers · Sarasota

This book may be available in an electronic edition.

21 20 19 18 17 16   6 5 4 3 2 1

First cloth printing, 2014
First paperback printing, 2016

Library of Congress Control Number: 2014937652
ISBN 978-0-8130-6000-2 (cloth)
ISBN 978-0-8130-5402-5 (pbk.)

The University Press of Florida is the scholarly publishing agency
for the State University System of Florida, comprising Florida
A&M University, Florida Atlantic University, Florida Gulf Coast
University, Florida International University, Florida State University,
New College of Florida, University of Central Florida, University of
Florida, University of North Florida, University of South Florida,
and University of West Florida.

University Press of Florida
15 Northwest 15th Street
Gainesville, FL 32611-2079
http://www.upf.com

Contents

Illustrations

Acknowledgments

The idea for this book originally emerged out of a panel of the Annual Conference of the British Society for Latin American Studies held at the University of Bristol in 2010, although the editors of this book go back even further to their PhDs in history at University College London.

Over the months and years, we assembled a group of contributors that would allow us to cover the broadest ground possible in the history of immigration to Latin America; we are, above all, immensely grateful to our contributors, some of whom have been willing to make time in their busy schedules at extremely short notice to produce a chapter for this book, as well as to the peer reviewers who provided such insightful comments.

The book would have been impossible without institutional and financial support through a Marie Curie Career Integration Grant and a John F. Kennedy Fellowship at the Center for European Studies, Harvard University, which allowed Michael Goebel to find time and financial support for this book.

Nicola Foote is grateful to Florida Gulf Coast University (FGCU) for the award of sabbatical leave for the 2012–13 academic year, which provided the time away from teaching responsibilities necessary to complete this book. Thanks also to Dean Donna Henry and to Eric Strahorn for providing travel money for archival work related to this project in 2010 and 2011. The library staff at FGCU was essential to this project. Thanks to Rachel Tait for her help with interlibrary loan, and to Rachel Cooke for obtaining manuscript materials from the National Archives. Thanks to Erik Carlson for pushing for funding for library materials that supported this project. Thanks to Tim Shannon for help with formatting illustrations.

Nicola Foote was also able to benefit from the wonderful resources at the Smathers Latin America Collection at the University of Florida. Thanks especially to Paul Losch and Richard Phillips for their helpful suggestions and encouragement during multiple research trips. Thanks also to Marcel Carter for help with transportation to and from the library.

Several research assistants helped with the preparation of this volume. Thanks to Philine Apenburg, Norma Ladewig, and Tristan Oestermann at Freie Universität Berlin, whose assistance was financed through the Marie Curie Grant. Thanks also to Michael Rodriguez of FGCU, who did amazing work in compiling the bibliography and helping to format the manuscript. Thanks also to John Cox who helped with proofreading the volume proposal.

Thanks to Duke University Press for permission to publish maps previously published in Lara Putnam's chapter "The Making and Unmaking of the Circum-Caribbean Migratory Sphere: Mobility, Sex across Boundaries, and Collective Destinies, 1840–1940, in Dirk Hoerder and Nora Faires, eds., *Migrants and Migration in Modern North America: Cross-Border Lives, Labor Markets, and Politics in Canada, the Caribbean, Mexico, and the United States* (Durham, N.C.: Duke University Press, 2011). Thanks also to Daniel Sacroisky for permission to publish his cartoon that originally appeared in *Plural JAI*, Buenos Aries, May 5, 2012.

At University Press of Florida, Amy Gorelick was a wonderful source of help and support as we developed this project, and we are grateful for her enthusiasm for the volume. Meredith Babb has been an excellent editor and extremely helpful in the later stages of this project. Thanks also to Sian Hunter and Dennis Lloyd for their assistance with this volume.

On a personal note, Nicola would like to thank Carlos King for being such a wonderful, supportive, and loving husband during the preparation of this volume, as well as her parents, Margaret and Jeff Foote, for allowing their holidays to be diverted to Gainesville so that she could do some library work for this project.

Introduction

Reconceptualizing Diasporas and National Identities in Latin America and the Caribbean, 1850–1950

MICHAEL GOEBEL

What's the recipe for a Turk? Take the 25 de Março Street cocktail shaker and put in a Syrian, an Armenian, a Persian, an Egyptian, a Kurd. Shake it up really well and—boom—out comes a Turk.

Guilherme de Almeida, 1929

Migrations to Latin America and the Caribbean, 1850–1950

Even though Latin America has been a continent primarily of emigration during the last decades, historically the region has been one of mass immigration. One aim of this book is to provide an overview of the history of migrations to Latin America between 1850 and 1950. In contrast to much of the previous scholarship, this volume does so by specifically examining the interaction between transnational migrations and the formation of national identities. Building on the fields of migration studies and nationalism theory, neither the nation-states from which migrants came nor those to which they moved are seen as preexisting but are rather in a continual processes of being (re)defined. By analyzing these processes from a comparative angle, the book seeks to engage Latin American and Caribbean history more firmly with recent approaches to the history of global migrations at the height of the worldwide spread of nationalism. In order to make room for examining less-studied groups such as the Chinese, and for analyzing the long-term repercussions of immigration to Latin America, the book chooses the unusual time frame of 1850–1950 instead of the more common 1870–1930, the period during which the largest numbers of foreign immigrants arrived.

Although the well-known arrival of conquistadors and African slaves during the period of the Iberian empires had turned Latin America, strictly speaking, into a region of "immigration" well before the period studied in this volume, the inflow of peoples between 1850 and 1950 (concentrated especially in the six decades after 1870) was quantitatively unprecedented, embedded within a larger set of global migrations, of which those across the Atlantic were only the best known.[1] The main destinations within Latin America were, in descending order, Argentina, Brazil, Cuba, Uruguay, and Chile. Roughly 4 million immigrants settled permanently in Argentina between 1870 and 1930, 2 million to 3 million in Brazil, and perhaps 1 million in Cuba and 300,000 in Uruguay. Since in some countries, such as Argentina and Uruguay, the preexisting population was small, the relative impact of these immigrations was sometimes greater than the impact of immigrations to the United States. Uruguay's population grew sevenfold in the second half of the nineteenth century, and Argentina's quadrupled, mainly due to immigration.[2] As was the case in the United States, Europe furnished the greatest numbers of immigrants in Latin America, with Italy and Spain being the two most important sending countries in quantitative terms, followed by a number of other European countries, such as Portugal, Germany, the British Isles, and France. In addition, especially after World War I, there were growing numbers of Eastern Europeans, among them many Jews, migrating to Latin America just as they did to the United States.

But Europe was by no means the only sending region of migrants to Latin America. From the 1850s Chinese workers went to Cuba, other Caribbean countries, and Peru. After 1900 Peru and especially Brazil began to receive significant numbers of Japanese. Middle Easterners, mainly from today's Lebanon and Syria, arrived in virtually all Latin American countries, and in especially large numbers in Argentina and Brazil. Armenians, too, came to settle in cities such as Buenos Aires, São Paulo, and Montevideo. Migrants from the British West Indies, often working for North American railway or fruit companies, began to form significant, if marginalized, parts of the populations of countries such as Costa Rica, Panama, and Ecuador, while many Haitians went to neighboring Cuba. Colonial Caribbean countries, meanwhile, saw the mass arrival of Asian indentured laborers, who altered the population structure of Surinam, British Guiana, and Trinidad.

Furthermore, migrations within Latin America, both internal and between countries, often neighboring ones, set in on a larger scale, leading to the growth of urban centers such as Mexico City, São Paulo, or Buenos Aires, the latter two of which had initially expanded mainly due to transatlantic migrations. All these movements had far-reaching impacts on the national identities of virtually all Latin American countries, which at the same time were being constructed and continually renegotiated.

Although the broadest population movements are well known to specialists, the histories of the many migrations into Latin America and the Caribbean between 1850 and 1950 remain understudied when compared to the parallel experience of the United States. While there are countless studies of individual migrations, much of the literature on the topic is compartmentalized into individual case studies. In spite of a body of comparative scholarship slowly building up,[3] a large proportion of studies, many of which are written by the descendants of immigrants themselves, continue to focus on one "ethnic" or "national" group within one receiving nation-state because of a lack of funds for cross-national research in Latin American universities and the ongoing weight of methodological nationalism both within Latin America and among historians outside the region, who tend to be specialized in individual national histories. As a consequence of this as well as the overwhelming global power of Anglo-American academe in terms of theory-building, Latin American migratory histories have had a limited impact compared to those of the United States. Though in declining measure, theoretical models derived from the Chicago School of sociology—especially the opposition between "assimilation" and "pluralism"—continue to be the framework in which historical migration to Latin America is mostly being discussed. Since mass migration to Latin America declined sharply from 1930, the scholarship on historical migrations to Latin America, eventually left to historians alone, has been less influenced by more recent theoretical models than by the historiography on migration to the United States, where, due to ongoing immigration, disciplines other than history continued to influence the methods and approaches of migration studies. This disjunction is all the more regrettable because the nature of Latin America's immigration histories can tell us a great deal about migratory processes more generally. Building on a growing literature that complicates straightforward assumptions about the relationship between migrations and national identities, this book seeks to contribute to redressing this problem.

Migration Studies and Theories of Nationalism

One obstacle to setting this right is that, in spite of their obvious related-ness, migration studies and theories of nationalism have developed in a curious separation from one another. The major paradigms of migration studies were long informed by the experience of migration to the United States, in particular the so-called second wave that set in around 1890 and brought primarily Southern and Eastern Europeans to North America. From the 1920s the Chicago School of sociology dominated the field for several decades by studying the "assimilation" of these immigrants into American society. Although the ideas of this school were not monolithic internally, most of the scholars associated with it—ranging from Robert E. Park and W. I. Thomas to Louis Wirth and Milton Gordon—studied the degree to which immigrants retained or gave up their cultural bag-gage in the process of fusing into what was frequently called the "American mainstream."[4] The thrust of the underlying assumptions was that immi-grants should and eventually would shed their old-world habits in order to achieve social upward mobility as well as to allow for the creation of a viable American identity.

From the 1960s such arguments were challenged by a new generation of migration scholars, sometimes called "pluralists" or "retentionists." Al-though, ironically, "assimilation" as understood by the Chicago School had by then arguably become a reality of American society, the pluralists pro-claimed that assimilation was neither realistic nor desirable.[5] Instead of focusing on macro social developments and statistics, which appeared to corroborate the decline of the importance of distinctions based on ethnic origin, these authors concentrated on the micro level of migratory chains and networks, which they found helped the survival of the immigrants' and their descendants' cultural and ethnic particularities. It was no coin-cidence that this paradigm change in migration studies came alongside the civil rights movement and a general upsurge in identity politics. Being a backlash against earlier assumptions of Anglo-conformity, the writings of "pluralists" sometimes stressed the "roots" of immigrants and "ethnics" as if these were primordial and unchangeable.[6] Yet both "assimilationists" and "pluralists" spent little time on conceptualizing the "mainstream." This shortcoming has been pointed out in relation to the Chicago School, but it can also be extended to its "pluralist" challengers.[7] The problem could well be attributed to a much broader one identified by Nina Glick Schiller and Andreas Wimmer—namely, the blind eye of mainstream sociology for the rise and ongoing importance of nationalism owing to an implicit and unacknowledged methodological nationalism.[8]

Thinking about the "mainstream" was left to a different field of study: that of nationalism. Similarly to migration studies, theories of nationalism have been bedeviled by a dichotomy, dividing "constructivists" or "modernists" such as Benedict Anderson, Ernest Gellner, and Eric Hobsbawm from "primordialists," "perennialists" or "ethno-symbolists" such as Anthony Smith. Whereas the former have insisted that nations are "invented" or "imagined" and that "it is nationalism which engenders nations and not the other way round," the latter have typically stressed that such inventions are restricted by the available "raw material" from which nationalism is built and that "a state's ethnic core shapes the character and boundaries of a nation."[9] Ironically, the constructivist viewpoint in theories of nationalism predominated in the 1970s and '80s, precisely at the time when the arguably more primordially inclined "retentionists" seemed to be carrying the day in migration studies. Communication between these fields was minimal, further limited by disciplinary boundaries (the best-known migration scholars were often sociologists, while the major theorists of nationalism came more often from history, political science, or anthropology) as well as geographical separation (migration studies were dominated by American academics, while British-based scholars made a greater impact in theories of nationalism).

Just as the most influential authors on migrations showed little concern to conceptualize nationalism, the most-read scholars of nationalism rarely had a major interest in migrations.[10] Although theorists of nationalism such as Anderson, Craig Calhoun, or Elie Kedourie studied how the idea of the nation—what Anderson has called the "modular" form of nationalism—traveled around the globe, they related these movements to intellectual transfers rather than the mass flows of peoples that interested students of migration.[11] Moreover, as Rogers Brubaker has remarked, an overriding concern with the *origins* of nations and nationalism gave rise to an implicit tendency, even among constructivists, to see nations as relatively stable entities once they had been invented by nationalists.[12] If migrants did come into the picture, their role was that of real or potential challengers of an already existing national identity.

Over the last two decades, the dichotomous structuring of both migration studies and nationalism theories has largely been worn away. Migration scholars who had been trying to reappraise the concept of "assimilation" are now stressing that this term cannot be understood without granting serious attention to the transformations of the "mainstream" as a result of migrations.[13] Numerous studies have shown that, depending on context-specific variables, there is no strict opposition between the retention of ethnic networks and the adjustment into receiving societies. In many instances ethnic networks worked as promoters of, not as obstacles to, assimilation.[14] Nor was there a straightforward relationship between the declining importance of ethnic distinctions and socioeconomic upward mobility.[15] Historians of migrations, including those to Latin America, have moved away from privileging either macro social phenomena or a micro approach. By integrating the two, they have arrived at more nuanced interpretations of how migrations were open-ended processes shaped by conditions in a number of interlinked localities instead of a definite movement from one place to another with a fixed outcome.[16] In theories of nationalism, the old divide between "perennialists" and "constructivists" has survived to this day. But when it comes to concrete historical studies, most scholars would now pursue a combined approach that examines the interaction between the efforts of the state and intellectuals to forge national identities and the popular customs that they belabor.[17]

Parallel to the development of theoretically more open frameworks, historical studies of both immigrations and the formation of national identities in Latin America have expanded enormously over the last decades. Nonetheless, in both fields the dearth of historical scholarship on Latin America in comparison to other world regions and, particularly, the limited impact of studies on the region's history on theory-building continue to be rightfully lamented. The major theorists of nationalism have relegated Latin America to a few uneasy footnotes, admitting that its history may sit uncomfortably with their overarching frameworks. But this has rarely impelled them to question their models.[18] Likewise, the region's immigration history has usually at best served as a counterexample to the North American case with which it has been compared in terms of the relative "integration" of immigrants into the receiving societies. As summarized by Eduardo Míguez, the most prominent argument has been that "it is likely that the integration of immigrants into the local society was faster and more successful in many of the migrant flows that arrived in Spanish and Portuguese America than in their North American counterparts."[19] Regardless of whether one concurs with this statement (or whether an agreement can be reached on what "integration" and "successful" mean), the contribution of studies on historical immigrations into Latin America to the conceptual tools of migration studies has been minimal.

More problematically still, notwithstanding the changes within both fields of study during recent decades, when immigration and nationalism have been studied together, the pair has usually been conceptualized in a binary opposition, where nationalism is almost equated with nativism and xenophobia. Apart from the exacerbating factor of the divide between migration studies and nationalism theories, three interrelated reasons are responsible for this tendency: first, the predominant focus in historical migration studies on the second wave of migrations to the United States and its related history of negative prejudice against immigrants perceived as ethnically different; second, contemporary public debates on immigration, especially in Europe and the United States, with their usual concentration on the question of the extent to which immigrants "fit" into presumably preexisting "national identities"; and third, partially a result of all the above, a frequent implicit narrowing down of the very term "migration" in scholarly as well as wider public debates to those migrations that cross national boundaries and are seen as culturally very different. The problem, therefore, is not a specifically Latin American one.[20]

Yet, if (European) immigrants to Latin America were—as much of the historiography comparing North America and South America has it—more often met with positive rather than negative prejudice, and if immigrant incorporation coincided with the clearer formulation of national identities across the region rather than succeeding it, then Latin American history might help complicate any plain dichotomy between migration and national identity. Historians of nationalism and national identity constructions in Latin America are in fact lamenting that there is too little transnational work in their field and that "we need to know far more about the international context in which national identities evolved, about the transfer of people, ideas and images in both directions."[21] Yet, in spite of such demands, most scholars continue to be steeped and interested in *either* migrations *or* the study of nationalism, and when attempts have been made to combine the two, this was done mostly through an opposition between migrations and national identities.

Interactions between Transnational Migrations and Constructions of National Identities in Latin America

To be sure, there are countless Latin American examples of discrimination, racism, xenophobia, and types of nationalism that advocated assimilationist policies toward immigrant communities and their descendants. Many of the contributions to this volume testify to the recurrence of prejudice against immigrants as outsiders. Although in the mid-nineteenth century many Latin American political elites were enthusiastic about "civilizing" or "whitening" their countries through European immigration, they grew more skeptical over time as results failed to yield the envisaged outcomes. As the chapters by Stefan Rinke and Frederik Schulze show, this change in attitudes affected even those who initially had been among the most coveted groups to "whiten" Latin American countries, such as the Germans. In the eyes of Brazilian elites, Germans turned into dangerously isolationist aliens, especially during World War I. Jeane DeLaney's contribution in this volume on Argentine elites' attitudes toward immigration reveals a similar change over time. The writer-statesman Domingo Faustino Sarmiento, for example, was a fervent advocate of (ideally northern) European immigration in the 1850s and '60s, but by the 1880s he railed against the "Italianization" of Argentina.[22] Against the background of anarchist political activities, the Argentine government of Julio A. Roca passed a residency law in 1902 allowing for the easier expulsion of foreigners.[23] In several countries, various forms of anti-Semitism developed alongside right-wing Catholic nationalisms, erupting in serious ethnic violence during Argentina's so-called tragic week in 1919.[24]

The majority of chapters in this volume also mention that by the 1930s governments enacted laws to curb the entry of migrants.[25] Even long before then, discriminatory legislation existed in some places. As early as 1890, the supposedly liberal Uruguayan state enacted a law that tried to stimulate the immigration of Europeans but specifically forbade the entry of Africans, Asians, and "Gypsies," which had little effect in practice because none of these three groups intended to migrate to Uruguay in large numbers at the time. The measures of the 1930s, however, did affect many immigrants. The authoritarian regime of Brazil led by Getúlio Vargas, dealt with by Schulze, was a typical case, trying to "Brazilianize" immigrants already in the country, for example, by closing down foreign-language schools and outlawing "foreign" organizations, such as Zionist political associations.[26] Unsurprisingly, migrants perceived as religiously, racially, or ethnically "different" or "inferior" according to globally circulating ideas about race were targeted more than others, as becomes particularly clear in the chapters by Lara Putnam and Nicola Foote, which both deal with migrants from the British Caribbean. In the 1930s the Cuban governments of Ramón Grau San Martín and Fulgencio Batista deported more than 25,000 Haitians in an attempt to "Cubanize" the labor force.[27] Postrevolutionary Mexico—whether in spite, because, or regardless of its limited number of immigrants—witnessed a great deal of working-class and peasant xenophobia directed especially against the Spanish and the Chinese but also against Arabs, who were accused of "suck[ing] the few available resources" (*chupan las pocas economías*)—a xenophobia addressed by Jürgen Buchenau and Kathy Lopez in this volume.[28] As Buchenau underlines in his chapter on Mexico, the notion of an unchangingly xenophilic Latin America versus a xenophobic North America has to be treated with great caution. In many instances national identities were construed or mobilized in opposition to migrations.

However, the contributions to this volume as a whole, in addition to an ever-growing number of studies, also show that the increasing movement of peoples, and with them goods and ideas, into Latin America—engaging flows in the opposite direction as well as within Latin America and on to other places—interacted with the global spread of nationalism and ideas about nationhood in much more complicated ways than any simple compilation of anti-immigrant sentiments would suggest. On the one hand, it could be argued that it was only through conceptualizing the world as one divided into nations that migrations really became understood as such. As even the most superficial survey of the field of migration studies as well as public debates will quickly reveal, the very term "migration" has for a long time almost been equated with "inter*national*" or "trans*national*" migration. The world's leading journal in the field, the *International Migration Review*, is mainly concerned with movements of peoples crossing national boundaries. There are studies of other migrations, labeled "internal," but these are typically left to demographers, sociologists, or historians working within the framework of individual nation-states. In a sense, therefore, it was nationalism that made migrations visible. Moreover, migratory flows themselves can be determined by various forms of nationalism. Exclusionary or discriminatory nationalisms can work as "push factors." The drawing and establishment of national boundaries, in turn, can sometimes work as "pull factors," as they did in those cases where migrants specifically went to border areas for economic purposes such as smuggling—undermining but sometimes unintentionally consolidating these boundaries. The Chinese in northern Mexico and southern Peru (who were particularly targeted in xenophobic attacks, according to Lopez in this volume) were an example of this.[29]

On the other hand, migrations made and reshaped national imaginaries and nationalisms because they involved sweeping global demographic shifts. As José Moya has underlined, the unprecedented scale of movements of people across the Atlantic easily exceeded the grip of policymakers in any particular nation-state trying either to kindle or to withhold them.[30] Many transnational migrations were preceded (and followed) by what in hindsight has been classified as "internal" migration, modifying the social fabric and the economies as well as the national imaginaries of the sending areas. They were also intimately interwoven with large-scale migrations across national boundaries in the larger supranational sending areas, for example, Europe or the Caribbean.[31] In the receiving context of the Americas, wide-ranging and hardly controllable changes were brought about. The former colonial peripheries (such as Argentina, Uruguay, southern Brazil or the northern and western parts of the United States) were transformed into the economically most dynamic regions of the hemisphere, while the economic heartlands of the former colonies based on mining or plantations (from the southern United States via Haiti, central Mexico, and Peru to the Brazilian northeast) declined. Those areas where many migrants went became more urbanized and industrialized—and vice versa; migrants went to the urbanizing and industrializing regions. Lara Putnam's argument in this volume—that mass migration in the Caribbean, at least until the turn of the century, was driven by economic forces rather than by the racial fantasies of intellectual or political elites—could easily be extended to most of the cases studied in this book.

These large-scale movements had far-reaching implications for the construction of national identities, both in international comparison—with some countries construed as more "modern," "white," or "dynamic" than others, which were cast as "backward" or "racially inferior"—and by internally reshuffling imagined boundaries of centers and peripheries. The question of whether a country's national identity was coded as primarily "ethnic" or "civic," if one wants to work with this classic distinction in studies of nationalism, was as closely related to migratory flows as it was to the question of whether the state preceded nationalism or vice versa, as Rogers Brubaker has argued in his comparative study of citizenship and nationhood in France and Germany.[32] Most European sending countries adopted one form or another of the jus sanguinis (conferment of citizenship based on descent) in order not to lose their overseas denizens, while virtually all American countries adhered to the jus soli (citizenship based on place of birth), which led to frequent diplomatic conflicts.[33] The point may sound banal today, but it is still worth making: the mass movements of people preceded the formation of national identities—Putnam's Caribbean in this volume being a clear case in point—as often as they followed on its heels.

The significance of migratory flows for the construction of national identities, however, did not always correlate directly with their size. For Mexico, Jürgen Buchenau has convincingly pointed out that "small numbers" could have a "big impact."[34] Some of the most illuminating studies to analyze the intersection between migrations and national identities concern smaller groups, a good example of which is migrants from the Middle East. Steven Hyland's chapter in this book shows particularly well how migrants from that region debated the constant (re)drawing of imperial, colonial, or national boundaries in their home countries. Although the first immigrants from Arab lands to Brazil were Moroccan Jews in the wake of the Spanish-Moroccan war of 1859–60, in both Argentina and Brazil immigrants from Arab countries from the 1890s were summarily called "Turks" (*turcos*) because they mainly came from the Ottoman Empire. This category included Arab Christians and (fewer) Muslims from today's Lebanon and Syria, and Jews from across the Ottoman Empire as well as Armenians but hardly any people who today or in historical settings other than Latin America would be labeled Turks. Depending on their place of origin and ethnic and religious factors, these migrants and their descendants subsequently "acquired" other identities: Armenians understandably (and successfully) disentangled themselves from the term "*turco*," as did many Jews, especially after the foundation of the state of Israel in 1948, while Arab Christians and Muslims became "Syrian-Lebanese" in Argentina and Brazil, "Palestinians" in Honduras, and "Lebanese" in Mexico and Ecuador.[35]

In virtually all other areas of origin, too, the nationality of the emigrants was open to negotiation before and after migration. In Brazil and especially Peru a large proportion of "the Japanese" were not necessarily regarded as such in Honshū, since many came from Okinawa, which had been colonized by the Meiji Empire only in 1879. The islands' inhabitants underwent a forced "Japanization" from 1890 onward, perhaps contributing to emigration, but in itself undertaken by the authorities with an eye on how overseas Okinawans might fit into Japan's imperial political designs.[36] Many of Argentina's "Germans," especially in the province of Entre Ríos, came from the lower Volga area of Russia, where they had settled since the late eighteenth century.[37] The "nationality" of the few thousand Cape Verdeans who went to Argentina between the 1920s and 1940s was hard to establish for immigration officials, too, even if their passports unmistakably identified them as Portuguese. Making their appearance in Foote's and Put-nam's chapters, the more numerous Anglophone West Indians who spread across the Hispanic Caribbean between 1900 and 1930 of course did so as British subjects—in contrast to Haitians, who seem to have suffered heavier discrimination in part because they lacked this link to the British crown.[38]

The roughly 12,000 Irish who settled permanently in Argentina during the nineteenth century also came as British subjects, but in contrast to both West Indians in Spanish America and the Irish in the United States, they were subsumed under the label "English" (*ingleses*) by many Argentines—an etiquette that they increasingly rejected from the 1880s as nationalism surged back home, but that they also learned to use creatively when it promised socioeconomic benefits.[39] Conversely, one could debate whether the roughly 270,000 Spaniards who came to Cuba during the nineteenth century should be classified under the rubric of "transnational migrations" since Cuba was still a Spanish colony then. The 60,000 who arrived between 1800 and 1850, to be sure, were "transnational" migrants in the sense that they came mainly from recently independent Spanish American countries, such as Mexico and Venezuela. Between 1850 and 1898, in turn, many came as soldiers from the Iberian Peninsula to fight against Cuban aspirations for independence.[40]

Skeptics may dismiss such examples as fascinating yet quantitatively minor exceptions. They should be reminded, however, that virtually all the "nation-states" that sent migrants to Latin America between 1850 and 1950 were themselves being formed or at least (re)negotiated and contested. Before 1861 and 1871, respectively, "Italians" and "Germans" did not arrive as such, but as Ligurians, Piedmontese, Bavarians, and so forth. The "French" who in the second half of the nineteenth century came in large numbers to Argentina and Uruguay were mainly from the Basque Country, and if their marriage patterns (in Uruguay) are anything to go by, they socialized with other Basques, including those from across the Franco-Spanish border.[41] The "Spanish" who went to Argentina, Cuba, and Uruguay in the late nineteenth and early twentieth centuries were primarily Galicians (around 65 percent of the total), Basques, Catalans, and Canary Islanders (in Cuba and Uruguay) whose "Spanishness" was as questionable as the quandary's solution adopted by "Argentines," "Cubans," and "Uruguayans," who for reasons of simplicity resorted to using the shorthand *gallegos* for all of them.[42] These Latin American nationalities may well be put in quotation marks, too, since by the beginning of World War I, over half of the populations of Argentina and Uruguay were first- and second-generation immigrants while Cuba, besides containing a large immigrant contingent, had until recently itself been that "most faithful island" pertaining to Spain.

Moreover, migrants constantly crossed boundaries within Latin America. As Lara Putnam reminds us in her chapter, in some Latin American countries the largest groups of foreigners in the early twentieth century came from neighboring republics. But classic immigration countries in South America also saw much cross-border movement. Uruguay, which an Italian diplomat in the 1890s doubted was "anything more than a bridge between the ocean and Argentina" (though a heavily frequented one), was a particularly clear case in point.[43] In 1908, 18,600 "Argentines" and 27,800 "Brazilians" lived in Uruguay, but their parents (especially parents of Argentines) were mainly Europeans, while a few of Uruguay's Spanish citizens were born in Cuba. Most of those listed as U.S. citizens who married in Montevideo during the first three decades of the twentieth century had at least one parent born either in Italy or Spanish America, or else came from Puerto Rico.[44] In turn, around 100,000 Uruguayans—almost a tenth of the country's population—lived in Argentina in 1907.[45] As a consequence of such movements, Italian sources rarely differentiated between the River Plate countries until after the unification of Italy.[46] But in people's minds, even the distinction between North America and South America may have been blurred at times. "America" meant rather different things in different regions of Italy, depending on where emigrants went to *fare l'America*. German emigration records did not distinguish between Argentina and Brazil, both Südamerika, until World War I.[47] Only once clearer information spread through the networks formed by the migratory process did the contours of American nation-states become more precise in European people's minds.

Migrations also contributed to the establishment, (re)drawing, and consolidation of national boundaries on a less imaginary level. In the Caribbean, where nation-states formed only during or after the century at which this volume looks, this was especially clear. But even with regard to continental Latin America, the political map of 1850 looked different from that of 1950. Changes concerned especially the interior borders of South America pertaining to areas that were difficult to access and claimed by various neighboring countries. In other places, such as the Caribbean lands of Central American countries or the southern parts of Argentina and Chile populated by indigenous peoples, certain territories formally belonged to the nation-state, but they were barely integrated into the nation's social, economic, cultural, and political life. State- or company-fostered transnational migrations frequently played a crucial role in the "nation-alization" of such territories. After the 1860s, Germans, Swiss, and others were attracted to southern Chile and a Welsh community began to settle in Argentine Patagonia, partly as a result of state attempts to diminish the weight of indigenous populations.[48] In the course of the Amazonian rubber boom, a highly multinational workforce, including laborers from various Asian, European, and British Caribbean countries (especially Barbadians) helped to "Brazilianize" the infrastructure of territories whose status was previously disputed or formally belonged to Spanish American countries.[49] Something similar could be said about marginal areas of Costa Rica or Panama, mentioned by Foote and Putnam.

Several chapters in this volume highlight that wars constituted an important litmus test for migrations as well as debates around nationality. Even if the relative absence of border conflicts, separatist movements, and international wars in Latin America in comparison to other world regions is sometimes noted by scholars of nationalism, they were intimately connected to nation-building and the formation of national myths, with immigrants frequently wound up in them.[50] In her chapter comparing Chinese immigrants in three Latin American countries, Kathy Lopez demonstrates that the participation of Chinese in the Cuban war of independence earned them a more favorable position in Cuban society than was the case in Peru, where many Chinese were associated with Chile during the War of the Pacific, or in the heated climate of revolutionary Mexico. The restrictions of German community life during World War I, outlined by Rinke and Schulze, are another good example. In the Chaco War of 1932–35, which resulted in Bolivia having to cede large swathes of territory to Paraguay, German-speaking Mennonites who had recently come from Canada and Russia proved a crucial factor in swaying the war's outcome.[51] By then, immigrants had long become actors in the national life of most Latin American countries.

Diaspora Nationalisms and Homeland Relations

Another issue to consider is that of "diaspora nationalism" or "long-distance nationalism," which Steven Hyland and I deal with in this volume. Its study, with the classic diasporic cases of Greeks, Jews, Armenians, and to some extent Chinese and Indian expatriates in mind, was advocated already by Gellner as a peculiar case where a national identity is construed without a state fostering nationalization through education and where, as a result, the idea of the nation becomes particularly imaginary and deter-ritorialized.[52] The term "diaspora" has been popularized enormously in the last two decades to include a majority of migrant communities. If the most commonly applied yardsticks are taken, most of Latin America's immigrant communities between 1850 and 1950 could indeed be called "diasporas": they all were dispersed over several nation-states, even though the ele-ment of trauma and forcefulness in this dispersal obviously varied; they all developed some sort of awareness of themselves as a community distinct from others surrounding them, combined with varying degrees of bound-ary maintenance; and there was longing for a real or imagined homeland.[53] One might lament that through the proliferation of the term "diaspora" it loses its specificity to describe those who might now be called "victim dia-sporas." But the term's heuristic benefit is that we gain a greater deal of sen-sitivity to the multisited nature of transnational connections of migrants and their relationship with an imagined or real homeland, both factors that historiographies focusing exclusively on the nation-state have obscured.

Diasporic nationalisms engage many different and shifting types of identity constructions. First, in the host societies, they interact (or don't interact) with the various identities—regional, national, supranational, religious, ethnic, or racial—of co-migrants who come to be construed as co-nationals, co-ethnics, and so forth. Zionism, discussed in passing by Jeffrey Lesser and Raanan Rein in this volume, is perhaps the best-known case of diasporic nationalism. But it has also been shown that Sicilians or Calabrians really became "Italians" in the Americas (as well as "Ameri-cans" or New Yorkers or Argentines or *porteños*), even if they mainly mi-grated there after the unification of Italy. This process happened in part through heteroreferential adscription, as in the common discrimination as "dagoes" in the United States or in the slightly less malign gringos and *tanos* of the River Plate. But this process also worked through a gradual replace-ment of regional attachments (to "Neapolitan" associations or newspapers, for instance) with national ones ("Italian"). This becoming national in the diaspora was frequently kindled through external events, such as World War I.[54]

Campanilismo (the Italian word for emotional attachment to the local bell tower) or *Kleinstaaterei* (German for the division into small states of what should be, according to the term's implication, a larger nation-state) are often seen as competitors or obstacles to a unified "national identity" in such contexts. But subnational regionalism and nationalism frequently interacted in mutually reinforcing ways. As José Moya has shown, Basques and Catalans may have involuntarily turned into *gallegos* upon arrival in Buenos Aires, but the myriad of their regionally based associations actually formed the bedrock for the emergence of a more unified "Spanish" associationist culture too.[55] In some cases this process occurred because administrative deals with national (e.g., Italian or Spanish) authorities were more practical and they were able to provide a greater deal of protection and rights than associations based on regional origin. In other instances the very fact of living abroad reinforced a common sense of belonging among groups that were earlier stratified along regional divisions.

Second, diasporic nationalisms invariably engaged constructions of national identity in the homeland regardless of whether this existed as a nation-state or not. Again, the Jewish diaspora's role in the foundation of Israel and the ensuing Middle East conflict or the Armenian diaspora's importance in the country's independence and the conflict in Nagorno-Karabakh are only the best known of a great many possible examples. One important driving force in diaspora-homeland connections was that, contrary to common perceptions of migrations as straightforward and definite movements from one nation-state to another, they always involved much return migration (on average probably nearly 50 percent for the migrations discussed in this volume) as well as back and forth movements and on-migrations, all within much larger circuits.[56] As scholars are becoming increasingly aware of this multisitedness, issues such as the transnational dimensions of Giuseppe Mazzini's ideas, including in Latin America, or the importance of Giuseppe Garibaldi's stay in South America for the unification of Italy are increasingly being researched.[57]

Chinese diaspora nationalism is another good case. Sun Yat-sen, who founded his Revive China Society in Hawaii in 1894, had a keen interest in the exploitation of Chinese Coolies in Peru and Cuba, as revealed by his library, which contained books based on the testimonies of returnees. Famously, he called the overseas Chinese "the mother of the revolution [of 1911]." A seminal Chinese nationalist tract from 1903 referred to Cuba as evidence that "fellow countrymen" were "ill-treated abroad." Although the overwhelming majority of Chinese in Latin America at the time came from Canton, forms of nationalism derived from the diasporic experience gained an ever widening spatial circulation back in China.[58] The Syrian Social Nationalist Party, in turn, was founded in Lebanon in 1932 by Antun Saadeh upon his return from São Paulo, where he had developed a nationalist consciousness in part through engagement with the texts of German

Romanticism as well as more recent race theories of the extreme right.[59] The living conditions of German immigrants in southern Brazil in turn buoyed the imagination of ethnic nationalists in the German Empire, who were in search of a traditional ideal untainted by the supposedly corrupting forces of modernity they believed were plaguing central Europe.[60] During the Weimar Republic (in varying degrees and depending on the political conjunctures at home) and the Third Reich (far more aggressively), German policymakers sought to galvanize "their" communities together with Latin American intellectual elites for Germany's political aims in Europe, usually in contradistinction to anything perceived as "French."[61] The Italian fascist state also directed propaganda efforts toward "its" diaspora, with especially intense efforts surrounding the Italian-Ethiopian war of 1935, as my own chapter outlines.[62]

Third, owing to the multidirectional movements of diasporas, diasporic nationalisms tend to promote or at least interact with the creation of supra- or pan-national identities, which are usually based on linguistic, religious, ethnic, or racial criteria. In fact, diasporic nationalism and pan-nationalism are often close relatives, so a clear-cut distinction between them is difficult to establish. It could be argued that the nationalism of the African diaspora, if it has ever existed in the singular, is much the same as pan-Africanism—if by this latter term we do not refer primarily to attempts to create supranational political structures uniting African nation-states. Latin America is not usually treated as a privileged site for the study of pan-African ideas since there exists an ongoing perception (or myth, if we prefer) that, in comparison to the United States or the Anglophone Caribbean, the national identities of African Latin Americans—as Brazilians, Colombians, or Cubans—trumped their racial identities.[63] Regardless of whether one shares this understanding or not, Latin America unquestionably mattered for the history of pan-Africanism. Marcus Garvey's travels to Costa Rica and Panama between 1910 and 1912 exerted a crucial influence on the development of his ideas as well as his Universal Negro Improvement Association, which—as Lara Putnam and Nicola Foote both discuss—opened branches in most Hispanic Caribbean countries in the 1910s. Many of its members, including Garvey himself, meanwhile, learned to draw on the resource of their British citizenship (perhaps not quite a pan-national but in hindsight arguably transnational identity) when this appeared to be useful. The disappointing results of this strategy then helped discredit British colonialism in Jamaica or Barbados, where many migrant workers returned in the 1930s, coinciding with the stirring of pan-African solidarities and anticolonialism that the war in Ethiopia provoked in this setting (not to mention the earlier impact of the Harlem Renaissance).[64]

A pan-national concept that is of particular interest here is that of hispanidad. After first being used by a Spanish priest in Buenos Aires in 1926, the concept came to rally a long-existing pan-Hispanic nationalism, which was popularized by the right-wing Catholic intellectual Ramiro de Maeztu, who had served as Spain's ambassador to Argentina from 1928 to 1931, through his 1934 book, *Defensa de la hispanidad*. The celebrations of October 12 (the day on which Columbus first landed in the Americas) in many Spanish-speaking countries were subsequently labeled as Día de la hispanidad. Although the concept was nourished by earlier ideals of *hispanoamericanismo*, the repercussions of the Spanish civil war added a marked association of the term with the extreme nationalist right and with Catholicism in different settings. In Peru it served to lodge a distinction between right-wing *hispanistas* and left-wing *indigenistas*. In Argentina it was (paradoxically, one might think) always used in opposition to "cosmo-politanism" and sometimes tied into anti-Semitism or invoked as a coun-terweight to "Italianization," as Jeane DeLaney shows in her chapter in this volume.[65]

All of these examples demonstrate that national identities were not for-mulated only in opposition to migrations but rather in their course. Vari-ous identities—including those coded as national—oftentimes overlapped rather than excluded each other. Contrary to what some Chicago School theorists would make us believe, there was no strict correlation between the degree of "assimilation" or "integration" and socioeconomic upward mobility. Nor did "culturally similar" immigrants necessarily assimilate more easily or fully. If this had been the case, on the basis of concepts such as hispanidad, one would have to assume Spanish immigrants to be more "assimilated," "adjusted," or "integrated" than others in Spanish America, and the Portuguese to blend "more successfully" with Brazilians than other immigrants. However, the Spanish and the Portuguese often scored higher than others on the paradigmatic proxies for exclusion and separateness, such as levels of in-marriage, residential segregation, propensity to crime, or socioeconomic marginalization, all of which have been and continue to be seen by policymakers and much of the public at large as inimical to "inte-gration" and the formulation of a "cohesive" national identity. Thus, in spite of their heavily male sex ratio, Portuguese immigrants in late nineteenth- and early twentieth-century Brazil in-married more often, were poorer on average, and more often imprisoned than most other "foreigners." On those same criteria as well as residence patterns, Montevideo's Spanish were more "excluded" than its Italians. Nonetheless, travelers described the city as "typically" Spanish, and in the writings of local social chroniclers the label "immigration" itself seemed to be reserved for non-Spanish-speaking groups.[66]

Conversely, perhaps because they felt they had to, ostensibly "more different" groups were often keen to stress the cultural similarities between their home regions and the receiving society. For example, as political developments in the Middle East, mediated through what Brubaker has called "ethnopolitical entrepreneurs," began to stimulate pan-Arab feelings in Latin America's Syrian and Lebanese communities, the same "entrepreneurs" construed genealogies between Arab and Hispanic or Portuguese culture, in the process drawing on concepts such as hispanidad, or, as happened in Argentina in the 1950s and '60s, seeking to engage Catholic and anti-Semitic strands of nationalism.[67] Diasporic nationalisms therefore need not be construed in opposition to nationalisms of the host countries. Again, this can happen as DeLaney and Schulze suggest in their contributions. The chapters, however, provide many examples of compatibility or mutual reinforcements of various kinds of national identification. My own chapter, for instance, underlines the close overlaps between Italian Risorgimento exiles and nineteenth-century nation-building in the Rio de la Plata. Jeff Lesser and Raanan Rein mention Zionism as a vehicle to become Argentine since it gave Jews the kind of homeland that other Argentines—of Italian, Spanish, Portuguese descent—had too. Kathy Lopez shows in her chapter how Chinese immigrants and their descendants in Cuba sought to construe analogies between the Cuban independence hero Carlos Manuel de Céspedes and "their" national hero Sun Yat-sen.

Migrations and Comparison

Such manifold and varying relationships between migrations and the (re)reformulation of nationalisms in their global embedding must lead us to reconceptualize clean oppositions and dichotomies. Borrowing Peggy Levitt and Nina Glick Schiller's words, such rethinking indicates "that the incorporation of individuals into nation-states and the maintenance of transnational connections are not contradictory social processes. . . . Migrant incorporation into a new land and transnational connections to a homeland or to dispersed networks of family, compatriots, or persons who share a religious or ethnic identity can occur at the same time and reinforce each other."[68] There was not "less" nationality A if there was "more" nationality B, but rather there was often "more" A *and* B as a result of migrations. As demanded by Jeffrey Lesser and Raanan Rein for the study of Jewish Latin Americans, the "nation" can and should still retain "a prominent position" in studies of such connections. Like ethnicity, religion, race, or gender, "nation" is one—and an important—"piece within a broader identity mosaic," whose constituent elements can be mutually exclusive but also compatible or reciprocally reinforcing.[69]

The very term "transnational," the use of which in social sciences and the humanities has risen spectacularly in recent years, serves us well as a starting point to think about how national identities were themselves formed only in the process of being transgressed. As Kiran Patel has underlined, the concept should not tempt us into a "postnational, historically teleological wishful thinking that seeks to abolish nationalism and nation-states altogether by denying their importance as subject matters of analysis." After all, "the very logic of the term" implies that "the nation-state or an elaborated national consciousness represent a certain point of reference."[70] Bringing to the fore the case of immigration to Latin America, the aim of this volume, therefore, is not to minimize the historical importance of nation-states and national identities but rather to conceptualize them as "processual," undermined but equally importantly constituted through movements and shifts that crossed their boundaries. "Transnational" communities were "transnational" only because they engaged with national boundaries. For this purpose, the authors present the insights that can be gleaned from migration studies and from nationalism theories together.[71]

While recent developments in the discipline of history, with its newfound interest in far-flung global connections and flows, have doubtless contributed a great deal to complicating previous master narratives about the world's division into nation-states, they have arguably been weaker in postulating structural and causal factors leading to change than earlier theoretical models such as modernization theory, which is often cast as its archenemy. Yet the search for causation might still be seen as part and parcel of the historian's job. In order to prevent the danger of the history of migrations and national identities from falling apart into an infinite number of anecdotally fascinating but explanatorily weak series of connections and spreads without specific spatial grounding, each of the chapters of this volume adopts an explicitly comparative angle—whether by comparing different communities within one setting or a community that has become coded as such in different settings. The volume thereby seeks to meet a frequently made but rarely implemented demand of historians of both migrations and nationalism for a comparative framework.[72] The goal, to be sure, is not merely additive but is to compare systematically similarities and differences between cases in order learn cumulatively about the relative weight of structural variables in shaping outcomes. In other words, a transnational perspective is not seen as a deadly antidote to the alleged ills that some proponents of transnational history believe to have detected in historical comparison but is instead a necessary, complementary element.[73] Because of its *longue durée* history of overlapping, blending, and competing national identities through migrations, the study of such movements in Latin America between 1850 and 1950 can make an especially interesting contribution to an emergent field of study thus defined.[74]

This volume is therefore divided into two parts that are designed to cover the history of immigration in Latin America and the Caribbean as comprehensively as possible and to test different ways of how comparison can further our understanding of this historical topic. The first part—consisting of chapters by Lara Putnam, Jürgen Buchenau, Jeane DeLaney, and Frederik Schulze—deals with geographical contexts, comparing various immigrant groups within that space. Putnam surveys the entangled histories of in- and out-migration in the circum-Caribbean. Since she concentrates on the British Caribbean, her chapter provides a welcome example of a context where the very term "nation" grew in importance only during or after the period of mass migration. Buchenau focuses on the untypical case of Mexico, drawing out examples of both xenophilia and xenophobia, which appeared to be rather often a popular affair directed against relatively wealthy immigrants in the Mexican context. Jeane DeLaney scrutinizes the changing attitudes of Argentine elites toward immigrants, which informed the rise of Argentine cultural nationalism from around 1880 onward, while Frederik Schulze contrasts various nationalisms enmeshed in southern Brazil—that of German and Japanese immigrants and that of Brazilian elites that over time became wary of immigration.

The second part, consisting of six chapters, looks at one "group" in different settings. In their contribution on Jews in Brazil and Argentina, Jeffrey Lesser and Raanan Rein put forward a forceful argument against the myth of Jewish exceptionalism—or, indeed, the exceptionalism of any immigrant group. Fitting well with some of the arguments made in this introduction, they stress that being Jewish did not usually mean being less Argentine or Brazilian in any way. Stefan Rinke, meanwhile, concentrates on a particular moment in the history of German Latin Americans—mainly in Argentina, Brazil, and Chile. During World War I, Rinke demonstrates, they were subjected to various degrees of hostility, most notably in Brazil. The chapter is a useful reminder that community identity does not necessarily decline with the length of stay in the host country but can be powerfully reinforced due to external pressures. Kathy Lopez compares the history of Chinese immigrants in Cuba, Mexico, and Peru. While she stresses that they were subjected to discrimination in all three contexts, due to hemispherically circulating discourses about the "yellow peril," there were also significant differences. Her chapter is thus a showcase of how the attribution of certain characteristics to a particular group interacts with the political embedding in different settings.

Nicola Foote builds on this theme in her assessment of the experiences of British Caribbean immigrants in Latin America. Drawing on the often neglected case studies of Peru, Ecuador, Brazil, and Venezuela in addition to the more familiar examples of Central America and Cuba, her chapter highlights how the critical contribution British West Indians made to nationalist modernization projects was complicated by the negative ideologies associated with blackness as well as by the close connection of Caribbean migrants to imperialist powers—exacerbated in many cases by forms of diasporic nationalisms that emphasized a "British" identity and that foregrounded the English language and Protestant religions. Her chapter underlines the tragic consequences of racism and xenophobia at the level of lived experience but demonstrates that even exclusionary and discriminatory nationalisms were shaped and informed by the actions of migrants themselves, who were not passive agents in the process of identity formation.

Finally, Steven Hyland's chapter and my own chapter deal more specifically with diasporic nationalisms, focusing on the Syrian-Lebanese and the Italian case, respectively. Hyland's contribution, in particular, stresses the heterogeneity of diasporic nationalisms among Arab communities in Latin America. Given the fragmented religious, ethnic, and political landscape of the post-Ottoman Levant, migrants in Latin America debated fiercely over what political course their homelands should take. If Schulze's chapter emphasizes the social heterogeneity of immigrant groups, Hyland's underlines that their visions of national identity were just as multifarious. My own contribution adopts a similar view but highlights the long-term role of migratory flows and demographics. Comparing diasporic nationalisms among Italians in Argentina, Uruguay, and Brazil, I arrive at the conclusion that the timing of migration played a crucial role in determining the politics of Italian communities in the Americas.

Notes

Epigraph: Guilherme de Almeida, quoted in Lesser, "(Re)Creating Ethnicity," 58.

1. For a concise overview, see McKeown, "Global Migration." A useful survey of the height of migrations from Europe to the Americas is Nugent, *Crossings*.

2. Figures vary widely. For an overview, see Sánchez Albornoz, "Population of Latin America, 1850–1930," 130, who probably overstates the numbers. Moya gives higher figures about the destination of European emigrants, but these exclude return migration (*Cousins and Strangers*, 46).

3. Much of this scholarship is comparative in the sense of edited volumes or special issues of journals in which each article treats specific, usually nationally framed, cases: e.g., Klich and Lesser, *Arab and Jewish Immigrants*; Fausto, *Fazer a América*; Baily and Míguez, *Mass Migration*; Anderson and Lee, *Displacements and Diasporas*; Lesser and Rein, *Rethinking Jewish-Latin Americans*; and the special issues of *Americas* 53, no. 1 (1996), on Middle Easterners; *Caribbean Studies* 31, no. 3 (2003), on Garveyism in the Hispanic Caribbean; *Latin American Perspectives* 31, no. 3 (2004), on East Asians; *Hispanic American Historical Review* 86, no. 1 (2006), on various groups in various countries; and *Portuguese Studies Review* 14, no. 2 (2006), on the Portuguese. In turn, monographs that are in themselves explicitly comparative remain rare. The most important are Baily, *Immigrants*; Franzina, *L'America gringa*; McKeown, *Chinese Migrant Networks*; and Masterson and Funada-Classen, *Japanese in Latin America*. The study of different groups within one national setting is still less frequent in the English-language scholarship. Exceptions are Lesser, *Negotiating National Identity*; and Goebel, "*Gauchos, Gringos* and *Gallegos*." While there are plenty of studies in languages other than English, some of which compare various groups within one national setting (a good survey on the best-known case—Argentina—is Devoto, *Historia de la inmigración*), the Latin American scholarship comparing different settings within Latin America beyond one nation-state remains extremely thin. As this overview underlines, the comparative literature has a bias toward smaller immigrant communities that are perceived as more "exotic" on racial, ethnic, or religious grounds. An important precursor of much of the scholarship mentioned here was the short survey by Mörner, *Adventurers and Proletarians*.

4. The best-known works are Park and Miller, *Old World Traits Transplanted*; Wirth, *Ghetto*; Warner and Srole, *Social Systems*; and Gordon, *Assimilation*.

5. The classic formulation of this idea can be found in Glazer and Moynihan, *Beyond the Melting Pot*.

6. An extreme, more autobiographical or political than scholarly example is Novak, *Rise of the Unmeltable Ethnics*. In hindsight, this book's methodological nationalism, with its square focus on U.S. (identity) politics, is as striking as its ethnic essentialism. The author's irate denial of "Americanization," in my view, makes for a peculiarly "American" book, arguably bespeaking an acculturation of sorts.

7. E.g., Persons, *Ethnic Studies at Chicago*, 87–89; and Kazal, "Revisiting Assimilation," 446.

8. Wimmer and Glick Schiller, "Methodological Nationalism."

9. Gellner, *Nations and Nationalism*, 55; Smith, *National Identity*, 39; Anderson, *Imagined Communities*; and Hobsbawm and Ranger, *Invention of Tradition*.

10. Of course, there were always prominent exceptions—for example, John Higham or, for Argentina, Sam Baily—but even they have usually treated nationalism/nativism and migrations in separate studies: Baily, *Labor, Nationalism, and Politics* and Baily, *Immigrants*. A fruitful attempt truly to integrate the two fields in Latin American history are the writings by Lesser, especially his *Negotiating National Identity*, although it is arguably more indebted to cultural or intellectual history than to social history.

11. Anderson, *Imagined Communities*, 81; Calhoun, *Nationalism*; and Kedourie, *Nationalism in Asia and Africa*, 1–152.

12. Brubaker, "Ethnicity, Race, and Nationalism," 28–30.

13. E.g., Brubaker, "The Return of Assimilation?"; and Alba and Nee, *Remaking the American Mainstream*.

14. Such findings are summarized by Gans, "Toward a Reconciliation."

15. An important article for this thesis is Portes and Zhou, "New Second Generation."

16. A good example is Moya, *Cousins and Strangers*.

17. For Spanish American history, see the discussion in Miller, *In the Shadow*, esp. 32–42.

18. Colom González, "La imaginación nacional"; and Miller, "Historiography of Nationalism," esp. 203–7, both make this observation.

19. Míguez, "Introduction: Foreign Mass Migration," xxii. The classic North American–South American comparison is between Italians in the United States and Argentina: Klein, "Integration of Italians"; and Baily, *Immigrants*.

20. Even sophisticated works such as Portes and Rumbaut, *Immigrant America*, since their aim is "focusing on major aspects of the adaptation experience" (34), suffer from a lack of conceptual interest in nationalism, discussing it mainly as nativism (346–49). A classic in Latin American history from such a perspective is Solberg, *Immigration and Nationalism*.

21. Miller, "Historiography of Nationalism," 216.

22. Sarmiento, *Conflicto y armonía*. On anxieties about Argentina's "Italianization" more generally, see Bertoni, *Patriotas*.

23. Costanzo, *Los indeseables*.

24. See Lvovich, *Nacionalismo y antisemitismo*, ch. 3. A good hemispheric comparison is Tucci Carneiro, *O anti-semitismo*.

25. Some of these measures were similar to the Immigration Act of 1924 in the United States, but most of them were passed after 1930, when the global economic crisis had already significantly reduced the number of immigrants anyway. There were, however, many mutual influences across countries of the Americas in directing migratory flows and legislation; see Bejarano, "La inmigración a Cuba."

26. See, e.g., Gertz, *O perigo alemão*; and Lesser, *Welcoming the Undesirables*, 105.

27. Carr, "Identity, Class, and Nation"; and McLeod, "Undesirable Aliens."

28. Alfaro-Velcamp, *So Far from Allah*, 116; on the other cases, see Hu-DeHart, "Racism"; and Yankelevich, "Hispanofobia."

29. On their role as border communities, see Curtis, "Mexicali's Chinatown"; and McKeown, "Conceptualizing Chinese Diasporas," 321.

30. Moya connects what he casts as primarily transatlantic migrations to what Kenneth Pomeranz has called the "great divergence," which economically left China to trail behind Europe from around 1800 (Moya, "Continent of Immigrants," 4; Pomeranz, *Great Divergence*). By contrast, McKeown, in "Global Migration," points to the sizeable movement of peoples across Asia.

31. A well-known case is that of the Italians, who until the 1870s and after World War I in their majority went to other European countries but in between primarily went to the Americas. See, generally, Gabaccia, *Italy's Many Diasporas*.

32. Brubaker, *Citizenship and Nationhood*, 1–17. Brubaker later dismissed the whole distinction, however, in "Manichean Myth."

33. Álvarez, "Latin America and International Law," esp. 305–6. On how understandings and laws of citizenship were made *through* migrations between Argentina, Italy, and Spain, see Cook-Martín, "Soldiers and Wayward Women."

34. Buchenau, "Small Numbers, Great Impact."

35. On Moroccan Jews in the Amazon, see Benchimol, *Eretz Amazônia*; generally, see Klich and Lesser, "'Turco' Immigrants."

36. Apart from Masterson and Funada-Classen, *Japanese in Latin America*, see also, on Japanese immigration in Peru and Brazil, Takenaka, "Japanese in Peru"; Lone, *Japanese Community*; and Lesser, *Searching for Home Abroad*; and especially the article by Mori, "Identity Transformations among Okinawans," 47–66. On the role of Okinawa in Meiji constructions of "Japaneseness," see Morris-Suzuki, *Re-Inventing Japan*, esp. 26–34.

37. Bosch, "La colonización"; and Albaladejo, "Les descendants des Allemands."

38. Maffia, "La migración caboverdeana"; and McLeod, "Undesirable Aliens."

39. Kelly, *Irish 'Ingleses'*; see also Sábato and Korol, *¿Cómo fue?*.

40. Moya, "Spanish Emigration," 16.

41. Within a sample of 5,056 marriage records compiled from four Uruguayan departments between 1880 and 1930 (see Goebel, "Gauchos, Gringos and Gallegos," 194–96 for the sampling method) there were 67 Basque Frenchmen, of whom 34 married Frenchwomen. Only one of these Frenchwomen was not Basque (compared to 30 percent of non-Basques among the whole sample of Frenchwomen). Of the remaining 33 male French from the Basque Country, 7 married Spanish women (all Basques) and 20 married Uruguayan women, all but 2 of whom had at least one Spanish or French parent. Although the regional origin of the parents could not be ascertained, one would suspect a Basque involvement there too.

42. Moya, "Spanish Emigration," 20.

43. Quoted in Oddone, "La politica e le immagini," 98. Guy Bourdé estimates that about 17 percent of the approximately 7.6 million European arrivals to Buenos Aires between 1857 and 1930 (of whom many left again) came from Montevideo; Bourdé, *Urbanisation et immigration*, 162.

44. *Anuario Estadístico de la República Oriental del Uruguay*; and Goebel, "Gauchos, Gringos and Gallegos."

45. Vanger, *Model Country*, 17.

46. Devoto, "Un caso di migrazione precoce," 15.

47. Nugent, *Crossings*, 66.

48. Blancpain, *Les Allemands*, 450–53; and Williams, "Welsh Settlers."

49. Greenfield, "Barbadians."

50. E.g., Hobsbawm, "Nationalism and National Identity."

51. Hughes, "Logistics," esp. 436–37. The Bolivian campaign in turn was led by the retired German general Hans Kundt; for an introduction to his role in the conflict, see Farcau, *Chaco War*, 87–98.

52. Gellner, *Nations and Nationalism*, 101–9. The second term is preferred by Nina Glick Schiller; see "Long-Distance Nationalism."

53. The most important introductions to definitions of the term and its relation with nationalism are Tölölyan, "Rethinking Diaspora(s)"; Cohen, *Global Diasporas*; Brubaker, "'Diaspora' Diaspora"; Gal, Leoussi, and Smith, *Call of the Homeland*; and Bauböck and Faist, *Diaspora and Transnationalism*.

54. E.g., Cinel, *From Italy to San Francisco*, 228–55; and Luconi, *From Paesani to White Ethnics*. A good Latin American regional case study is Zanini, *Italianidade*.

55. Moya, *Cousins and Strangers*, 277–331.

56. For obvious reasons, this is less valid for the classic (victim) diasporas.

57. Bayly and Biagini, *Giuseppe Mazzini*. The general idea is well elaborated by Choate, *Emigrant Nation*.

58. McKeown, *Chinese Migrant Networks*, 85–99; for the Sun quote, see Lum and Lum, *Sun Yat-sen*, xv; on Sun's library containing the 1860-book *Bitter Society*, see T'sai, "Chinese Emigration," 398; and Tsou and Lust, *Chinese Revolutionary Army*, 73. An important article to stimulate research in this area, though not in relation to Latin America, is Duara, "Transnationalism."

59. Lesser, *Negotiating National Identity*, 62–63; and Schumann, "Nationalism," esp. 601–3.

60. Conrad, *Globalisierung und Nation*, 229–78. In an interesting contrast to the predominant view of an "assimilationist" Brazil versus a "pluralist" or segregationist United States, pan-German nationalists loathed the United States, as opposed to Brazil, as a "mass grave of Germandom," due to assimilation; Chickering, *We Men Who Feel Most German*, 88.

61. The literature on these topics, especially the Nazis, is obviously very broad. See, e.g., Rinke, *"Der letzte freie Kontinent"*; Goebel, "Decentring"; Brepohl de Magalhães, *Pangermanismo e nazismo*; Newton, *"Nazi Menace"*; and Mitchell, *The Danger of Dreams*.

62. Bertonha, "Italiani nel mondo"; and Scarzanella, *Fascistas en América del Sur*.

63. The comparison of race relations in Brazil and the United States is a classic in the literature at least since the days of the Brazilian intellectual Gilberto Freyre, who, in his 1933 book, *Casa-Grande e Senzala* (The masters and the slaves), favorably compared Brazil's alleged "racial democracy" to North American racism. For a brief overview of mutual Brazilian–U.S. influences see Andrews, "Brazilian Racial Democracy."

64. See the contributions in *Caribbean Studies* 31, no. 3 (2003): Harpelle analyzes how Garvey organized a celebration for King Edward's coronation in Costa Rica ("Cross Currents," 48), and Hill argues that "the returning emigrants were a testament to the failure of imperial citizenship," kindling an anticolonial nationalism that was stirred further by the

war in Ethiopia ("Boundaries of Belonging," 15–16). See also Lewis, *Marcus Garvey*, ch. 7 on Garvey's travels.

65. See, generally, Falcoff and Pike, *Spanish Civil War*; Pérez Herrero and Tabanera, *España-América Latina*; Moya, *Cousins and Strangers*, 332–84; and González Cuevas, *Maeztu*.

66. Klein, "Social and Economic Integration"; Florentino and Machado, "Ensaio"; and Goebel, "*Gauchos, Gringos* and *Gallegos*."

67. Lesser, "(Re)Creating Ethnicity," 47–48; and Goebel, "Von der *hispanidad*." On "ethnopolitical entrepreneurs," see Brubaker, "Ethnicity without Groups," 166.

68. Levitt and Glick Schiller, "Conceptualizing Simultaneity," 1003.

69. Lesser and Rein, "Challenging Particularity," 250–51.

70. Patel, "Transatlantische Perspektiven," 628–29.

71. For a similar demand concerning the "processual" character of ethnicity, see Brubaker, "Ethnicity without Groups"; and for an integrated field of study, see his "Ethnicity, Race, and Nationalism." In history, such an approach to nationalism is proposed by Duara, "Historicizing National Identity."

72. Green, "L'histoire comparative"; and Stearns, "Nationalisms."

73. The different positions are laid out in the following two articles: Seigel, "Beyond Compare," who appears to want to abolish comparisons with the help of the "transnational turn"; and Kocka, "Comparison and Beyond," who argues in favor of an integration of the two. An earlier significant challenge to comparison is Espagne, "Sur les limites."

74. Alba and Nee speculate that racial and ethnic stratifications in the United States in the near future "could begin to resemble in certain aspects those of Latin America" in that "race/ethnicity will lose some of its clear-cut, categorical character," but they do not delve into the history through which these stratifications developed in Latin America (*Remaking the American Mainstream*, 290).

I

Spaces of Migration

1

Migrants, Nations, and Empires in Transition

Native Claims in the Greater Caribbean, 1850s–1930s

LARA PUTNAM

The notion of "entangled history" has recently been put forward to label studies that trace interdependent social, cultural, and political processes within two or more countries. The crucial claim is not that processes were similar—they may or may not have been—but that they were connected: that their causes and consequences can only be understood in the context of the multilayered connections between the locales. This chapter argues that the histories of the islands and the rimlands of the Greater Caribbean (including the United States) were entangled in precisely this way from the mid-nineteenth to mid-twentieth centuries. Within Latin American history the construction of racial hierarchies, the assertion of national identities, and the emergence of populist coalitions have generally been treated as national-level dynamics: developing across the region at similar times for similar reasons. Yet I argue that in the Greater Caribbean these were not merely parallel but *entangled* developments—reflecting connections that spanned the region and encompassed anglophone and francophone islands as well as Spanish-speaking islands and rimlands. And in the entangled histories of race, nation, and state formation here, matters of migration played a central role.

This chapter traces the evolving politics of immigration in the Spanish-speaking rimlands and islands; the British colonies, both mainland and insular; and the northernmost pole of the circum-Caribbean migratory system: the United States. (The French colonies and the independent republic of Haiti also make brief appearances.) These lands comprised a shifting mix of republics, protectorates, and colonies. Likewise, the political communities imagined (and defended, and transformed) by residents and sojourners in the Greater Caribbean came in many shapes and sizes.

The pages that follow highlight three basic subthemes: the importance of the international gaze, the class divide over race, and the inconsistent significance of "nation." In regard to the first, by the dawn of the twentieth century immigration law was everywhere understood as a component of international positioning, and the polities of the Greater Caribbean were all too aware of their own subordination within geopolitical structures. Spanish American statesmen worried openly about the threat of U.S. expansionism. Both the optics and the substance of unbarred frontiers, they feared, served to heighten that vulnerability.

Leaders in the British colonies, meanwhile, debated immigration control in terms of their place within a formal rather than informal empire, drawing comparison to the racially exclusionary policies enacted by the "white dominions" of Canada and Australia in particular. Even more importantly, the British Caribbean colonies were fundamentally sending societies, with rates of emigration reaching as high as the one-quarter of working-age Barbadian men who departed for Panama during canal construction. As circum-Caribbean receiving societies (like Panama) raised barriers against British West Indians in the 1920s, this regional panorama became the main international frame against which British Caribbean immigration laws were debated. Some voices argued that first-hand experience of discrimination elsewhere should make British Caribbeans loathe to build barriers themselves. But as antiblack laws elsewhere and economic hardship increased in tandem, answering nativism with nativism instead became the order of the day.

The second subtheme tracks the class dynamics of ideas about race. These class dynamics differed in the Spanish American republics and the British colonies, yet by moving in opposite directions they converged over time. In Spanish America, from start of independent life, elites talked openly about racial difference: they saw changing the racial makeup of the pueblo as crucial to national advance. European immigration must be encouraged; Asians and Africans barred. Among the Spanish American rural and urban working classes, in contrast, race was not initially prominent within discussions of difference or justice. By the 1920s and 1930s, though, popular movements increasingly adopted the elite rhetoric of scientific racism and "assimilability" as they sought support for banning the foreign workers they saw as undercutting wages and taking jobs.

In contrast, in the British colonies, across the nineteenth century racial hierarchies and allegiances were openly important to the working classes, who saw themselves as categorically separate from the white elites whose power survived the end of slavery intact and from the indentured East Indian "coolies" whose labor planters' profits now relied on. Yet elites here, in contrast to the Spanish American republics, were loathe to talk about race in public—they didn't identify with the destiny of these pueblos, and they harbored few optimistic fantasies about whitening the islands' black masses. By the 1920s and 1930s, though, seeking to co-opt the nativist language with which popular leaders denounced antiblack immigration bans elsewhere, British Caribbean elites grew to tolerate and in some cases propagate race-based rhetoric—as long as it denounced Chinese and Syrians rather than British or local whites as the enemy.

The third subtheme regards use of the term "nation." *Nación* and *nacionalismo* were continually invoked in political rhetoric in the Spanish American republics in this era, and their referents were relatively clear. "Nationalism" in Cuba was about love and loyalty among Cubans. "La nación" in Panama meant Panama. In the British Caribbean colonies, and among British Caribbeans abroad, things were not so simple. Insular identities (Grenadian; Barbadian) were sometimes referred to as "national." The British West Indies as a unit was sometimes labeled a "nation." Most of all, especially in the decades after the Great War, "nation" referenced global collectives identified by race: the "Negro" or "African" people worldwide, and increasingly "the Indian people" at home and abroad as well. The spirit of nationalism was essential to modern progress, all agreed. But which kind of "nation" would be the nation of the future? The answer was entirely unclear as the decade of the 1930s and the long heyday of interregional migration drew to a close.

Finally, the pages that follow also capture three constants true across the countries studied and over the decades we track. First, employers did not let politicians' noise about preferences for this or that group interfere with the bottom line, which was access to workers willing to work. Second, Chinese and Middle Eastern trading diasporas were the most tempting scapegoats when times got hard. Third, immigrants from adjacent countries invariably outnumbered all others. Yet for long stretches these "near neighbor" migrants went unremarked in political debate, despite their highly visible presence in working-class communities near borders and within capital cities. Only occasionally were they more systematically targeted, and the results could be tragic.

Throughout, this regional story was shaped by shifts beyond the region's borders. The transition of empires under way in the years covered included three components: the end of Spanish imperial rule on the mainland in the first decades of the nineteenth century and in Cuba and Puerto Rico by century's end; the emergence and extension of U.S. informal empire, ranging from heavy-handed support for U.S. investors abroad to military interventions to formal dominion over Puerto Rico from 1898 forward; and the waning of the British West Indies from centerpiece to backwater of the British Empire, culminating in decolonization in the decades after World War II. Such was the international context of regional entanglement.

A Region Remade: Islands and Rimlands as the Spanish Empire Receded and U.S. Dominion Expanded, 1850s–1900s

In the wake of independence in the Spanish American rimlands (1810s–1820s) and emancipation in the British Caribbean (1830s), those who sought opportunity in and around the Greater Caribbean faced few barriers to mobility and encountered only rudimentary state oversight upon arrival. The newly empowered elites ruling Spanish American republics fantasized about European immigrants who would advance agriculture and offer a civilized example to the unruly mestizo and *mulato* masses. Capturing the conventional wisdom, Venezuelan Carlos Gómez argued in his 1906 dissertation that only mass European immigration could erase via "wise ethnic fusion" (that is, sexual mixing) the "ugly heritage of vice and illness that the Castilian, Indian, and black has left us" and replace it with "a peaceful, prudent, and hardworking character."[1] In contrast to such concern, British Caribbean elites rarely discussed their islands' populations as anything other than brute labor power; when they did so, they put their faith in transformation through Christian instruction rather than immigration and "ethnic fusion."

In neither case, however, did these elite imaginings have much impact on state practices, which pursued export-driven profits first and foremost. By the final decades of the nineteenth century, Spanish American elites saw infrastructure expansion and foreign investment as keys to national progress. Employers looked to nearby islands for a low-cost, mobile labor force. Conceived of as a short-term means to a long-term end, this nonwhite immigration occasioned few qualms among Spanish American elites even though it contradicted their fantasies of whiter futures. The new projects and plantations were often located in sparsely populated coastal lowlands that had long been linked to the insular Caribbean by small-scale migration. Thousands of Windward Islanders and British Guianese provided the bulk of laborers for gold fields in El Callao, Venezuela, in the 1850s, even

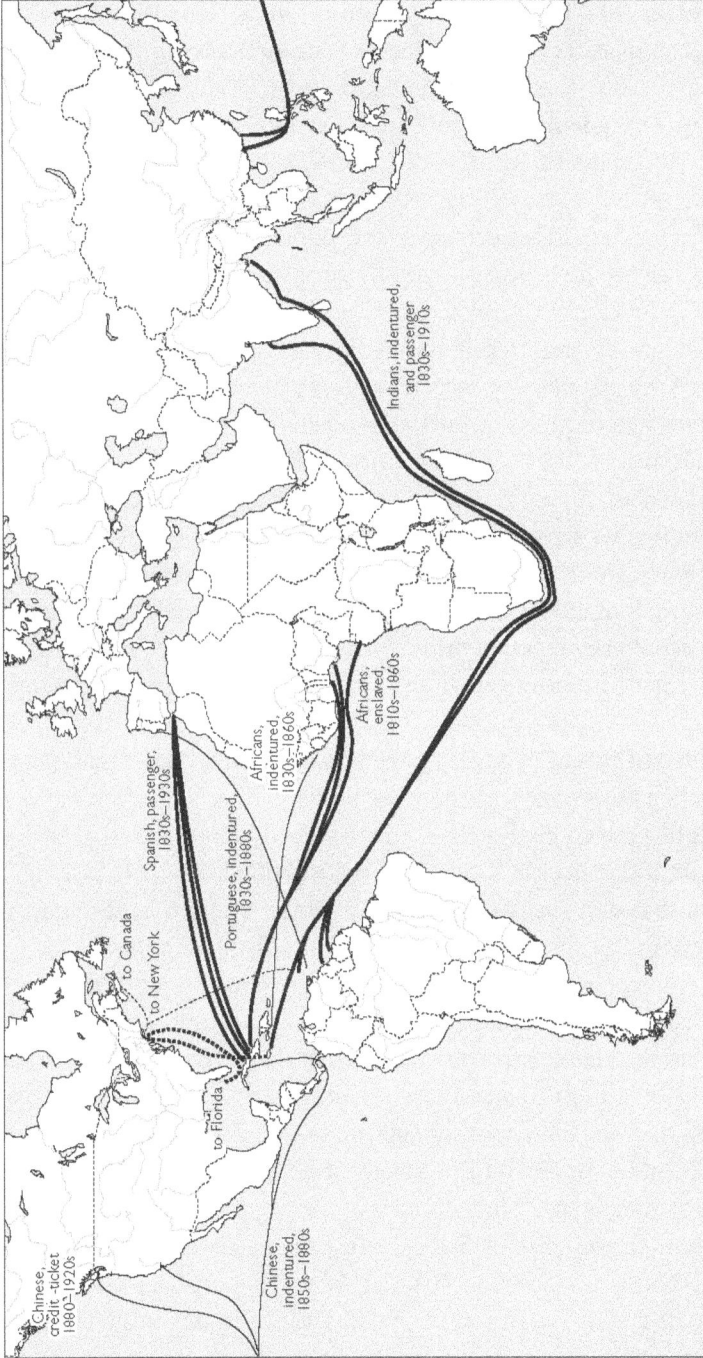

Figure 1.1. Map depicting migration within and around the Greater Caribbean, 1840s–1920s. Map created by Lara Putnam and Bill Nelson. Permission granted by Duke University Press.

as thousands of Jamaicans did likewise for the Panama Railroad. French-patois speakers of African ancestry from the small islands of the Eastern Caribbean cultivated cacao in northeast Venezuela and northern Trinidad alike. In a parallel development in the western rimlands, English-patois speakers of African ancestry pioneered the cultivation of bananas for export in eastern Jamaica, northeast Panama, and Honduras's north coast alike.[2]

With by far the largest economy and population of the islands at the end of the nineteenth century—indeed, surpassing in population all of the rimland republics except Mexico, Colombia, and Venezuela—Cuba was both central to regional trends and exceptional in multiple ways. Seeking to preserve the stability of sugar plantations powered by enslaved labor, Cuban elites had declined to pursue independence during the rupture of Spanish authority at the start of the nineteenth century. Across the ensuing generations labor supply remained the primordial concern of plantation elites. After further arrivals of enslaved Africans were definitively curtailed at mid century, some 125,000 to 150,000 Chinese workers were brought in under contracts of indenture. Slavery would not end here until 1886. Independence would be nipped in the bud a decade later, as U.S. troops stepped into the struggle between Cuban patriots, loyalists, and Spanish troops in 1898.[3]

The outsized power of sugar interests redoubled as U.S. investment in Cuba reached new heights in the wake of 1898. Thus, although Cuban intellectuals like the young Fernando Ortiz voiced in 1906 the same biological and cultural concerns about immigration policy as Carlos Gómez in Venezuela that same year—insisting that "race is the most fundamental aspect we should consider in the immigrant," dismissing the "black" and "yellow" as "races well-known to be backwards," and pondering the relative merits of Northern and Southern Europeans—it was sugar planters' labor needs rather than eugenic considerations that shaped de facto immigration policy.[4] The booming Cuban economy continued to draw Spanish migrants as it had in the past, more than 800,000 across the first three decades of the twentieth century (many returned home, harvest earnings in hand; some stayed). But already in the first decades of the twentieth century thousands of Afro-Antilleans arrived to cut cane in Cuba, even though the entry of contract laborers was formally banned. When sugar prices soared in the wake of World War I, even this formal hindrance would be altered at employers' behest.[5]

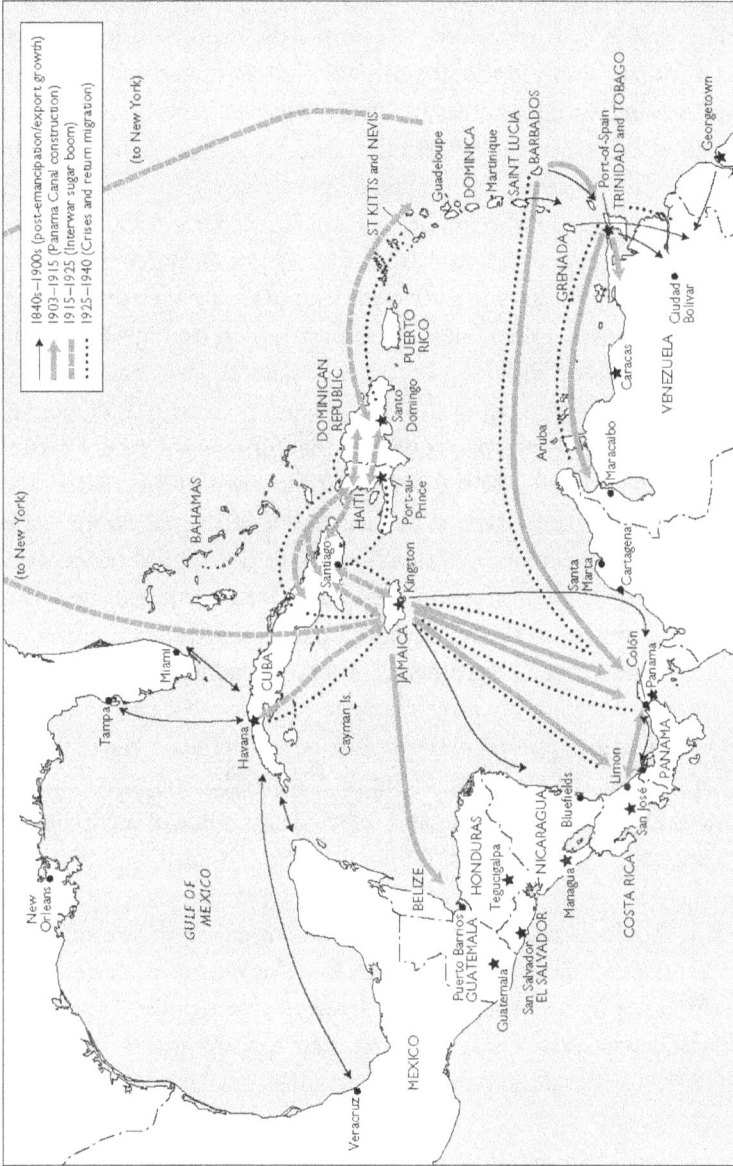

Figure 1.2. Map depicting migration into and out of the Greater Caribbean, 1850s–1930s. Map created by Lara Putnam and Bill Nelson. Permission granted by Duke University Press.

Similar elite demand for cheap labor in the wake of abolition brought indentured workers to British colonies in the mid-nineteenth century. Indentured immigration provided unfree workers at fixed wages, postponing the restructuring of labor relations that the end of slavery would otherwise have required. British-ruled South Asia proved the steadiest supply. Indentured East Indian migration began in 1845 and continued for three generations, until Indian nationalists (in India) succeeded in ending recruitment for good in 1917. In all, 239,000 East Indians reached British Guiana; 144,000, Trinidad; 36,000, Jamaica; and 6,000, Grenada.[6]

Whereas in the rimland republics the lands receiving Afro-Caribbean immigrants were generally distant from the centers of native population, and therefore immigration's impact on working-class wages disguised, in the British islands the role of subsidized East Indian immigration in undercutting the position of freed people's descendants was clear. As a 1904 editorial in an opposition paper in Port of Spain pointed out, democracy didn't work like this. "When one considers that for many years the Australian Government, yielding to the pressure of the working-class vote, has refused to permit the importation of cheap labour from the South Sea Islands, and the strict regulation of immigration in the interest of the working population which is in force in the United States, one sees how large a share of representation the labouring population acquires under a real system of representative Government."[7] The Trinidad legislature's support of state-aided immigration was prima facie evidence that the "unofficial" members supposedly appointed to speak on behalf of the people in fact did nothing of the kind. "If the Administration assume that they have successfully achieved their alleged object and selected an unofficial section that is truly representative of all classes of the population, it must appear strange to them that the agricultural labourers, who form the great bulk of the population, should, through their representatives, insist on keeping down wages."[8] Yet the editorialists' calls to "check . . . coolie immigration" made barely a ripple in public debate and no impact on crown policy.[9] The annual allocation of newly arrived indentured workers to waiting plantations continued; for planters and their allies, this was the only "immigration question" that mattered.

Thus, even as East Indian laborers flowed in, Afro-Caribbean laborers flowed out, seeking the cash earnings that might bolster a family's precarious autonomy. Jamaicans built railroads in Costa Rica in the 1870s and in Ecuador in 1900; emigrants from Guadeloupe and Martinique and more Jamaicans labored in Panama on the French-run canal effort in the 1880s;

Windward Islanders harvested cacao in northeast Venezuela and joined the second Orinoco gold boom by the thousands in the 1880s.

The Heyday of Labor Migration, 1900s–1920s

As we already previewed in the case of Cuba after 1898, the expansion of U.S. investment went hand in hand with an expansion of U.S. political sway. Sometimes this was effected through direct colonial possession, as in Puerto Rico after 1898 and the Panama Canal Zone after 1903, and other times through the threat or reality of military occupation, as in Cuba, the Dominican Republic, Haiti, and Nicaragua. The completion of the Panama Canal under U.S. control between 1903 and 1914 was both harbinger and accelerator of this process. Ensuing cycles of boom and bust drew thousands of migrants from the islands to Central American banana plantations; Cuban and Dominican sugar plantations; and oil camps in Trinidad, Mexico, and Venezuela.

Even more than Spanish American elites, Yankee employers sought labor supplies with an eye to short-term production and profits rather than the moral and biological legacies that concerned men like Carlos Gómez and Fernando Ortiz. By the 1920s a new generation of nationalist reformers in the Spanish American republics would make this the centerpiece of their twinned denunciations of "foreign capital" and the "foreign workers" it had "imported."[10] Such critiques captured the relationship between informal empire and local transformation but massively overstated the extent of employer control. The great bulk of circum-Caribbean migration remained self-directed, guided by networks of kith and kin rather than employer contracting abroad.[11]

Port cities adjacent to centers of economic dynamism—Port of Spain, Ciudad Bolívar, Carúpano, Barranquilla, Panamá, Colón, Bocas del Toro, Port Limon, Veracruz, New Orleans, Havana, Santiago de Cuba—became polyglot nodes in trading networks large and small. Those buying were as cosmopolitan as those selling. On Port of Spain's streets, wrote one traveler in 1917, "a score of races" were on display: "half-naked, spindle legged Hindus with huge turbans, stolid Chinese, herculean negroes, fiercely mustached Latin-Americans, French, Spanish, Italian, Portuguese, English, Americans, Dutch, Irish, Scotch, Norwegians, every race and nation save Germans, are there, as well as innumerable unidentifiable individuals in whose veins runs the blood of half the nations of Europe and varying quantity of Africa."[12]

Struck though this traveler was by the range of Europeans he perceived in Port of Spain, in numerical terms such migratory streams were negligible in the plantation tropics, as census data makes clear (see table 1.1).[13] Cuba was the only exception: 1931 found more than 257,000 Spanish immigrants there, easily outnumbering the 28,000 British West Indians and 77,000 Haitians tallied in the same year.[14] Elsewhere Afro-Caribbean immigrants swamped European arrivals. The Republic of Panama circa 1930 was home to 23,000 island-born British West Indians and Costa Rica, 11,000 (with, in each case, a second generation almost as large surrounding them); neither Panama nor Costa Rica counted more than 3,000 European immigrants in its population. The Dominican Republic in 1935, for all its Europhile hispanidad, counted 52,000 Haitian-born residents, 9,000 British Caribbeans, and only 3,000 Europeans in all (see table 1.1).

Meanwhile, throughout the period covered in this chapter, immigration from adjacent territories that shared a language and cultural heritage—reflecting a common imperial past—outstripped all other migratory movements. These were people who crossed borders of recent origin and intermittent salience. Ever since independence, the largest numbers of foreigners arriving in Venezuela had been Colombians in the Andean border region, 19,000 of them resident in Venezuelan territory in 1936. In turn, Venezuelans outnumbered all other immigrants in Colombia. The pattern was replicated around the rimlands. Colombians outnumbered all but Jamaicans and Barbadians in Panama, Nicaraguans matched British West Indians in Costa Rica, Hondurans swamped all others in Nicaragua, Salvadorans even more so in Honduras, Mexicans outweighed all others in Guatemala, and Guatemalans in British Honduras (see table 1.1). In Great Britain's Eastern Caribbean colonies the same held true: immigrants from nearby Windward Islands in Trinidad in 1911 included over 19,000 Barbadians, 10,000 Vincentians, and 8,000 Grenadians. Ten years later the total of Barbadian-born had fallen to 16,000 (Panama and Cuba and now New York City had become popular alternatives to Trinidad) but the total of Grenadians had risen above 12,000.[15]

In general, political elites ignored this kind of migration. Certainly they declined to legislate against it. Movement across these particular borders often antedated the borders' existence and was crucial to yearly agricultural cycles and the long-term economic and demographic growth of border regions. These "near neighbor" migrants occupied a contradictory position in the territories where they sojourned. They intermixed and intermarried with far greater ease than did foreigners more alien in appearance, language, and habits. Yet their numbers and occupational overlap with local populations made them conspicuous targets for working-class hostility. Intimacy and animosity thus went hand in hand. Stereotypes of impoverished near-neighbor immigrants allowed almost equally impoverished locals to assert their own superior virtue. This was true of Guatemalans in southern Mexico; Mexicans in eastern Guatemala; Salvadorans in Honduras; Nicaraguans in Costa Rica; Colombians in Venezuela; Barbadians, Grenadians, and Vincentians in Trinidad; and Haitians in the Dominican Republic's northwest *frontera*.[16]

Such migrants might face abuse but it was often of the same kind that illiterate or rural migrants of any birthplace faced in the same societies. A Port of Spain journalist in 1920 recorded an outburst from a local magistrate upon hearing that a defendant hailed "from Grenada, sir." "Why can't you people from Grenada keep out of the island. We don't want you here. I have scarcely passed one single person from Grenada who was not a rascal. Why can't you keep to your blessed country? Pay £10 or do three months' hard labour."[17] The immigrant sweating through three months' hard labor doubtless found the exchange less amusing than the journalist did. But, ultimately, the ire of cranky judges was something that Port of Spain's poor had in common, whatever their island of birth.

Near-neighbor tensions could become explosive, however, when center-state politicians needed a scapegoat or distraction. Most tragically, Dominican dictator Rafael Trujillo's efforts to create a stark border out of a blended near-neighbor frontier would lead to mass slaughter of Haitian immigrants and Dominicans of Haitian ancestry in 1937, as I discuss later.[18]

The Temptation of Anti-Asian Demagoguery: 1900s–1920s

In the first decades of the twentieth century several hundred thousand British Caribbeans traveled to Panama, Costa Rica, Cuba, New York City, and Venezuela, while an even larger number of men and women crossed the borders of near-neighbor states for some portion of their lives. In contrast to these major population movements, East Asian and Middle Eastern immigrants tallied only a handful, even fewer in number than the European immigrants the Greater Caribbean's Spanish American elites so desired. Yet Asian migrants drew an extraordinary amount of attention from both lawmakers and the public in colonies and republics alike.

Table 1.1. Immigrant populations of the greater Caribbean, ca. 1930

	Year	Total population	Total born elsewhere (%)
BRITISH COLONIES			
Jamaica	1921	858,118	18,096 (2%)
British Guiana	1921	297,691	53,966 (18%)
Trinidad & Tobago	1921	243,796	57,509 (24%)
Barbados	1921	156,774	5,373 (3%)
British Honduras	1921	45,317	7,000 (15%)
SPANISH-SPEAKING ISLANDS			
Cuba	1931	3,962,344	436,897 (11%)
Dominican Republic	1935	1,479,417	73,070 (5%)
Puerto Rico	1920	1,299,809	8,167 (1%)
RIMLANDS			
Venezuela	1936	3,467,839	45,484 (1%)
Colombia	1928	7,851,000	35,251 (0.4%)
Panama	1930	467,459	47,144 (10%)
Canal Zone	1930	39,467	33,193 (84%)
Costa Rica	1927	471,524	29,265 (6%)
Nicaragua	1920	638,119	10,375 (2%)
Honduras	1930	854,184	42,280 (5%)
Guatemala	1921	2,004,900	16,814 (1%)

Sources: Kuczynski, Demographic Survey, 79–80, 156, 198–99, 341; Cuba, Comité Estatal, Memorias iné-ditas, 74; Cuba, Dirección General del Censo, Censo de 1943, 888–89; República Dominicana, Dirección General, Población de la República Dominicana, 2, 5; U.S. Bureau of the Census, Fifteenth Census, 328, 334–35; Venezuela, Ministerio de Fomento, Sexto Censo de Población, 540–41; Colombia, Contraloría General de la República, Memoria y cuadros del Censo de 1928, 39; Panamá, Secretaría de Agricultura, 1930 Censo Demográfico, 17, 21–23; Costa Rica, Base de datos del Censo de 1927, http://ccp.ucr.ac.cr/censos/; Nicaragua, Censo General de 1920, 4; Honduras, Dirección General de Estadística, Resumen del censo general, 32; Guatemala, Ministerio de Fomento, Censo de la población, 1:139, 2:57.

External birthplaces and number of residents from each								
Top three external birthplaces / number of residents						Europe total	Syria/ Turco[a]	China
India	7,145	Great Britain	2,410	China	2,302	2,612	245	2,302
India	39,965	British Caribbean	10,128	Portugal	1,170	2,653	n/a	376
British Caribbean	46,411	India	37,341	Venezuela	4,135	2,287	112	1,334
British Caribbean	3,020	USA	706	Latin America	627	336	n/a	1
Guatemala	2,540	Mexico	1,391	Honduras	1,350	362	48	12
Spain	257,596	Haiti	77,535	British Caribbean	28,206	266,863	n/a	24,647
Haiti	52,657	Britain/ British Caribbean	9,272	Puerto Rico	3,221	2,926	1,242	312
Spain	4,975	USA	1,617	Virgin Islands	663	6,144	186	n/a
Colombia	18,872	Spain	5,506	British Caribbean	5,261	12,916	2,167	935
Venezuela	14,748	Syria	2,967	Spain	2,465	7,499[b]	2,967	n/a
British Caribbean	23,075	Colombia	6,083	French Caribbean	2,690	3,062	294	2,742
USA	15,166	British Caribbean	8,011[c]	Central America	6,568	1,437	n/a	88
British Caribbean	10,595	Nicaragua	9,296	Panama	2,982	2,865	72	483
Honduras	5,019	Britain/ British Caribbean	1,576	El Salvador	748	961	106	462
El Salvador	18,522	Guatemala	7,885	Nicaragua	5,907	1,412	788	269
Mexico	5,043	El Salvador	2,948	Honduras	2,390	2,824	669	759

Notes: a. Includes all labeled Syrian, Turkish, Lebanese, Palestinian, Arab, and (in cases where Chinese and Japanese listed separately) "Other Asiatics."
b. Includes 1,436 "English," many of whom may have been British Caribbean.
c. Includes 509 native French speakers, likely most from French Caribbean.

The first wave of anti-Chinese laws in the Greater Caribbean followed immediately upon those in the United States and Canada in the 1880s. But the movement of racial ideologies and restrictionist legal forms was not a one-way street from north to south. In fact, as historian Erika Lee points out, awareness of Chinese labor on Cuban sugar plantations and of British debates over indentured labor in the postemancipation Caribbean were part of the mix of ideas that went into North American debates over what came to be called the "Yellow Peril."[19] By the first decade of the twentieth century, immigration laws in the Spanish-speaking republics of the Greater Caribbean barred entry to an expanding list of Asian and Middle Eastern "races," "nations," or "peoples."[20]

Yet settlers from these lands arrived in small numbers before, during, and after such prohibitions were imposed. By dint of hard work, intraethnic commercial networks, and a willingness to stump through rural areas that local elites disdained, they carved their niche in small-scale trade. Indeed, in many cases they came to dominate retail in the very same export zones where Afro-Caribbean sojourners labored. This was true of Chinese grocers and "turco" peddlers in Costa Rica's Caribbean banana zone, "Palestinians" on the north coast of Honduras, turcos in the Atlantic slopes of Colombia, and libaneses or sirios in northeast Venezuela.[21] Arab communities of the Greater Caribbean were so small they barely merited the term "community." A given secondary city might be home to a handful of extended families hailing from one or, at most, two towns in the Levant. Nothing in the Greater Caribbean compared to the 65,000-strong Syro-Lebanese community of Argentina in 1914 (discussed in chapter 10).[22] Yet the notice they drew was large.

Although in some cases—Honduras, the Dominican Republic, Colombia—these merchant diasporas became securely consolidated as junior partners to local elites, they repeatedly proved to be tempting targets for populist outrage and mob violence. "Native" elites proved willing to whip up popular hostility toward these "alien" merchants whenever economic downturns threatened to push class conflict simmering between locals to a boil. In turn-of-the-century Haiti, for instance, police and politicians openly fanned popular anti-Syrianism with the encouragement of the Haitian bourgeoisie. There was even a short-lived newspaper named L'Anti-Syrien.[23] An official commission in 1903 denounced the Syrians on both populist and culturalist grounds: they had ruined rural marketwomen's livelihood; they "always remained strangers in Hayti, sticking to their own customs and living lives entirely different to the Haytians."[24]

Here too we see the international reverberation of anti-Asian laws. As historian Brenda Plummer explains, "Haiti sought a precedent in the Chinese exclusion laws of the United States, Australia and Cuba," arguing "that these states had reserved the right to bar nationalities deemed unassimilable and harmful to national interests. Why then should Haiti be prevented from doing the same?"[25] However, in this case U.S. interests were firmly aligned with the Syrians, who had come to provide a crucial channel for U.S. exports to Haiti. Newspaper reports captured the dual role of a government that, having spurred popular resentment, found itself pushed to act as the immigrants' protector as well. President Pierre Nord Alexis "paraded through the streets of the city today, throwing money to the natives running behind his carriage. The people fought for the coins, at the same time crying 'Long life to Nord and down with the Syrians.' The Syrians are terror-stricken and do not leave their houses."[26] But foreign diplomatic pressure averted mass expulsion, and profitable commerce continued.

In the British colonies as well, the position of East Asian and Middle Eastern immigrants was shaped by multiple, partially countervailing pressures. Within the popular classes, resentment against petty retailers whose prices pinched could build into outright violence, as in the rioting against Jamaica's eight-thousand-strong Chinese community in 1918 that left Chinese-owned shops across the island looted and destroyed.[27] Oral histories convey the perception of top-down encouragement: people heard both that a "chiney man" had shot an Afro-Jamaican man over a love triangle, and that in response "the government seh dem must mash down every damn chiney man shop."[28] As we shall see, some Jamaican elites indeed sought to align themselves with popular hostility to Chinese immigrants. But elite opinion was hardly united. Some British Caribbean elites did not think their islands' populaces any better than the Asian immigrants other states sought to keep out. Meanwhile, as in Haiti, although the example of states elsewhere might spur restrictionism, the ability of local elites to act against immigrants was hampered by geopolitical constraints: all the more so in the British islands, which were not self-governing republics but colonial possessions.

Six months before the 1918 riot, the parochial board of St. James had already undertaken to debate the frontiers of native rights and the possibilities of exclusion within empire. Board member and wealthy Afro-Jamaican planter A. B. Lowe denounced Chinese shop owners' supposed dishonesty and vice and concluded, "it was unfair that our sons should go away from this country in order that Chinese should supersede them." In contrast, board member Brown—a white planter—insisted that racial divisions did not exist within empire (a claim many less privileged than he would have found laughable).[29] "Supposing the people of Jamaica don't want Chinese," he argued, still "they must subordinate their desires and requirements for the welfare of the Empire as a whole." Division would be bad for empire, would be forbidden by imperial authorities, and was wrong to boot. "What about Cuban prejudices? What about American prejudices? Now that our sons are going north or south of the United States how would we appreciate the banning of the Jamaican immigrant? In America the so-called Jamaican is only a little less unpopular than the Chinese, and if it were not for the raising of 'a stink' they would not allow us to land."[30] Here, as in scores of other debates of its kind in the interwar British Caribbean, we see debate over immigration entangled with emigrants' experiences of racism abroad. In this case, Brown used discrimination elsewhere to argue against discrimination at home. But as we shall see, within the decade some working-men's leaders would argue the opposite, and some elites like Brown would choose to go along.

Conspicuously absent from the 1918 debate in St. James was Latin American leaders' faith that the masses could be improved by "wise fusion" with certain immigrants and avoidance of others. On the contrary, the Jamaican masses' mixed blood and questionable morals were for Brown the final argument against exclusion. "Is a country consisting of English, Irish, Americans, Indians and all classes of people going to determine who should or should not be allowed to come here? . . . He did not think that it was for the natives of Jamaica, with all our shortcomings—with our statistics of marriages and births and criminal statistics also—to throw stones at the Chinese."[31] For Spanish American statesmen such as Gómez and Ortiz, the "shortcomings" of the "natives" could not be accepted so blithely: they believed they had nations to build out of these pueblos.

For the moment, Lowe's 1918 proposal to exclude outsiders and protect the masses did not prosper. Jumping to attest to Chinese merchants' merits and Jamaican peasants' fecklessness, the parish fathers roundly defeated his motion. The following year, in the wake of the anti-Chinese riots, the island's legislative council adopted an immigration law that required "all aliens" to pass a "dictation test" by proving the ability to read aloud in English, French, or Spanish.[32] With the imperial government's acquiescence, this common international mechanism was used in its accustomed role, limiting Asian entry without mention of race or nationality.

But what of the largest immigrant group from Asia to be found in the British Caribbean in these years—indeed, the largest immigrant group there, period: the East Indians whose arrival had been not merely countenanced but organized by the colonial government? In the Spanish-speaking rimlands, as in the United States, Canada, and other self-proclaimed "white republics," South Asians were generally stereotyped—and barred—alongside East Asians, Arabs, and other "Orientals."[33] However, within the British Caribbean in this era, East Indians were not lumped with "alien" Chinese or Syrians. To be sure, East Indians too were potential targets for hostility from the Afro-Creole masses whose wages the indenture scheme systematically undercut. But the contours of debate were far different.

In Trinidad and Guiana, East Indians and their descendants made up over a third of local populations by 1921, and their labor remained essential to planters' plans. Indentured immigration was halted by Great Britain in 1917 not in response to workingmen's complaints in the colonies but in response to pressure from Indian nationalists who were long concerned over the treatment of their countrymen abroad. Only one-third of East Indian immigrants to Jamaica, one-fourth of immigrants to Guiana, and one-fifth of immigrants to Trinidad returned to India upon completion of their term of indenture.[34] In other words, over the half century of indentureship, more than three hundred thousand had stayed. Some of them and their descendants remained on sugar plantations as resident workers; others had acquired land through purchase or in exchange for forfeited return passage, creating small farming communities.

In the wake of indentureship's abolition, Caribbean elites congratulated themselves on the "high degree of prosperity" that "free Indian communities" had attained.[35] Simultaneously, the same elites imposed draconian vagrancy laws to ensure that those prosperous Indian peasants could not decline wage work entirely. They also cast about for some new immigration scheme that would bring at least temporarily dependent laborers from India. That is, elites up through the early 1920s remained more worried about having enough workers to keep wages low than about having enough jobs to keep workers quiet.[36] Even the question of immigrants mixing with locals through sex—the centerpiece of eugenicists' hopes and fears elsewhere—was treated by British Caribbean elites as a matter of labor supply. Given the numerical predominance of men among East Indian immigrants and of women within Afro-Caribbean communities shaped by outmigration to Panama and Cuba, "effort has been made" (explained a commentator in 1917) to "bring . . . about unions between East Indian men and negro women." But, alas, "race prejudice has proven too strong": "they do not mix."[37]

Certainly there were exceptions, but on balance he was right. Afro-Caribbeans and Indo-Caribbeans coalesced as two separate collectives. The perceived distance between them helped to paper over the heterogeneity within each. Grenadian and Barbadian immigrants in Trinidad might face stereotypes or mockery, but at the end of the day all were "creole" (understood as Afro-Creole) people. Hindu and Muslim families might worship separately in Trinidad, but at the end of the day all were "Indian people," and they came to share rituals and symbols that back in India instead marked divides between Hindu and Muslim.[38] British Caribbean elites could lament popular "race prejudice," but it was the outcome of the postemancipation labor system they themselves had created.

The Interwar Rise of Restrictionist Regimes: The Geopolitics and Labor Politics of Biopolitics

In the two decades after the Great War, immigration control became an evermore prominent component of nation-state formation, both institutionally and symbolically.[39] This international trend played out here with regional specificities. National elites across the Greater Caribbean's republics insisted that only by controlling their borders and ensuring that their populations evolved in "eugenic" directions would they be able to protect their nations against U.S. expansion. Reinforcing this conviction, leading U.S. restrictionists in the 1920s worked actively to systematize immigration bans across the Americas. Spanish American elites began to prioritize long-term population "hygiene" over the immediate joys of cheap labor, not only in rhetoric now but in practice. And working-class leaders increasingly adopted the same racialized rhetoric to push for workingmen's rights.

The populist and eugenicist cases for immigration restriction, now working hand in hand, echoed across the circum-Caribbean receiving societies whose politics were so entangled. In his widely read 1920 jeremiad *The Rising Tide of Color against White World Supremacy*, Lothrop Stoddard denounced the greedy white "employers of labor" who "put private interest above racial duty." In his analysis, as in the Trinidadian opposition press a generation before, open doors were the weapon of the wealthy. "Barring a handful of sincere but misguided cosmopolitan enthusiasts, it is unscrupulous business interests which are behind every white proposal to relax the exclusion laws protecting white areas."[40]

In the United States, class-focused and race-focused nativist arguments together culminated in the Johnson-Reed Act of 1924, hailed by one breathless supporter in the pages of *Foreign Affairs* as "a turning point in American civilization": "an emphatic national decision that, to quote President Coolidge, 'America must be kept American.'"[41] The act reduced downward wage pressures by capping overall immigration and addressed eugenicists' concern over the "dysgenic" impact of particular "stocks" by allocating slots to "Nordics" rather than Italians, Slavs, Jews, and other southern and eastern Europeans. While the act's impact on European immigrants absorbed public debate, the impact on nonwhite immigrants was in fact more drastic. Entry by any groups ineligible for citizenship—which is to say, all Asians— was barred. Meanwhile, "non-self-governing" colonial possessions in the Americas were placed under quota control for the first time. Then, simply by not extending quota numbers to consulates in the Caribbean, the United States in essence barred British Caribbean immigration, which fell from more than twelve thousand immigrants in the first half of 1924 to fewer than eight hundred in all of 1925.[42]

U.S. restrictionism added fuel to similar movements around the region. Across the Latin American republics, new groups were rising to challenge old elites, promoting a nationalist reorientation of economy and society that similarly combined class-based and race-based arguments. The new groups did not simply ape the North Atlantic eugenicism that predicted for their Afro-Indo-Latin populaces perpetual decay. Mestizo populists were at once racist and antiracist, rejecting biological essentialism while fetishizing "national" essences, with nonwhite immigrants as a frequent foil.[43] "Neither nations nor individuals are more or less intelligent, nor more or less valiant, nor more or less apt for civilization because they belong to this or the other race," wrote Venezuelan intellectual Laureano Vallenilla Lanz in 1930.[44] Rather than "Race" one "should speak of Society, *Pueblo*, Nation," and then recognize that "the sentiment of nationality and *Patria*, the 'organic solidarity,' are as deeply rooted and solidly established among us as in any of the older nationalities . . . in spite of our ethnic mosaic and young age."[45] All the more important, Vallenilla concluded—pivoting from antiracism to racism—to prevent immigrants of "African" blood from disrupting Venezuela's "organic solidarity."

"We must ban yellow and [South Asian] Indian immigration and restrict black as much as possible, even if at the start those preferences may be costly for us," wrote future Venezuelan minister of agriculture and minister of hacienda Alberto Adriani a few years later.[46] Afro-Caribbean immigrants "would undeniably contribute to the prosperity of the foreign capital that exploits our mineral resources, and certainly would help to increase our production, but at the cost of greater damages to our national life, for these are people whose level of life is almost always inferior to ours, who are in any case inassimilable, who bring no stimulus toward progress, who threaten our *social compact* and weaken our international situation."[47]

This last warning pointed to the external rather than internal consequences of open borders. These were the geopolitics of biopolitics, and they resonated in public debates in Santo Domingo, Havana, San José, and Caracas alike. Everyone knew that the United States had been "especially harsh, even unscrupulous," in its treatment of countries with Afro-descended populations, like Haiti and the Dominican Republic, reminded Adriani. "There is every reason to believe that the yankees will be inexorable against *pueblos* composed of races they consider inferior, like the black race, or future enemies, like the yellow."[48] Countries seeking to advance in the congress of nations must note the immigration policies of their aspirational peers. "Chinese and Hindus are inassimilable immigrants," banned in the United States, Argentina, Australia, New Zealand, and South Africa, warned Adriani.[49] Did Venezuela want to be among the ban-ers or the banned?

Meanwhile, around the region, organized workers embraced nationalism and often nativism as they struggled for jobs, pay, and rights. The Republic of Panama in the 1920s and 1930s saw multiple popular mobilizations, with allies ranging from local radicals with Comintern ties to junior military officers resentful of U.S. domination to American Federation of Labor (AFL) leader Samuel Gompers. The one issue on which all could agree was that the blatant privileging of foreign capital over local labor must change, and all except the Communists agreed that British West Indian workers, even those locally born, did not count as local labor. A drastic immigration ban passed in 1926 had originally been framed to target those stalwart scapegoats the Syrians, Turks, and Chinese but was revised to include West Indian Negroes, East Indians, and Japanese. Hispanic Panamanian commentators echoed the eugenicist/populist fusion heard from California to Caracas in the same years: selective immigration restriction was about placing the long-term needs of the pueblo over the short-term desire for profits. What Panama needed was not cheap labor but "families who will benefit us not only by means of material success but principally by means of morals and race."[50]

Although state rhetoric across the region now insisted that the hiring preferences of transnational employers were no longer paramount, state practice told a different tale. As a British diplomat in Bogotá explained to his superiors, Colombia's 1923 immigration law stipulated "that immigrants, whose admittance should be ethnically undesirable by reason of their race being such as would derange the proportion of races forming the Colombian stock, may be admitted or refused at the discretion of the Ministry for Foreign Affairs. This gives the Government a free hand, and as it is not its policy to encourage coloured immigration, it may be said that immigration of British West Indians, in the strict sense of the word, is practically prohibited." Yet somehow the United Fruit Company was routinely able to acquire visas for the "coloured employees" it sought to bring in to work on its Colombian enterprises.[51] The scenario repeated in republic after republic. Popular xenophobia made its way into law, yet enforcement left the bottom-line interests of powerful employers untouched.[52]

Although anti-immigrant and anti-imperialist rhetoric often went hand in hand, black immigrants made more tempting targets than Yankee interlopers did. In 1924 the Panamanian Federación de Obreros denounced the employment of "Jamaican and Barbadoes workers, whose inclination is towards abjection and slavery, and whose productiveness as workers can by no means be compared with that of the workers of Panama" in a report to the AFL-dominated Pan-American Federation of Labor: it was adopted unanimously. Two years later the Federación de Obreros sought AFL support as they petitioned the U.S. government that in the Canal Zone "preference be given the natives *in positions not occupied by American workers* [my emphasis] and that the West Indian workers who are not needed be repatriated to their place of origin."[53] That is, booting out dark-skinned immigrants and their children was a battle Panamanian *obreros* thought they could win. In contrast, the "American workers" who monopolized the choicest jobs in the Canal Zone looked unassailable—and remained unassailed.

Eugenicist alliances ultimately undercut labor agendas, however compatible they appeared. This was clear to some observers at the time. As the British Caribbean-run, Panama-based *Workman* declared in 1924 with regard to xenophobic agitation in Cuba, "if a surplus of West Indian labour should menace the economic interests of Cubans" it was "only fair that they protect themselves by restricting immigration from the West Indies." But to ban West Indians "to make room and give preference to Spaniards and Italians," as in practice was done, was both insulting and self-defeating.[54]

Leaving the prerogatives of foreign-born whites untouched, restrictionist bargains often succeeded in excluding foreign-born blacks while rarely securing for the native-born working class the advantages they sought.

The "Blaze of Nationalism" among British West Indians at Home and Abroad

This high-pressure era saw a wide variety of collective identities asserted by British Caribbeans, especially overseas. They faced a world in which individual mobility increasingly depended on international negotiations and in which nationalist claims had become a key resource in class struggle. Yet British Caribbean emigrants had no nation-state to call their own.

Seeking cross-island alliance in support of demands for representative government, intellectuals and activists of color had begun to preach the virtues of federation among the British colonies. Men like Grenada's pioneering journalist T. A. Marryshow saw unity as essential for advance within the empire. "When the consciousness of oneness is sufficiently awakened in the various islands," argued Marryshow in 1915,

> the West Indies will automatically come into its own as political entity and a component part in the fabric of the British Empire. There should be neither Grenadians, nor Barbadians, not Trinidadians, nor any such "ians" among us, but *West Indians* and, fundamentally, none other. . . . Only in this way can a West Indian Dominion come into being which will cause us to be a respectable force in the affairs of the world. We should all leave the "out grown shell" of insular limitations and aspire to the more "stately mansions,"—the mansions of nationality.[55]

Nationality, in this formulation, meant British West Indian unity, incompatible with (smaller) island loyalties but compatible with (larger) imperial ones.

Yet, for migrants in overseas British West Indian communities, those small loyalties loomed large. In Panama, Jamaica-born journalist Sidney Young lamented in 1927 that "twenty-three years of residence in a foreign country under singularly repressive conditions have not served to bring the people of the various [island] groups into the close kinship which the bonds of race, color, and nationality would warrant."[56] As with the "near neighbor" migrants discussed earlier, it was precisely because "the average Barbadian, St. Lucian, Jamaican, Trinidadian, Grenadian, Antiguan" in Panama shared so much that the differences between them—"national customs and particularities," Young called them—stood out in the fabric of daily life.[57] Note that in Young's first sentence, "nationality" references the collective of British West Indians, while in the second, the "national" is island-specific: this in the writings of a single author discussing a single topic.

Young railed against "the miserable doctrine of Insularity" that shaped British Caribbean civic life in Panama.[58] Yet for the migrants who read Young's pages, the reliable solidarity of home island associations—the Sons and Daughters of Barbados, the Grenadian Benevolent Society—was a crucial shelter rather than an "out grown shell." Contrary to Young's fears, however, home island solidarity proved fully compatible with larger collectives. Indeed, the avid associationism of British West Indians abroad spurred rather than hindered the spectacular growth of the most influential association of all, Marcus Garvey's Universal Negro Improvement Association (UNIA).

Founded by Garvey in Kingston in 1917 after his travels had taken him through Costa Rica, Panama, and London, and refounded after his emigration to New York in 1918, the UNIA by 1923 claimed two million "active, dues-paying members" around the Atlantic. The largest numbers of chapters were in the United States, Cuba, Panama, Costa Rica, and Trinidad: that is, precisely the top British Caribbean immigrant receiving societies. Preaching racial solidarity, "Negro Nationhood," and freedom of movement, the UNIA bore the mark of this particular moment of mass emigration, race-based mobility bans, and race-conscious nativist claims. By 1927 Garvey had been deported from the United States, and U.S.-based UNIA chapters fragmented and faltered. But within the Greater Caribbean both the UNIA and other black internationalisms surged onward.[59]

Across the 1920s and 1930s, the proudly "race conscious" newspapers run by men like T. A. Marryshow and Sidney Young routinely labeled the collective made up of the Negro Race worldwide a "nation" as well. Proper race-wide "nationalism," author after author declared, was a spiritual necessity in the modern world. But structures mattered as well as sentiments within this modern world, they knew, and what this meant for the Negro Nation was unclear. In places like Venezuela, Panama, and Cuba, British Caribbean migrants were confronted not only by mestizo nationalist hostility but by concrete state power. Could Our Nation become Our State? A typical reader's contribution to the British West Indian-run *Limon* (Costa Rica) *Searchlight* in 1931 argued that members of "the Black Race" should embrace the spirit of "Nationalism"; an appended editorial pointed to the institutional crux of the matter. "Nationalize how, where, by what means, because it seems to us for a people to Nationalize they must have a country to do so in."[60] This was the very dilemma, the editor explained, that Marcus Garvey had sought to answer in preaching "Africa for the Africans, at home and abroad."

"Nationalize how, where, by what means?" The question was on target. In the 1930s there was no polity offering British West Indians full political membership in any of the imagined communities they meant when they spoke of "nationalism," be it the Garveyites' worldwide "Negro Nationhood," Marryshow's British West Indies–wide "mansions of nationality," or the individual islands whose "national customs" Sidney Young saw as distractions from Pan–West Indian unity. What was on offer instead, as we shall see, was an island-specific nativism—Jamaica for the Jamaicans, Trinidad for the Trinidadians—that elites in the British colonies now embraced in rhetoric while still refusing to offer political rights for the Jamaican or Trinidadian masses.

Nativism without Populism: The British Caribbean, 1920s–1930s

As restrictionism spread across the Greater Caribbean's receiving societies, middle-class politicians in the region's sending societies embraced the time-honored strategy of scapegoating "alien" shopkeepers. Meanwhile they utterly failed to address the genuine crisis created by the closure of labor outlets abroad. Even more than with anti-Antillean agitation in Panama, Costa Rica, Venezuela, and the Dominican Republic, xenophobic rhetoric in the British colonies substituted for rather than accompanied populist shifts. High property requirements for voting and the lack of self-government meant that workingmen and women here had fewer levers to use. Social guarantees were not forthcoming; labor protections and political rights did not expand. As race-based restrictionism in the surrounding republics hit working-class households across the British colonies, British Caribbean elites performed nationalist concern while refusing even to debate real structural or constitutional change. Once again, East Asian and Middle Eastern immigrants found themselves at center stage in the political theater.

The international moment had shifted, argued the *Kingston Daily Gleaner*—voice of the island's merchants, professionals, and resident plantation owners—in October 1924. The U.S. Johnson-Reed Act, implemented a month before, was taking a toll both materially and symbolically. No more could the common shelter of empire be taken to disallow all barriers. Emulating "America, Australia, Canada, [and] New Zealand," Jamaica too must move to "protect [her] nationals against the severe and desperate competition of outsiders, even if some of these happen to be British subjects."[61] As had so often happened elsewhere, Chinese shopkeepers would be made the scapegoat for political and economic trends they had done nothing to foster. Even the Jamaican Imperial Association—mouthpiece of the wealthiest and whitest elites least concerned with the complaints of the masses—now urged "vigorous enforcement" of the existing immigration law: "which of course," they were quick to underline, "would not apply to persons from the Mother Country, the self-Governing Dominions and the United States of America."[62] Nativist immigration laws now seemed a reasonable bargain—as long as they did not undercut white privilege.

With increasing intensity from the mid-1920s into the 1930s, politicians in the British Caribbean—Jamaica and Trinidad in particular—followed legislators in Canada, South Africa, and Australia in proposing race-based immigration restraints. They did so in response to ever-louder street politics that demanded anti-Chinese exclusion at home in response to anti-black exclusion abroad. A typical 1925 letter to the editor (signed by "A NATIVE") declared that the masses were mobilized: if the governor "fails in this representation of the feelings of the natives over this Alien menace, then every native is quite prepared to subscribe his quota towards the cost of a strong and responsible deputation to England on the matter."[63]

Encouraging popular hostility to focus on Asian and Middle Eastern shopkeepers rather than on planter hegemony or electoral disenfranchisement was a win-win proposition for the white and near-white elite and middling sectors on islands like Jamaica and Trinidad, who themselves did compete with hard-driving immigrant merchants. British officials struggled to balance that calculus against the diplomatic complications discriminatory legislation brought. The Colonial Office stalled proposed legislation from the colonies for long months or even years as they fielded complaints from Chinese diplomats and sought euphemistic language that would work as nativist window dressing while not openly insulting any "Alien" race.[64]

Strikingly, South Asian immigrants and their children remained at the margins of these impassioned debates over insular belonging and native rights. They were not scapegoated as alien usurpers as were the Chinese and Syrians, yet they were not positioned to claim "Native" rights as some Afro-Caribbeans (in line with workers from Panama to Pittsburgh) attempted in these years. Proponents of anti-Chinese action in 1930s Jamaica formed the Jamaica Native Defenders Committee (JNDC); returnees from Panama, Cuba, and Costa Rica were prominent among its leaders, as were former or current Garveyites. A typically fiery JNDC speech from 1931 threatened that if the government refused to act against the Chinese, "people will think about cutting throats, burning down shops and do all sorts of things.... We are out to agitate for something, and that is to bid chinese goodbye."[65] Yet JNDC speakers went out of their way to clarify that "when speaking of aliens" they "meant specially the Chinese and Syrians; they did not refer to the Indians, called 'coolies.' These last mentioned people were agriculturally inclined and as the country was an agricultural one they fitted in well."[66] East Indians were not quite natives, but not quite aliens.

However, the same currents that encouraged Afro-Caribbeans in this era to define themselves as part of a supranational "Negro Race"—a collective shaped by history, united in sentiment, and struggling together against global oppression—impacted East Indians as well. The resultant essentialist internationalisms tended to reify ethnic divides. Increasingly, some East Indian elites proclaimed race- and culture-based reasons why East Indians did not belong in the Caribbean—or certainly did not belong as part of the political projects Afro-Creole politicians sought to lead.

When a British parliamentary commission visited Trinidad in 1922 to assess possibilities for constitutional change, the East Indian leaders they interviewed shared the goal of political integration: although some favored formal communal representation, others argued the trend toward "denationalization" and absorption into the Afro-Creole populace—which they viewed with equanimity—would make communal representation unnecessary. By the 1930s things were different. In dialogue with emissaries from the anti-imperial Indian nationalist movement, East Indian leaders discovered "a new spirit of renaissance or race determination or race consciousness," as one participant gushed in 1929. Both the vocabulary and the ideas echoed the black internationalisms of which Marcus Garvey's UNIA had been a harbinger a decade before. By 1936, at an "All Indian Round Table Conference" organized in Trinidad, East Indian elites from across the ideological spectrum spoke of "denationalization" as a specter to be avoided at all cost.[67]

Nevertheless, in the same era of the 1930s, in both Trinidad and Guiana, hard-hit East Indian cane workers joined forces with Afro-Creole organizers to demand food, shelter, and voice.[68] Multiple kinds of political community were imaginable at this moment, and which would predominate was unclear.

Anti-Immigrant Action, Return Migration, and the Dawn of New Nations, 1930s–1950s

What kinds of societies did the early-twentieth-century heyday of circum-Caribbean migration leave in its wake? A survey of the region circa 1930 shows us, first, a large group of emigrant-sending societies where immigrants rarely came to stay (Jamaica, Barbados, Puerto Rico, and all of the Leewards and Windwards: each with only 1 to 3 percent of total population born elsewhere); second, many countries where immigrants, although highly visible in specific regions, made little dent in national-level figures (Colombia, Venezuela, Guatemala, Nicaragua, Dominican Republic, Honduras, and Costa Rica: 1 to 6 percent born elsewhere); third, a handful of immigrant-heavy societies, where mass arrivals of foreign-born had been fundamental to the preceding decades of growth (Panama, Cuba, the United States, and British Honduras: 10 to 15 percent born elsewhere); and fourth, outdoing them all, British Guiana and Trinidad: 18 and 24 percent born elsewhere, reflecting the presence in each case of some 40,000 South Asia-born residents, joined in Trinidad's case by an equivalent total composed of Barbadians, Vincentians, and Grenadians (see table 1.1).

As the eugenicist/populist frameworks developed in the 1920s collided with global economic crisis in the 1930s, anti-immigrant nativism moved from rhetoric to practice at a growing number of sites. European immigrants—as we have seen, only present in truly sizable numbers in Cuba—were not targets. On the contrary, they remained highly sought-after, the desirables against whom "undesirable" aliens were defined. (The working-class Cubans whose chance at upward mobility Spanish immigrants usurped felt differently, and for a brief populist moment in 1933, the "Nationalization of Labor Law" was enforced to give Cubans preference over Spaniards as well as over Haitians and British West Indians.[69]) In some places, Chinese and Middle Eastern merchants drew renewed hostility; this was true of Chinese and "Turco" shopkeepers in El Salvador, culminating in the mass closure of businesses and threatened expulsion of the Chinese (but not the Arabs) in 1931.[70] Similarly, when labor riots broke out among the suffering masses of Jamaica in 1938, Chinese shops were destroyed across the island.

But most pervasively, it was Afro-Antillean immigrants and their children who bore the brunt of anti-immigrant action as the Great Depression dug in. To labor leaders seeking to ensure jobs for "native" workers and to eugenicist elites seeking to guard the "blood stocks" against "Negro contamination," exclusionary laws no longer seemed sufficient. Four decades of circum-Caribbean labor migration had created large, multigenerational Afro-Antillean populations in Venezuela, Panama, Costa Rica, Cuba, and the Dominican Republic. In each case, in the 1930s the national state undertook an array of actions both legal and extralegal to marginalize or remove Caribbean immigrants and their children. Deportations on grounds of current unemployment or supposedly illegal original entry occurred sporadically from Mexico to Venezuela. More systematic mass deportations were threatened against British Caribbeans in the Dominican Republic, Cuba, and Panama and were carried out against Haitians in Cuba and the Dominican Republic.[71]

Made pervasively unwelcome, scores of emigrants and their foreign-born children streamed back to Jamaica, Barbados, and Haiti. Smaller numbers returned to the Leeward and Windward Islands, but their proportional impact was even greater. The practices of "indoor gate-keeping" that drove them out of the Spanish American republics included workplace-specific employment quotas, increased fees and fines, and plain old violence. Extralegal coercion was often left in the hands of local officials, allowing center-state politicians to deny responsibility for what they dismissed as isolated abuses.

The pattern was common to many of the Greater Caribbean's porous and heterogeneous borderlands, including eastern Cuba and northeast Venezuela. But it reached its tragic apogee with the massacre of some 15,000 residents of Haitian ancestry in the Dominican *frontera* region in 1937. Locals of varied and mixed origin had long moved back and forth through the Haitian-Dominican borderlands. Indeed the border's demarcation had not been settled until 1936. This was a classic case of the "near neighbor" transnational movement so characteristic of Greater Caribbean frontiers. Or at least it was until October 3, 1937, when General Rafael Trujillo sent troops to the region with orders to kill all "Haitians" found. For five days they did so, using machetes rather than bullets to disguise official involvement.

Three months later, as testimonies trickled out describing families herded en masse into the woods for slaughter and refugees hacked to death on the river bank as they sought to flee to Haiti, Trujillo still insisted that any violence had been "a purely local incident, which is not international or even national"—and moreover had been entirely provoked by illegal Haitian border-crossing. Ultimately the guilt lay with the "100,000 Haitians on Dominican soil taking employment from Dominicans and using our land and resources."[72] The death toll was staggering, and sui generis, but the justification was absolutely typical of the era.

Action against black and Asian immigrants was just one strand of a broader reframing of national communities in the entangled Greater Caribbean in the 1930s. The story of the era is one of new inclusions and exclusions at once. As global economic crisis shook regimes, the new nationalist alliances opened the way for genuine, if not always permanent, reforms. Across the region, in republics and colonies, Spanish-, English-, and French-speaking alike, the late 1930s saw large-scale labor unrest. In the republics—without the backstop of empire—this often triggered regime change as self-described nationalist reformers within the military stepped in to replace elites whose control over the political system was fracturing. The equivalent dynamic in the colonies saw imperial warships rushed to provide support to colonial governments threatened by strikes and riots in Trinidad, Barbados, Jamaica, and British Honduras. Regime change would come here, too, but through a slower process of negotiated decolonization.[73]

Exactly what form would the new states take? Where would the internal and external boundaries of "nation" be drawn? The outcomes were far from predetermined, yet the conflicts over return migration and immigrant rights in the 1930s foretold divisions to come. The restriction of return migration to island of origin presaged a divided archipelago rather than a unified federation. And the street-level hostility toward Asian denizens in Jamaica and Trinidad suggested that forging "national" solidarity across lines of race and class would be challenging indeed.

The entanglements of immigration and political belonging in the Greater Caribbean sat front and center in an analysis by Marcus Garvey in 1940. He had jumped to offer evidence to the Royal Commission investigating the causes of the popular uprisings that had shaken Port of Spain, Bridgetown, and Kingston from 1935 to 1938. Garvey explained the crisis of imperial rule as the culmination of a multisited saga of elite power, popular mobility, and rising exclusion. He began with the remaking of labor regimes in the wake of slavery. The "importation" of "coolie immigrants" had depressed wages and "forced the ambitious labouring natives to seize the opportunity of going abroad."[74]

Here, as elsewhere, Garvey used the term "native" for Caribbean people of African ancestry. And throughout the rest of his testimony, in keeping with the patterns of the preceding two decades, Garvey denounced anti-black nativism in the receiving societies only to embrace anti-Asian nativism at home. "After the closing down of work in the respective countries with prejudice drawn against the West Indians, large numbers of people who went abroad returned to their respective homes and particularly Jamaica, to be confronted with, in Jamaica, the country being dominated by Chinese, Assyrians, and in some respects Indians, and to find no opportunity for work, employment, or business, in the land of their nativity."[75]

The category of "nativity" was fundamental to Garvey's argument, and there was no possibility that it could be acquired by birth alone. Indians born in Jamaica did not count. It was the West Indies' destiny to be peopled by "Negroes," whose struggle against the "Asiatic races" was inevitable. For Garvey, history mattered and labor struggles mattered, but ultimately ancestry and political community must coincide. "There is no doubt that the question is basically racial." Jamaica "is really economically monopolized by the Asiatic races and one may mention prominently the Syrians, in combination with the Jews. In Trinidad and British Guiana there is a similar influence, particularly among the East Indians, that affects the good and well being of the Negro race."[76] Echoing rhetoric that rang across Europe at this moment—a week before the partition of Czechoslovakia in Munich and two months before the Kristallnacht—Garvey saw races as actors in a long-term battle for territory. The West Indies, like all countries, must inevitably "grow into might[y] native centres which will not offer any peaceful relationships between ambitious groups of opposite races."[77]

The story of Caribbean nationhood is often used to counter such claims. "Out of Many, One People," holds Jamaica's national motto. Yet the history of the region is still being written, and the complexities of exclusion and belonging that shaped the transition to independence were real and enduring.[78] As noted earlier, popular mobilizations in the British Caribbean in the late 1930s saw multiple instances of alliance between East Indians and Afro-descendants, all the more impressive because they cut across not only the racial divide that preoccupied Garvey but also divisions of residence, economic sector, language, and religion. However, such alliances proved hard to sustain. Just like British West Indians born in Central America, East Indians born in the British Caribbean were leery of radical political movements that reached out for their support in times of need, given how often they had been treated as alien by "local" working classes despite their own local birth.

Worried that steps toward representative government might leave them without political influence in these lands of their birth, East Indians tended to support incremental reform and communal representation rather than immediate decolonization and universal suffrage. In turn, worried that East Indian "chauvinism" or "conservatism" might hamstring economic reform, some Afro-Creole reformers supported language tests or literacy tests that would exclude many from voting. The devil of democracy would be in the details, and the details reflected disputes over race, culture, and belonging that had been shaped by local class dynamics and region-wide state-making alike.[79]

Conclusion

The politics of immigration and nationalism in the islands and rimlands of the Greater Caribbean during the heyday of transoceanic migration were entangled in multiple ways. Those who debated barriers to entry did so with explicit reference to international comparisons and geopolitical consequences. For Spanish American republics, the frame that mattered was U.S. economic hegemony and military threat. For British Caribbeans, the relevant frames were provided by the British Empire on the one hand and the surrounding circum-Caribbean republics on the other (the latter including the United States, but from this vantage as pioneer of anti-immigrant bans rather than source of menacing marines).

We began by noting regional differences in the class dynamics of explicit race talk. We then saw a major convergence in the 1930s as mestizo nationalists, Afro-Creole advocates, and Hindu renovators all seemed to agree on just how different they were from each other. In the international heyday of romantic territorialist nationalism, everyone from canny elites to insurgent middle sectors to hard-pressed masses spoke of nativity, nativism, and nation as they staked their claims to a piece of the pie. Actors from Marcus Garvey to Panamanian labor leaders reflect this supraregional trend. But whereas within the Spanish-speaking republics the heyday of mestizo populism brought at least rhetorical agreement on the inclusivity of "the nation" by the 1930s (although in practice racism and poverty still barred full participation by many), within the Caribbean's British colonies the meaning of nation was far less clear. Individual islands, the British West Indies as a whole, and supraterritorial collectives like "Our Negro Race" and "Our Indian People" all were called "nation" on a regular basis in this era. Which collective should be the "self" on whose behalf "self-government" should be sought would be the vexing question of the generation that followed.

Acknowledgments

The two maps in this chapter were designed by Lara Putnam and executed by Bill Nelson. They appeared originally in Lara Putnam, "The Making and Unmaking of the Circum-Caribbean Migratory Sphere: Mobility, Sex across Boundaries, and Collective Destinies, 1840–1940," in *Migrants and Migration in Modern North America: Cross-Border Lives, Labor Markets, and Politics in Canada, the Caribbean, Mexico, and the United States*, ed. Dirk Hoerder and Nora Faires (Durham, NC: Duke University Press, 2011), and appear here by permission of the publisher.

Notes

1. Gómez, *Contribución al estudio*, 9. See also Palmer, "Racismo intelectual en Costa Rica y Guatemala."
2. Petras, *Jamaican Labor Migration*; Salas, *Enduring Legacy*; McGuinness, *Path of Empire*; and Soluri, *Banana Cultures*, ch. 1.
3. Scott, *Slave Emancipation in Cuba*; Corbitt, "Immigration in Cuba"; and Chinea, "Race, Colonial Exploitation and West Indian Immigration," esp. 514–15.
4. Ortiz, "Inmigración desde el punto de vista criminológico," 55.
5. De la Fuente, *A Nation for All*; and Casey, "Haitian Migrants in Cuba."
6. Laurence, "Importation of Labour; and Roberts, *Population of Jamaica*, 128.
7. Editorial, "Our Unofficial Legislators," *Port of Spain Daily Mirror,* November 14, 1904, 6.
8. Ibid.
9. Ibid. See discussion in Brereton, *History of Modern Trinidad*, 114–15.
10. Colby, *Business of Empire*; Bourgois, *Ethnicity at Work*; and Chomsky, "'Barbados or Canada?'"
11. E.g., Putnam, *Company They Kept*; Charlton, "'Cat Born in Oven Is not Bread'"; and Putnam, *Radical Moves*, ch. 1.
12. Verrill, *Book of the West Indies*, 150.
13. See analysis in Moya, "A Continent of Immigrants."
14. Ferenczi and Willcox, *International Migrations*, 1:525–27; de la Fuente, *A Nation for All*, 101.
15. Kuczynski, *Demographic Survey*, 3:11.
16. See, e.g., Quirós, "Inmigración e identidad nacional"; Edelman, " Central American Genocide"; and Sandoval García, *Otros amenazantes*.
17. "A 'Systematic' Impostor. The Magistrate on Grenadians," *Port of Spain Weekly Guardian*, February 14, 1920, 9.

18. Derby, "Haitians, Magic, and Money"; and Turits, "A World Destroyed, A Nation Imposed."

19. Lee, "The 'Yellow Peril.'" See also Hu-DeHart, "Indispensable Enemy or Convenient Scapegoat?"; and, for an even broader context, McKeown, *Melancholy Order*; and Lake and Reynolds, *Drawing the Global Colour Line*.

20. Putnam, "Eventually Alien."

21. Klich and Lesser, "Introduction: '*Turco*' Immigrants"; Foroohar, "Palestinians in Central America"; Bruckmayr, "Syro-Lebanese Migration"; and Guzmán, *A Century of Palestinian Immigration*.

22. Klich, "Argentine-Ottoman Relations," esp. 179.

23. Plummer, "Race, Nationality, and Trade," esp. 523–24.

24. "Deep Unrest in Haiti," *Port of Spain Daily Mirror*, August 18, 1904, 2–3.

25. Plummer, "Race, Nationality, and Trade," 525.

26. "Deep Unrest in Haiti," *Port of Spain Daily Mirror*, August 18, 1904, 2–3.

27. Johnson, "Anti-Chinese Riots." See also Bouknight-Davis, "Chinese Economic Development."

28. Johnson, "Anti-Chinese Riots," 20.

29. "Parochial Board of St. James," *Kingston Daily Gleaner*, January 7, 1918, 13.

30. Ibid.

31. Ibid.

32. Bouknight-Davis, "Chinese Economic Development," 87. See also discussion in National Archives of the United Kingdom, Colonial Office [henceforth, CO] 295/596/17: Criticisms by the Chinese Government of the immigration legislation recently enacted by the Government of Trinidad (1937).

33. Lake and Reynolds, *Drawing the Global Colour Line*; and Mongia, "Race, Nationality, Mobility."

34. Roberts and Byrne, "Summary Statistics," 132.

35. "A Settlement Scheme for East Indians," *Kingston Daily Gleaner*, February 22, 1918, 7.

36. Brereton, *History of Modern Trinidad*, 158–60.

37. "Progress of East Indians in the West Indies," *Kingston Daily Gleaner*, August 15, 1917, 11.

38. Williams, *Stains on My Name*; Munasinghe, *Callaloo or Tossed Salad?*; and Khan, *Callaloo Nation*.

39. Fahrmeir, *Citizenship*; and Zolberg, *Nation by Design*.

40. Stoddard, *Rising Tide of Color*, 276.

41. Ward, "Our New Immigration Policy," 110 and 104.

42. Zolberg, *Nation by Design*; Ngai, *Impossible Subjects*; Putnam, "Unspoken Exclusions"; and Putnam, *Radical Moves*, ch. 3.

43. Stepan, *"Hour of Eugenics"*; and Putnam, "Eventually Alien."

44. Vallenilla Lanz, "Disgregación e integración," 325, 326.

45. Ibid., 333.

46. Adriani, *Labor Venezolanista*, 150.

47. Ibid., 149. See also Pellegrino, *Historia de la inmigración*, 1:148–58, 171–72; and Wright, *Café con Leche*, 76–94.

48. Adriani, *Labor Venezolanista*, 149.

49. Ibid., 148.

50. "Panama's Immigration Need Is Discussed by 'El Diario': Spanish Daily Says Country Needs Brawn but not from the West Indies," *Panama American*, December 29, 1926; see also "West Indian Negroes Excluded in Drastic Immigration Bill: Chinese, Syrians, Turks and East Indians Also Barred," *Panama American*, September 19, 1926.

51. CO 318/406/1: Immigration of British West Indians in Central and South America: Letter to Foreign Office from British legation in Bogotá, March 29, 1932.

52. See discussion in Putnam, *Radical Moves*, ch. 3.

53. *Report of the Proceedings*, 130; and "Mr. Adames letter to Mr. Hushing," *Panama American*, March 3, 1926.

54. "West Indian Labourers in the Republics: Views Expressed in Editorial Published in 'The Workman' of Panama," *Kingston Daily Gleaner*, September 5, 1924, 3.

55. Editorial, "West Indians and the West Indies," *West Indian* (St. George's, Grenada), February 20, 1915, 2.

56. Sidney A. Young, "A Deplorable Trend," *Panama American* West Indian Page, February 10, 1927.

57. Sidney A. Young, "Blocking Progress," *Panama American* West Indian Page, December 4, 1926.

58. Ibid.

59. Hill, *Marcus Garvey and UNIA Papers*, vol. 11; Martin, *Race First*; and Ottley, *New World A'Coming*, 68–81.

60. "Nationalism and the Black Race," *Limón Searchlight*, February 7, 1931, 5.

61. "The First Question," *Kingston Daily Gleaner*, October 11, 1924, 12. On anti-Chinese political debates in this era, see Carnegie, *Some Aspects*; on anti-Chinese popular mobilization, see Post, *Arise Ye Starvelings*.

62. "Points Placed before the New Governor," *Kingston Daily Gleaner*, October 1, 1924, 7.

63. "The Alien Question," *Kingston Daily Gleaner*, May 15, 1925, 8.

64. See Putnam, *Radical Moves*, ch. 3.

65. "Another Sedition Case," *Limon Searchlight*, June 6, 1931, 2. See also Carnegie, *Some Aspects*, 99–111; and Post, *Arise Ye Starvelings*, 208–12.

66. "Enter Protest Dissolution of the Council," *Kingston Daily Gleaner*, September 16, 1930, 14.

67. Singh, "Conflict and Collaboration," 234, 237, 240; Samaroo, "Indian Connection"; and Munasinghe, *Callaloo or Tossed Salad?*, 191. See also Shepherd, "Dynamics," esp. 19.

68. Bolland, *Politics of Labour*, 252–57, 336–56; Lewis, *Labour in the West Indies*; and Basdeo, "Indian Participation."

69. McGillivray, *Blazing Cane*; and de la Fuente, *A Nation for All*.

70. Suter, "'Pernicious Aliens.'"

71. Extensive evidence in support of this and the following paragraph is presented in Putnam, *Radical Moves*, chs. 3 and 6.

72. "Dominican President Refuses to Arbitrate: Says Incident 'Purely Local,'" *Pittsburgh Courier*, December 25, 1937, 7. See Turits, "A World Destroyed, A Nation Imposed."

73. For a synthetic overview, see Bolland, "Labor Protests, Rebellions."

74. CO 950/44: Mr. Marcus Garvey (Universal Negro Improvement Association): Memorandum of Evidence, Letter from Marcus Garvey to WIRC, September 21, 1938.

75. Ibid.

76. Ibid.

77. CO 950/44: Mr. Marcus Garvey (Universal Negro Improvement Association): Memorandum of Evidence, Letter from Marcus Garvey to Lloyd, Secretary, WIRC, September 24, 1938.

78. Khan, "Journey to the Center of the Earth"; see also Mohammed, "Asian Other."

79. Singh, "Conflict and Collaboration," 242. On current tensions in Trinidad, see Brereton, "All ah we is not one"; and Cudjoe, "Multiculturalism."

2

The Limits of the Cosmic Race

Immigrant and Nation in Mexico, 1850–1950

JÜRGEN BUCHENAU

For Mexico is a land in which men have survived against heavy odds, like a cactus in the desert or a golden dome built far from civilization.

Irene Nicholson, 1965

The two most prominent Mexicans of the twenty-first century are sons of immigrants. With a net worth of approximately US$60 billion, the world's wealthiest individual is Carlos Slim Helú, a Lebanese Mexican. And in July 2000 Vicente Fox, the son of Irish and Spanish immigrants, won election to the presidency of Mexico, thus ending the seventy-one-year rule of the Partido Revolucionario Institucional. To the casual observer, Slim's enormous wealth and Fox's political triumph appeared to show that Mexico, like Argentina, Brazil, and the United States, had at last become a nation of immigrants.[1]

In fact, however, Slim's and Fox's examples proved epiphenomenal rather than paradigmatic. Whereas Argentina, Brazil, Canada, and the United States received millions of newcomers during the heyday of transatlantic migration in the period 1820–1930, only 270,000, or 0.5 percent of all European immigrants in the New World, settled in Mexico (see table 2.1). In 1930 immigrants made up less than 1 percent of the Mexican population.[2] To be sure, this small number made a big difference. In the course of the late nineteenth century, European and Chinese immigrants seized control of banking and commerce, and French and Spanish families pioneered industrialization. In the twentieth century, immigrants came to play important roles in academia and the arts.[3] Contributions from immigrants have greatly shaped our understanding of the past century, especially the

Table 2.1. European migration to Mexico in comparative perspective, 1820–1932

Receiving Country	Number of European Immigrants	Percentage of total European overseas immigration
United States	32,564,000	57.9
Argentina	6,501,000	11.6
Canada	5,073,000	9.0
Brazil	4,361,000	7.8
Cuba	1,394,000	2.5
Mexico	**270,000**	**0.5**
Peru	30,000	0.05
Other countries	7,677,000	10.65

Source: Adapted from Moya, *Cousins and Strangers*, 46. These figures exclude return migration.

writings of the Polish-born writer Elena Poniatowska, now adopted as one of Mexico's own. Still, in light of the presence of 31.7 million Mexicans and their descendants in the United States as of 2009, one would be hard pressed to disagree with the assessment of historian Moisés González Navarro that Mexico is "a country of emigration rather than immigration."[4]

This small yet influential immigrant population assimilated, but slowly. This chapter builds upon my previously published work that focused on European immigrants' practices of self-exclusion, a product of their widely held sense of racial and cultural superiority.[5] Expanding the purview beyond merely European immigration, and taking into account the significant scholarship that has appeared in the last decade, it analyzes endogenous factors that affected the degree of integration of immigrants into the national polity. The complex relationship between Mexico and its immigrants complicates the stereotype of a xenophilic country serving as "mother of foreigners and stepmother of Mexicans," a stereotype pertaining both to the modernizing dictatorship of José de la Cruz Porfirio Díaz and to the neoliberal regimes that have governed the country since 1982. Thus, elite xenophilia contrasted with widespread popular xenophobia, a legal framework that discriminated against foreign-born residents throughout most of the twentieth century, and constructions of Mexican nationalism that excluded immigrants.[6]

Immigration into Mexico therefore does not fit into either standard narratives of Mexican identity or other New World paradigms. It provides a counterpoint to the hypothesis quoted in the introduction to this volume that "the integration of immigrants into the local society was faster and more successful in many of the migrant flows that arrived in Spanish and Portuguese America than in their North American counterparts."[7] As recently as 2010, the agency of the national government charged with preventing discrimination reported that "the prevalent image of Mexico as a country in solidarity with and open toward foreigners is debatable."[8]

A Nation of Spaniards, "Indians," and Mestizos

Unlike North Americans and the inhabitants of the Southern Cone, Mexicans have not imagined their country as a nation of immigrants. Their historical memory focused on the experience of the Spanish-indigenous encounter in the sixteenth century, and particularly the construction of an exploitative colonial state on the ruins of the once-proud Mexica Empire. Whereas North American whites traced their roots to a succession of largely voluntary European migrations, and African Americans derived their own identity from the legacy of the transatlantic slave trade, Mexicans (as well as the inhabitants of other nations with large indigenous populations) imagined themselves as the products of the Spanish sexual conquest of indigenous Mesoamerica. Forged in the crucible of racial miscegenation—and particularly, as Mexicans imagined it, the union of Spanish conquistadors and indigenous women—was the mestizo, the prime exponent of the national character. Mexico thus displayed what Estelle Tarica has labeled "mestizo nationalism": the identification of *mexicanidad* with the miscegenation of the conquerors and the conquered, which produced a new mestizo race.[9] Of course, this imagining also included the nonmiscegenated elements of Mexican society: the *indios*, who continued to make up approximately 15 percent of the population and retained their languages and customs; and the creoles, the descendants of the Spaniards who occupied privileged political and economic positions. Although a quarter-million African slaves had also arrived during the colonial period, contributing to the ethnic mix particularly on both coasts and in many of the cities, their legacy remained almost forgotten in the national period until José Vasconcelos included them in his representation of the "cosmic race"—and, even then, in a merely marginal representation.[10]

In the colonial era, creole efforts at maintaining their dominance in a multiethnic society contributed to constructions of national identity that excluded immigrants. The creoles imagined themselves as the representatives of a Spanish Roman Catholic community as embodied in the Virgin of Guadalupe.[11] By identifying themselves as "americanos"—or, as historian

Mark Burkholder has argued, "native sons"—the creoles defied the *peninsulares*, the native-born Spaniards who held the most important political positions, and did not relinquish their association with the Spanish heritage.[12] In this view, all those not of Spanish culture ("Indians" as well as foreigners, particularly Protestants, Jews, and members of other faiths) remained outsiders. The *peninsulares*, also pejoratively called *gachupines*, were the only immigrant group recognized in this imaginary, and hardly in a favorable light. Meanwhile, the growing group of mestizos assumed a position in the middle of the Mexican social pyramid, and their sense of themselves as products of the Spanish-indigenous encounter dovetailed with the creoles' imaginary world made up of Spaniards, "indios," and those in between.

Mexico also posed specific obstacles for immigrants. Despite the optimism of German geologist Alexander von Humboldt, whose monumental *Political Essay on the Kingdom of New Spain* predicted great agricultural wealth, Mexico offered few opportunities for immigrant farmers.[13] Regionally diverse but predominantly dry and mountainous, the country possessed relatively little farmland. Even more importantly, land was not widely available. Prior to the 1850s, half of the arable land was the patrimony of the Catholic Church, and a small creole elite owned much of the remainder. A prospective farmer who came without financial resources therefore competed for jobs with the peasantry and led, more often than not, a life of material deprivation. In addition, Roman Catholicism remained the state religion through 1857, discouraging the immigration of those of different faiths. Workers found low wages; artisans, competition from a glut of skilled crafts people; and entrepreneurs, occasional efforts to outlaw foreign ownership of retail businesses.[14] For the first seventy years after independence, the country's political and economic problems added to these factors that discouraged immigration. The Wars of Independence (1810–21) left the economy ruined and political authority severely weakened. In the succeeding decades, the country experienced four major foreign invasions, including the U.S.–Mexican War, which led to the loss of half of the nation's territory. Thereafter, the disastrous War of the Reform (1858–61), followed by the French occupation and the war against Maximilian's empire (1862–67), wreaked havoc once again. To top it off, newcomers who might have desired to settle in the temperate zones in the mountains first had to pass through the tropical coastal areas, risking diseases such as yellow fever and malaria.

As a result, the sparse foreign-born population of nineteenth-century Mexico—composed primarily of the aforementioned Spaniards, U.S.

farmers, Guatemalan refugees, and European merchants—either came from neighboring countries or counted on effective protection by fortune and family networks. Even more strikingly, the presence of the first three of these groups markedly increased the anti-immigrant tendencies of the ruling class.

The case of the Spaniards is particularly instructive in this regard. Immigrants from Spain had come since the days of Hernán Cortés, and their descendants had formed the creole elite that owned New Spain's most precious land. Excluded from the highest colonial offices, the creoles had grown to resent more recent arrivals, especially during the Bourbon Reforms of the late eighteenth century. During that era, ten thousand Spaniards arrived, many of whom took advantage of family ties to become merchants and landowners. Not only did most *peninsulares* boast indisputable *limpieza de sangre*, or purity of blood, but peninsular merchants also found themselves in a fierce rivalry with the creoles. Anti-Spanish sentiments served as one of the causes of the Wars of Independence, and they intensified during the wars as Spanish troops brutally suppressed the insurrections. The achievement of independence signaled the hour of payback. In 1828 the government decreed the expulsion of all Spaniards, a decree enforced the following year when Spain's failed attempt at a reconquest led to the departure of more than seven thousand *peninsulares*.[15]

U.S. immigration proved even more ominous. Recognizing the specter of U.S. territorial expansion, late colonial authorities had invited English-speaking Roman Catholic settlers to live in the sparsely populated northeastern province of Téjas. In 1824 the national government of Guadalupe Victoria renewed this invitation, although signs already pointed to an unregulated influx of Protestant immigrants from the southern United States. By 1833 the situation had gotten out of hand. More than thirty thousand English speakers in Texas, a majority of whom did not respect Mexican law, confronted approximately nine thousand Spanish speakers, and three years later the Anglos launched a successful war of secession. The Texas secession and the subsequent war with the United States demonstrated that the threat of U.S. land grabbing outweighed any possible benefits of immigration as long as political instability continued. Ironically, the annexations also demonstrated the viability of immigration, as the United States soon succeeded where Mexico had failed. After the war the United States funneled hundreds of thousands of people into the old Mexican northwest, many of them European immigrants. These areas—particularly California and Texas—constituted the promising, exploitable frontier that could have invited widespread immigration.[16]

The presence of a Guatemalan minority in the southeastern state of Chiapas constituted the mirror image of the Texas question. The westernmost province of the old Captaincy General of Guatemala, Chiapas had not joined the United Provinces of the Center of America that had emerged from the collapse of Spanish colonial authority. While the other provinces had joined Guatemala City in forming the new federation, Chiapas did not follow suit. The creoles in the highlands of Chiapas favored annexation by Mexico, while those in the lowlands preferred association with Guatemala. In 1842, several years after the disintegration of the United Provinces, Mexico annexed Chiapas. For decades thereafter, thousands of Chiapanecos still thought of themselves as Guatemalans.[17] Just as Mexicans native to California and Texas became "foreigners" by means of shifting borders, so did Guatemalans native to Chiapas—an intriguing case of transforming identities by moving boundaries rather than people.

Finally, immigrants from central and western Europe—particularly those whom historian Walther Bernecker has called the "trade conquistadors"—acquired an influence disproportionate to their small numbers.[18] The trade conquistadors came in order to advance the economic interests of their families. Armed with investment capital, they soon dominated mining, money lending, and wholesale trading. By 1850 a small group of British investors owned most of the privately held mines. Moreover, the Europeans took advantage of the prejudice of the upper classes against banking and commerce to seize control over those sectors as well. Whereas investors from London and Paris founded the first modern banks, French, German, and Spanish merchants owned most of the warehouse stores that formed the hubs of an extensive wholesale network. These bankers, merchants, and miners far outnumbered the types of immigrants who dominated the migrant flow to the United States—for example, peasant farmers and intellectuals fleeing the stifling political climate in Europe.[19]

Nineteenth-century immigration to Mexico therefore followed a pattern common to most of the Central American and Andean nations rather than the one defining what we might call the "mass immigrant nations." In Canada, the Southern Cone, and the United States, most immigrants were migrants of need who fled persecution or poverty in their home country. Most of the immigrants who came to Mexico, on the other hand, were migrants of choice. Like other heavily indigenous and mestizo nations characterized by intense struggles over land, Mexico followed a pattern of "qualitative" rather than "quantitative" immigration. The major historical drama of the nineteenth century involved the unsuccessful incorporation into the national body of a racially diverse population that spoke more than one hundred indigenous dialects and languages rather than the creation of what historian Alfred Crosby has called "neo-Europes" by means of a mass influx of European immigrants.[20]

"Whitening" the Mestizo Nation?

Beginning in the mid-1850s and culminating in the long reign of General Porfírio Díaz (1876–80 and 1884–1911), liberal modernization redefined both the idea of the nation and the country's approach to the issue of immigration. Following the mantra of the nineteenth-century Argentine statesman Juan Bautista Alberdi that "to govern was to populate," the liberal regimes encouraged immigration as a way to unlock what they saw as their nation's enormous potential, to discourage further U.S. annexations, and to "whiten" the population. Three ironies marked this strategy. First, the loss of land to the United States shifted the consensus within the Mexican government toward an acceptance of immigration. Second, Díaz's policies facilitated East Asian and Middle Eastern immigration (especially as what historian Theresa Alfaro-Velcamp has called the "back door to the United States") more so they did than European immigration.[21] Third—and perhaps most importantly—the liberals coveted foreign investments much more than they did immigration.

The Liberal Reforma of the 1850s provided the legal and institutional background to an era of contradictions that witnessed both the rapid growth of foreign influence and the rise of popular xenophobia—contradictions that were to contribute decisively to the Revolution of 1910. Seeking to emulate the U.S. economic success that the liberals believed to be based on yeoman farming, the Ley Lerdo of 1856 disentailed the lands of the Church and invited Europeans to colonize these vast territories. The ideology of reformers such as Benito Juárez emphasized immigration as a way of infusing his country's mestizo and indigenous population with such Protestant virtues as thrift, industriousness, and discipline. Himself a Zapotec Indian who only learned Spanish at the age of six, Juárez displayed an abiding belief in European models. Therefore, the liberals invited more immigrants to come to rural Mexico. Nonetheless, they could not persuade more than a few thousand, as civil war and foreign intervention continued to ravage the country until 1867. Moreover, the liberals feared the influence of foreigners they considered "pernicious"—above all, foreign-born representatives of the Church—to the extent that Article 33 of the Constitution of 1857 threatened them with expulsion.[22]

The long-lived dictatorship of Porfirio Díaz witnessed a more sustained attempt. What came to be known as the Porfiriato sponsored immigration as key to its project of state and nation building. The Díaz regime advertised Mexico as a land of unlimited opportunities for immigrants. The Porfirians hoped that immigrants would bring modern agricultural practices to the countryside. Moreover, the Díaz regime sought to settle the arid north, a sparsely populated expanse with tenuous links to the capital. Finally, the Díaz regime viewed immigration as a way of "whitening" a heavily miscegenated population.

However, the Porfirian idea of whitening involved a cultural rather than a strictly biological construction of race and ethnicity, contributing to an emphasis on foreign investments over immigration. In contrast to the widespread North American consumption of the social Darwinist thought of Herbert Spencer—the notion that race and sex, as biologically constructed, determine the struggle for survival—French positivism as defined by Auguste Comte remained more prominent in Mexico. Positivism emphasized cultural and economic "development" as measured by European models rather than biological categories. To the Porfirian elite, whitening thus meant the infusion of European money, education, and customs into a countryside populated by supposedly indolent and ignorant indigenous people. Being white, they believed, was a stage of civilization and a class marker more than it was a biological condition. As skin color, ethnicity, and class coincided to a great extent, this positivist orientation had little practical effect on the way the elite viewed the poor majority, but it did imply a prioritization of economic development.[23]

When Porfirians considered the benefits of immigration for the modernization of their country, they were thus more interested in the influx of immigrants' capital and expertise than in their physical presence. Hence, the most transformative foreign influence came by way of direct investment by faraway investors and corporations; witness the U.S.- and British-financed construction of the railroad system, the transformation of Sonora by U.S. copper barons such as William Greene, or Weetman Pearson's role in advancing British investments in the oil industry. Nonetheless, immigration served, in the words of historian Adina Cimet, to "avoid a direct confrontation of how to incorporate the indigenous population into the

body politic."[24] The influential education undersecretary Justo Sierra portrayed white immigration as a civilizing influence and ultimately as a step
toward the eventual cultural and racial fusion of the creole, mestizo, and
indigenous people.[25]

Therefore, foreign capital—not immigration, as in Argentina, for example—formed the core of the Porfirian strategy. This strategy sought to take
advantage of the rapid expansion of industrial production and the construction of efficient patterns of global exchange, which assigned to Mexico
the role of a raw material producer in the emerging global division of labor.
Countries that fell into this category not only furnished the industrializing
economies of the North Atlantic with metals, minerals, and foodstuffs; they
also became targets for investment capital as well as important markets for
surplus industrial products. Díaz and his allies believed that the surplus
capital generated by such export-led development would eventually lead
to industrialization. They envisioned Mexico as a modern nation sharing
in the prosperity of the North Atlantic economies—one that borrowed
freely from European and North American cultural and economic models while expressing pride in its historical heritage, as evidenced by Díaz's
commission of a statue of the Aztec emperor Cuauhtémoc on the capital's
main boulevard. Indeed, foreign capital flowed freely into Mexico in the
late nineteenth and early twentieth centuries, building up an impressive
railroad network, modernizing the infrastructure (particularly in the ports
and major cities), and creating a sizable urban middle class.[26]

As investments and foreigners arrived together in many cases, foreign
residents reached the high point of their presence in the Porfirian era.[27] Immigrants and their descendants were well represented in the Díaz cabinet:
the secretary of finance, José Y. Limantour, came from a French family,
and the secretary of foreign relations, Ignacio Mariscal, was married to a
woman from Baltimore. The *peninsulares*, who had completed their demographic recovery from the expulsions of the 1820s by the time of the 1910
census, married into Mexico City's most distinguished creole families. Even
more importantly, the trade conquistadors ventured into industrial manu-
facturing. In particular, French textile manufacturers formed a powerful
industrial conglomerate in Orizaba, Veracruz, while Spanish merchants
joined influential creole families in the northern city of Monterrey in setting up the beginnings of a steel industry.[28]

Encouraged by the impact of the foreigners already present, the Díaz
regime pursued a three-pronged strategy to lure more immigrants. The first
aspect of this strategy consisted of rural colonization projects. To encourage

rural immigration, the Porfirians sent agents to Europe to promote a sani-
tized version of Mexican reality. The most important of these agents, German-born Heinrich Lemcke, traveled through Europe with a pamphlet that
portrayed Mexico as a country with wide-open spaces, abundant farmland,
and a scarcity of people to work the land other than those whom Lemcke
described as the somnolent, lazy, and superstitious "Indians." It promised
generous government subsidies to prospective settler colonies, including
tax breaks and the provision of needed infrastructure. In 1882 much fan-
fare accompanied the launching of the most significant of these colonies,
six settlements whose inhabitants totaled more than 2,600 Italians. A few
decades later, four of these colonies had disappeared, as most of the Italians
had either returned home or moved to the United States.[29]

The second strategy entailed the recruitment of foreign workers and professionals, an issue that dovetailed with the influx of foreign investments.
When British and U.S. companies built the railroad lines that connected the
U.S. border with Mexico City and the major mining centers, a large number
of Chinese and Italian coolies moved south from the United States or from
their countries of origin to do the actual work. Moreover, foreign mining
and oil companies brought their own engineers and overseers, individuals
who were paid many times as much as the Mexicans working alongside
them.[30]

Finally, a reform of immigration law that suited the needs of foreign
capitalists and immigrant farmers alike constituted the third prong of Porfirian immigration policy. In 1883 the Mexican government passed legislation allowing foreigners the right to own land and subsoil resources. The
infamous "Law of Fallow Land" permitted private investors to scoop up
property declared "public," much of it land taken from indigenous communities. Three years later, the "Law of Foreignness and Naturalization"
established jus sanguinis as the guiding principle of Mexican citizenship
for the children of foreign nationals. Although the Mexican Constitution
of 1857 espoused the principle of jus soli—the idea that one's place of birth
determines one's nationality—the 1886 law allowed Mexican-born children
of foreigners to retain their father's citizenship so long as they claimed that
citizenship by the age of majority.[31]

What was curiously absent from all of these measures was a plan to assimilate foreign nationals, or at least to make them into what one thinker
called "the new creoles."[32] Indeed, the sizable foreign communities in the
capital became more rather than less isolated as the Porfiriato progressed.
In the 1890s these communities acquired a critical mass in Mexico City,

where members of the most sizable foreign communities established institutions such as schools, churches, and social clubs that allowed them to raise their families in the host country. Correspondingly, the wall that had always separated these communities from Mexican society grew much higher. By 1900 the wealthiest and most conspicuous foreign diasporas in Mexico City—the American, the British, the French, the German, and the Spanish—had become enclaves, or "colonies." In the words of a U.S. sociologist who grew up in Mexico City, a colony consisted of "those who seek to maintain their own racial and cultural integrity although living in an alien land which has an independent government."[33] This effort involved a sense of superiority over the host society, the spirit of belonging to a close-knit community, and the notion that the colony constituted an integral part of the home country even though its members lived in a different society. For example, instruction at the Colegio Alejandro von Humboldt, the German school in Mexico City, endeavored to "preserve . . . children for German culture."[34]

Immigration thus resulted in unassimilated ethnic enclaves rather than the whitening of Mexico, as little cultural transfer took place, least of all in the cities. Similar enclaves also existed in southern Brazil, Chile, and Argentina—but there they included rural areas, such as the environs of the city of Blumenau in Santa Catarina, Brazil, which became one of the largest German enclaves in Latin America, complete with schools that educated the young in German culture until President Getúlio Vargas enforced "Brazilianization" in the World War II era.

The raw numbers of immigration were even more disappointing. While direct foreign investment into Mexico grew by a factor of twenty between 1880 and 1910, the owners of much of the money remained in Europe and the United States. According to the census records between 1895 (the first official census) and 1910, the number of foreign-born immigrants doubled during these fifteen years—a far cry from the exponential growth of foreign-born residents of Argentina, Canada, and the United States. Immigrants founded only thirty-seven rural colonies in the Díaz era, and most of them failed due to lack of government support, indigenous resistance, and results that did not satisfy the inhabitants.[35] As we have seen, these disappointing results in part corresponded to an ambivalent attitude toward immigration.

Porfirian attitudes toward Chinese (and, to a lesser extent, Japanese) immigration are a good case in point because these populations could not "whiten" Mexico the way that Europeans could. Chinese immigrants arrived in ever greater numbers after the Chinese Exclusion Act diverted them south from the United States, their preferred destination. Between 1882 and 1910, an estimated sixty thousand Chinese immigrated, two-thirds of whom continued on to the United States or returned to their country of origin.[36] Initially the Porfirians showed themselves favorably disposed toward the Chinese, whom they considered hard-working, disciplined, and thrifty—all qualities they believed to be lacking among most Mexicans. They also considered the Chinese particularly well suited for Mexico's climate. For example, Secretary of Fomento Matías Romero, who owned several coffee fincas in Chiapas, believed that "the only colonists who could . . . work on our coasts are Asians, coming from climates similar to ours, primarily China. The great population of that vast empire, the fact that many of them are agriculturalists, the relatively low wages they earn, and the proximity of our coast to Asia mean that Chinese immigration would be the easiest and most convenient."[37] Romero's viewpoint corresponded to a widely held belief among hacendados and industrialists that Chinese immigrants were well suited as laborers. But Chinese immigrants did not follow the script assigned to them, acquiring a predominant role in the dry goods trade and lending in northwestern Mexico, particularly in the state of Sonora. As a result, they provided stiff competition to the middle classes, engendering hatred and xenophobia.

Following an outbreak of bubonic plague on the Pacific coast in 1903, Díaz decided to reevaluate East Asian immigration. The year 1908 saw the publication of the nation's very first immigration law, which prohibited the entry of Asians with communicable diseases. The Porfirians also commissioned a report on the socioeconomic impact of Chinese immigration. Among the more pro-Chinese committee members, one wrote that "the Chinese and the Westerner are fundamentally different" but that "we need their cooperation as an indispensable condition for development." Another committee member, however, labeled the Chinese population "a noxious element because of its low conditions and its repugnant customs." The report contrasted Chinese immigration with "desirable"—in other words, European—immigration, which cultivated the frontiers of both North America and South America.[38]

The xenophobic angst that accompanied Chinese immigration revealed both racist attitudes and an awareness of the growing number of Chinese vis-à-vis European immigrants. While the number of Europeans grew from about 26,000 to 47,000 between the 1895 and 1910 censuses, the East Asian population catapulted from 1,500 to 15,000. In Sonora alone, the Chinese

Table 2.2. Selected foreign nationals in the Mexican censuses, 1895–1970 (in thousands)

	1895	1900	1910	1921	1930	1940	1950	1960	1970
British	3	3	5	4	5	4	2	2	1
Chinese	1	3	13	14	19	7	6	5	2
French	4	4	5	4	5	3	3	4	3
Germans	2	3	4	4	7	4	5	7	5
Guatemalans	14	5	22	14	17	8	8	9	7
Japanese	—	—	2	2	4	2	2	2	2
Syrio/Lebanese	—	—	—	—	4	4	5	4	2
Spaniards	13	16	30	29	47	29	37	50	31
U.S. Citizens	12	15	21	11	12	19[a]	83[b]	98[b]	97[b]

Source: Mexican census records.

Notes: a. Misleading or missing census data.

b. The figures for U.S. citizens include resident retirees who responded to the census. This population burgeoned after World War II.

community was estimated at 4,486 individuals in 1910—by far the largest foreign colony in that state. The actual number may have been far higher because many Chinese crossed the U.S.–Mexican border, back and forth. With good reason, historian Grace Peña Delgado has analyzed the Chinese Mexican community as a transnational one that straddled the borderlands.[39] The Japanese immigrants who settled in Mexico's Pacific port cities maintained similarly intimate ties with Japanese communities on the West Coast of the United States (see table 2.2).

Although xenophilic in comparison, the Porfirians failed to attract significant immigration for a variety of reasons. In the first place, they remained ambivalent about its benefits. Second, Mexico remained a relatively unattractive target for immigrants. As land and work remained abundant in North America and the Southern Cone, newcomers continued to flock to these traditional targets of immigration, beckoned by relatives and friends who already lived in those areas. The disentailment of millions of acres of Church and peasant land led not to the development of a rural middle class that would have proved inviting to foreign immigrants but to the enrichment of wealthy hacienda owners and the impoverishment of the peasantry. In the view of one historian, Porfirian policies produced a chasm between the "modern" city and the "traditional" countryside—an area that remained neglected and undercapitalized and therefore a poor choice for a prospective immigrant.[40] Actively discouraged by European governments as well as the press, the colonization schemes only attracted small groups of colonists. Finally, the Díaz regime itself became leery of foreign influence; in the last years before his fall, don Porfirio nationalized the railroads, signed restrictive immigration legislation, and developed an anti-imperialist foreign policy.[41] In the end, the failure of the immigration project highlighted the deficiencies of the Porfirian model—a model that had vastly increased foreign influence without leading to more prosperity for all.

Revolutionary Nationalism and the Closing of the "Cosmic Race"

The period since 1910 has witnessed the end of pro-immigration sentiment in Mexico and the beginning of an era in which the government has focused on the natural growth of the population. The Mexican Revolution (1910–20), the Great Depression, and the two world wars combined to discredit the notion that European immigration could solve the country's woes. In addition, non-European immigrant communities—particularly the Chinese—found themselves racialized and oppressed in an atmosphere of open xenophobia.

Accompanied by calls for land reform and an end to foreign privileges, the revolution reminded the foreigners of their status as outsiders. As such, they became targets of a wide variety of social movements that agreed on limiting foreign influence. In 1907 a serious economic crisis had highlighted the privileged position of foreign workers and professionals. This recession intensified two responses to the foreign presence that had long simmered in the Porfiriato: elite economic nationalism and popular xenophobia.[42] While John M. Hart's claim that the revolution was a war of national liberation against U.S. imperialism appears overstated, most foreigners feared conditions resembling those of the xenophobic Boxer Rebellion in China.[43] These fears proved exaggerated because most foreign communities suffered limited casualties during the ten years of civil war compared to the native population, with total deaths of foreigners estimated at 1,477.[44] In other words, it was safer to be a foreigner in the Mexican Revolution than to be a Mexican.

However, there was one group that faced conditions resembling the Boxer Rebellion: ironically, it was the Chinese immigrants. The Chinese in Mexico found themselves subject to widespread lynching, robberies, and even murder. On May 15, 1911, just weeks before the triumph of the revolutionary coalition under the leadership of Francisco I. Madero, a mob of four thousand revolutionaries committed the single worst act of violence against an immigrant community in the Americas when they murdered 303 foreign residents, a majority of them Chinese, in the northern town of Torreón, Coahuila. Over the next eight years, another 257 documented murders occurred, although estimates of the total casualty rate for the 1910s ascend to 814. When the violence subsided, Sonora again became the epi-center of anti-Chinese activity. In February 1916 Sinophobes founded the Junta Comercial y de Hombres de Negocios (Commercial Union and of Businessmen) in the town of Magdalena, which marked the beginning of a campaign that would culminate in the expulsion of the Chinese from Sonora fifteen years later.[45] Under the motto "por la patria y la raza" (for the fatherland and [our] race), this campaign enjoyed broad middle-class support, including the collaboration of people who would go on to play important roles in the emergent postrevolutionary state. For example, the bullfighter Luis L. León, who would go on to serve as one of the founders of Mexico's official revolutionary party in 1929, wrote that "a true nationalism, aimed at destroying, not only the eminent Chinese monopoly, but also even the monopoly over the fountains of wealth of the state of other foreigners, such as the North American companies, will . . . give us strong sympathy in all of the republic."[46] Fortunately for the Chinese, they initially received some measure of protection from the state government, especially from Gov. Plutarco Elías Calles and his associates. A revolutionary commander who had made a name for himself in part by waging war on the Yaqui in-digenous population, Calles—himself no friend of the Chinese—desired to avoid a second ethnic-based war in Sonora and aimed to uphold law and order. He therefore instructed the municipal president of Magdalena "to give protection to those foreigners [or] you will suffer the consequences."[47] However, Calles also suppressed further immigration.[48]

While the extreme response to the Chinese served as the tip of the ice-berg, all immigrants came to realize that the xenophilic rhetoric of the Porfiriato was a thing of the past. In April 1914 the U.S. occupation of the port of Veracruz produced shrill denunciations on the part of both the incumbent dictator, Victoriano Huerta, and one of his main opponents, Venustiano Carranza. More than two years later, when Carranza's victori-ous faction convened a constitutional convention after the defeat of both Huerta and Pancho Villa, the convention met in the shadow of the Puni-tive Expedition, U.S. president Woodrow Wilson's feeble attempt to pun-ish Villa for his attack on Columbus, New Mexico. Not surprisingly, the assembled delegates pursued a nationalist agenda designed to end the easy ride of foreign interests. This agenda led to the inclusion of three articles that made Mexico the first nation with a constitution that strove to protect its citizens from foreign exploitation. Article 27 of the 1917 Constitution declared land and mineral resources the patrimony of the nation. The article also required all foreign nationals to forsake the diplomatic protection of their home governments in questions relating to the private ownership of natural resources. In a reformulation of the 1857 Constitution, Article 33 threatened recalcitrant foreigners with expulsion: "The Federal Executive shall have the exclusive power to compel any foreigner whose remaining it may deem inexpedient to abandon the national territory immediately and without the necessity of previous legal action." Finally, Article 123 outlawed the preferential treatment of foreign workers. Nonetheless, foreign economic interests remained dominant, and U.S. direct investment doubled between 1910 and 1920.[49]

Article 33 played a particularly important role in targeting Spaniards. Although liberal modernization had greatly softened the Hispanophobia of the early republic, the revolution once again brought such sentiments to the fore. Between 30,000 and 50,000 strong, the Spanish community was the largest foreign community, and many of its members held exalted positions in economic and cultural life. Of the approximately 1,200 expulsion orders under Article 33, Spaniards accounted for the single greatest number, or 32 percent of the total, compared to 19 percent for the Chinese and 11 percent for U.S. citizens. Although these numbers were not large, the fact that the federal government (not state or local authorities) decreed expulsion under Article 33 illustrated that the government considered Hispanophobia politically expedient, reflecting tens of thousands of lesser affronts to the Chinese perpetrated by lower-level authorities and at the grass roots.[50]

After 1920 the reform agenda of the winners of the revolution posed new challenges to foreign immigrants. Although Articles 27 and 123 of the Constitution of 1917 still awaited full implementation, the governments of Alvaro Obregón (1920–24) and Plutarco Elías Calles (1924–28) professed the desire to implement some of the significant social and economic provisions of these articles. In addition, foreign entrepreneurs feared the possibility of outright expropriation and, secondarily, the prospect of debilitating strikes, protracted labor disputes, high taxation, and stifling government regulations. During Obregón's tenure, foreign merchants began to found chambers of commerce along national lines that (unlike individual entrepreneurs) could appeal for diplomatic protection. For his part, Calles struck a formal alliance with a major labor organization, and his efforts to regulate the foreign-owned oil industry provoked a grave crisis with the United States. Even more importantly, as president and as *jefe máximo* (1928–34), when he continued to influence national politics from behind the scenes, Calles pursued a campaign to eliminate the influence of the Catholic Church, citing the fact that foreigners (i.e., the Vatican) directed that Church as one of its many vices. At its height, the Church–state conflict led to the expulsion or execution of foreign-born priests and the suspension of all official religious services in Mexico. Finally, just as foreigners believed that the worst lay behind them, along came President Lázaro Cárdenas (1934–40). The Cardenistas built a populist state with the support of workers' and peasant organizations and embarked on a reform program that ended with the expropriation of the oil industry and the distribution of 49 million acres of former hacienda land to peasants. To be sure, all of these governments retained a capitalist blueprint, and none of them ever considered Soviet-style expropriations.[51]

The Obregón and Calles administrations also signaled the coming of a new era by their promotion of a program of cultural and racial nationalism that could incorporate the indigenous population into the state. In particular, the concept of *indigenismo* sought to redeem the heritage of the indigenous population. In the words of Manuel Gamio, a prominent *indigenista*, the postrevolutionary regimes were "forging a fatherland."[52] As Gamio wrote in 1948, "indigenous culture is the true base of nationality in almost all Latin American countries."[53] Gamio's remarks again illustrated that the cultural elites conceived of their nation as the heir of the Aztecs rather than a melting pot in which immigrants played a prominent role. This rhetoric—like that of the Constitution—cloaked a different purpose, in this case the incorporation of the "Indians" into society rather than the restoration of their lands at the expense of hacendados and privileged foreigners.[54] Put another way, *indigenismo* aimed "to short-circuit the racial distinctions differentiating individual citizens and determining their place in a divided and hierarchical space by promoting an overriding collective mission embodied in the national mystique."[55]

Regarding the immigrants, an even more important concept for the repositioning of national identity was that of the "cosmic race" propagated by Obregón's secretary of public education, José Vasconcelos. Vasconcelos followed in Justo Sierra's footsteps when he talked about a cosmic mestizo race: a race superior to its indigenous, European, and African components. He expressly included immigrants in his imagining of the nation when he argued that "the advantage of our tradition is that it has greater facility of sympathy toward strangers. . . . This implies that our civilization, with all of its defects, may be the chosen one to assimilate and to transform mankind into a new type; that within our civilization, the warp, the multiple and rich plasma of future humanity is being prepared."[56] For both Vasconcelos and the mass education program he oversaw, the mestizo stood at the core of this cosmic race, and the issue of incorporating and Hispanicizing the foreign immigrant formed symmetry with the incorporation and Hispanicization of the "*indio*." Therefore, foreigners remained welcome as long as they displayed a willingness to join the cosmic race and thus abandon their own cultural heritage.

This rhetoric aside, foreign immigration continued to increase during the 1920s. As ever more stringent immigration restrictions diverted migrant flows away from the United States, Mexico became the new home of tens of thousands of mostly lower-class immigrants. Many of the new immigrants were Eastern Europeans, Jewish refugees, and Middle Eastern immigrants. In addition, Obregón invited a group of German-speaking Mennonites to settle in a remote area of Chihuahua, the home state of his archenemy, Pancho Villa. By the late 1920s almost 10,000 Mennonites lived in Chihuahua. All told, the 1930 census counted almost 160,000 foreigners, up from barely above 100,000 nine years before. The 1920s were a historical moment in which Mexico appeared to be a haven for immigrants during an era in which U.S. immigration policy became much more restrictive.[57]

Middle Eastern immigrants experienced the greatest increase—almost 300 percent—during the 1920s. During the Porfirian era, the northern border region and some of the major cities had witnessed the influx of a few hundred merchants from the Ottoman Empire. Commonly called *turcos*, or Turks, these immigrants were in fact a diverse lot, including Druze Christians, Muslims, and Jews from a variety of geographical origins. Most of them were sojourners, or newcomers who returned to their place of origin after establishing their commercial interests. Following the dissolution of the Ottoman Empire after World War I, Middle Eastern immigrants permanently settled in Mexico, assuming important positions in the same merchant and other middle-class professions that also sustained the Chinese community. Like the Chinese, the Middle Easterners crossed the U.S. border back and forth, maximizing their commercial opportunities on both sides. Many Mexicans mistrusted the Middle Eastern immigrants, particularly the Jews and Muslims among them. Over time, the term "*turco*" came to stand for someone difficult to trust or to figure out. For example, President Calles, a stern man with a steely, austere gaze, had long been known as "el turco." Much historical scholarship has continued to perpetuate the myth that he was indeed of Middle Eastern origin, claiming that he was of Jewish or Muslim descent. To be sure, Calles's paternal family name was Elías; he was from Sonora; like the Middle Eastern merchants, he had operated a succession of mercantile businesses along the border; and he displayed a strong antipathy toward the Catholic Church. Nonetheless, his paternal ancestry from a creole Sonoran family remains beyond doubt.[58]

It was Calles who presided over the first significant attempt to limit immigration—an attempt directed particularly against poor immigrants. In March 1926 the government approved the Ley de Migración, or Immigration Law. Based in part upon its 1908 predecessor, the law again cited public health concerns as a reason to restrict immigration. Even more importantly, the new law authorized the government to restrict immigration in times of high unemployment and required would-be immigrants to present written offer of employments to obtain permanent residency permits. The following year the government prohibited the immigration of persons of Middle Eastern origin, excepting only immediate family members of those already in Mexico.[59]

Beginning in 1929 the Great Depression induced the government to adopt even more stringent restrictions. In this endeavor, the Chinese community fared worse than any other. In 1931 the Sonoran state government expelled all Chinese. That same year a report by a government commission labeled Chinese immigration "an invasion as in a conquered nation." As in the case of the 1911 massacre, the Chinese found themselves singled out based not only on their commercial success but also on frank racism.[60] In the waning years of *jefe máximo* Calles, the national government also sought to keep out refugees fleeing the fascist and Nazi dictatorships in Europe. In 1933 a directive of the Secretaría de Gobernación aimed to "attack the problem created by Jewish immigration, which more than any other, because of its psychological and moral characteristics, and because of the type of activities to which it dedicates and the procedures it follows in pressing business of commercial nature that is inevitably its choice comes to be undesirable."[61]

However, the administration of Lázaro Cárdenas proved more receptive, and the specter of totalitarianism prompted an inclusion of humanitarian concerns in this policy of selective immigration. Between 1937 and 1948, more than eighteen thousand Spanish Republicans arrived, fleeing the dictatorship of Francisco Franco. With these left-leaning Spaniards,

Mexico received a group of white and well-educated immigrants, many of them scholars and artists. Although marginalized equally by the conservative Spanish colony and anti-*gachupín* Mexicans, this group achieved an important position in society. Republican Spaniards founded what would later be called the Colegio de México, the country's finest academic institution devoted to research and teaching in history, literature, and the social sciences. They also enriched the life of virtually every major university and cultural institution. Less important in quantitative terms but equally active in cultural life was a group of Jewish refugees who escaped the Holocaust.[62]

The Mexican government also made a half-hearted attempt to encourage the assimilation of the foreign residents. In 1933 a law imposed jus soli on the children of immigrants, and three years later Cárdenas signed a law that promoted the miscegenation of the foreign communities by waiving immigration restrictions for those who married women of "Mexican origin."[63] These efforts at assimilation, however, ultimately failed. Despite the talk of a cosmic race, Mexico remained a land of unhyphenated identities. Both the disadvantaged indigenous societies and the privileged foreign colonies remained separate from Spanish-speaking Mexico, and in the absence of a hyphen, the road to assimilation led only over the chasm defined by the dichotomy of *mexicano* and *extranjero*. Indeed, the revolutionary rhetoric widened this chasm, and immigrant communities—particularly the German community, which fell under the sway of Nazi propaganda—reinforced the structures of self-segregation.[64]

Although the Mexican government could not assimilate the foreign colonies, the internal cohesion of some of these colonies began to fray at the edges. Already, the French colony had seen its glory days slip away with the departure of the Francophile Porfirians, and the British colony had likewise faded into the background. Beginning in the 1920s other colonies confronted a different threat: the disunity brought about by social differentiation and political conflict. The conservative and elitist German and Spanish merchant families, most of whom lived in the glory of an imperial past and backed the Franco and Hitler regimes, found themselves threatened by the influx of antifascist refugees.[65]

World War II gave further impetus to the dissolution of the foreign ethnic enclaves by leading to efforts to curtail the activities of the German, Italian, and Japanese communities. Because of Mexico's proximity to the United States, the U.S. government did not tolerate what it labeled "fifth column" activities. Even before Pearl Harbor, FBI agents were at work against Axis infiltration, the U.S. government issued a blacklist of "enemy nationals" in Latin America, and the administration of Franklin D. Roosevelt pressured President Manuel Ávila Camacho to join the Allied camp. After the German sinking of two Mexican vessels resulted in Mexico's declaration of war on the Axis powers, the Mexican government seized all companies belonging to ethnic Germans, Italians, and Japanese, and the Ávila Camacho regime also jailed hundreds of Axis sailors and presumed spies.[66]

In the wake of this process, the only foreign community that continued to prosper was the so-called American colony. In a larger sense, the Americanization of Mexico proved that the revolution remained as receptive to foreign influences as the Porfiriato had been. During the thirties, U.S. citizens—already the largest group of foreign residents—replaced the Chinese as the fastest-growing immigrant community. As part of this migration, U.S. cultural pilgrims, fascinated by Mexico's revolution and rich cultural heritage, came to complement their country's economic influence. Other North American residents in Mexico included retirees, entrepreneurs, and professionals. In the interwar years, what Helen Delpar has called the "enormous vogue of things Mexican" stood juxtaposed with an equally enormous vogue of things "American," as returning workers, the radio, and motion pictures brought U.S. culture closer to Mexico. According to one estimate, the number of U.S. citizens in Mexico quadrupled to forty-eight thousand during the 1930s, though this figure very likely includes numerous U.S. citizens of Mexican descent, many of whom were forcibly "repatriated" during the Great Depression regardless of their nationality.[67]

By the forties, the Mexicans had learned that their country—unlike the vast neighbor to the north—was a net exporter rather than importer of migrants. Under the bracero program, thousands of Mexicans packed up and moved to the United States, where they joined a Mexican American community that had already greatly increased in number due to the exodus of Mexicans fleeing the revolution, notwithstanding the mass repatriation of Mexicans and Mexican Americans during the Great Depression.[68] Not surprisingly, many Mexicans came to the conclusion that their government needed to assist the native-born rather than the foreign-born population.

Such was the background of the 1947 Ley General de Población, which formally ended the official pro-immigrant orientation commenced in the Liberal Reforma of the 1850s. Emphasizing the natural growth of the Mexican population, this law tore down the last vestiges of policies designed to "whiten" the population. The law stipulated public health and literacy programs designed to reduce the steep mortality rates of Mexican children, and it made immigration a secondary priority. It also contained incentives for Mexican workers in the United States—the so-called lost sons—to return.

The law highlighted Mexico's predicament as a newly industrializing society. As elsewhere in Latin America, the scarcity of manufactured products during World War II had jumpstarted a national import-substitution program to offset the declining terms of trade for raw materials. But Mexico remained a predominantly rural country, and the age of internal migration to Mexico City and the provincial capitals was still in its beginnings. The Ley General de Población implied that Mexico would find enough workers through natural growth and not through immigration. By the late seventies, only refugees from the South American and Central American military dictatorships were granted immigrant visas on a regular basis.[69]

It was only in the forties that the process of assimilation picked up steam. Particularly in the larger cities, where foreign colonies had lived a life of self-segregation, the lines between the colonies and Mexican society at large began to blur. To begin with, industrialization swelled the ranks of the middle class, whose members no longer accepted the artificial barriers the foreign enclaves had erected to keep Mexican culture out of their communities. As more Mexican families began to enjoy a higher income, many of them enrolled their children in the schools of the foreign colonies that enjoyed an excellent reputation for their stringent curriculum and their bilingual education—and as the percentage of Mexicans in these schools increased, the use of Spanish in the schools increased as well. In addition, the emergent mass culture—music and motion pictures, in particular—appealed to the children and grandchildren of foreign immigrants. When young Mexicans used the new media to articulate their own version of the wave of counterculture made in the United States, their peers from foreign families discovered that it was "hip" to be Mexican.[70]

Theresa Velcamp's "multicultural Mexico," a nation in which immigrants and their descendants are freely accepted and assimilated, is therefore of very recent vintage.[71] Throughout the period 1850–1950, the Mexican government displayed an ambivalent attitude toward the relatively few immigrants who arrived in the nation during that century. Whether the Porfirian dictatorship, which was devoted to opening its borders to foreign investment, or the postrevolutionary administrations that struggled with the effects of natural population growth, popular xenophobia, and revolutionary nationalism, Mexicans and their government found themselves caught between the enticing prospects of immigration for economic development and demographic, cultural, and political realities that left little room for such immigration.

Notes

1. On Slim, see Alfaro-Velcamp, *So Far from Allah*, 9. On Latin American countries that have experienced mass immigration, see Baily, *Immigrants in the Lands of Promise*; Baily and Míguez, *Mass Migration to Modern Latin America*; Lesser, *Negotiating National Identity*; and Moya, *Cousins and Strangers*.

2. Secretaría de Gobernación, *Quinto censo de población*, vol. 1: *Resumen General* (Mexico City: Dirección General de Estadística, 1934), 8.

3. Salazar Anaya, *La población extranjera*.

4. González Navarro, *Los extranjeros en México*, back cover and passim; see also Yankelevich, "Mexico for the Mexicans." The statistics on Mexican immigration to the United States come from the Pew Research Center; see Dockterman, "Hispanics of Mexican Origin."

5. Significant portions of this chapter were previously published in Buchenau, "Small Numbers, Great Impact," 23–49. See also Buchenau, *Tools of Progress*.

6. For case studies, see Salazar, *Xenofobia y xenofilia*.

7. Míguez, "Introduction: Foreign Mass Migration," xxii.

8. Quoted in Yankelevich, *Deseables o inconvenientes*, 14. All translations are my own unless otherwise indicated.

9. Tarica, *Inner Life of Mestizo Nationalism*.

10. Vasconcelos, *La raza cósmica*.

11. Brading, *Los orígenes del nacionalismo mexicano*; and Lafaye, *Quetzalcóatl and Guadalupe*.

12. Knight, "Racism, Revolution, and *Indigenismo*," 72–73; Anderson, *Imagined Communities*; and Burkholder, *Spaniards in the Colonial Empire*.

13. Originally published as Alexander von Humboldt, *Essai politique sur le royaume de la Nouvelle-Espagne*, 5 vols. (Paris: Schoell, 1811).

14. Berninger, *La inmigración en México*; and Bernecker, *Die Handelskonquistadoren*, 564–67.

15. Sims, *Expulsion of Mexico's Spaniards*; Flores Caballero, *Counterrevolution*, 14–40; and Lida, "Los españoles en México," 429.

16. Benson, "Territorial Integrity in Mexican Politics"; and Brack, *Mexico Views Manifest Destiny*.

17. Benjamin, *A Rich Land, A Poor People*, 7–9; and Zorrilla, *Relaciones de México*, 148–67.

18. The term comes from the title of Bernecker, *Die Handelskonquistadoren*.

19. See also Von Mentz et al., *Los pioneros del imperialismo alemán*; and Meyer, "Les français au Mexique," 52–60.

20. Lida, "Los españoles en México," 435–36; and Crosby, *Ecological Imperialism*.

21. Alfaro-Velcamp, *So Far from Allah*, 31.

22. Olliff, *Reforma Mexico and the United States*, 17–18; González Navarro, *Los*

extranjeros en México, 1:230–353; and Brading, "Creole Nationalism and Mexican Liberalism," 139–90.

23. Raat, *El positivismo durante el porfiriato*.

24. Cimet, *Ashkenazi Jews in Mexico*, 20.

25. Raat, "Ideas and Society in Don Porfirio's Mexico," 32–53.

26. Katz, "Liberal Republic and Porfiriato," 57.

27. Foreign investors who lived outside Mexico were another matter, as the investments of large corporations continued to increase throughout the twentieth century.

28. Meyer, "Les français au Mexique," 62–64; and Herrero, "Algunas hipótesis de trabajo sobre."

29. González Navarro, *Población y sociedad en México*, 2:117.

30. Brown, "Foreign and Native-Born Workers," 786–818. For the example of the oil industry, see Brown, *Oil and Revolution in Mexico*, chap. 1.

31. González Navarro, *Los extranjeros en México*, 2:82–122.

32. Molina Enríquez, *Los grandes problemas nacionales*, 146.

33. Davis, "American Colony in Mexico City," ii.

34. Quoted in Buchenau, *Tools of Progress*, 46.

35. Salazar Anaya, "Migration," 883–84.

36. Romero, *Chinese in Mexico*, 1.

37. Quoted in ibid., 176.

38. Quoted in Yankelevich, *Deseables o inconvenientes*, 26; and Romero, *Chinese in Mexico*, 180–81.

39. Delgado, *Making the Chinese Mexican*.

40. Guerra, *Le Mexique*, vol. 1. Guerra's conceptualization cannot account for the highly commercialized and profitable agribusiness estates in Mexico.

41. Buchenau, *In the Shadow of the Giant*, chaps. 3 and 4.

42. For this distinction between elite economic nationalism and popular xenophobia, see Knight, *U.S.-Mexican Relations*, 55.

43. Hart, *Revolutionary Mexico*. For a critique of Hart's views, see Knight, "United States and the Mexican Peasantry." For the reference to the Boxer Rebellion, see Katz, *Secret War in Mexico*, 75.

44. González Navarro, *Los extranjeros en México*, 2:48–49.

45. Romero, *Chinese in Mexico*, 147–57.

46. Quoted in ibid., 157.

47. Fideicomiso Archivos Plutarco Elías Calles y Fernando Torreblanca, Mexico City (FAPECFT), Archivo Plutarco Elías Calles, Fondo Plutarco Elías Calles, serie 0204, gav. 86, exp. 56, inv. 1082, Calles to Nicolás Burgos, Hermosillo, January 2, 1918.

48. On Sinophobia in revolutionary Sonora, see also Réñique, "Race, Region, and Nation."

49. Niemeyer, *Revolution at Querétaro*; and Womack, "Mexican Economy," 80–123.

50. Yankelevich, "Hispanofobia y revolución," 31–33.

51. Collado Herrera, *Empresarios y políticos*, 18–26, 124–25. On Calles, see Buchenau, *Plutarco Elías Calles*, chaps. 5 and 6; on Cárdenas, see Knight, "Cardenismo," 73–107.

52. Gamio, *Forjando Patria*.

53. Gamio, *Consideraciones sobre el problema indígena*, 8.

54. Knight, "Racism, Revolution, and *Indigenismo*," 71–113.

55. Tarica, *Inner Life of Mestizo Nationalism*, xxx.

56. Quoted in Alfaro-Velcamp, "Immigrant Positioning," 65.

57. Departamento de la Estadística Nacional, *Censo general de habitantes*; Secretaría de Gobernación, *Quinto censo de población*; and Oeste de Bopp, "Die Deutschen in Mexico," 495–96.

58. Alfaro-Velcamp, *So Far from Allah*, 45–109. On the idea of Calles as a *turco*, see Buchenau, *Plutarco Elías Calles*, 8–9.

59. "Ley de Migración de los Estados Unidos Mexicanos," *Diario Oficial de la Federación*, March 13, 1926; and Alfaro-Velcamp, *So Far From Allah*, 102–3.

60. Romero, *Chinese in Mexico*, 183.

61. González Navarro, *Población y sociedad en México*, 2:34–56; and Cimet, *Ashkenazi Jews in Mexico*, 13.

62. Lida, "Los españoles en México," 434–44; and Von zur Mühlen, *Fluchtziel Lateinamerika*.

63. González Navarro, *Población y sociedad en México*, 2:45–52.

64. See also Yankelevich, *Deseables o inconvenientes*, 31–32.

65. Proal and Charpenel, *Los barcelonnettes en México*, 71–75; Meyer, *Su majestad británica y la Revolución Mexicana*; and Oeste de Bopp, "Die Deutschen in Mexico."

66. Paz, *Strategy, Security, and Spies*. See also Niblo, *War, Diplomacy, and Development*, 3–62.

67. Delpar, *Enormous Vogue of Things Mexican*, 15–53; Schmidt, *Roots of "Lo Mexicano,"* 98; and Camposortega Cruz, "Análisis demográfico," 37.

68. Guerin-González, "Repatriación de familias."

69. Salazar Anaya, "Migration," 885; and Palma Mora, "Inmigrantes extranjeros," 83–132.

70. Scanlon, *Un enclave cultural*; Zolov, *Refried Elvis*; and Monsiváis, "Tantos millones de hombres."

71. Alfaro-Velcamp, "Immigrant Positioning," 61–62.

3

Immigration, Identity, and Nationalism in Argentina, 1850–1950

JEANE DELANEY

Argentina stands out as one of the Latin American nations most deeply reshaped by postindependence immigration. Like their counterparts in many other countries in the region, Argentina's nineteenth-century liberals saw European immigrants as bearers of the values needed to construct a modern, prosperous nation that would belong within the orbit of Western civilization. Yet with the exception of neighboring Uruguay, only Argentina realized the ambition to become a nation virtually remade by immigrants. A vast, sparsely populated country occupying almost a third of the continent's east coast, Argentina became the preferred destination for millions of Europeans who crossed the Atlantic during the late nineteenth- and early-twentieth centuries in search of opportunity. Attracted by a booming economy based upon the export of grains, wool, and beef, over 4 million immigrants permanently settled in Argentina between 1870 and 1930. This massive influx was the driving force behind the country's explosive growth in population, which rose from 1,737,923 in 1869 to just under 6 million in 1947.[1] Just as dramatic was the number of immigrants versus the number of native-borne. By 1914 almost 30 percent of the Argentine population was estimated to be foreign-born, with much higher rates in key cities such as Buenos Aires and Rosario.[2]

The arrival of millions of newcomers during these decades caused many to rethink the country's long-standing open-door policy and to ask whether the state should impose new restrictions on who could immigrate. Indeed, much attention has been paid to the rise of anti-immigrant sentiment among the Argentine elite during the early twentieth century, and certainly there is abundant evidence of such feelings.[3] But what should be remembered is that even during the years of peak influx, the overwhelming majority of the Argentine upper class remained convinced that theirs was an underpopulated country whose future depended upon attracting immigrants. By necessity, then, Argentine nationalism often—although certainly not always—took an *inclusive* form, one in which immigrants continued to be welcomed and were expected to become part of the national community. But just how this process of "Argentinization" was to occur was a judgment that changed over time, as understandings of Argentineness evolved.

In what follows, I argue that the experience of mass immigration during the period 1880–1930 helped precipitate a significant and long-lasting shift in notions of Argentine identity. Although ideas about *anything*—let alone about something as elusive as national identity—are never uniformly shared, it is possible to chart a broad transformation in how the nation's leading intellectuals, opinion makers, and key political figures spoke and wrote about the nature of Argentine nationality. During much of the nineteenth century, the country's liberal elite defined Argentineness primarily in political terms. In other words, they believed that the basis of Argentine identity was, or should be, Argentines' qualities as citizens: their love of liberty, their basic sense of egalitarianism, and their loyalty to the Argentine state.[4] As the century progressed, cultural aspects of Argentine identity came to be emphasized, but the equation of "citizenship" and "nationality" still held, and the terms continued to be used interchangeably.[5] The onslaught of massive immigration, however, prompted early-twentieth-century intellectuals to discard these earlier, more politically based definitions of Argentine identity in favor of new essentialist understandings of nationality. Inspired by Romantic nationalist currents from abroad and grappling with the impact of mass immigration at home, these intellectuals stressed the supposedly inherent cultural and ethnic qualities of the Argentine people and posited the existence of a distinctive, homogeneous national character.

Yet as these ideas about a supposedly unitary national character gained greater acceptance, a new series of debates erupted over the nature of this putative character and the role the immigrants played in its shaping. Were the millions of immigrants flooding onto Argentine shores a key ingredient of an emerging Argentine nationality, or were they contaminants? Just as important for the immigrants themselves was the question of whether becoming a true Argentine required the shedding of prior ethnic and religious identities. Could one be a Protestant or a Jew, or conserve one's German or Italian heritage, and still be a true Argentine?

Immigrants themselves were not passive observers of these debates. As they struggled to establish homes, find jobs, and develop friendships, the newcomers also wrestled with their own identities and their places in their adopted society. Some embraced their new country wholeheartedly and sought to shed all aspects of their prior lives; others saw themselves as birds of passage who were in Argentina only long enough to return home with money in their pockets. A large number, particularly the Spaniards and Italians who formed the bulk of the immigratory stream, chose to live in neighborhoods of newcomers with similar origins. Within these neighborhoods, they formed their own banks, ran their own schools, and established mutual aid societies. Individually and through these institutions, they organized civic and cultural festivals, promoted their interests, pressured politicians, and manifested their allegiance to their new homeland. With the passage of time, some—or, more often, their children—also became respected intellectuals who participated in the lively identity debates of the day. Thus, through their actions and ideas, immigrants sought to make their own contributions to the meaning of Argentineness, and in some cases to fight for a more pluralistic definition of what it meant to be Argentine.

The Nineteenth-Century Background

Throughout most of the nineteenth century Argentina's liberal elite saw European immigration as the solution to two perceived problems. The first problem was that of peopling the country's vast territory. Endowed with the second-largest landmass of all the Latin American nations, Argentina lacked the large indigenous population that provided the initial demographic base of such countries as Mexico, Peru, and Bolivia. Spanish settlement during much of the colonial period was similarly sparse, and only in the final decades of the eighteenth century did the area begin to experience substantial growth. Still, at the time of independence the territory that would become Argentina had only an estimated 400,000 souls.[6] The second problem the liberal elite sought to solve with European immigration was the supposedly inferior quality of the existing population or creoles. Creoles, these modernizers believed, suffered under the double burden of an obscurantist Spanish cultural legacy and the supposedly negative effects of racial mixture between Spaniards, Africans, and Indians. Accordingly, they saw immigration from Protestant Europe as the surest means to whiten the population and build a prosperous, democratic society.

This pro-immigration stance, evident from the very beginnings of the republic, became one of the central preoccupations of the liberal Generation of 1837. Including such individuals as Domingo F. Sarmiento, Juan Bautista Alberdi, and Bartolomé Mitre, this group, along with political allies, gained ascendency after the ouster of dictator Juan Manuel de Rosas in 1852. It was Sarmiento, who served as Argentine president from 1868–72, who produced the most famous expression of his generation's faith in the benefits of European immigration. Published in 1845, his *Facundo: Civilización y barbarie* (*Facundo: Civilization and Barbarism*) directly linked the vast emptiness of the Argentine pampas or plains to what he believed to be the violent and primitive lives of the rural creoles. Sarmiento affirmed that the right kind of immigrants would allow the country to overcome the cultural and racial legacies of the colonial past and to create a new, authentically Argentine culture.[7] Alberdi echoed this view. Like Sarmiento, he hoped the influx of Europeans would inject Argentina with a "new spirit" and introduce new attitudes toward work and progress. In a famous tract that would serve as the basis of Argentina's 1853 Constitution, Alberdi expressed his conviction that Europeans' "habits of order, of discipline and of industry" would prove infectious.[8] For Argentina's mid-nineteenth-century intellectual and political elite, then, immigration was understood to be the key to building a new nation, one they hoped would be radically different from that forged during the colonial period.[9]

The liberal faith in mass immigration as the most important engine of Argentine progress raises the following questions: Just how did this nineteenth-century elite envision the process by which immigrants would become Argentines? Were immigrants expected to shed their former cultural identities and national allegiances in favor of a new homogeneous Argentine identity, or would a certain degree of ethnic and religious pluralism be tolerated? Clearly, nineteenth-century liberals neither expected nor wanted these newcomers to assimilate *culturally* into domestic society. Rather, as noted, they saw European immigrants as agents of change that would help sweep away the Spanish colonial heritage and bring with them the values necessary to create a new national culture. Yet just how uniform or all-encompassing did liberals believe this new common culture should be? And what of the legal status of the newcomers?

Mónica Quijada has stressed that Latin America's nineteenth-century liberals followed the model of the French Revolution in identifying the nation with an equal and sovereign people. With such a vision of the nation, she argues, came the drive to erase ethnic and racial differences and to create a homogeneous people who would share a common culture. In the Argentine case, this meant the creation of a racially white, Europeanized population that effectively erased (either through extermination or biological absorption) peoples of African and indigenous blood.[10]

Quijada is certainly correct in noting the homogenizing impulse behind nineteenth-century Argentine liberalism, especially as it relates to racial whitening. Yet in the case of European immigrants, the realities on the ground meant that demanding complete cultural and ethnic uniformity was impossible. Beggars, of course, cannot be choosers, and in seeking to attract massive numbers of European immigrants, Argentine leaders were forced to open the transatlantic door as widely as possible. Thus, in contrast to the United States, throughout the period of mass immigration Argentina never seriously entertained restricting immigration on the basis of ethnicity.[11] Moreover, the Argentine state offered newcomers a range of protections that would allow them to decide the degree to which they wished to retain prior identities and loyalties.

Religious tolerance and educational freedom provide obvious examples. Although the 1853 Constitution declared that the Argentine state "sustained" the Catholic religion, it also guaranteed freedom of worship.[12] Protestants were of course welcome, but so were Jews, at least officially. In 1881, for example, the government sent a special envoy to Europe with the aim of fomenting the immigration of Russian Jews fleeing persecution in their homeland.[13] Religious pluralism was further affirmed in 1884 with the passage of Law 1420, which prohibited religious (i.e., Catholic) instruction in the public schools during regular school hours. Meanwhile, immigrants enjoyed the right to establish their own private schools where students could receive both religious instruction and lessons in their parents' native tongue. Although criticism of these schools mounted toward the end of the nineteenth century as their numbers increased, the national government yielded to immigrant pressure and continued to permit them.[14]

Given this acceptance of religious and ethnic pluralism, albeit within the racial parameters of "whiteness" (a category that proved elastic), and their own tendency to associate nationality with citizenship, nineteenth-century liberals not unexpectedly stressed the need for immigrants to integrate politically into their adopted homeland by becoming naturalized citizens. Argentina had a long history of offering an easy path to citizenship, and the 1853 Constitution continued that trend by requiring only a two-year period of residency. In 1869 new rules allowed even this provision to be waived in certain circumstances and, as a further enticement, exempted new citizens from military service for a ten-year period. Few were tempted, however, and naturalization rates in Argentina remained extremely low, hovering around 5 percent between 1850 and 1930.[15]

Immigrants at Last

Despite the pro-immigration schemes of Argentine liberals, few Europeans made their way to the nation's shores during first seven decades following independence. All this would change by the nineteenth century's end, when in a matter of decades Europe's surging demand for grains, beef, and wool enabled Argentina to boast one of the world's fastest-growing economies. Beginning around 1870, what had been a small trickle of immigrants swelled first to a respectable stream and then to a veritable flood.

The impact of this human tidal wave on Argentina society, culture, and identity is difficult to overstate. While few members of the native-born elite questioned the need for cheap European labor, the massive influx of foreigners raised fears on a number of fronts. One source of concern was the nature of the immigrants themselves. Whereas nineteenth-century leaders such as Sarmiento and Alberdi had hoped to attract yeoman farmers from Protestant Europe, the immigrants who began to arrive at the close of the nineteenth century were of a different sort. Predominately from Italy and Spain, these often uneducated newcomers formed the basis of the nascent urban working class and often provoked more disdain than admiration from native Argentines. Immigrant militancy was another worry. Many immigrants brought with them socialist and anarchist ideas, and elites often blamed them for labor unrest. The massive influx also awakened racial anxieties, which were often tied to concerns over the social question. Although the vast majority of Argentina's immigrants were from southern Europe and therefore considered "white," native elites worried that many of the new arrivals represented the dregs of their societies. Accordingly, they urged the state to prohibit the entry of such undesirables, whom they blamed for the rising social unrest, crime, disease, and delinquency.[16] Finally, immigrants came under fire for their supposed "materialism," excessive greed, and utilitarian approach to life. Such a mindset, critics maintained, threatened to undermine the traditional Argentine values of honor, generosity, and simplicity by infecting the native population with these new pernicious values.[17]

Taken together, these concerns about the negative impact of immigration represent a remarkable reversal both in attitudes toward the immigrant and in perceptions of the nation's identity. Whereas liberal leaders previously had seen European immigrants as bringing civilizing values to a backward society, turn-of-the-century elites assessed the value of the newcomers from a very different position. Buoyed by their country's stunning economic success and steeped in nostalgia for a rapidly disappearing past, many native-born Argentines now viewed immigrants as a threat to a national culture worth defending rather than erasing. Yet despite these new attitudes toward immigrants, there remained the conviction that Argentina still needed Europeans to prosper. The problem now became how to incorporate millions of newcomers while preserving—or creating—a coherent national identity. The solution was in no way straightforward and inevitably hinged on shifting and often divergent understandings of what it meant to be Argentine.

One response to the challenge of mass immigration harkened back to the traditional liberal view that identified Argentineness with citizenship. As the growing immigrant population failed to naturalize, traditional liberals became increasingly concerned about the impact on the nation's political institutions. Renowned jurist Estanislao Zeballos, for example, complained that unless the immigrant could be persuaded to naturalize, Argentina would be bereft of the citizens necessary to "use, defend, and perfect" the nation's political institutions.[18] In 1887 both he and Sarmiento joined other prominent members of Argentine society to form the Comité Patriótico, whose aim was to promote naturalization. Widely read newspapers such as *La Prensa* supported these efforts, calling naturalization "a supreme necessity of the nationality."[19] Various proposals were put forth to deal with the problem, including automatically granting citizenship to all immigrants who had resided in the country for seven consecutive years. This plan ran aground in large part because of fears that such policies would actually discourage potential immigrants.[20]

Official interest in promoting naturalization peaked in the early 1890s. From that point on, only Argentina's Socialist Party would actively push the issue. Instead, the state pursued an energetic program of patriotic education aimed at instilling immigrant schoolchildren with a love of the fatherland. Interest in using the public schools to create a sense of national identity surfaced as early as the mid-1880s, when reformers mandated the teaching of new courses on Argentine history and geography, imposed new regulations requiring that schools display the national flag, and ordered schools to officially observe Argentina's two independence days.[21] These efforts continued well into the new century. Of particular importance was the leadership of José María Ramos Mejía, a prominent sociologist and president of the National Council of Education (CNE). As head of the CNE from 1908 to 1912, Ramos Mejía urged schools to adopt texts authored by Argentines rather than foreigners, and encouraged administrators and teachers to organize frequent patriotic festivals.[22]

How did the immigrant children themselves react to these obligatory patriotic celebrations? Contemporary accounts suggest that they did so with enthusiasm. Although certainly not an unbiased observer, Ramos Mejía's description of immigrant school children raptly listening to "the heroic episodes" of Argentine history and singing patriotic songs "with their faces scrunched [in concentration]" does give the sense that these were more than rote exercises. Indeed, so taken was Ramos Mejía by the immigrant children's obvious enjoyment of civic festivals that he confidently lauded them as "the Argentine[s] of the future" who would soon be the "depositor[ies] of the future sentiment of the nationality."[23] Another account by Enrique Dickmann, a Russian-born Jew who became one of the first members of the Socialist Party to be elected to Congress, is interesting both because it suggests enthusiasm on the part of the students and because of Dickmann's own reaction. In a speech before Congress, Dickmann described attending a school program where "children of all races . . . and all nations" rose together to sing a rousing rendition of the national anthem. Dickmann professed himself to be so deeply moved by the experience that his "eyes filled with tears" at the sight of this new generation of Argentines, whose very lives were evidence of the deepening of Argentine democracy.[24]

As Dickmann's comments suggest, adult immigrants also exhibited enthusiasm for patriotic festivals and often actively sought ways to identify with Argentina. Despite their reluctance to become naturalized citizens (a step Dickmann himself took), immigrants did mobilize around issues that mattered to them directly. Beginning in the latter half of the nineteenth century, Buenos Aires witnessed frequent mass meetings and demonstrations as people from a variety of social backgrounds and professions organized to protest an unpopular policy, express their support for a particular cause, or seek solutions to common problems. As is evident from press reports, immigrants—both as individuals and in organized groups—were prominent participants in these events, and in doing so sought to exercise their influence in, and become a part of, their adopted homeland.[25]

Immigrants also demonstrated their sense of belonging by participating in patriotic festivals organized by both the state and private civic groups. During the 1890s festivals celebrating important dates such as May 25 (the anniversary of the 1810 May Revolution) and July 9 (Independence Day) became an important part of civic life in Argentina. Immigrant organizations, including groups of Italians, Spaniards, French, Austria-Hungarians, Portuguese, and Jews, would regularly participate, a fact commented on with pride by the national press.[26] Describing one such celebration, one newspaper enthused that "when rendering tribute to the cult of their adopted country, foreigners, like the sons of the country are all one, are all Argentines."[27]

Less formal cultural activities also provided ways in which the foreign-born could identify with their adopted homeland. Among the most prominent were the *círculos criollos* or "creole clubs" that sprang up in Buenos Aires at the turn of the century.[28] These clubs, formed mostly by immigrant youths, were social organizations through which members gathered to recreate a rural atmosphere and practice the musical arts, dress, and lifestyle of the Argentine gaucho. The gaucho had been despised by nineteenth-century liberals as the embodiment of native barbarism. But by the end of the century, the herdsman enjoyed a reversal in image as intellectuals began to tout this traditional figure as the symbol of Argentine nationality. Urban immigrants also embraced the rural herdsman with gusto. The initial spark for the gaucho's sudden appeal among the urban popular classes was the appearance, during the 1880s, of a new mass-produced literature called the "gauchesque." Cheaply printed and written in a feuilleton style, gauchesque literature proved wildly popular among urban immigrants and was quickly adapted to the stage for audiences who eagerly followed the exploits of such characters as the gaucho hero Juan Moreira and the outlandish "Cocoliche," a maladroit Italian immigrant whose bumbling attempts to imitate gaucho speech and clothing were played up for comedic effect. Besides their sheer entertainment value, gauchesque literature and theater gave immigrants a means to identify with their adopted homeland and provided, as Adolfo Prieto has argued, "immediate and visible form of assimilation, a credential of citizenship" with which immigrants could integrate themselves into the broader society.[29]

This immigrant fascination with the gaucho was often scorned by elites, some of whom decried the gauchesque genre as a vulgar parody of true gaucho culture. Worse still, some believed the popular celebration of gauchos as outlaws led to delinquency among young immigrants.[30] But other elites held more positive views. Some, such as writers Manuel Gálvez and Eduardo Schiaffino, praised the popular version of the gauchesque for its human warmth and capacity to evoke national sentiments (in themselves, and presumably in immigrants).[31] Elites also sometimes praised the immigrants themselves for their enthusiasm for what had now become a national icon. One of the highlights of Buenos Aires' yearly carnival was gaucho performances by the creole clubs, which invariably won enthusiastic applause from observers and accolades in the national press. Reporting on the 1901 festival, for example, *La Prensa* lauded one group for the authenticity of its performance, noting that it was carried out "with all the faithfulness of someone who has really lived the life of the *gaucho*." Members of another group won well-deserved applause, the newspaper reported, for their "genuine *criollo*" verses.[32]

Tango was another cultural form in which immigrants played a central role. Both a style of dance and music, tango emerged during the final decades of the nineteenth century from the slums and brothels of Buenos Aires. Embraced by the immigrant and native poor alike, it grew out of the same musical tradition as the late nineteenth-century gauchesque, as popular singer-songwriters of that genre began to incorporate urban themes and explore the shady underside of the city.[33] Given that many prominent tango singers (including, of course, the legendary Carlos Gardel) were themselves immigrants or first-generation Argentines, it is not surprising that lyrics often focused on the clash and fusion of cultures as the newcomers and their Argentine-born children made their way in the city. Initially associated with crime and prostitution, tango was at first shunned by the middle- and upper-class natives. Although many elites remained hostile to tango, others came to laud it as an authentically Argentine art form, and by the 1920s it had gained widespread acceptance among Argentina's middle class as a symbol of national identity.[34]

Taken together, these diverse activities and utterances suggest an open, inclusive vision of Argentine identity that was shared by immigrants and at least some natives. Although many Argentines did indeed worry about the Babel-like heterogeneity of their cities, when we consider the educational program of the state, the myriad ways in which immigrants sought to identify with their adopted homeland, and the positive responses of mainstream newspapers like *La Prensa*, it is clear that important sectors of Argentine society believed that immigrants could be transformed into loyal Argentines, and that these newcomers could strengthen rather than weaken the nation's identity. What comes through as well is a degree of tolerance for pluralism and the idea that becoming an Argentine was first and foremost a question of loyalty. Immigrants themselves undoubtedly helped promote this view. As they confidently marched in civic parades or performed in gaucho festivals as part of Italian, Spanish, French, or Jewish immigrant associations, they physically exhibited their conviction that one could be both a member of an ethnic community as well as a loyal Argentine.

Complicating—and ultimately competing with—this inclusive and at least partially pluralistic vision of Argentineness was the emergence of a new intellectual movement that posited a narrower, unitary, and essentialist notion of identity and nationality. As is well known, the opening years of the twentieth century witnessed the emergence of Hispanism, a movement defined by its sympathy toward Spain and the belief that Spain and its former colonies formed a single spiritual and ethnic community. Hispanism flourished throughout Latin America, fueled in part by Spain's swift defeat by the United States in 1898. Although most Latin Americans sympathized with the Cuban cause, the U.S. intervention sparked fears of further U.S. aggression in the region and produced a new sympathy for Spain. The result was what Mónica Quijada has called a "sharpening of Hispanic American ethno-cultural consciousness" and a growing belief that Hispanics should strive to preserve their unique way of being or cultural essence.[35]

Intellectual influences from Spain also played a role. The ideas of Spain's famed Generation of 1898, all energetic proponents of Hispanism, were widely disseminated in Argentina and had a direct impact on a young generation of intellectuals known today as the cultural nationalists. At the core of this group were Ricardo Rojas and Manuel Gálvez, both of whom explicitly acknowledged their debt to the Spaniards, especially to Miguel de Unamuno and Ángel Ganivet. A devout Catholic, Gálvez visited Spain twice as a young adult and would become became one of the most important Hispanicists of his day. One of his earliest and most influential works was his 1913 *El solar de la raza* (The Ancestral Home of the Race). In this work Gálvez lauded Spaniards for their "mystical, Catholic" character and proclaimed that Spain was the country that had best preserved the essence of *latinidad*.[36] *El solar* struck a resonant chord with the reading public and quickly sold out its first edition of four thousand copies.[37] In a similar vein, fellow cultural nationalist Emilio Becher urged his countrymen to return to their Spanish roots. Despite the massive influx of immigrants, Becher affirmed that "our civilization has not changed at its core." Still, he believed it was necessary to "strengthen our society on the cement of solid tradition" and to embrace "the indestructible soul of [Argentines'] Hispanic ancestry."[38]

Spanish immigrants themselves helped promote Hispanism. Having long encountered the generalized anti-Spanish attitudes of Argentine society, the new insistence that Argentina should defend its Hispanic character provided Spanish immigrants with a new boost in their collective self-esteem. During the 1910 centennial celebrations of Argentina's first act of independence, approximately 100,000 Spanish immigrants turned out in full force to welcome the Infanta Isabela, exhibit their pride in their roots, and display their loyalty to their adopted country. Leaders within the Spanish immigrant community also worked to promote the notion of Hispanism by sponsoring and funding the visits of prominent intellectuals from the peninsula.[39]

In considering the overall importance of Hispanism and its impact on attitudes toward immigration, however, it is important to note that this identification of Argentineness with Spanish ancestry and culture was but a single thread within the broader tendency of what might be called the increasing "ethnicization" of Argentine identity. As the twentieth century unfolded, we begin to see a more generalized influence of European ethnic nationalist currents on Argentine thought as an increasing number of intellectuals began to posit the existence of a distinctive *raza argentina*, or Argentine race. According to this essentialist vision of nationality, nations were understood to be distinctive, internally homogenous ethnic communities whose members share intrinsic mental and emotional traits and whose culture is unitary and immutable. That these ideas gained traction at this time is not surprising. Indeed, as Argentina faced the influx of new peoples, rapid modernization, and the rise of new social classes, it was experiencing many of the same phenomena that had fueled ethnic nationalism in late-nineteenth-century Europe.[40]

Writing about these new conceptions of nationality, historian Lilia Ana Bertoni has characterized the early twentieth century as a moment when Argentina's tradition of "inclusive patriotism," which respected a degree of internal religious and ethnic pluralism, gave way to a "defensive and exclusivist" form of nationalism that demanded cultural "homogeneity, purity and invariability."[41] If referring only to the phenomenon of Hispanism, Bertoni's verdict is certainly accurate. Undoubtedly, for Argentina's non-Spanish immigrants, the drive to define the nation as Hispanic and Catholic certainly felt exclusive. Thus, it was no longer enough to march in civic parades as part of a French mutual aid society or an association of Italian sailors, nor would decking out in gaucho attire turn Jewish colonists into Argentines. In other words, full-fledged membership in the national community was a matter of ancestry rather than of mere feeling or conscious choice. But as noted, Hispanism was not the only variant of ethnic nationalism to emerge during these years. Indeed, I argue that it remained subordinate to a broader tendency to see the Argentine race as still evolving, and whose final form would incorporate all of the nationalities that were pouring onto Argentine shores. Thus, Bertoni's judgment should be modified: while promoters of the idea of the Argentine people as a still evolving race clearly envisioned a national identity founded upon a fixed, unitary culture, the fact that the elite continued to believe that Argentina still needed immigrants meant that most strains of the new nationalism had an inclusive rather than exclusive thrust.

This inclusive notion of Argentine race-in-formation had several variations. Ricardo Rojas, for example, believed the new race had been largely formed but was still in the process of absorbing the new waves of immigrants. One of the most important intellectuals of his generation, Rojas argued that Argentina's national race was the result of the centuries-long contact between Europeans and conquered indigenous peoples. He maintained, however, that this process was much more than simply the biological mixing of invaders and natives. Deeply influenced by European Romantic nationalism, Rojas posited the existence of invisible telluric forces emanating from the soil that over time transformed the disparate peoples living within the Argentine territory into a "homogenous race, and thus a nationality."[42] The most national or representative human product of this mystical blending, he maintained, was the Argentine gaucho or cowboy, whom he described as the archetype of the Argentine race.[43] Most importantly for our purposes was Rojas' insistence that Spain had contributed but one element of the Argentine race, and his refusal to identify Argentineness with Catholicism. Thus, in his view all European immigrants, regardless of nationality or religion, could be easily incorporated into the putative national race. At the same time, however, Rojas made clear his belief that the immigrants would be absorbed into a preexisting national mold and would play no role in shaping the still evolving Argentine race.

Other participants in the identity debates of the period took the idea of Argentina as a race-in-formation a step further, believing that this race was still in its infancy. Embracing a kind of melting pot model, but one infused with essentialist meanings, they downplayed or rejected the notion of a preexisting ethnic core into which the current wave of immigrants would be absorbed. Writing in 1915, for example, prominent anthropologist Salvador Debenedetti insisted on this point by proclaiming that the "soul" of this "future race" was currently "shaping itself [*plasmándose*] . . . under the influence of the social medium and the environment."[44] The son of an

Italian immigrant of Jewish extraction, Debenedetti had good reason to see this race as both still unformed and capacious enough to include individuals of disparate ethnicities. A similar impulse may have informed the thinking of writer Juan Más y Pi. A Catalan who spent much of his adult life in Argentina, Más y Pi's origins may have made him especially sensitive to the hegemonic pretensions inherent in Hispanism. In any event, he seemed to exult in Argentina's contemporary heterogeneity, describing the country as one of "great ethnic confusion, [an] enormous conglomerate of all the races and castes." And it was from this "confused conglomeration," he optimistically affirmed, that "a great race ... would inevitably emerge."[45]

Clearly, then, the spread of the essentialist notion of *la raza argentina* encompassed a variety of ways of imagining Argentine identity, including ways that immigrants themselves (or their children) sometimes helped shape. And while there were certainly exclusivist, narrow definitions of Argentineness, others, such as the one articulated by Debenedetti and Más y Pi (and even, to lesser extent, by such intellectuals as Rojas), were much more inclusive. Indeed, it is perhaps the very capaciousness of this construct that was the source of its broad appeal, allowing it to gain acceptance among individuals who might otherwise have championed the more traditional liberal vision of Argentine identity that emphasized common political values and loyalties rather than an imagined uniformity of being.

Identity and Immigration in the Post-1930 Period

How would attitudes toward immigration change in the 1930s, and what would be the longer-term legacies of the early twentieth-century shift toward ethnic or racial understandings of national identity? In answering this question, it is first important to note the precipitous drop in the influx of Europeans into Argentina, first as a result of the worldwide economic crisis and then due to the outbreak of war. In 1933, for example, Argentina received only 24,345 European immigrants, a number representing just a fraction of the previous decade's peak year of 1923, when more than 195,063 arrived.[46] Immigration rates would remain low until the second half of the 1940s, when the end of the war and a new economic boom once again made Argentina an important destination for European emigrants. This prolonged slowdown almost certainly led to a blurring of internal ethnic identities as the lack of a constant stream of new arrivals lessened immigrants' ties to their native countries. Matthew Karush has also emphasized how new forms of communication and entertainment, such as radio and cinema, worked to create a more integrated society during the 1930s. According to Karush, mass entertainment helped all Argentines develop common cultural reference points while leading to increased class polarization due to different tastes and consumption patterns.[47] In any event, both of these outcomes very likely worked to weaken immigrant identities by consolidating new ones. Finally, concerns over the corrosive impact of European immigration on Argentine identity were probably lessened by another demographic trend that gained importance by the mid-1930s: the rapid rise of rural to urban migration. During the second half of the decade, the growth of light industry in the cities served as a magnet for rural people seeking employment. By 1947 an estimated 37 percent of the population of greater Buenos Aires had migrated from rural areas.[48]

The easing of the immigrant "problem," however, did not mean a lessening of the tendency—by now widespread among educated Argentines—to conceptualize the nation in essentialist, unitary terms. To be sure, during the 1930s the term "Argentine race" began to fade from identity discourse. While never disappearing entirely, it would become less common as native intellectuals became less obsessed with the problem of incorporating massive numbers of foreigners into an imagined national ethnic group. But despite the loss of the initial trigger that prompted Argentina's early-twentieth-century flirtation with ethnic nationalism, much of the conceptual framework emerging from these decades proved enduring and continued to shape how Argentines thought about their identity. Thus we see during the 1930s increasing references to Argentina's *índole nacional* (inherent national character) and *ser nacional* (national being or soul). Carrying many of the same essentialist meanings as "Argentine race," these terms referred to the supposedly immutable core essence of the Argentine people that was believed to form the basis of their unique identity. Even as early twentieth-century Argentines had disagreed over the nature of the imagined Argentine race, so too was the content of the equally imaginary *ser nacional* hotly contested.

One vision of the Argentine *ser* that gained force during the 1930s, and which persists to this day among certain nationalist sectors, was the identification of Argentineness with Catholicism and—in some versions—with the nation's Latin or Spanish heritage. In many ways a continuation of Hispanism, this understanding of the nation's identity was, not surprisingly, championed by the Argentine Catholic Church. Determined to strike back at Argentina's tradition of liberal secularism, the Church entered a new period of activism during the early 1920s as it sought to convince Argentines that Catholicism formed the essential bedrock of the nation's identity or, in the words of one prominent priest, the "diamond axis of our being."[49] Central to this effort was the establishment in 1922 of the Cursos de Cultura Católica, a Catholic educational institute conceived as an alternative to the liberal-dominated public universities. Under the leadership of such key nationalist figures as Fathers Leonardo Castellani, Julio Meinvielle, and Spanish cleric Zacarías de Vizcarra, the Cursos would become, in the words of Loris Zanatta, "a study group for young nationalists" of the period.[50] Indeed, several individuals with ties to the Cursos, including Ernesto Palacio and Julio Irazusta, would become close associates of Gen. José Félix Uriburu, the nationalist leader of the 1930 military coup against democratically elected president Hipólito Yrigoyen. Deeply hostile toward any threats to what they saw as Argentina's inherently Catholic character, these intellectuals proclaimed that all of Argentine society was "formed in accordance with the laws of Catholicism," and that "a true Argentine is born, lives and dies within the sacrament of the Church."[51] Some adherents of this Catholic vision of Argentine identity, such as Palacio, stressed ethnicity as well, proclaiming that Argentines' Spanish heritage formed the "invariable substance" of the nation's identity.[52]

Although constitutional order was restored in 1932, right-wing nationalist groups would proliferate during the 1930s and '40s. The crisis caused by the world depression injected a new element into nationalist rhetoric as key intellectuals such as Julio and Rodolfo Irazusta began to tie the defense of Argentina's supposed Catholic *ser nacional* to the defense of the country's economic sovereignty. Liberalism—both political and economic—came under attack as nationalists argued that Argentina's model of capitalist development had stymied the growth of domestic industry and left it dependent upon external markets for primary goods. It was in this context that we see the rise of anti-British sentiment, especially in the wake of the 1933 trade agreement with Great Britain known as the Roca-Runciman Agreement. This pact, which guaranteed Argentina continued access to British markets provided that that all proceeds from these sales be used to purchase British manufactures, incensed nationalists who accused Argentine liberals of colluding with Britain to exploit the country and erase its Catholic character.[53]

Contributing to the increasing nationalist rejection of liberalism were intellectual influences from Europe, especially the ideas of Charles Maurras. Italian fascism also became an important inspiration. This was particularly true of a subset of the clergy who believed that Argentina should develop its own variant of Catholic fascism. In their view, this form of fascism would function as a tool to rid Argentina of antinational liberalism in all its forms and return the nation to its true Catholic being.[54] Naturally, this brand of nationalism, and the vision of the Argentine *ser nacional* that informed it, was deeply anti-Semitic and hostile to pluralism.

The 1930s, however, witnessed the emergence of a competing vision of Argentine identity, that, while still positing the existence of a unitary national essence also insisted on a more inclusive approach that took into account the hybrid nature of Argentine society. Like the earlier and most inclusive versions of Argentina as a race-in-formation, this vision of the *ser nacional* saw immigrants as an essential ingredient of a new nation, and indeed went further by explicitly embracing the urban masses as the core of the nation's identity. The most influential formulation of this hybrid vision of Argentine identity came from the pen of celebrated writer Raúl Scalabrini Ortiz. The son of an Argentine mother and an Italian-born father, Scalabrini became a respected writer during the 1920s. In 1931 he published what was to be his most famous work, a book-length meditation on Argentine identity titled *El hombre que está solo y espera* (The Man Who Is Alone and Waits). Wildly successful, *El hombre* went through four printings in the first five months, winning Scalabrini instant and enduring fame.

Scalabrini, like elite writer Ricardo Rojas before him, believed in the existence of a national archetype that had emerged from the union of local and foreign elements. Yet for the younger thinker, this archetype had been produced by the fusion of the native creoles and the recent waves of immigrants that had swept onto Argentine shores. Employing the metaphor of the water droplet, he argued that the contemporary Argentine was a "chemical combination of races" that, like the fusion of hydrogen and oxygen in the chemist's test tube, had come together to create a substance completely different from its constituent parts.[55] This "chemical combination of races," Scalabrini believed, had created a new national archetype that was uniquely Argentine and utterly different from other nationalities. Just as important for our purposes was Scalabrini's insistence that this new archetype was the anonymous denizen of Buenos Aires, where this fusion between creole and immigrant had supposedly taken place. Affirming his appreciation for the new urban culture formed during the period of mass immigration, Scalabrini believed that the truest expression of the authentic Argentina could be found in tango lyrics and the "stuttered scenes of the *sainetes*" (popular plays) so beloved by ordinary people.[56]

Given the enormous commercial success of *El hombre*, it is clear that

Scalabrini's popular, inclusive (albeit unitary) vision of Argentine identity struck a resonant chord with much of the reading public. It also was to become more than a mere literary phenomenon. In the years following *El hombre*'s publication, Scalabrini underwent a conversion of sorts and joined the Irazusta brothers in becoming an outspoken critic of British economic imperialism. Through his friendship with Arturo Jauretche, Scalabrini became intimately involved with the left-wing nationalist organization La Fuerza de Orientación Radical de la Joven Argentina (FORJA) and served as its key theorist. Formed by dissident members of the Radical Party, FORJA championed a variant of nationalism that was populist, antiliberal, and anti-imperialist. Like their right-wing counterparts, Forjistas embraced the idea of a unitary national character or essence and frequently referred to the *ser nacional* or Argentine "soul."[57] But, for these nationalists as for Scalabrini, this putative national essence was unavoidably the product of a mixture whose ingredients included the diverse peoples who had come to Argentina during the period of mass immigration. Thus, according to one FORJA manifesto, Argentina was a nation "rooted in and nourished by all the pueblos of diverse ancestries [*estirpes*] that had contributed to our development."[58] FORJA leader Jauretche concurred. While he at times praised right-wing nationalists for contributing to the "revalorization of the Hispanic American roots of Argentina," it was clear that he viewed the Spanish legacy as only one element of the nation's identity.[59] The real Argentina, he insisted, was the Argentina of the "multitudes," one that was in the process of creating, "according to the modalities of its realities," something "authentic and original."[60]

What of the traditional liberal vision of Argentine nationality that stressed that the basis of the nation's identity were political values and loyalties rather than a unitary collective essence? Argentine liberalism had entered the 1930s in disarray. Although liberals had successfully forced the return to constitutional rule in 1932, they were sharply divided between a conservative faction that controlled the presidency through a coalition known as the *concordancia* and their sometime allies, a more progressive branch that included elements of Radicalism, the Socialists, and a new party known as the Progressive Democrats.[61] Although this latter group sought to defend Argentina's tradition of secularism, many of the conservative liberals had strong ties with Catholic nationalists and shared the latter's anti-Semitism. In the cultural field, this period also witnessed the emergence of publications such as the famous magazine *Sur* and groups such as the Colegio Libre de Estudios Superiores that supported the cause of liberalism and

antifascism both in Argentina and abroad.[62] But even here there were contradictions. Many of these liberal intellectuals, especially those associated
with *Sur*, were deeply elitist and looked back with nostalgia at an allegedly
purer, more authentic, more Argentine past. According to this view, most
forcefully articulated by famed liberal writer Eduardo Mallea, who himself
exhibited essentialist tendencies, the great waves of immigrants had weakened "our spiritual form, our inheritance [*acervo*] of soul and conscience."[63]
For various reasons, then, 1930s liberals were unable or unwilling to revive
the early, more inclusive liberal vision that stressed shared political values
and loyalties as the basis of Argentine identity.

In any event, any attempts to do so would have been cut short by the 1943
military coup. Carried out by a nationalist faction within the military called
the Grupo de Oficiales Unidos (GOU), the coup brought to power a regime
that sought to impose from above its vision of Argentina as a Catholic Hispanic nation. Pledging to restore Argentina's traditional values and to fight
the "sinister" groups and policies that had weakened the nation's Catholic
identity, the regime rolled back the liberal educational reforms of 1884 and
made Catholic religious instruction in the public schools mandatory.[64] This
policy was the brainchild of novelist Gustavo Martínez Zuviría, the newly
appointed minister of justice and education and a well-known anti-Semite.
The regime also sought to protect the Hispanic character of Argentine society by prohibiting parents from giving their children non-Spanish first
names. In October 1943 it promulgated Decree 11.609, which required all
individuals born in Argentina to receive proper Spanish names, or names
that had been "Castellanized" by common usage.[65]

The regime's obsession with defending its Hispano-Catholic version of
Argentine identity spilled over into immigration policy. In 1945 de facto
president Gen. Edelmiro Farrell appointed anthropologist and Nazi sym-
pathizer Santiago Peralta to head the General Direction of Migrations
(GDM). At his urging, Farrell authorized the creation of the Office of Ethnography (later the National Ethnic Institute), also headed by Peralta and
under the jurisdiction of the GDM. Such a move reflected Peralta's intense
concern with promoting and defending Argentina's ethnic and religious
unity. Looking at horror at Yugoslavia, which encompassed a veritable
"checkerboard" of peoples of different "nationalities, religions, races and
cultures," he affirmed that it should be the function of the state to manage
immigration flows in order to "perpetuate the native *pueblo*, defending its
culture in all its aspects: language, art, science, ethical and religious morality, institutions, justice, history, traditions . . . [all of which] are a blood

inheritance, the pride of the nation."[66] Accordingly, Peralta sought to take
a systematic approach to regulating immigration that would favor white
immigrants, who he thought would help to further erase Argentina's indigenous peoples and could be easily assimilated into the existing population.
This policy meant encouraging the better-quality immigrants from Mediterranean countries and prohibiting the influx of those who possessed "a
cultural heritage that could be transmitted [through the blood]."[67] Jews, in
other words.

The military government came to an end in 1946 when popular protests
forced the regime to hold elections. Won by the charismatic Juan Perón,
the elections marked a turning point in the country's history. Perón's vision of Argentine identity was complex and sometimes contradictory. A
prominent figure in the regime that took power following the 1943 coup,
Perón had made his career in the Argentine military at the moment when
the Church's influence within that institution had reached new heights. Not
surprisingly, he had internalized many elements of what Loris Zanatta has
called the "myth of the Catholic nation." At the same time, however, Perón
very quickly expanded his vision of the Argentineness, and like FORJA,
which disbanded in 1945 in order to free its members to support the Peronist cause, he stressed its popular content. Having gained power through
the support of the urban working class, Perón celebrated the masses—
which included recent arrivals, their children, and the mixed-race migrants
from the interior—as the embodiment of the real or authentic Argentina.

In doing so, he sometimes adopted language that suggested an essential-
ized, static, and unitary notion of Argentine identity. In a 1946 message to
Congress, for example, Perón complained that the elite's efforts to force the
people "to assimilate an alien culture" had damaged the "national soul,"
resulting in a lessening of Argentina's "unique characteristics." The masses,
however, had finally rebelled and thus begun to reclaim "the intimate being
of this soul of ours."[68]

At other times, however, Perón embraced a notion of identity that placed
more emphasis on political loyalties rather than a unitary essence, thereby
accepting a degree of pluralism. As Mariano Ben Plotkin has argued, Perón
conceived his movement as an all-encompassing civic religion in which
to be a good Argentine was to be good Peronist, a status open to all regardless of place of birth or ethnicity.[69] Accordingly, Perón actively courted
Argentina's Jewish leaders and, indeed, appointed several Jews to his administration. Many of his public statements also reflected a more open,
pluralistic vision of Argentineness. In his 1948 speech at the headquarters

of the Asociación Israelita Argentina, for example, Perón insisted that anti-Semitism and Argentineness were incompatible. "How can it be accepted," he asked rhetorically, "that there would be anti-Semitism in Argentina? In Argentina there should be no more than a single class of men: men who work for the national good, without distinctions. [Individuals] are good Argentines, whatever their place of origin, race or religion, when they work daily for the greatness of the nation."[70]

Perón's immigration policies provide yet another twist to what seemed to have been his protean vision of Argentineness. During the postwar economic boom, his government actively promoted immigration, and once more Argentina became an important destination for emigrating Europeans. Between 1946 and 1955 net European immigration to Argentina reached approximately 806,000.[71] But who were these immigrants? Despite the crisis of European Jewry and the country's expressed willingness to work with resettlement agencies such as the International Refugee Organization (IRO), the vast majority of this new wave of immigrants came from Spain and Italy.[72] This was by design. Taking an active role in the immigration process, the Peronist state signed special bilateral agreements with Spain and Italy while at the same time imposing new restrictions on the entry of refugees.[73] By 1949 Argentina had accepted only 32,172 refugees through the IRO. Of these, the overwhelming majority were Catholics from Eastern Europe.[74] The tensions in Perón's attitudes toward immigration and nationality are on full display in the text of his 1946 law regulating immigration. According to this decree, "in no case will immigration be restricted or prohibited on the basis of origin or credo of any kind." However, the text continued, "preference will be given to immigrants whose origin, habits, customs and language will facilitate assimilation with the ethnic, cultural and spiritual characteristics of Argentina."[75]

The years following the war would be the last time Argentina would be a favored destination for Europeans as the country's economic problems and political instability led prospective immigrants to look elsewhere for opportunity. Since 1950 the immigrants who have come of Argentina have come—usually illegally—from neighboring, poorer nations such as Paraguay and Bolivia. But the experience of mass European immigration continues to echo in Argentina in a singular way. The arrival of millions of immigrants into a country with a small population and whose identity was still in flux created, in many ways, an entirely new society. And perhaps as importantly, the native elite's resistance to this fact reshaped the country's intellectual and even political history. The result was the emergence and widespread acceptance of new conceptions of Argentineness that weakened the country's nineteenth-century liberal tradition and helped fuel narrower, less tolerant interpretations of the nation's identity.

Notes

1. These figures come from Solberg, "Mass Migrations in Argentina," 148 and 15.

2. Ibid., 150.

3. A classic treatment in English is Solberg, *Immigration and Nationalism*.

4. Myers, "Language, History, and Politics," 122.

5. On the growing importance of culture in defining Argentine identity, see Myers, "Language, History, and Politics," 122. On the continual identification of citizenship with nationality, see Pacecca "El fantasma en la maquina," 118.

6. Myers, "Language, History, and Politics," 120.

7. Ibid., 126.

8. Alberdi, *Bases*, 74.

9. Myers, "Language, History, and Politics," 126.

10. Quijada, "El paradigma de la homogeneidad."

11. Devoto, "El revés de la trama," 284.

12. The link between religious freedom and Argentina's ability to attract suitable immigrants is expressly made by Alberdi. See *Bases*, 77.

13. Lvovich, "Argentina," 27.

14. For the late nineteenth-century struggles over immigrant schools, see Bertoni, *Patriotas*, 64–77.

15. Rock, *Argentina*, 143.

16. Zimmermann, "Racial Ideas," 36.

17. DeLaney, "Making Sense of Modernity."

18. Estanislao Zeballos, *Diario de Sesiones*, Cámara de Diputados, October 21, 1887. Quoted in Bertoni, *Patriotas*, 124.

19. "Editorial," *La Prensa*, October 25, 1887. Quoted in Bertoni, *Patriotas*, 126.

20. Gandolfo, "Inmigrantes y política en Argentina."

21. Bertoni, *Patriotas*, 45.

22. Halperín Donghi, "¿Para qué la inmigración?," 479.

23. Ramos Mejía, quoted in Prieto, *El discurso criollista*, 32–33.

24. Enrique Dickmann, quoted in Dickmann, *Nacionalismo y socialismo*, 50.

25. See Sábato, *Many and the Few*, esp. ch. 7.

26. Bertoni, *Patriotas*, 83–84. For accounts of the participation of Jewish immigrants in these festivals, see Deutsch, *Crossing Borders*, ch. 1.

27. Quoted in Bertoni, *Patriotas*, 98.

28. Micol Seigel estimates that at the turn of the century, there were about fifty such clubs that actively participated in the yearly carnival festivities in Buenos Aires. Seigel, "Cocoliche's Romp," 59.

29. Prieto, *El discurso*, 18–19.

30. On fears of delinquency, see ibid., 147–48.

31. Ibid., 158–59.

32. *La Prensa*, February 18, 1901, 4–5. Quoted in Seigel, "Cocoliche's Romp," 60.

33. For an innovative analysis of this process, see Bockelman, "Between the Gaucho and the Tango," 591–99.

34. Vila, "Tango to Folk," 107.

35. Quijada, "Latinos y Anglosajones," 599, 603.

36. Gálvez, *El solar de la raza*, 27.

37. Gálvez, *El mundo de los seres ficticios*, 12.

38. Emilio Becher, in *La Nación*, June 20, 1906. Quoted in Rock, *Authoritarian Argentina*, 351.

39. Moya, *Cousins and Strangers*, 352–53.

40. On the factors leading to the rise of ethnic nationalism in Europe, see Hobsbawm, *Nations and Nationalism*, 109.

41. Bertoni, *Patriotas*, 316. The term "inclusive patriotism" comes from p. 13.

42. Rojas, *Los gauchescos*, 114.

43. For Rojas' concept of "Eurindia," see his *Eurindia*. For his ideas about the gaucho, see *Historia de la literatura argentina*.

44. Debenedetti, "Sobre la formación," 416–17.

45. Más y Pi, "El arte en la Argentina."

46. This occurred in 1923. See Devoto, "El revés de la trama," 287.

47. Karush, "Melodramatic Nation."

48. Solberg, "Mass Migrations," 153.

49. G. Riesco, "El eje diamantino de nuestro ser," *El Pueblo*, October 12, 1941. Quoted in Zanatta, *Del estado liberal*, 295.

50. Zanatta, *Del estado liberal*, 45.

51. Rodolfo Irazusta, "Las relaciones entre la iglesical y el estado," *La Nueva Republica*, May 5, 1928; reproduced in Irazusta, *El pensamiento político nacionalista*, 108.

52. Palacio, *La historia falsificada*, 63.

53. The Irazusta brothers' 1934 work *La Argentina y el imperialismo británico. Los eslabones de una cadena. 1806–1933* was instrumental in fanning hostility to the treaty and toward Great Britain more generally. From that point on, the theme of British imperialism was central to Argentine nationalist thought. Such anger, however, did not seem to translate into hostility toward British immigrants, who—particularly after 1890—represented only a small portion of the foreign-born. In 1895, immigrants from Great Britain (including the Irish), comprised 2.2 percent of Argentina's immigrant population. This percentage dipped steadily throughout the twentieth century, reaching 0.5 percent in 1947. Bailey and Seibert, "Inmigración y relaciones étnicas," 543.

54. Finchelstein, *Transatlantic Fascism*, 136–37.

55. Scalabrini et al., *El hombre que está solo y espera*, 41.

56. Ibid., 87.

57. See, for example, Amable Gutiérrez Diez, "Repudiamos el Frente Popular," *FORJA*, num. 1 (September 14, 1936), quoted in Scenna, 206; Gabriel del Mazo, "Yrigoyen," *Forjando*, vol. 1, no. 2, August 27, 1940, 2; and Atilio García Mellid, "La abstención electoral y el comicio de Buenos Aires, *Forjando*, vol. 2, no. 11, January 1942, 1.

58. "La falsa opción de los dos colonialismos," Organización Universitaria de FORJA, 1943. Reprinted in Jauretche, *FORJA y la década*, 102–7. Quoted material from p. 103.

59. Jauretche, *FORJA y la década*, 15n2.

60. Ibid., 17.

61. Nállim, *Transformations and Crisis*, 64.

62. Ibid., 67–85.

63. Mallea, *Historia de una pasión*, 71. For a fuller discussion of Mallea's vision, see Senkman, "Nacionalismo e inmigración."

64. Pedro Pablo Ramírez, "Carta del Excmo. Sr. Presidente de la Nación Pedro Pablo Ramírez al director del *Criterio*, monseñor Gustavo J. Franceschi," June 22, 1943, published in *Criterio*, July 1, 1943. Reprinted in García and Rodríguez Molas, *Textos y documentos*, 225–26.

65. After coming to power, Perón upheld Decree 11.609 but would issue a new decree exempting diplomats and functionaries from the restriction.

66. Santiago Peralta, *Conceptos sobre la inmigración (instrucciones de difusión al personal)*, pamphlet (Buenos Aires: Dirección de Migraciones, 1946), 6, 8. Quoted in Senkman, "Etnicidad e inmigración." Ellipses are Senkman's.

67. Peralta, quoted in Senkman, "Etnicidad e inmigración."

68. Perón, "Mensaje del Señor Presidente," 40.

69. Plotkin, *Mañana es San Perón*.

70. Juan Perón, Speech of August 20, 1948. Quoted in Buchrucker, *Nacionalismo y peronismo*, 355.

71. Solberg, "Mass Migrations in Argentina," 155.

72. For the years 1946–55, Italians made up about 45 percent of total net European immigration, with Spaniards making up about 23 percent.

73. Senkman, "Etnicidad e inmigración," 11–12.

74. Ibid., 15.

75. Quoted in Avni, *Argentina and the Jews*, 184.

4

Nation and Migration

German-Speaking and Japanese Immigrants in Brazil, 1850–1945

FREDERIK SCHULZE

In January and February 1940 Brazilian army officer major Aristoteles de Lima Câmara and the sociologist Arthur Hehl Neiva visited several rural settlements of Japanese, Polish, and German immigrants in the Brazilian states of São Paulo, Paraná, and Santa Catarina on behalf of the Council for Immigration and Colonization (*Conselho de Imigração e Colonização*, CIC). The purpose of the trip was to evaluate the integration of the immigrants into Brazilian society. The CIC was part of the nationalistic immigration policy of the authoritarian government led by Getúlio Vargas, which demanded the assimilation of immigrants into the nation. In 1941 Lima Câmara and Hehl Neiva published a report about their trip in the *Revista de Imigração e Colonização*—the official organ of the CIC—and stated the following about the Japanese and German immigrants: "In Brazil there are various cores of high concentration of alien elements and ethnics different from the Brazilian which, pure or mixed in the most varied proportions with indigenous or Negro African elements, constitute the substratum of nationality. These cores, true racial, psychological, linguistic, cultural and social cysts, in the broadest sense of this last term, including therefore economic, moral and even political peculiarities, are, more or less, resistant against the assimilation to the national milieu."[1] The scientists described an antagonism between certain groups of immigrants—most notably, Japanese and Germans—and the Brazilian nation and considered the "assimilation" of the immigrants advisable and necessary.

Although the immigrants were not sufficiently assimilated and adapted to the Brazilian nation—at least in the eyes of Brazilian political leaders, proponents of German cultural policy in Brazil in turn bemoaned that the German immigrants were losing their so-called Deutschtum ("German-ness"). One of these actors was Gottlieb Funcke, since 1929 the permanent representative of the Federation of German Evangelical Churches (Deutscher Evangelischer Kirchenbund) for Brazil in Porto Alegre, a federation to which the German-speaking protestant synods in Brazil were affiliated. In a speech in 1932 Funcke stressed the necessity to preserve Deutschtum but noted that the immigrants had little enthusiasm for their German heritage and culture. The contact with Brazilian society led, in his opinion, to the "Brazilianization" (Verbrasilianerung) of the "Germans": "Not only the intimate German mother tongue, but also the good German tradition and the honest German conscience among us is undeniably and widely threatened by disintegration."[2]

These examples highlight the way that in Brazil different actors thought about issues of immigration and nation as intimately and inextricably entwined. However, Brazilian and ethnic leaders used divergent concepts of what the nation was, and they differed with respect to their political goals and their evaluation of the situation of the settlers. The various notions of the meaning of "nation" used in these debates constructed certain national groups as "imagined communities" to which the immigrants should affiliate—either to the Brazilian nation, which was engaged in a process of nation building promoted by Brazilian intellectuals since the independence in 1822 and again after the proclamation of the Republic in 1889; or to the German nation, which German nationalists and colonialists defined as a global community of descent; or to the Japanese nation, which served as an organizer of emigration as well as an ideational point of reference for the immigrants.[3] The immigrants themselves were co-opted by nationalist actors but rarely got a chance to articulate their own opinion. It is vital, therefore, not only to analyze the globally circulating nationalist discourses that homogenized the immigrants as groups with a common national descent but also to point to the regional, local, and social heterogeneity of the immigrants.

This chapter will show how "nation" and "immigration" were discussed in relation to one another in Brazil. Which actors debated the role of the immigrants for the nation? Which were the competing nationalist discourses on immigration to Brazil? And in what relationship to these discourses did the immigrants themselves stand? My main examples are German and Japanese immigrants in Brazil who experienced most of the conflicts related to issues of nationality and nationalism. Although Portuguese, Italian, and Spanish immigration were much more important in terms of sheer quantity, German and Japanese migrants provide a unique window into the negotiation of nationality because their ethnic leaders emphasized a "proper" national group identity while Brazilian politicians and intellectuals perceived them as a direct threat to Brazilian nationality. Through studying the example of the two groups, the conflictive relationship between "nation" and "immigration" can be shown particularly well.

This chapter begins with a short overview of immigration to Brazil between 1850 and 1945 in which the motivations of the Brazilian state to promote immigration are discussed. Subsequently, the chapter describes how the two groups of immigrants—or, to be more precise, certain actors from these groups—positioned themselves toward the Brazilian nation and their nation of origin. Finally, it examines the role of immigration sociology and immigration policy in Brazilian nation building after 1930.

Mass Immigration to Brazil, 1850–1945

It was not just in 1850 that Brazil became a country of immigration. Nevertheless, this year was a watershed for Brazilian demographic development because the country finally abolished the slave trade. As early as 1822, when Brazil achieved independence from Portugal, Great Britain had insisted on the abolition of the slave trade. When normal diplomacy brought no results—the Brazilian government refused a renewal of the unequal Portuguese–British treaties and did not implement several agreements—the British exercised gunboat diplomacy.[4] But domestic economic and political reasons, too, led to a rethinking of the elites in the Brazilian Empire on this question. In particular, the coffee planters from São Paulo and Minas Gerais began to realize that they had to change the labor system on the plantations as slavery came to appear an anachronistic and outdated model. This perception was boosted by global shifts away from chattel slavery and developing discourses of progress and modernity as well as the resistance of enslaved people themselves, who time and again escaped and organized uprisings. After 1850 the forced immigration of African slaves was replaced by—usually voluntary—European and, later, Asian immigration.

Until 1850 Brazil was, as compared to the United States, an insignificant destination for the transatlantic emigration wave from Europe. The country had been open to immigrants since 1818, but until the end of the 1850s only a little more than 135,000 people immigrated to Brazil, among them barely 65,000 Portuguese and 23,000 German-speaking people.[5] In the

1860s 110,000 immigrants entered Brazil; in the 1870s, 194,000; and in the last decade of the empire, 444,000. This increase originated mainly from Italian immigration. Apart from the Portuguese, Spanish immigrants also began to arrive in larger numbers. German immigration reached a first climax between 1880 and 1889 with almost 19,000 arrivals. Other major groups were the British, the French, the Austrians, and the Swiss. During the First Republic (1889–1930), Brazil continued to be a country of immigrants with nearly 4 million entries in this period. The peak of immigration to Brazil was reached in the 1890s with around 1.2 million arrivals, including 690,000 Italians, 195,600 Portuguese and 113,000 Spaniards. The migrant flow stopped during World War I, when transport routes were interrupted. Between 1910 and 1929, the Portuguese again constituted the largest group of immigrants with 620,000 persons, followed by Spaniards and Italians. German immigration peaked at almost 76,000 migrants. In 1908 the Japanese influx started, numbering 180,000 migrants by 1941.[6] In addition, 80,000 Arabs, the so-called *sírio-libaneses*, entered the country after 1900.

Just as the immigrants' countries of origin differed, so too did their motivations to move as well as their social, economic, religious, and political backgrounds. Most of the immigrants decided to migrate due to economic reasons, trying to escape poverty, supply shortfalls, or overpopulation. Others fled political or religious persecution. In Brazil, they took heterogeneous life paths, depending on the kind of immigration and the target regions. An important migrant group was the educated middle class of British, French, German-speaking, and U.S. merchants who established themselves after 1818 in port cities such Rio de Janeiro, Salvador, Recife, Porto Alegre, and Belém as well as the inland city of São Paulo. Merchants were joined by diplomats, journalists, clergymen, and, later, industrialists. These expatriates kept in touch with their countries of origin and founded clubs, societies, church congregations, and newspapers. Among those whose migration was not temporary, some engaged in local politics.

Urban immigration developed a high visibility but was secondary in terms of quantity compared to rural immigration. The majority of the immigrants were poor and mostly illiterate peasants. Brazil pursued an active colonization policy to promote rural immigration and to these ends employed immigration agents in Europe, published advertising, subsidized the passage immigrants, and offered state-owned parcels of land to the so-called colonists (*colonos*). Emperor Dom Pedro I initiated this policy to colonize the three southernmost provinces of Brazil—Rio Grande do Sul,

Santa Catarina, and Paraná—which, as well as Espírito Santo in the southeast, were only sparsely populated. The south was chosen due to the mild, nontropical climate and in order to consolidate Brazilian claims in the region against Argentina. The settlers cleared the forest off their small parcels in order to carry out subsistence agriculture. In the course of time, provincial governments took over the colonization activities, established state colonies, and distributed land.[7] In addition, private colonization societies founded settlements such as Blumenau, established in Santa Catarina in 1850, which was meant to receive German-speaking colonists. This colonization policy could lead to problems. The government did not always keep its promises to the immigrants, and non-Catholics were not equal before the law during the Brazilian Empire. Other problems could occur on the spot: some settlers had difficulties in adapting to the new environment or to the new labor conditions. Lower-class immigrants, mainly artisans and servants before the onset of industrialization, went instead to the cities.

A third form of immigration was established in order to cultivate the coffee plantations in São Paulo. In 1846 coffee planter Nicolau Pereira de Campos Vergueiro started the implementation of a special kind of leasing system (*parceria*).[8] German-speaking immigrants were recruited to work on the coffee plantations. They were supposed to pay off their debts—including the cost of their passages and the leasing price for the land—with the coffee crops they produced over several years. In fact, however, the system led to an exorbitant indebtedness of the tenants, and the living conditions were precarious too. When the realities of the practice became known in Prussia, the Prussian government prohibited in 1859 the active recruitment of Prussian immigrants for Brazil. After that Prussian immigration to Brazil could occur only on one's own initiative. Not until 1895 was the ban lifted. Thus, during the First Republic it was primarily Italians, Spaniards, Portuguese, and Japanese who worked in the coffee production of São Paulo. They harvested coffee as tenants within an improved leasing system (*colonato*) that enabled them to practice subsistence farming, or the immigrants bought land and worked on their own coffee plantations.[9] Other immigrants went to the cities as workers. Immigration caused social changes in Brazilian society: the labor system on the plantations and in the industrial sector underwent changes, urbanization began, and the immigrated workers stimulated the foundation of labor unions and other social movements such as the women's movement.

In 1937 Getúlio Vargas, who had been president since 1930, issued a new constitution that proclaimed the authoritarian period of Estado Novo. This regime regulated and restricted immigration by law. Still, some 333,000 people immigrated in the 1930s and around 114,000 in the 1940s, including a few thousand refugees from Europe, among them many Jews.[10] The beginning of World War II eventually halted immigration; the era of large-scale immigration had come to an end. The year 1945 marked not only the end of the Estado Novo through a military coup but also a new perspective on immigration among Brazilian intellectuals: sociologists such as Gilberto Freyre, although still propagating a Portuguese-dominated culture, acknowledged for the first time the value of minority cultures for the nation.

Whitening the Nation

Beginning in the early nineteenth century and increasingly during the reign of Dom Pedro II (1840–89) Brazilian politicians and intellectuals discussed what the Brazilian nation was meant to be.[11] European, North American, and Hispanic American national discourses were stimulating for these debates, and so were the recently established sciences such as national historiography, ethnography, or geography. In 1838 the Brazilian Historical and Geographical Institute (Instituto Histórico e Geográfico Brasileiro, IHGB) was founded in Rio de Janeiro as an intellectual space for the discussion of national issues.[12] In this context Brazilian national literature and, later on, other art forms such as painting emerged. In literature, Indianism (*indianismo*) became important. Its exponents, José de Alencar or Gonçalves de Magalhães, created the noble savage as founding myth of the Brazilian nation despite the marginalization of indigenous peoples from Brazilian national realities in the nineteenth century.

The idea of the "nation" served to affirm national unity and to demarcate boundaries against the Latin American republics and the old colonial power Portugal. Another European concept that gained in importance in Brazil was "race."[13] Arthur de Gobineau, one of the most prominent proponents of racial theory, went to Brazil as a French diplomatic representative and befriended Dom Pedro II. European racial theories provoked discussions among Brazilian intellectuals because the construction and rating of different races seemed to directly concern everyday reality in Brazil. Not only were the so-called Ethiopian race and American race described as inferior to the so-called white race, but mixture between distinct races, too, was rejected as the fountainhead of degeneration.[14] "Civilization," progress, and technical development, as the imperialist sciences of the West tried to persuade, were only possible for the "white race." The Brazilian elites of

European descent were facing a dilemma: on the one hand, they yearned for an advanced nation that should be as close as possible to European "civilization." On the other hand, they had to integrate the contradictory everyday reality of Brazil into their national project. In the eyes of racial theorists, the large share of Afro-Brazilians among the population, the continued presence of the indigenous population, and, most of all the high percentage of the so-called racially mixed led them to the pessimistic conclusion that Brazil was incapable of achieving European "civilization."

Brazilian intellectuals replied to this dilemma with two strategies: first, they tried to interpret the "racial mixture" as a positive and unique characteristic of the Brazilian nation. By doing that, they adopted European racial theories but updated them with new content. Bavarian biologist Carl Friedrich Philipp von Martius, who became acquainted with Brazil during his extensive travels in the 1810s, formulated this idea for the first time in his text "Remarks on the Writing of a History of Brazil" (Bemerkungen über die Verfassung einer Geschichte Brasiliens), which he submitted as his entry for an IHGB competition in 1843 about how to write Brazilian national history.[15] With this text he laid the base for the influential studies by Sérgio Buarque de Holanda and Gilberto Freyre, who described the "racial mixture" as constituent for Brazil.[16]

Second, many intellectuals simply adopted wholesale the European racial theory. Following social evolutionary theory, they interpreted the Afro-Brazilian population as an obstacle for Brazil's development. These thinkers for the most part uncritically linked "nation," "race," and "progress" with the issue of immigration. Whereas the Brazilian state initially promoted immigration in order to develop southern Brazil economically, to protect its Southern territory against Argentina and Uruguay, and to replace slavery by wage labor, some Brazilian intellectuals assigned European immigrants an important role in the "civilizing" of the nation they envisaged. The immigrants should not only guarantee the technical and social progress of the nation but also "whiten up" the population over time—that is, eliminate and dissolve by "racial mixture" those segments of the population defined as inferior, such as the slaves and their descendants.[17] The "whitening ideology" (branqueamento) tied in with Martius insofar as "racial mixture" was reinterpreted as reasonable or even desirable—as long as Europeans were the main factor in the mix.

In the high esteem with which they perceived European immigrants, Brazilian thinkers were part of a global discourse that was circulating also in the Latin American republics. As early as 1852 the Argentine writer Juan

Figure 4.1. Modesto Brocos, *The Redemption of Ham* (A redenção de cam), 1895. Image available at Wikicommons.

Bautista Alberdi called for a strong European immigration in order to civilize the Argentine nation.[18] Fears of non-European migration can also be seen in the Chinese Exclusion Act passed by the United States in 1882.

All these discourses classified not only Afro-Latin Americans but also Chinese "coolies" as backward, racially inferior, and nationally inadequate.[19] Although some intellectuals supported Chinese immigration, the anti-Chinese discourse was predominant in Brazil, so the "coolies" did not play a significant role in Brazil. Japanese immigration did not occur during the nineteenth century and, therefore, was not yet discussed.

During the First Republic the concept of whitening continued to be prevalent.[20] Important proponents were sociologist Francisco José de Oliveira Vianna, philosopher and literary critic Sílvio Romero, and the director of the National Museum in Rio de Janeiro, João Batista de Lacerda. The only thing they could not agree upon was how long the process of whitening would last. Painter Modesto Brocos put the ideology of whitening in a nutshell. His 1895 painting "The Redemption of Ham" (A redenção de Cam) shows, beginning on the left, three generations of Afro-Brazilians who are getting whiter and whiter by "racial mixture" (see figure 4.1). In the center we see a couple of an already light-skinned Afro-Brazilian woman and a European immigrant whose child is very light-skinned. The Afro-Brazilian grandmother on the left side of the picture thanks God for the redemption of the curse that Noah declared on his son Ham, and with which the dark skin color of African people was explained since antiquity. Crucially, it was European immigrants who were able to lift this curse.

"Germanness" in Brazil

According to the whitening ideology, German-speaking immigrants were considered desirable additions to the Brazilian nation. Nevertheless, conflicts arose because German immigrant elites had their own nationalist ideas and because the integration of the immigrated Germans into Brazilian society followed multiple paths. During the Brazilian Empire, private societies and church authorities from Germany were actively engaged in policies to maintain Deutschtum abroad—that is, to preserve the German language and culture of the emigrants (Deutschtumspolitik).[21] The idea behind this was to use emigrated Germans and the so-called Germans abroad (Auslandsdeutsche) for the expansion of German economic interests and informal empire. German economists and geographers supported this idea before 1871, and after the foundation of the German Empire several middle-class intellectuals and politicians demanded more engagement in the colonial policy and discovered the "Germans abroad" as a surrogate for German colonies. These publicists observed the British advance in colonialism and developed two aspirations: on the one hand, they called for the redirecting of the German-speaking emigration away from its principal destination, the United States, toward southern Brazil. Travel reports from the 1850s and 1860s suggested that Deutschtum could be preserved particularly well in southern Brazil because the settlers had almost no contact with Brazilian society so that a "New Germany" could emerge.[22] Emigration to the United States, by contrast, appeared less desirable to German nationalists because they considered that the migrants' Deutschtum was too quickly diluted there because the Anglo-Saxon culture was seen as very dominant and absorbent.

On the other hand, the German actors started to work actively in favor of the preservation of the German language and culture in southern Brazil. In 1864 Friedrich Fabri, the superintendent of the Rhenish Missionary Society, founded a committee that in 1881 changed its name to Evangelical Society for the Protestant Germans in America (*Evangelische Gesellschaft für die protestantischen Deutschen in Amerika*). By 1911 this evangelical society had sent 102 German priests to Brazil in order to ensure ecclesiastical and educational support for the immigrated protestant Germans (almost half of all emigrants).[23] In the eyes of Fabri, the Evangelical Society contributed in this way to German colonial policy. Like Fabri's 1879 book, *Bedarf Deutschland der Colonien?* ("Does Germany Need Colonies?"), many Protestant texts from Brazil emphasized the colonial aspect of their authors' ecclesiastical work. "It is in fact a quite patriotic enterprise when we try to preserve a part of the emigrants . . . for our fatherland. How important it is to have a German brother tribe across the Ocean which thinks and acts in a German way, which is sympathetic to us in trade and politics and which defends our interests in all cases, is recognized by experts by now."[24] Robert Jannasch, an important German economist, fostered emigration propaganda and the economic relations to southern Brazil with his "Central Society for Trade Geography and the Promotion of German Interests Abroad" (*Centralverein für Handelsgeographie und zur Förderung deutscher Interessen im Ausland*).[25] These and other globally active propagandists and societies, such as the Society for Germanness Abroad (*Verein für das Deutschtum im Ausland*), were well interlinked and connected with the German-speaking elite of southern Brazil. They initiated an extensive activity in support of Deutschtum, which included the establishment of churches, schools, local societies, and German-speaking newspapers. After the foundation of the German Empire in 1871, government agencies also got involved in the preservation of German language and culture; among such agencies were the Imperial School Fund (*Reichsschulfond*), the Evangelical Church of Prussia, and German diplomatic missions in Brazil. After an interruption during World War I, German initiatives to foster Deutschtum in Brazil continued until 1937.

But what did these actors consider as German? What kind of connection did they envision between immigrants and the "German nation," and what role did the new host nation Brazil play in these thoughts? Wholly in the spirit of German nationalism in the nineteenth century, which the historiography has described, as ethnic nationalism based on the jus sanguinis, Deutschtum was for a long time defined as an ethnic community with common descent.[26] It was constructed in a very affirmative, positive manner by using certain characteristics such as industriousness, punctuality, order, cleanliness, loyalty, and morality. To make this self-image plausible, negative counterimages of the Brazilians were constructed. This led to an image of a homogenous German group in Brazil, a group that was depicted as superior compared to the inferior other, Brazil. Germans were also envisioned as bearers of a cultural mission and civilizing task in Brazil. The idea of a cultural mission was connected to the "cultural work" of the German farmers in the Brazilian jungle and endorsed civilizing and whitening discourses:

> The South American man . . . becomes accessible to the influence of the Germanic cultural sphere. Therefore, the overall objective of all aspirations on the mission territory in South America must be that the immigrated protestants are brought firmly together in Church and school, . . . so that the declined South American nationality is reinforced by the example of Germanic life and receives from its example and teaching the revitalization and the fertilization which it needs in its own judgment.[27]

From this perception of nationality, certain consequences arose for the situation of the "Germans" in Brazil. Since the "Germans abroad" played a crucial role in German colonial designs, German nationalists not only recommended the preservation of German language and culture but also rejected the assimilation of immigrants into Brazilian society. Acquiring the Portuguese language, living in the Brazilian environment, marrying Brazilians, losing German citizenship (which happened with all immigrants due to the Brazilian naturalization program in 1889), and adapting Brazilian everyday culture—many Germans involved in the Deutschtumspolitik considered these processes a problem and called them "Brazilianization," or degeneration, or "de-Germanization."[28] According to these German thinkers, the change or the blending of German nationality had to be prevented at all costs. The notion that Germans in Brazil might end up serving as a "national fertilizer" (Völkerdünger) for the host country—improving Brazil without benefit to Germany—came under particular attack.[29] Similarly, German nationalists rejected the idea that they should help Brazil to "whiten" its society, fearing that doing so would lead to their own "racial degeneration": "there are Brazilians who think that they can use the strong, blond and non-degenerated German to regenerate the Brazilian blood. But for such experiments only the last-ditch quality of German scum prostitutes itself. . . . At least we have come this far that even the smallest colonist knows which evils result from such a blending."[30]

Hence, some members of the intellectual elite of German immigrants strongly opposed acculturation in Brazil. But in Brazil the local everyday reality of the German-speaking people hardly corresponded with the homogenizing discourses of Deutschtum. On the contrary, the immigrants were settling into Brazilian society and were forging a new life far away from Germany in various and individual ways. As Jeffrey Lesser has argued, immigrants of various national origins created their own spaces for negotiating identities in Brazil, which differed from hegemonic identity conceptions, whether those of Brazilian nationalists or of ethnic leaders of the respective immigrant groups.[31] The German settlers were also not as isolated as the colonial discourses suggested—recent historiography has disproved that myth and shown various forms of exchange processes between the settlers and the Brazilian society.[32] German immigrants, for instance, adapted Brazilian cultural practices such as language, alimentation, agricultural techniques, and forms of religiosity, to name a few. Other German-speaking immigrants married Brazilians or were engaged in Brazilian politics.[33] Reports written by German priests in Brazil criticized such changes of culture and behavior. After their arrival in Brazil, they quickly felt disappointed and frustrated about the behavior of German emigrants and, thus, constructed them as missionaries to preserve a culture they saw as all too easily lost without their activities. However, the immigrants had organized themselves independently during the first years in Brazil, had found parishes, and had elected their own pastors. When the German clergymen came to Brazil, many settlers defended themselves against the ecclesiastical attempt of social disciplining.[34]

The implementation of the Deutschtumspolitik was complicated by such concrete conflicts and by the fact that many colonists were acculturating themselves into the new society. It was also challenged by the heterogeneity of the immigrants.[35] If one bears in mind the different regions of origin of the migrants, who in many cases emigrated long before the German Empire was founded and only spoke dialects, it becomes evident that we should not talk about the "German" immigrants in Brazil as a singular unit. Other differences existed in terms of religion, social status, regions of settlement, the type and timing of immigration, and the diversity between urban and rural immigration. Only with time did the Deutschtumspolitik lead to a certain degree of homogenization of the immigrants.

Even urban German-speaking elites, large parts of which basically agreed with German state policy, recognized their own acculturation and created a new identity, calling themselves "Teuto-Brazilians" (*teuto-brasileiros*).[36] They felt still part of the German nation but identified themselves also with their new home society, Brazil. As Giralda Seyferth has suggested, by reference to Fredrik Barth's concept of ethnicity from 1969, the Teuto-Brazilian identity conjured up by intellectuals was a construction, but it also had "real" aspects.[37] As Seyferth has shown, ideas of Deutschtum and of Brazilian citizenship were amalgamated.

Recent historiography has criticized this concept of ethnicity as too static. The identity of immigrants should be understood not only as an ethnic one but also as connected to other components such as social status, religion, gender, and regional identification.[38] As a matter of fact, this objection confronts us with a dilemma. On the one hand, we encounter certain concepts like "nation," "ethnicity," Deutschtum, or "diaspora" in the source material.[39] These terms are part of homogenizing discourses that intend to structure and construct reality but that do not necessarily reflect reality. On the other hand, historians need group definitions in order to be able to talk about history.

Moreover, it is necessary to stress the fact that reality was always more heterogeneous, complex, and conflictive than these discourses suggest and suggested. Homogenizing concepts, therefore, should be used as historical terms but not as scientific concepts. Otherwise we run the risk of repeating problematic discourses of the past. It is indeed quite difficult to assume a single Teuto-Brazilian ethnicity, as the discourses of Deutschtum suggested over decades. Instead of repeating these homogenizing concepts developed by German-speaking urban elites, we should emphasize the heterogeneity of the immigrants and their experiences. A similarly problematic concept is "diaspora," which is equally homogenizing and was used for that purpose by German clergymen.[40]

The Japanese in Brazil

Japanese immigration to Brazil occurred relatively late in comparison with German immigration.[41] It also differed regarding its organization. After 1908 Japanese migrants arrived mainly as coffee pickers; they therefore developed a "sojourner mentality."[42] Although they did not plan to stay in Brazil forever and did not naturalize as Brazilian citizens, many Japanese purchased land. In the mid-1920s some changes occurred when the Japanese state, in cooperation with Brazilian authorities, became to main organizer of Japanese migration to Brazil. The Japanese government tried to protect its emigrants and established purely Japanese settlements in Brazil, the so-called colonial cores (*núcleos coloniais*). Célia Sakurai has called this "patronized immigration."[43] Japan wanted to not only relieve its population pressure but also to create a new market for its products.[44] At the same time, the Japanese state intended to promote a positive and modern image of Japan overseas with the help of its emigrants.[45]

In fact, Japan and Japanese culture often fared badly in Western imperialist discourses, as can be seen from the catchword "yellow peril" or the U.S. Immigration Act of 1924, which prohibited Japanese immigration. At the same time, Japan developed since the Meiji-era (1868–1912) expansionist and imperialist activities in Asia and opened itself to industrialization. In addition, there was a racial nationalism—for example, directed against China—that sought to draw on aspects of "Western modernity." Japan's emigration policy was part of that nationalism, which strived to overcome the Western racism and negative stereotypes of Japan. The Japanese perception of immigration as a nationalist tool seemed to fit well with the Brazilian ideas of immigration as a means to economic and cultural advancement. As was the case with the Germans, the Japanese came up with the idea of a cultural mission that even ordinary immigrants accepted: "Our immigration will mean something only if our blood purifies the Brazilian impurity with our superior tradition."[46]

To avoid the scenario of the United States, with its hostility to Japanese immigration, Japan decided to cooperate closely with the Brazilian government. It promised Brazil industrious, adaptable, and docile settlers who would be different, for example, from the "defiant" German immigrants whose ethnic leaders refused the assimilation into Brazilian society.[47] Furthermore, the settlers were supposed to stay permanently in Brazil. Brazil was interested in the new immigration and participated in its organization. In the early years of the First Republic, Japanophile voices prevailed over those that warned against Asians. The Republican government pushed forward the rapprochement with Japan with the signing of a treaty of friendship in 1895, and the positive image of the country gained in strength through the Japanese victory in the Russo-Japanese War (1904–5).[48] The measures of the Italian government against emigration to Brazil led to a decrease of the Italian influx and, therefore, to Brazil's opening to Japanese migrants.

In Japan, emigration offices were founded and placed under the authority of the Federation of Immigration Cooperative Societies in 1927. In Brazil, the colonization society Burajiru Takushoku Kumiai (BRATAC) acquired land in the states of São Paulo and Paraná with government bonds and private capital from Japan. Then BRATAC resold the land to immigrant families and built the infrastructure of the settlements, including Japanese schools. Japanese cultural societies, youth groups, and newspapers were founded too.[49] The colonization policy resulted in homogeneous Japanese settlements such as Bastos in São Paulo. This and the growing Japanese imperialism that accentuated Japanese nationalist pride as well as religious adherences meant that immigrant elites still identified with the Japanese nation and the emperor.[50] Even so, the Japanese immigrants soon entered an acculturation process. The naturalized Japanese immigrants called themselves Nikkei. Hereafter, as had occurred with German-speaking immigrants, Japanese ethnic leaders created the idea of a mixed nationality. As a representative of the Japanese Student League of São Paulo proclaimed, "We are proud and happy of being born in Brazil. Even though the blood of the Japanese nation runs in our veins, our heart throbs with patriotism for Brazil."[51] In a similar way, the magazine Transição, founded in São Paulo in 1939 by Japanese immigrants, tried to strengthen the identification of the immigrants with Brazil.[52]

While the Nikkei stressed their loyalty to the Brazilian state, nationalist groups supported the preservation of Japanese culture and language and promoted the Japanese emperor and his policy in the Japanese-language press in Brazil, primarily during World War II.[53] Some radicals even founded secret societies that outlived the war. In summer 1945 the group Shindo Renmei appeared for the first time in public by denying the Japanese defeat.[54] The group subsequently published evidence for the Japanese victory and committed several homicides. As a reaction of these actions, riots against Japanese-looking persons occurred in summer 1947, and four hundred supporters of Shindo Renmei were arrested. From the 1950s on, this kind of nationalism lost significance, not least because of a new wave of immigration from Okinawa.

Assimilation to the Brazilian Nation: Policies toward Immigrants, 1900–1945

Although many Brazilian politicians and intellectuals supported immigration in principle, they voiced reservations against certain groups of immigrants, among them Germans and Japanese. Criticism leveled against German immigration stemmed from Brazilian perceptions of the Deutschtumspolitik since the German voices that refused "integration" seemed to jeopardize the idea of "civilizing" and "whitening" the nation. To this end, it was vital that the colonists became Brazilians and established members of the society. Consequently, already during the nineteenth century, Brazilians demanded the assimilation of the German-speaking settlers.

Around 1900 such debates intensified under the impression of the increasing Deutschtumspolitik, and the Brazilian press discussed at length the so-called German peril (*perigo alemão*) based on perceptions of the expansionist plans of the German Empire in southern Brazil as well as the lack of integration of the immigrants.[55] Journalists and intellectuals such as Sílvio Romero, who actually favored the "whitening" of Brazil, were not satisfied with the situation and, upon worriedly noticing German nationalist discourses, warned against the "German peril."[56] German-speaking journalists in Brazil in turn accused the Brazilian journalists of being nativist and xenophobe and named them "Pan-Brazilianists" who neglected Brazil's cultural diversity.[57] When the German Empire torpedoed Brazilian vessels during World War I, Brazil declared war on Germany, and violent riots against German businesses occurred in southern Brazil. The use of the German language in public and in the German press were forbidden. The war thus served as a catalyst for a conflict between two nations in which many immigrants were caught between the fronts.[58]

In the 1920s the Japanese, too, were perceived as a threat. While the Japanophiles dominated the debate around 1900, the opponents of Asian immigration gained in strength as Japanese immigration picked up. Brazilian observers were worried because the foundation of purely Japanese settlements with schools and societies, promoted by the Japanese state, reminded them of the behavior of the Germans. Similarly to the German precedent, Brazilian concerns were reinforced by Japanese imperialist activities in Asia. Another reason was that racialist discourses continued to be influential. As in the United States, where an anti-Japanese immigration policy was adopted, the catchword of the "yellow peril" became commonplace.[59] Brazilian politicians criticized the lack of integration of Japanese immigrants as well as Japanese attempts at political meddling in Brazilian affairs.[60] A heated debate ensued between journalists and politicians such as Alexandre Konder and José de Oliveira Botelho, who defended Japanese immigration, and Miguel Couto and Vivaldo Coaracy, who were supporters of the anti-Japanese discourse and warned against the "infiltration of the yellows" creating a "racial problem" for the future.[61]

From the 1930s anti-immigrant prejudices were tied into a much broader nationalist discourse and immigration policy when Getúlio Vargas successfully seized power in a coup d'état and ushered in a new vision of the Brazilian nation. The Vargas regime replaced the oligarchic First Republic (1889–1930), which had granted a large degree of autonomy to the federal states. The two strongest states, São Paulo and Minas Gerais, had pushed through their own interests, based on the coffee sector, and formed the so-called coffee with milk alliance (café com leite). Vargas, who came from Rio Grande do Sul, tried to strengthen the national government. For this purpose, he passed a new constitution in 1934, which was intended to formalize his authoritarian-style governance. In 1937 Vargas staged another coup and proclaimed the authoritarian Estado Novo. All democratic institutions were abolished. After 1937 Vargas tried to unify and vitalize the "nation." To this end he stressed the importance of the sense of community, the family, and brasilidade ("Brazilianness"). During the Estado Novo, Vargas introduced a number of nationalist practices, including national holidays (for instance, "Flag Day" [Dia da Bandeira] with parades in honor of the Brazilian flag) and a language reform in order to demarcate boundaries between Brazilian and Continental Portuguese. Likewise, Brazilian history was instrumentalized for patriotic purposes—in 1937, for example, the National Institute of Historic and Artistic Heritage was founded.

One piece of this nationalism was a new immigration policy.[62] The constitution of 1934 had already affirmed the necessity that immigrants "assimilate," and had decreed "necessary restrictions to ensure the ethnic integration . . . of the immigrant."[63] In 1938 the CIC was founded to discuss the immigration question, to draft new laws, and to press ahead with the assimilation of the settlers. Employees of the CIC, such as Lima Câmara and Hehl Neiva, closely followed the migration theories of the Chicago School, considered modern at the time, and tried to apply them to Brazil. Robert E. Park and Ernest Burgess had developed a theory of assimilation in the 1920s. They envisaged an ideal integration of immigrants in the host society and assumed that total assimilation would be desirable.[64] Such theories fit into the CIC's policy and its demands for assimilation of the immigrants to

Brazilian national culture. Problematic cases were, in the eyes of the CIC, the "reluctant" German and Japanese migrants. To solve this "problem," Lima Câmara and Hehl Neiva recommended "priests, teachers, schools, press, radio, cinema, societies, soaked by the spirit of *brasilidade* extensive intermixture with genuinely Brazilian elements."[65] Following such recommendations, Brazilian migration legislation set quotas against "undesirable" immigrants, specifically targeting the Japanese, and in favor of those who could enrich the Brazilian nation. Even though the regulations were not strictly implemented because Brazil did not want to compromise the good trade relations with Japan, immigration from Japan clearly declined.[66] In addition to the quotas, Brazil implemented the nationalization of certain immigrant groups.[67] In 1938 and 1939 various laws came into effect at federal and federal state levels, nationalizing the foreign-language immigrant schools. The teaching language had to be Portuguese and the content of teaching was supposed to foster *brasilidade*. The foreign-language press and the use of foreign languages in public were prohibited in 1939. Mixed settlements should prevent so-called ethnic cysts for the future. All these measures put an end to the preservation of the German and Japanese languages and cultures.

With the start of World War II and with the Brazilian entry into the war in 1942, the immigration issue became a question of national security. Now the German-speaking, Japanese-speaking, and Italian-speaking immigrants were considered "internal enemies" and "fifth columns." This seemed plausible since the Foreign Organization of the German Nazi party (NSDAP/AO) behaved aggressively in southern Brazil since the mid-1930s and sought to manipulate also those German-speakers who did not have German citizenship.[68] In 1938 the organization was declared illegal, and the Brazilian police authorities arrested its members, including German priests, who were then detained in camps. Even if the NSDAP/AO was unable to mobilize the broad masses of the German-speaking population, spectacular newspaper articles and police reports on German espionage and Nazi activities suggested the opposite.[69] Such police actions also hit the Japanese and Italian communities.[70] The discourse of the "yellow peril" or the "Japanese peril," mixed with war rhetoric, alleged a conspiracy of the Japanese immigrants.[71] Some German and Japanese immigrants were indeed sympathetic to Japan and Germany, but the generalized condemnation of the immigrants affected thousands of noninvolved Brazilian citizens who lived in the country for generations, who were considered still "Germans" in that situation, and who suffered from the nationalization campaign. As examples from the Japanese community demonstrate, the aggressive nationalization policy sometimes had effects that were opposite to what was intended, leading in some cases to a reidentification of the migrants with their nations of origin.[72]

There were also Brazilian intellectuals whose understanding of immigration and its relation to *brasilidade* differed from that proposed by the CIC during the Estado Novo. Gilberto Freyre, for instance, who published his best-known work "The Masters and the Slaves" (*Casa-Grande e Senzala*) in 1933, developed the ideas of the Brazilian "racial democracy" (*democracia racial*) and the Lusotropicalism.[73] According to Freyre, one of Brazil's key characteristics was that all its "races" lived together peacefully, which in his view was due to the special ability of the Portuguese to create civilizations in the tropics. These civilizations, Freyre held, were free of racism and provided equal rights for all population groups. In the eyes of Freyre, Brazilian culture was a predominantly Portuguese one, which "ha[s] succeeded in assimilating not only the Amerindians . . . , but also the African slaves . . . and, more recently, Spanish, Italian, German, Polish, Syrian, Japanese and other immigrants."[74] Like his colleagues from the CIC, Freyre pleaded for the assimilation of immigrants.[75] He underlined that "such attempts by German or Japanese or Polish sub-groups to lead in Brazil a separate life as super-groups—based on a *mystique* of being not only *different*, but also superior, to the Luso-Brazilian community—have failed."[76] This was, he observed, facilitated by the nationalization campaign by Vargas and led to the social advancement of the immigrants in the new society. On the other hand, Freyre admitted that the immigrant groups contributed with their culture to Brazilian society and encouraged, later on, even the bilingualism of the descendants of the German-speaking immigrants.[77]

Unlike Freyre, who read the Brazilian assimilation policy as a success story of national unity, German sociologist Emilio Willems focused on the problems of minority groups.[78] Willems, who worked in Brazil and migrated in 1949 to the United States, adapted the acculturation theory by the American anthropologist Melville Herskovits, who took into account that the host society is also subject to changes as result of the presence of immigrants. This understanding implied that not only the immigrants had to assimilate.[79] Willems devoted himself in particular to the study of hybrid minority subcultures and analyzed processes of change. He showed how immigrants used Brazilian cultural techniques and mixed them with their original everyday culture—for example, in cuisine or language—and how the Brazilian society adopted cultural practices by the immigrants.

Conclusion

Between 1850 and 1945 "immigration," "nation," and "race" were key issues in Brazilian public debates. Since the nineteenth century Brazilian intellectuals and politicians discussed the nature and destination of the Brazilian nation and wished for a nation as European, "civilized," and "progressive" as possible. European immigration gained in importance for the desired building of a Brazilian nation. While Brazilians welcomed immigration in order to "better" and "whiten" their nation, opposite ideas circulated in Germany and Japan. Most notably, German nationalists at home and overseas intended to instrumentalize the emigrants for German imperialist designs. This led to a so-called Deutschtumspolitik in Brazil that increasingly contradicted, with its emphasis on the preservation of Deutschtum and its warnings against "Brazilianization," the goals of Brazilian political and intellectual elites. Although the majority of immigrants followed individual ways of acculturation and identified with Brazil, the Brazilian critique homogenized—similar to German policy—the heterogeneous group of the settlers by calling them "Germans." Even if a policy equal to the Deutschtumspolitik was missing in the Japanese case, the Japanese government's commitment to the immigrants' cultural preservation, by founding schools, societies, and nationalistic groups in Brazil, strengthened the close ties and the identification of the immigrated people with Japan. Notwithstanding the fact that many Japanese were acculturating themselves in Brazil, Brazilian criticism emerged against the Japanese immigrants as well, lamenting their poor assimilation. In the Vargas years, Brazil implemented a decidedly nationalistic immigration policy, which adopted measures against both immigrant groups.

Nationalist discourses used "nation" as an exclusive concept. As the nationalist intellectuals perceived it, the immigrants should preserve the nation or assimilate to it. Therefore, immigrants in Brazil got caught between two distinct national concepts, which developed homogenous group categories and tried to classify the immigrants as "Japanese" or "German." The majority of the colonists, however, often could not express their opinions in the issue. Some immigrants followed the ethnic leaders and became more "German" or "Japanese," others actively tried to acculturate in Brazil, others—such as the "Teuto-Brazilians"—constructed their own hybrid spaces of identity, and others simply chose individual courses of life. Immigration was a practice that both affirmed and challenged the idea of the nation. Various conflicts resulted from this ambivalence because many nationalists had difficulties in accepting forms of difference, dissolution, and blending of fixed categories.

Migration played a crucial role in Brazilian nation building. While the perception of migration during the nineteenth century was dominated by European concepts such as "race" and "civilization," Brazil developed in the first half of the twentieth century its own scientific and politic forms of dealing with the topic, often in a nationalistic way. By doing so, Brazil strengthened its national identity and was able to face Western hegemonic behavior such as the German Deutschtumspolitik. Brazil, far from being a country on the periphery, established its own powerful *loci* of enunciation in a globalizing world.

Notes

1. Lima Câmara and Hehl Neiva, "Colonizações nipônica e germânica," 96.

2. Funcke to the Deutscher Evangelischer Kirchenausschuss, Porto Alegre, May 13, 1932. Enclosure: Kirche und Volkstum, Vortrag, gehalten auf der Synodaltagung der Deutschen Ev. Kirche von Rio Grande do Sul, 16, in *Evangelisches Zentralarchiv Berlin 5–2243: Kirchenbundesamt. Akten betreffend: die Riograndenser Synode, 1931–1933*.

3. "Nation" as a constructed category was theorized by Anderson, *Imagined Communities*; and Hobsbawm and Ranger, *Invention of Tradition*.

4. Bethell, *Abolition of the Brazilian Slave Trade*.

5. These and the following figures only consider arrivals and are approximate only. Due to incomplete source material and a considerable remigration, there are no absolute immigration figures for Brazil. The figures are taken from Asdrúbal Silva, *Inmigración y estadísticas*, 149–57. An introduction to Brazilian immigration history can be found in Fausto, *Fazer a América*. Immigration history enjoys great popularity among Brazilian scholars. Hundreds of books, articles, and theses on immigration history have been published in the last twenty years.

6. Masterson and Funada-Classen, *Japanese in Latin America*, 74.

7. Brazilian immigration policy is analyzed in Browne, "Government Immigration Policy"; Seyferth, "Colonização e política imigratória"; and González Martínez, *La inmigración esperada*.

8. Wagner, *Deutsche als Ersatz*.

9. Immigration into the coffee regions and the resulting social and economic transformations are described by Holloway, *Immigrants on the Land*; and Font, *Coffee and Transformation*.

10. Numbers are from Merrick and Graham, *Population and Economic Development*, 91.

11. Good overviews on Brazilian nationalism and nation-concepts are Moreira Leite, *O caráter nacional*; and Burns, *Nationalism in Brazil*.

12. See Salgado Guimarães, "Nação e civilização."

13. On the perception of racial theories in Brazil, see Skidmore, *Black into White*; and Schwarcz, *Spectacle of the Races*.

14. The terms "Ethiopian race," "American race," and "Caucasian race" were used by European racial theorists like Blumenbach. See Blumenbach, *Über die natürlichen Verschiedenheiten*, 204.

15. Von Martius, "Bemerkungen."

16. See Freyre, *Masters and the Slaves*; and Buarque de Holanda, *Raizes do Brasil*.

17. On guaranteeing the technical and social progress of the nation, see Browne, "Government Immigration Policy."

18. Alberdi, *Bases*.

19. Dezem, *Matizes do "amarelo,"* 45–108; and Lesser, *Negotiating National Identity*, 13–39. Notably, the anti-indigenous sentiment that was so preponderant in other parts of Latin America at this time was not a significant factor in Brazilian racial ideology. Instead the romantic ideology of Indianism predominated.

20. Skidmore, *Black into White*, 53–69.

21. The German activities in Brazil are portrayed by Brunn, *Deutschland und Brasilien*; Dreher, *Kirche und Deutschtum*; Kloosterhuis, *"Friedliche Imperialisten"*; and Rinke, *"Der letzte freie Kontinent."* See also Conrad, *Globalisierung und Nation*.

22. Two influential travel accounts were Avé-Lallemant, *Reise durch Süd-Brasilien*; and Epp, *Rio Grande do Sul*.

23. Wachholz, *"Atravessem e ajudem-nos."*

24. *Die Arbeit*, 45.

25. Kloosterhuis, *"Friedliche Imperialisten,"* 361–65.

26. Jus sanguinis (right of blood) determines nationality by descent, while jus soli (right of the soil) means that everyone born inside a national territory is considered a national. Rogers Brubaker recently questioned the distinction between ethnic and civic nationalism based on these different judicial regimes: Brubaker, "Manichean Myth." See also Berger, "Germany."

27. "Umfassende Missionsprojekte der Nordamerikaner in Südamerika," *Der deutsche Ansiedler* 28, no. 12 (1890), 91.

28. See Spliesgart, *"Verbrasilianerung."*

29. "Der gegenwärtige Stand der Einwanderungsfrage in Brasilien," *Export* 9, no. 17 (1887), 263.

30. Kunert, "Aus der deutschen Kolonie," 13.

31. This complex of themes is discussed by Lesser, *Negotiating National Identity*.

32. Tramontini, *A organização social*; and Witt, *Em busca*.

33. Acculturation is described in Spliesgart, *"Verbrasilianerung."*

34. See Schulze, "O discurso protestante," 21–28.

35. René Gertz repeatedly called attention to this; see Gertz, *O fascismo*.

36. On the creation of Teuto-Brazilian identity, see Seyferth, *Nacionalismo e identidade étnica*; and Gans, *Presença teuta*, 111–210.

37. Barth, *Ethnic Groups and Boundaries*, 9–38; Seyferth, *Nacionalismo e identidade étnica*; Seyferth, "A colonização alemã no Brasil"; Seyferth, "German Immigration and Brazil's Colonization Policy"; and Seyferth, "Imigração e (re)construção de identidades étnicas."

38. Kleber da Silva and Arendt, *Representações*. Lesser uses the term "ethnicity" to emphasize the fluidity of migration identities and the agency of immigrants which challenges

national and racial concepts. See Lesser, *Negotiating National Identity*. The concept of multiple ethnic identities is strengthened also in the recent publications by Seyferth, e.g., her "Imigração e (re)construção."

39. "Diaspora" was used already by German clergymen to homogenize the "German" protestant experience abroad. Borchard, *Die deutsche evangelische Diaspora*.

40. Ibid.

41. For the following see Sakurai, "Imigração japonesa para o Brasil"; Lone, *Japanese Community in Brazil*; Masterson and Funada-Classen, *Japanese in Latin America*, 73–85; and the excellent volume Carneiro and Takeuchi, eds., *Imigrantes japoneses no Brasil*.

42. Ibid., 73.

43. Sakurai, "Imigração japonesa," 202.

44. Masterson and Funada-Classen, *Japanese in Latin America*, 79.

45. Dezem, *Matizes do "amarelo,"* 121–59, especially, 133–34.

46. Gaimusho Ryoji Iiju-bu, *Waga kokumin no kaigai hatten: Iiju hyakunen no ayumi* (Tokyo: Ministry of Foreign Affairs, 1971), 141; quoted in Masterson and Funada-Classen, *Japanese in Latin America*, 84–85.

47. See Lesser, "Japanese, Brazilians, Nikkei," 5.

48. Dezem, *Matizes do "amarelo,"* 109–20 and 257–85.

49. About the press and everyday life, see Handa, *O imigrante japonês*.

50. See Maeyama, "Ancestor, Emperor, and Immigrant"; and Reichl, "Stages."

51. Tschuida, "Japanese in Brazil," 193.

52. See Lesser, *Negotiating National Identity*, 130–31.

53. See Lone, *Japanese Community in Brazil, 150–59*.

54. See Lesser, "Japanese, Brazilians, Nikkei," 10–12; and Dezem, "Hi-no-maru manchado de sangue."

55. Brunn, *Deutschland und Brasilien*, 201–18.

56. Romero, "O allemanismo no sul do Brasil."

57. An example is "Etwas Nativistisches," *Deutsches Volksblatt*, May 4, 1914, 1.

58. Luebke, *Germans in Brazil*.

59. In 1907 the U.S. and Japanese governments agreed on preventing Japanese immigration to the United States on an informal basis. In 1924 Japanese immigration was banned by the Immigration Act. See also Dezem, *Matizes do "amarelo,"* 161–204.

60. Takeuchi, *O perigo amarelo*, 54–67.

61. Oliveira Botelho, *A imigração japoneza*, 53; Coaracy, *Problemas nacionaes*, 124. See also Takeuchi, *O perigo amarelo*, 67–122.

62. Good overviews on the immigration policy of the Vargas regime are González Martínez, *La inmigración esperada*, 183–200; Seyferth, "Os imigrantes e a campanha"; and Bernasconi and Truzzi, "Política imigratória no Brasil."

63. *Constituição da República*, 43.

64. Park and Burgess, *Introduction to the Science of Sociology*.

65. Lima Câmara and Hehl Neiva, "Colonizações nipônica e germânica," 109.

66. Lesser, "Japanese, Brazilians, Nikkei," 8–9.

67. About nationalization, see Harms-Baltzer, *Die Nationalisierung*; Seyferth, "Os imigrantes"; and Lesser, *Negotiating National Identity*, 115–46.

68. Bartelt, "Fünfte Kolonne ohne Plan"; and Müller, *Nationalsozialismus in Lateinamerika*.

69. An important report was Silva Py, *A 5ª coluna*. See also Dietrich, *Caça às suásticas*; and Ferreira Perazzo, *Prisioneiros da Guerra*.

70. Takeuchi, *O perigo amarelo*, 153–89; and Masterson and Funada-Classen, *Japanese in Latin America*, 130–40.

71. See Nucci, "O perigo japonês."

72. Lesser, "Japanese, Brazilians, Nikkei," 10–12.

73. Freyre, *Masters and the Slaves*; and Freyre, *New World*.

74. Freyre, *New World*, 147.

75. Ibid.

76. Ibid., 155.

77. Gilberto Freyre, "Discurso inaugural," in *I Colóquio de Estudos Teuto-Brasileiros*, 17–20.

78. Willems, *A aculturação*. On Japanese immigration, see Saito and Maeyama, *Assimilação e integração*.

79. Herskovits, Redfield, and Linton, "Memorandum for the Study of Acculturation."

II

MIGRATING PEOPLES

5

Motherlands of Choice

Ethnicity, Belonging, and Identities among Jewish Latin Americans

JEFFREY LESSER AND RAANAN REIN

> Germans always come in first place in the world, because of their minds. According to experts, they say that Germans have the best judgment in the world, and then come the Koreans, or rather the Japanese. And Paraguayans come in last place.
>
> Guillermo Fischer, a Paraguayan of German descent married to what he defines as an "authentic" Paraguayan, commenting on the relationship between ethnicity and national identity in 2013

Guillermo Fischer is a descendant of a group of German immigrants who migrated to Paraguay to form an Aryan stronghold called Nueva Germania (established 1887). His comments on why he is a "better" Paraguayan are not unusual in Latin America. Indeed, members of the many Latin American ethnicities that emerged following waves of immigration in the nineteenth and twentieth centuries tend to hail the national advantages of their exceptional foreignness. Like Fischer, ethnic group members (and their immigrant forbearers) habitually make reference to the cultural superiority of their real or imagined homeland (i.e., their premigratory roots) largely as an assertion of privilege over native peoples and those of African descent.

Fischer's comments are similar to professions of support for Zionism and Arab nationalism or the use of Italian or German or Japanese words across generations. In each case the speaker is doing more than simply performing an internal ethnic construction. Rather, the speaker is promoting "foreignness" as an asset in the service of national goals, a position that is resonant across class and social lines. No wonder that ethnic and national leaders consistently assert (as does Fischer implicitly) that their groups represent the best citizens because they combine national and foreign traits. From this perspective, Guillermo Fischer's ideas are not so different from the executives who produced an advertisement for one of Brazil's biggest banks, claiming that "We need more Brazilians like this Japanese."

These examples help us to understand why ethnicity is often presented as exceptional, a perspective often unchallenged by scholars. Much of the historiography on immigration to Latin America thus accepts the exceptionality position, notably by focusing on single groups with little or no reference to others.[1] This idea was reinforced because the study of immigration and ethnicity has traditionally been conducted by ethnic group members who sometimes emphasize xenophobic attitudes rather than integration. While the ethnic backgrounds of scholars have changed in the past two decades, the discourse about ethnic studies has remained quite static. Thus, many Latin American national historiographies (whether produced in the country or abroad) implicitly posit that the study of immigrants is primarily a personal topic.[2] Even today the majority of studies of Jews are written by those of Jewish descent; Arabs, by those of Arab descent; Japanese, by those of Japanese descent, and so on.

One of the ramifications of this relationship is that the study of immigrants and their descendants is frequently perceived via insider experiences. Time and again, research methods generate information on the discourses of primarily self-appointed community leaders. Newspapers and memos produced by community institutions that represent only small segments are overly privileged. In these documents, definitions of the ingroup are often extremely rigid, and the exceptionalist discourse is normalized. Academic research on Jewish Latin Americans often centers on synagogues, community centers, and Zionist organizations, even though most Jews do not belong to these institutions. Such scholarship may lead to a false impression of a cohesive and homogeneous Jewish population. The same is true in studies of Latin Americans of Arab, Japanese, Polish, Italian, and Portuguese descent. As a result, as Michael Goebel suggests in his introduction to this volume, ethnic groups are presented as so unique as to be unrepresentative of broad national experiences.

This essay takes a different approach. By thinking of immigrants as a privileged category deeply connected to both non-blackness and non-Indianness, we argue that the experiences of Jews in Argentina and Brazil help us to understand multiple aspects of national identity. Our focus is not on ritual specificity or charming food cultures but rather on the discourses that Jews, like others, have used to establish their place among those groups with the highest positions in the overlapping hierarchies that together create national identity in Brazil and Argentina. We are particularly interested in the majority of Jews in Latin America for whom "being Jewish" is a personal ethnic identification, not a statement of community belonging or religious faith. Finally, in a world characterized by globalization and transnationalism, this essay enlarges the territorial boundaries of "Latin America" to include Jewish Latin Americans who have relocated to various countries, including those who moved to or "made aliyah" to Israel.[3]

Our approach yields fascinating results. Take, for example, the recently built Jewish museum in Villa Clara, today a small town in the Argentine province of Entre Ríos. Villa Clara was founded in 1892 by the European-based Jewish Colonization Association (JCA) as an agricultural colony for refugee Jews. The colony originally had a few hundred Jewish settlers, and today the town of Villa Clara has a population of around three thousand, of whom about fifty trace their roots to the original Jewish colonists. The Museo Histórico Regional de Villa Clara (note that the word "Jewish" does not appear in the name of the museum) is constructed around a foundational claim made by those few descendants of the original Jewish farmers as well as by Jewish organizational leaders both in Argentina and abroad. They posit that Villa Clara was a wasteland before the arrival of their ancestors from eastern Europe. This position provoked a strong reaction on the part of Gaucho descendants in the region. They disputed the "Jewish version," emphasizing the existence of several rural hamlets with populations of both indigenous peoples and Gauchos before Jews arrived in large numbers.[4]

A traditional analysis of the Museo Histórico Regional de Villa Clara could take one of two approaches. The first could situate the museum within the context of Argentine Jewry and could likely leave unquestioned, as does the museum itself, the idea that Jewish immigrants settled an unpopulated territory. A broader yet still traditional approach might note that many Jewish museums in the Americas make agricultural settlement a foundational Jewish and national moment that led to individual success, either in making the land bloom (to follow a traditional Israeli Zionist narrative) or in providing the impetus for rapid migration to urban areas, where education and wealth were just a step away.

Yet an entirely different perspective appears when we compare the Museo Histórico Regional de Villa Clara to other immigrant or ethnic museums in Latin America. One ethnic group that has invested in museums are Nikkei, a generic term developed in Latin America to define those of Japanese descent.[5] In Brazil, Paraguay, and Peru, there are numerous Japanese immigration museums, each of which tells a story that would be recognizable to visitors to the Museo Histórico Regional de Villa Clara. In these museums, Japanese immigrants are presented as settling on uninhabited land given up by elites as unproductive. The newcomers struggled and made the land bloom. As the rural colonies expanded, the youth moved to the cities for education and to reposition not as farmers but as members of the dominant urban classes.[6]

Many of the exhibitions in "Jewish" and "Japanese" museums (we might call them Argentine or Brazilian museums) are interchangeable. Photos and dioramas of virgin forests are common, never including local peoples, whether gauchos, indigenous peoples, or those of mixed descent. There is a focus on tools, suggesting that immigrants brought modernity to their new countries and that success was achieved through merit, not through the luck of "racial" advantage of whiteness that Jews and Japanese entered with great rapidity in Latin America. The museums are also similar in that they display stories of success, even though historians would find in the documents of the colonization societies large numbers of complaints about poor conditions and lack of hope. In these documents, movement to the city, whether of Jews or Japanese, is represented as a failure, not as the natural progression that the museum exhibitions suggest.

Clandestine Practices and Other Colonial Experiences

In the colonial dependencies of the Spanish empire, immigration was restricted to Christians of "pure blood." Jews, converted Jews, and descendants of converted Jews were not allowed to settle. Neither were Moors and heretics, although this is often left out of accounts of the Inquisition in the New World. Laws, however, only tell us part of the story. In fact, a variety of public and secret ethnic rituals arrived in Latin America with the early European colonizers in the fifteenth and sixteenth centuries. While the research focus has been on Jews, often suggesting that something unique about members of the group allowed practices to continue across the oceans, new scholarship shows that Muslim practices arrived as well, not only among African slaves but also among Spaniards.[7] The Inquisition had forced much Jewish practice underground, and many of those characterized as "Jews" by Iberian political and religious leaders were actually the descendants of converted Jews. Variously called *judaizantes*, Marranos, conversos, and New Christians, they went to Latin America in small numbers to escape economic, social, and religious persecution.[8]

There is a heated debate in the historiography about how to define those in mid-sixteenth century New Spain (today's Mexico and Central America) whom the Inquisition categorized as Jewish or New Christians. Many of the accused were surely sincere Catholics. Some may have been crypto-Jews even though the evidence presented for the continuing existence of this group often fails the tests of conventional historians.[9] Others appear to have maintained a syncretic set of beliefs. An emblematic figure of presumed Jewish descent in colonial Mexico was Luis de Carvajal (1567–96), tried twice by the Inquisition and finally burned alive at the stake as an unrepentant "Judaizer." Carvajal composed—out of his own will, not under Inquisitorial pressure—his memoirs detailing his observance of Jewish customs.[10]

There were several mid-seventeenth-century waves of persecutions against supposed Judaizers in Mexico and Peru. These actions were often motivated by political and economic, rather than religious, reasons. This was also the case in Brazil, whose mother country, Portugal, had forced conversion of its Jews in 1497. While there was an important sixteenth-century Jewish presence in Brazil as a result of Portuguese colonial expansion, it would be inappropriate to characterize it as a "community" in the contemporary academic sense of the word, since practice, when it occurred, was clandestine. The one exception came in 1630, when the Dutch invaded northern Brazil and allowed the open practice of Judaism. Following the expulsion of the Dutch by the Portuguese in 1654, some practicing Jews became crypto-Jews, others moved to the Netherlands, and still others migrated to the Americas, notably the Dutch island of Curaçao, where a synagogue has been in continuous use since the mid-seventeenth century.[11]

The largest Jewish populations in eighteenth-century Latin America were composed primarily of Sephardic Jews (those of Iberian descent) in Surinam and Brazil. By the 1800s the vast majority of those of Jewish descent had assimilated. What has persisted is a focus on crypto-Jews, both among a small group of academics and a much larger group of ethnic Jews. Both seem to be looking for evidence of long-term settlement in the Americas in order to suggest that the masses arriving from Europe and the Middle East in the nineteenth century were simply another step in a five-hundred-year story of Jewish life in the Americas.

Those who study crypto-Jews often present the story as exceptional and part of a long history of Jewish victimization and resistance. Other groups, however, also make crypto claims. For decades, Peruvians of Japanese descent have posited that the Incas were a lost tribe of Japanese. Former president Alberto Fujimori mobilized this fiction for political purposes by dressing as both an Inca and a samurai during his campaign. Among Mexicans of Chinese descent comes a different kind of crypto claim. Some believe that following a great ancient sea battle against a superior enemy, a divine wind saved the Chinese navy by blowing it to a secret land, where the sailors found what has come to be known as the Aztec Empire. And among those of Middle Eastern non-Jewish descent comes a similar crypto claim involving a lost tribe of Arabs who sailed and populated the Amazon. In other words, the indigenous peoples of Brazil and Peru are in fact authentic Arabs (unless they were crypto-Jews or crypto-Japanese—how confusing).[12]

Much less is known about early Jewish communities in Latin America than the size of the historiography would suggest. Even so, it is clear that there is virtually no link between the contemporary communities formed by European and Middle Eastern Jewish immigrants to Latin America in the nineteenth and twentieth centuries and the small numbers of individuals who practiced Judaism openly or secretly during the colonial period. The colonial link allows ethnic groups to claim national authenticity. That Jews (or others) arrived in an unpopulated land and made it prosper is the discursive foundational bedrock for nineteenth- and twentieth-century national identity.

Multiple Motherlands in Argentina and Brazil

Argentina

Argentina has the largest number of Jews in Latin America, resulting from a great fifty-year wave of European immigration that began during the last quarter of the nineteenth century.[13] Jews in eastern Europe—especially in the Pale of Settlement—felt a growing pressure to seek a better future outside the continent. Physical harassment, social pressures, and economic plight all contributed to this situation. While a few Jews sought refuge in Palestine, most looked across the Atlantic for a home in the Americas. Jewish organizations created a number of settlement plans following Theodor Herzl's description of the choice facing the Jewish masses in eastern Europe as one between "Palestine or the Argentine." The agricultural settlements established in Argentina and Brazil, such as Villa Clara, seemed to offer a partial solution to the Jewish question.[14]

Just as Jews were looking for a safe haven outside Europe, Argentine authorities adopted a policy to encourage European entry. Elites desired to increase the relatively small population and to "whiten" it by bringing European immigrants who they hoped would ensure development. Modernization, which included a strong sense of racial exclusivity, was the main motivation behind the maxim coined in 1853 by the intellectual and politician Juan Bautista Alberdi: "*Gobernar es poblar*" (to govern is to populate).[15] Indeed, from the 1870s until the economic recession of the early 1930s, immigrants flooded onto Argentine shores. While Argentine leaders hoped to attract Northern Europeans, most in fact came from either southern or eastern Europe. As Catholics and speakers of a Romance language, Italians and Spaniards found their integration into Argentine society to be relatively smooth.

Other newcomers, notably urban and rural Jews from central and eastern Europe and Jews and Arabs from the Ottoman Empire, faced different issues. For most "Semitic" immigrants, Argentina proved to be a "promised land," and social and economic ascension went hand in hand, albeit with constant and at times violent reminders of their minority status. By the twentieth century, they had established communal institutions that satisfied many of their social, economic, and cultural needs. The immigrants and their descendants created a rich mosaic of social, cultural, political, and ideological life, which reflected a wide variety of faiths, identities, and social practices. At the same time, both Jews and Arabs faced similar stereotypes as to their "otherness."[16]

Chronologically, the first Jewish immigrants began to arrive in the 1840s, and the evidence of colonial-era conversos and crypto-Jews that exist for Brazil in a limited way cannot be found in the Argentine case. Like Brazil, however, Argentina's "pioneers" included Moroccan Jews, although this group arrived at the same time as did German Jews. An important milestone in Jewish immigration was recorded in 1881 when, following pogroms in Russia, the Argentine government decided to send a special emissary to tsarist Russia to encourage Jews to immigrate. The first organized group of 820 Russian Jews arrived in August 1889 on board the ship *Wesser*. They were sent to establish Jewish agricultural colonies, and some of its members founded the Moisesville agricultural settlement that became an important part of the Argentine national creation myth.[17] Arab immigrants did not establish agricultural colonies, but most of them did settle in the provinces in the interior and thus could claim pioneer status as well. In the second half of the nineteenth century, as Argentina emerged from a series of civil wars and provincial rebellions, Arabs and their social and commercial networks in the different provinces of the interior helped to shape a unified Argentina.

While mass Jewish immigration to Argentina was primarily Ashkenazi, Jews from Spanish Morocco also arrived in the mid-nineteenth century. They were later joined by Sephardim from the declining Ottoman Empire (especially from today's Syria) who arrived alongside waves from eastern and central Europe.[18] Sephardic Jewish immigrants often felt more comfortable among Arab Christians and Muslims than among Ashkenazi Jews.[19] They shared the same language, customs, food, and music with the Arabs and joined the same ethnic associations, especially outside of Buenos Aires.

The Argentine government's open immigration policy dramatically changed the demographic profile of the country, as became apparent in the 1914 census. Over twenty years, the country's population had almost doubled (to about 7.9 million), and more than a third of the inhabitants were foreign-born. In the capital city of Buenos Aires, this figure was around 50 percent. As for Jews, the rate of growth was much higher—between 1895 and 1919, the Jewish population increased from 6,000 to 125,000.[20]

The original elite vision of a focused and expanding Jewish agricultural enterprise did not last. In the late nineteenth century, most Jewish Argentines were concentrated in JCA colonies, but by the end of World War I the majority were urban dwellers, with Buenos Aires housing the largest Jewish population. In contrast to the limitations imposed by the United States and other countries, Argentina's open immigration policy remained almost unchanged with the exception of a temporary break during the Great War. It was only the world economic recession in the wake of the 1929 Wall Street crash that brought immigration to a virtual halt. The ensuing political upheaval provoked the first successful military coup in Argentina's history (September 1930), in turn reinforcing nationalist, Catholic, and xenophobic social tendencies.[21]

Xenophobic attitudes constituted obstacles for non-Catholic immigrants, not just Jews, because of their supposed difficulties in adjusting to Argentine society and culture. Furthermore, all newcomers—especially non-Catholics—were expected to abandon their customs in favor of the new culture that was emerging in Argentina as the twentieth century moved forward. In spite of (or perhaps because of) a population of close to 250,000 Jews in the 1930s, Argentina proved unwilling to open its gates to refugees during World War II, even though around 40,000 Jews entered (legally or illegally) between 1933 and 1945.[22] In the mid-1940s, following the end of hostilities in Europe, immigration to Argentina resumed, albeit in smaller numbers than in the past. The populist president, Juan Perón, lifted most immigration restrictions in 1947, and during the next three years more than 300,000 immigrants, primarily from Spain and Italy—the two "mother countries" of most Argentines—entered the country. While only 1,500 Jews entered Argentina in the second half of the 1940s, the Peronist regime did grant amnesty to all illegal residents, allowing some 10,000 Jews to obtain legal status. The 1950s witnessed the last wave of Jewish immigration to Argentina. These new arrivals were refugees from the Communist repression in Hungary in 1956 or Jews who had escaped from the hostile policy adopted by the Gamal Abdel Nasser regime in Egypt. From that point onward, the number of Jews in Argentina began to decline.

The size of the Jewish Argentine population and the relative ease of entry over the course of the nineteenth and twentieth centuries have not created a sense of comfort among many Jewish Argentines. Their continued sense of uncertain belonging helps to explain why research on Argentine Jewry is heavily focused on discrimination and racism. While evidence of anti-Semitic manifestations is easy to find, Jews (and Arabs) have successfully integrated into Argentine society. Polls in the past two decades emphasize that Jews and Arabs are hated less than relatively new immigrants from China, Bolivia, or Paraguay. Many Argentines also tell pollsters that they consider multinational corporations, the Catholic Church, banks, politicians, or the Army—and not Jews—as being "too powerful."

Government-sponsored anti-Semitism has been rare in Argentina. It manifested itself in the limitations imposed on Jewish immigration during the 1930s and the 1940s (restrictions similar to those in other American republics) and was also noticeable during the brutal military dictatorship that ruled the country between 1976 and 1983.[23] According to many testimonies, Jews arrested by the military suffered more than non-Jews. However, community institutions continued with their normal activities, no anti-Semitic laws were ever instituted, and Argentine relations with the State of Israel were excellent.[24]

The transition to democracy in the 1980s and 1990s witnessed the adoption of a more tolerant policy toward ethnic minorities and a growing awareness of the multicultural nature of Argentine society. This did not signal the complete disappearance of anti-Semitism or even of its occasional violent manifestations. The two bomb attacks on the Israeli Embassy and on the Jewish community center in Buenos Aires in 1992 and 1994, respectively, represented a different kind of danger for Jews in Argentina: transnational terror with local support. These bombings triggered grassroots mobilization and a continuing polemic among Argentine Jews as to their individual and collective identities, their place in Argentine society, and their relations with Israel, one of the many motherlands that Jewish Argentines choose.

Brazil

Academic literature on Brazilian Jewry often ties Inquisition-era Jews (and crypto-Jews) from Iberia with those masses from Poland and Germany who arrived after World War I. The fact that the Brazilian census of 1872 recorded no Jewish inhabitants is not an impediment to the connection drawn by those eager to suggest that Jews are more authentically Brazilian than pretender Catholics. A telling example comes with the first modern Jewish community (we use this term in the traditional sense here) in Brazil, a group of three thousand North African migrants attracted to the Amazon because of the rubber economy of the mid to late nineteenth century.

That this early and active Jewish community has been largely ignored by scholars speaks to a number of broad issues. The first is the multiple minority status of Sephardic Jewry, which diminishes scholarly interest much as it does for the Okinawans who make up the plurality of Japanese immigrants to Brazil. Second, North African Jews frequently intermarried in Brazil, using non-Halachic conversion techniques (in other words they did not strictly follow traditional Jewish law on the matter). The transgressive exogamic practices seem to have made these Moroccan Jews less worthy objects of analysis. While exogamy rates among those of Jewish, Arab, and Japanese descent in Brazil are around 50 percent (in fact, the most "closed" group in Brazil based on endogamy are rich, white Catholics), the academic production almost exclusively focuses on those who are members of the traditionally defined community.

The North African Jewish story also goes untold for methodological reasons. In Brazil and elsewhere, Sephardic Jews were often called "Arabs" (*turcos*); thus, finding them in the records demands more than simply looking for references to "Jews." Furthermore, many Jews returned to Morocco, leaving families behind. While out-migration from Brazil became, historiographically speaking, a move out of the interests of the nation, the

families with indigenous women heads of household do not fit into traditional concepts of Jewish studies. That Brazilian identity was maintained
both in familial and in citizenship categories, and that Jewish identity was
maintained transnationally, has been virtually ignored.

As the nineteenth century progressed, hundreds of Moroccan Jewish
families moved to Brazil, settling in both Rio de Janeiro and Belém do Para
(a large city at the mouth of the Amazon). The Spanish-Moroccan War
(1859–60) and a profound sense of minority status were the main catalysts
for this migration. The group's multilingualism—Arabic and Spanish were
used for business, French and Hebrew were learned at the Alliance Israélite
Universelle (AIU) schools, and Haquitia (Hispanic-Moroccan dialect) was
spoken at home—gave them a transnational perspective. Indeed, a report
from one of the AIU's directors noted that by the 1880s, 95 percent of the
boys completing an Alliance education migrated to South America.

By 1890 more than one thousand Jews had migrated to the Amazon,
where the rubber economy was booming. Many Arab Jews settled in small
towns along the banks of the river, where they traded urban products like
clothes, medicine, and tobacco for rural products like fish, Brazil nuts, and
rubber. Morocco's Arab Jews also discovered they could easily obtain Brazilian naturalization certificates, which gave them a means of economic
and social protection (as Brazilians) if they returned to Morocco, where local Jews were often the target of politicians. Many did go back to Morocco,
leaving in Brazil families with indigenous women who were converted to
Judaism; according to oral tradition the woman was brought into a room
blindfolded and told that a spoonful of molten gold would be put in her
mouth and that if she truly believed that the Jewish G-d was the one and
only G-d, the gold would taste as sweet as honey.[25]

In traditional scholarship, becoming Brazilian to return to Morocco
would likely be linked to Jewish refugee status in other times and places. Yet
thinking of that migration as a "Brazilian" (and not exclusively "Jewish")
topic, leads us in new directions. For example, since the late 1980s, 250,000
Japanese Brazilians have migrated to Japan as part of a special visa labor
program for those of Japanese descent.[26] Brazilian Nikkei often discover for
the first time what it is like to be considered unquestionably Brazilian, since
in Brazil there is no linguistic distinction between those from Japan and
those of Japanese descent—all are called "Japanese." From this perspective
Moroccan Jewish transmigration is a normative Brazilian experience, not
an exotic and exceptional ethnic one.

The largely forgotten story of the Moroccan Jews who migrated to Brazil

stands in contrast to the vibrant memory of Jewish immigration from eastern Europe. Perhaps this is because Ashkenazic Jews have been a large majority in twentieth-century Brazil. Perhaps it is because eastern European
Jews, like those in Villa Clara and unlike those in the Amazon, came as
farmers and thus fit one set of early-twentieth-century national goals.

Between 1904 and 1924 the JCA formed two agricultural colonies on the
frontier of Rio Grande do Sul, following the establishment of the Argentine JCA colonies discussed earlier.[27] The eastern European Jewish colonists who settled in Brazil never amounted to more than a few thousand
people. Yet as other countries in the Americas began to close their doors
to Jews after World War I (as they had previously with many Asian and
Middle Eastern groups), the numbers in Brazil began to rise. In fact, two
of the most noticeable new post–World War I groups who entered Brazil
were Jews and Japanese. These postwar immigrants differed in many ways
from the prewar group. Although Portuguese, Italian, Spanish, German,
and Middle Eastern immigrants continued to predominate, Japanese and
eastern Europeans (primarily Jews) challenged Brazilian national identity
in new yet similar ways.

Between 1924 and 1934 eastern European immigration to Brazil increased almost tenfold to over 93,000 persons. Jews made up about 45 percent to 50 percent of those immigrants, and by the mid-1920s, Brazil was
the destination for more than 10 percent of the Jews emigrating from Europe. By the early 1930s the Jewish population of Brazil approached 60,000
as the Japanese population approached three times that number.[28] Jews,
like Japanese and Arabs, became successful in part by negotiating their
non-blackness by refusing traditional immigrant roles as sharecroppers on
large plantations.

The combination of economic success and cultural difference made Jews,
Japanese, and Arabs particular targets of Brazilian nativists in the wake of
the Depression. Immigrants had been expected to save Brazil's agricultural
economy and Europeanize the culture at the same time. Jews (and others)
seemed to do neither. In 1934 immigration quotas were established as the
growing Jewish and Japanese immigrant population, a worsening economy,
and rising nativism made ethnicity an important topic among intellectuals, state politicians from urban areas, and federal leaders. Yet the growing public discourse opposing Jewish immigration and the resulting secret
prohibition on visas for "Semites" neither stopped Jewish entry nor particularly changed its pattern. One of the most important reasons was that
a philo-Semitic vision began to gain credence within the government.[29]

From this perspective German, Italian, and Austrian Jewish refugees were increasingly seen as bringing skills and capital to Brazil. International pressure to accept refugees was matched by a change in perception among some of Brazil's most important immigration policy makers. By 1938 new rules regarding Jewish immigration reopened Brazil's gates to such an extent that more Jews were to enter that year than in any of the ten years previously. These numbers mirror that of the Japanese whose legal entry exceeded the quota limits by between 200 and 300 percent through 1942.

In the 1950s Jews again began to immigrate to Brazil in significant numbers, this time from the Middle East, especially following the Suez Crisis of 1956. They came at the same time as Okinawans who had been forced off their land following the postwar United States occupation of that part of Japan. By 1960 Jewish Brazilians numbered about 100,000 but, as is the case throughout the Americas, disputes about population size abound. Information collected for the 2000 Brazilian census showed a Jewish population of 86,825, although Jewish organizations in Brazil place the number between 120,000 and 140,000. Some evangelical and Jewish groups use a much larger number by suggesting that most Portuguese colonizers were New Christians and extrapolating that number out to the current Brazilian population.

Approaches Old and New

Scholarly interest in Jews as a subject of Latin American studies has grown markedly in the last two decades, especially when compared to research on Latin American immigrant groups who trace their ancestry to the Middle East, Asia, or non-Jewish eastern Europe. The historiography on the Jewish presence in Latin America, however, is still characterized by essentialist concepts and overemphasizes particularity. Jews, the research seems to say, are a minority unlike other minorities. Thus, comparative frameworks tend to be diasporic and suggest that ethnicity is a nonnational phenomenon.

This tendency is not exclusive to scholarship on Jews, and a version of this chapter could easily have been written for those Latin Americans of Japanese, Chinese, or Lebanese descent. The dominance of transnational ethnicity over other components, including national identity, thus seems to be one aspect of ethnic identity performance in the Americas. Yet new research paradigms might focus on engagement in the national context in order to create comparison and contact zones with other ethnic minorities, such as Latin Americans of Polish, Japanese, Chinese, Syrian, or Lebanese descent. It might be useful to move beyond the binary view of ethnic minorities as *either* diasporic *or* national.

Research on ethnicity in Latin America often presumes that the children and grandchildren of immigrants feel a special relationship to their ancestors' place of birth or imagined homeland. Implicit in this assumption is the idea that ethnic minorities do not play a significant role in national identity formation in the host country. Some studies of Jewish Latin Americans, for example, assume that rank-and-file support of Zionist organizations is primarily related to loyalty to the State of Israel. Yet recent research suggests that conclusion is not the only one.[30] Indeed, Zionism appears to be one of the strategies espoused by Jews in order to become national citizens of Argentina and Brazil. Jewish Latin Americans needed to have a Madre Patria to be like Italian and Spanish immigrants (who had Italy and Spain). For Jews, who were at times excluded from national citizenship prior to migration, the imagined motherland became Zion, or Israel. From this perspective Israel was constructed as a nation of origin rather than as a political project to safeguard the future.[31]

The historiography also tends to assert that heritage makes one a member of an ethnic community. Yet many individuals do not see themselves (or wish to be seen) as members of a formally constituted ethnic or religious community.[32] There are many studies of ethnic community leaders and institutions, but few on the 50 percent (or more, in many places) of Jews not affiliated with Jewish institutions. The frequently used term "Jewish community" can be misleading when, without careful analysis, it refers only to those affiliated with Jewish organizations, synagogues, social clubs, or youth movements. Documenting life stories and reclaiming the memories of unaffiliated Jews will provide important lessons on the nature of national and ethnic identity. Studies might be conducted of Jews (or Arabs or Asians) married to people who identify themselves as having other origins, individuals who express ethnic identity based on rejection (what some scholars have termed "self-hatred"), and authors who do not explicitly express their Jewishness.

Much scholarship on Latin American ethnicity correctly notes that majority discourses are frequently racist. Yet there is often a gap between rhetoric and social practice. Indeed, racist manifestations have not prevented members of numerous Latin American ethnic groups from entering the dominant political, cultural, economic, and social sectors. Discourse-focused research tends to find victims and make racism appear an absolutely hegemonic structure. As a result, it is easy to connect ethnic identity

formation to discrimination and exclusion. Some scholars examining social status, on the other hand, have come to different conclusions. They suggest that success among Asian, Middle Eastern, and Jewish Latin Americans places them in the "white" category and thus as part of the dominant
classes.[33] Anti-Semitism has been a favored topic for scholars of Jewish
Latin America, but there is often little social and cultural research on the
ways in which Jews are embedded in prevailing national structures.

While studies on Jewish Latin Americans as members of the dominant
classes are rare, the literature does focus on economic success stories, often giving the impression of homogeneous, unstratified ethnic communities. Latin Americans of Asian and Middle Eastern descent seem to be
uniformly situated in the middle class or higher. This image is even stronger with regard to Jewish Latin Americans. Many scholars do not consider
research on the Jewish poor—possibly because these studies might shatter
myths that celebrate upward mobility as a unique ethnic trait.

Conclusion: Latin American Homelands Abroad

To make a single characterizing statement about contemporary Jewish
Latin Americans would be an error. Intermarriage rates are high, but so
is the growth of ultra religious worship.[34] Discourses about anti-Semitism
remain vibrant aspects of identity expressions, even though acts of violence
are rare. Zionist movements are strong among affiliated Jews throughout
Latin America, although aliyah rates are extremely low in Brazil compared
to Argentina. This difference is in part linked to how many Jews "feel" anti-
Semitism on a day-to-day basis. This "feeling" is at times economically
motivated, without the subject being a victim of xenophobic attitudes. Sebastian Klor convincingly shows that the many Argentines who migrated
to Israel during its first two decades of existence came largely from the
lower middle class while economically successful Jews were less likely to
migrate.[35]

The location of "Jewish Latin America" has expanded since the 1960s
to both Israel and to North America. The previously discussed strategy of
using an overseas motherland to create a claim of an exceptional national
identity thus continues in new forms. There are currently around one hundred thousand Israeli citizens of Latin American origin. Their integration
into Israeli society is considered a success story since many have attained
prominent positions in various fields. However, Latin American Israelis
do not promote group ethnicity, preferring individual mobility to group

assertiveness. Two major factors are at play here. First, there has never been a "wave" of immigration from Latin America to Israel, although there were peaks in the 1970s and 1980s, a time of military dictatorships in the Southern Cone. Second, there is wide spatial distribution of Latin American Israelis, thus no neighborhoods or towns are "Latin" in the way many are "Russian" or "Ethiopian."[36] Klor's argument about class also suggests that invisibility is part of a broader Israeli national ideal of marketing aliyah as a "prize" for successful Jews, not a "salvation" for less rich ones.

Latin American Israelis see their premigratory cultural orientation as an asset in the informal and improvisational climate of Israeli society. Latin American music, novels, and films have been popular in Israel for decades. Interest in Latin American culture grew dramatically in recent years as the number of Israeli youngsters traveling to South America increased. Today *telenovelas* have large audiences. Compared to many other newcomers to Israel, Latin American immigrants arrive with a stronger knowledge of Israel, Zionism, Judaism, and the Hebrew language. Quite recently there has been a dramatic increase in the number of Latin Israeli websites providing a space where Latin American identity can be asserted. As one of our informants told us, "It is cool to be Latino in Israel."[37]

This chapter argues that Jews are normative Latin Americans. It proposes that national categories such as "Argentine" and "Brazilian" include members of numerous "minority" groups, all of whom promote their attachment to multiple motherlands as critical to their status as national citizens. We have looked at some of the traditional academic ideas about Jewish Latin American life and have asked if new approaches might generate new data and new conclusions. We are interested in comparison within national boundaries and hope to see more research on those who define themselves as "ethnic" in noninstitutional ways. In this way we can begin to understand immigrants and their descendants not as *in* Latin America but *as* Latin America.

Recently the Israeli comedic television program *Eretz Nehederet* (Israel's version of *Saturday Night Live*) did a parody of the *Taglit* (Birthright) program, which "offers the gift of a free, 10-day educational trip to Israel for Jewish adults between the ages of 18 to 26."[38] The skit focused on four students, three from the United States and one from Brazil. The North Americans were couched in two ways: the girls/women were stereotyped Long Islanders desperately looking for their Jewish identity through Holocaust memory experiences, and the boy/man was from the Midwest and seemed to think he was in a summer camp. The Brazilian, however, was presented

Figure 5.1. "Reirse es Kosher." *Plural JAI*, Buenos Aries, May 5, 2012. Permission granted by cartoon author Daniel Sacroisky.

differently. At first he had nothing to say about Israel or Jewishness. Rather, he seemed obsessed with Brazil: his comments revolved exclusively around Brazilian *futebol*, Brazilian drinking rituals, and Brazilian sexuality. Yet the skit ended in an unexpected way as the group finds itself alone in a minefield. Suddenly the Brazilian was remade as the one who most readily adapts to the Israeli reality. He saved the others by teaching them to dance *capoeira* (an Afro-Brazilian martial art/dance) to the Michel Teló global mega-hit "Ai Se Eu Te Pego" (which references Brazilian *sertanejo* or "country" music). Latin American birth allows the negotiation of the Middle Eastern minefield.

This sense of Jewish Latin Americans as particularly prepared for integration into Israeli society is not without its discontents. In May 2012 the Buenos Aires–based Jewish Argentine online magazine *Plural JAI* ("Plural Lives") presented a cartoon that sums up the fluid nature of immigration, national identity, and ethnicity. In the first block (see figure 5.1), a Jewish Argentine is surrounded by his motherland choices: he sits in his home in Buenos Aires looking at a wall covered with Jewish and Israeli symbols, including the name of the country written in Hebrew, a photograph of Jerusalem, and a group of religious ritual implements. The second block shows the same person after having migrated to Israel. Now his wall is covered with a picture of tango star Carlos Gardel, a Boca Juniors pennant, and a photograph of Buenos Aires. His Jewish ritual implements have been replaced by ones of national identity—a *bombilla* to drink *mate* and a statue of tango dancing. The idea is not that he has exchanged one motherland for another. Rather, he has multiple motherlands, each of which he chooses to bring to the fore at different moments. In other words, he is a typical immigrant.

Notes

Epigraph: Nadia Sussman and Simon Romero. "A Lost Colony in Paraguay," *New York Times Video*, May 5, 2013. http://www.nytimes.com/video/2013/05/05/world/americas/1000 0000208901/a-lost-tribe-in-paraguay.html?ref=americas?ref=americas.

1. Recent examples include Schneider, *Futures Lost*; Rein, *Argentine Jews or Jewish Argentines?*; Buchenau, *Tools of Progress*; and Deutsch, *Crossing Borders*.

2. See, for example, Sociedade Brasileira de Cultural Japonesa, *Uma epopêia moderna*; or Kahan et al., *Marginados y consagrados*.

3. For an earlier discussion of these issues, see Lesser and Rein, "Challenging Particularity," 249–63.

4. Freidenberg, *Invention of the Jewish Gaucho*.

5. See Lesser, *Searching for Home Abroad*.

6. The historiography on the Jewish agricultural colonies in South America is constantly expanding. Among recent additions, see Cherjovsky, "La faz ideológica; and Flier, "Historia y memoria." See also the 2005 edition in Spanish of Avni's classic work, *Argentina y las migraciones judías*.

7. Reis, *Slave Rebellion*.

8. Bodian, *Dying in the Law of Moses*; and Kagan and Morgan, *Atlantic Diasporas*.

9. Neulander, "Crypto-Jews of the Southwest," 64–68.

10. On Carvajal and the Spanish Inquisition in Mexico, see Cohen, *Martyr*; and Lanyon, *Fire and Song*.

11. Wachtel, *Faith of Remembrance*.

12. Lesser, *Negotiating National Identity*.

13. On the discussions as to the number of Jews in Latin America in general and in individual countries, see Della Pergola, "Demographic Trends of Latin American Jewry."

14. Avni, *Argentina and the Jews*.

15. On Argentine immigration policy, see Solberg, *Immigration and Nationalism*.

16. Mirelman, *Jewish Buenos Aires*. On Arabs in Argentina, see the relevant essays in Akmir, *Los árabes*; and Agar, *Contribuciones árabes*; Klich, *Árabes y judíos*; and Rein, *Más allá del medio oriente*.

17. Gerchunoff, *The Jewish Gauchos*.

18. Bejarano and Aizenberg, *Contemporary Sephardic Identity*.

19. Klich, *Árabes y judíos*; Rein, *Árabes y judíos*; and Rein, *Más allá del medio oriente*.

20. Rein, *Argentine Jews or Jewish Argentines?*, 29–35.

21. Finchelstein, "Anti-Freudian Politics."

22. Senkman, *Argentina, la Segunda Guerra Mundial*.

23. Avni, "Antisemitism in Argentina."

24. Dobry, *Operación Israel.*

25. For an analysis of this story and its broader context about immigrant explanation of national authenticity, see Lesser, *Immigration, Ethnicity*, 116–49.

26. Lesser, *Searching for Home Abroad.*

27. Lesser and Rein, *Rethinking Jewish-Latin Americans.*

28. Levy, "O papel da migração," 71–73.

29. Lesser, *Welcoming the Undesirables.*

30. Nouwen and Rein, "Cultural Zionism."

31. Brodsky, "'Miss Sefaradí'"; and Nouwen and Rein, "Cultural Zionism."

32. Fishman, *Double or Nothing*; Cohen, *American Assimilation or Jewish Revival?*; Jmelnizky and Erdei, *La población judía*; and Karol and Moiguer, *Cultura de la diversidad.*

33. On Brazil, see Sociedade Brasileira de Cultural Japonesa, *Uma epopêia moderna*; and Sorj, "Brazilian Non-Anti-Semite Sociability." On Argentina, see Sofer, *From Pale to Pampa.*

34. Jacobson, *"Modernity, Conservative Religious Movements."*

35. Klor, "The Aliyah."

36. Roniger and Babis, "Latin American Israelis"; Bar-Gil, *We Started with a Dream*; Goldberg and Rozen, *Los latinoamericanos*; and Herman, *Latin American Community.*

37. Rein, *Argentine Jews or Jewish Argentines?* ch. 2.

38. Taglit-Birthright Israel, "About Us," http://www.birthrightisrael.com/site/Page Server?pagename=about_main (accessed May 21, 2012). For a discussion of a similar program for the Arab Diaspora, see Tofik Karam, *Another Arabesque.*

6

The Reconstruction of National Identity

German Minorities in Latin America during the First World War

STEFAN RINKE

TRANSLATED FROM GERMAN BY CHRISTOPHER REID

Over the course of the nineteenth century, some 150,000 Germans immigrated to Latin America, particularly to Brazil, Argentina and Chile. Compared to the size of the Spanish or Italian immigration, this number is relatively low.[1] Still, it seemed even to contemporaries and later generations of historians influenced by the paradigm of the nation that the German immigrants and their descendants occupied a peculiar place in society. They seemed to have a tendency to isolate themselves from the population and the politics of their host countries and to maintain a culturally and ethnically defined identity. It was argued that German immigrants' insistence on using their mother tongue and following German traditions and their consciousness of belonging to a German cultural community—albeit not precisely definable—made them stand out from other immigrant groups in Latin America. This was the case even when they no longer had German citizenship but instead officially identified themselves, or were identified as, Chilean or Brazilian, for example.

Before 1945 such an assessment was usually an expression of nationalist arrogance. This supported the view that the immigrants belonged to one of those rather remote "tribes" that supposedly composed the German nation.[2] In the lingo of the period, no matter whether they resided in Latin America or elsewhere in the world, these German immigrants were called "Germans abroad" (Auslandsdeutsche). At the time they were thought to be part of an almost mystical "Germanness" (Deutschtum) that transcended state borders and was responsible for—as it was sentimentally put—an "indissoluble bond" between all those who carried "German blood in their veins."[3] In this discourse, the host nation made demands regarding affiliation and ownership that, it is now known, became more forceful between the founding of the German Empire and the end of Nazi rule.

In particular, the establishment of numerous supposedly "typically German" associations and organizations was considered for some time to be evidence of an effort to maintain the German emigrants' group identity in Latin America.[4] Nonetheless, more far-sighted observers recognized early on that there was more to this lofty goal than "preserving Germanness." The establishment of schools and Protestant churches, the construction of hospitals, and the establishment of fire departments in fact made survival possible in a foreign and often repellent environment. The institutions and associations offered immigrants protection and social contacts in their new environment. Given the state's relative absence and the arbitrariness of the authorities, they also reflected an act of self-support. These institutions often nurtured an idealized image of Germany and the value of so-called Germanness abroad. It was against the backdrop of nationalist and racist ideas that the feeling of superiority over the Latin American population grew. This was particularly true for the decades following the founding of the German Reich, and especially the beginnings of the Kaiser's international and naval policy, a time when symbolic, self-affirmative municipal anniversaries and memorial projects celebrating German history were very common. German nationalism also found enthusiastic supporters in Latin America and was actively promoted by organizations in Germany.[5]

The national euphoria, however, affected only parts of the German minority in the Latin American countries. In social, religious, and ideological terms, the Germans were more (e.g., in Argentina) or less (e.g., in Chile) heterogeneous groups—despite the fact that the nationalist spokesmen would not acknowledge this and even though other parts of the population frequently perceived them as being a completely homogeneous, foreign, self-referential community. The German immigrants arrived at very different times, came from different regions, represented different religious confessions, and were recruited from diverse social strata. Recent research has increasingly emphasized the role of women, whose experiences often differed significantly from those of male migrants.[6]

The term "German colony" therefore had a leveling effect from the outset.[7] In addition, detailed historical studies show that acculturation and assimilation processes had begun among ethnic Germans in Latin America, which were accelerated by membership in the Catholic Church, migration to the cities, or marrying into the host society.[8] A German ethnic identity— with "ethnic" here understood as a nonpolitical category for distinguishing between groups—remained, and continues to remain, from one generation to the next.[9] In any case, there were few practical benefits to this. Even from a national (which is to say political) point of view, the blanket characterization about the "community of ethnic Germans," which was continually invoked in relevant commemorative publications, was a construction that increasingly diverged from reality.[10]

These heterogeneous groups of male and female emigrants from Germanic countries lived in Latin America in settlement colonies. Following the unification of Germany in 1871, they could also be understood as an "imperial diaspora," even though the German Reich did not have any formal colonial possessions in Latin America.[11] Just the same, these ethnic Germans cultivated their own ties between Germany and the host countries, which had varying degrees of intensity depending on the historical context. Simultaneously, the growing communication opportunities in the nineteenth century led to an increasingly close relationship with the old fatherland, which in turn had gained greater appeal as a reference point for emigrants since the Reich's founding. Thus, under the paradigm of the nation, an identifiable "discontinuous social space" of diaspora emerged at the end of the nineteenth century. The constructors of the space were aware of it and consciously reflected on it. This contributed to a brand of politics that was attuned to it, the so-called Deutschtumspolitik (policy of "Germanness").[12]

The outbreak of the First World War appears to have postponed the process once again. The war years continued long after to be recalled by ethnic Germans in Latin America as a period of great solidarity, and they were even romanticized in view of the internal conflicts of the 1920s and 1930s.[13] From this perspective, it seemed as though the class and party divisions between 1914 and 1918 had been reconciled by some kind of overseas truce or "überseeischer Burgfrieden." This was important for surviving in a suddenly adverse or even openly hostile environment, where ethnic Germans were increasingly perceived for various reasons as foreign nationals and thus a potentially dangerous group. The reconstruction of the national identity of an ethnic minority under conditions of crisis can be appreciated by focusing on the experience of the "Germans abroad" living in Latin America during the First World War.

The questions that are pursued in the following generally reflect two levels of analysis: the perspective of the Germans on the one hand, and that of the host countries on the other. In what ways did the war change the German populations in Argentina, Brazil, and Chile, the countries that are under examination here? What measures were taken by the governments in Latin America? To what extent did the behavior of Argentines, Brazilians, or Chileans change toward their fellow ethnic German citizens? Did the opinion of Latin Americans about the Germans fundamentally change? What effect did these relationships have on the self-confidence of ethnic German minorities and their sense of collective identity? What survival mechanisms did they develop? The preceding questions are addressed in what follows in three steps. First, I summarize how the German emigration to Latin America and the so-called Auslandsdeutschtum ("Germanness" abroad) constituted a motive for the German expansion in the long nineteenth century. Then I discuss the period of World War I and how the United States' entry into the war had a decisive impact on the attitude of many Latin American countries while marking a turning point in the situation for the German minorities.

German Emigration to Argentina, Brazil, and Chile

The German emigration to Latin America began soon after the independence wars in the early nineteenth century. It took place in three major waves until the outbreak of the First World War and was an expression of economic crises at home and the beginning of efforts to promote immigration in the countries of destination. The first of these waves occurred in the 1820s and mainly involved Brazil, which took in a large percentage of the total German emigrant population. The second phase was in the 1850s, in which more than 20,000 Germans immigrated to Latin America. Along with Brazil, their destination countries included Chile and Argentina. There was another surge to Latin America between 1866 and 1900, which, according to German statistics, peaked in 1890 with 5,924 emigrants. After the turn of the century, the number of emigrants to the subcontinent fell almost continuously, reaching an absolute low point of 579 in 1907. Numbers started to rise again slightly in the years preceding the outbreak of the war. The percentage of German overseas emigration to Latin America remained well below that of German emigration to the United States.[14]

The most important Latin American destination for German emigrants in the 1820s was Brazil. Chile and Argentina became more important later on, whereas larger German settlement projects only occurred in exceptional cases in the rest of Latin America. In Brazil, immigration was concentrated in the southern states of Rio Grande do Sul, Paraná, and Santa Catarina. In the areas that were still undeveloped, farm colonies emerged that soon created their own cultural institutions and small-scale industries. A similar pattern of German emigration could be found in southern Chile in the areas around the cities of Valdivia, Osorno, Temuco, Concepción, Lake Llanquihue, and, later on, the *frontera*. In Argentina, by contrast, closed German settlements, comparable to those in Brazil's southern states, were not established before the war. Some colonies were established in the provinces of Santa Fe and Entre Ríos. In 1914 about 40 percent of Germans lived in the growing capital, and many found employment with the numerous German-Argentine trading companies and other commercial enterprises. The governments in all three countries encouraged German immigration at least temporarily and more or less systematically through recruitment and the granting of certain benefits. Private shipping and settlement companies as well as emigration agencies also played a central role.[15]

In addition to the emigration of farmers and peasants to settled areas, the migration of German entrepreneurs, businessmen, engineers, and officers to the major cities, harbors, and trade centers in all the Latin American countries was already being observed in the nineteenth century as an important element of German emigration to the subcontinent. This "elite migration" was numerically insignificant but important in qualitative terms. In many cases these emigrants came from Hanseatic towns and belonged to internationally active trading companies, industrial concerns, or banks. The financial strength of this elite, which included the leading representatives of the expatriate German economy, gave them a wider leadership role. Their presence was especially influential regarding the relevant issues of the entire so-called German colony, the numerous German associations and organizations, communication with the German Reich's authorities, and in dealings with the ruling classes of their host country.[16]

After the negative experiences of settlers in Brazil, the Prussian and later German government adopted a restrictive emigration policy. This was reflected by the "von der Heydt rescript" from 1859, which prohibited the recruitment of emigrants to Brazil. It was also facilitated by the view, shared by German chancellor Otto von Bismarck, that emigration was fundamentally harmful to the economy. Nonetheless, in the 1870s the nationalist right started to demand taking control of the inevitable emigration to countries, notably Brazil, where the emigrants lived in closed settlements and were therefore able to preserve their national identity. Commercial, ideological, and political reasons went along with "world-political" motivations that ranged from exerting informal influence to creating a "new Germany." The revision of the emigration legislation in 1896–97, which made the routing of emigration to southern Brazil a national priority, was evidence of the changed view on emigration. However, as the number of emigrants continually decreased from the turn of the century, large-scale settlement projects could no longer be realized. The focus therefore turned more intensely toward the ethnic Germans already living abroad, who became the objects of a new policy of "Germanness" (Deutschtumspolitik).[17]

Advocates and opponents both agreed that the emigrants and their descendants—the "Germanness abroad"—had to maintain their national heritage (Volkstum). Otherwise they would simply be absorbed as "cultural fertilizer" by the host countries and ultimately be of no value to the German Reich. This belief was formed in the nineteenth century and was based on an ethnically oriented national consciousness, embodied in the definition of jus sanguinis set down in the Nationality Law of the German Empire and States of 1913. With the beginning of Wilhelminian "world politics" in 1890, the Germans abroad increasingly occupied the public's attention. The organizations of the political right such as the Pan-German League, the German Colonial Society, and the General German School Association found that "Germanness abroad" could serve as an instrument for the realization of their colonial aspirations. These were first aimed at informal expansion entailing territorial expansion over the long term. As the matter touched upon commercial interests, the export sector, in particular shipping lines and Hanseatic trading organizations, supported these circles.[18]

A variety of arguments were made about the significance of the Germans abroad. Thus, as consumers of German products and services, they would be able to boost the export sector while providing the raw materials the German Reich needed to confront international competition. Moreover, as pioneers and representatives of the German people overseas, the Germans abroad would be given the responsibility of improving the reputation of their homeland around the world and demonstrating the assumed superiority of the German culture and race. To this end, close cultural and religious ties were established between the Germans and the ethnic Germans outside of the country. This was made possible, for instance, through the support of German-language schools abroad, which were assigned the task of keeping alive the mother tongue. Latin America was thought of as a special target area. The prospect of creating isolated settlement structures was deemed essential to having an active policy of "Germanness" aimed at preserving the German national heritage.[19]

In this context, the organizations established by the Germans abroad played a central role. A large number of German associations were founded, especially in Argentina, Brazil, and Chile. The life of the expatriate German community was organized by associations. Recreational activities included gymnastics, shooting sports, bowling, and singing. There were also social services designed to support volunteer fire departments and health and burial funds as well as hospitals, schools, and churches. Military or veterans' associations considered it their mission to strengthen the patriotism of Germans abroad. In this, they were supported by an ever growing number of military officers from the Reich who since the late nineteenth century served as advisers in the armies of Argentina and Chile.[20] The urban ethnic German elite also created exclusive German associations or clubs that had their own buildings and whose rooms in turn were used by other associations. The heads of the German associations in the main cities also mostly understood themselves as representatives of the entire German "colony" of their respective countries. At the same time, these clubs were often in close contact with the social organizations of the Latin American elites.[21]

These associations were initially examples of self-support due to the absence of the state and the negligence and arbitrariness of the authorities. Beyond this, the associations represented meeting places with the more or less explicit self-understanding of contributing to the preservation of the German cultural identity or Deutschtum. This was accomplished by maintaining traditions, norms, and the German language, especially through institutions such as schools and churches. This aspiration was closely tied to a sense of cultural superiority. Pride was engendered through the power-political advancement of the old fatherland since the founding of the Reich but above all since the beginning of the Kaiser's "world politics." It was further bolstered by German advisers working in support of Latin America and the attractiveness of their schools and hospitals, even to non-German groups. Especially in urban environments such as Buenos Aires, where interaction with the foreign environment was inevitable and the proportion of German nationals in the German community was high, a self-image was cultivated of a closed, nonpolitical, respectable, and hardworking community.[22]

Nonetheless, the monolithic community—evoked by historical references and the very use of the term "Germanness" in commemorative publications or other elite bulletins—was an idealized construction. What is striking, rather, is the heterogeneity of the ethnic German groups. Membership to different social classes with conflicting policy objectives was particularly noteworthy. Further dividing lines included religious confession, regional distribution, the different experiences of life in the city versus the countryside, and the contrasts between German nationals and those of German descent.

A number of organizations and sociopolitical actors in the Reich saw it as their duty to oppose the acculturation and assimilation tendencies among the Germans abroad. An important role was played by the Association for Germanness Abroad (Verein für das Deutschtum im Ausland; VDA), which grew out of the General German School Association in 1908. Its goal was to preserve the national and cultural identity of ethnic Germans, above all through supporting German schools and awakening interest in the Reich in "Germanness abroad." The focal point of the VDA's work was the German minorities in Europe, although the local group in Hamburg founded in 1903 dealt specifically with supporting Latin America. After the turn of the century, there was a discernible increase within the context of "world politics" in the level of attention being directed overseas and a growing involvement in nationalist and pan-German agitation.[23]

In addition to the VDA, the churches were the most important transnational promoters of "Germanness" before the war. In many cases, the parish was in charge of the German-language schools and the German clergy were active as instructors. This political self-understanding of "Germanness" was especially pronounced in the Protestant church, whose goal of preserving belief among the Germans abroad was closely aligned with the effort to maintain the German national heritage (Volkstumsarbeit). Their primary area of activity in Latin America was in the southern Brazilian states. According to contemporary estimates, more than half of the Germans and German descendants in Brazil belonged to the Protestant faith. Spiritual care was mostly conducted by pastors who were sent from Prussia. Toward the end of the nineteenth century, a movement began toward greater centralization of the traditionally independent churches. The establishment of the Synod of Rio Grande in 1886 at the initiative of Wilhelm Rotermund was especially important in this regard. This undertaking intensified after the turn of the century. Thus, the German Evangelical Association of Parishioners of Santa Catarina and the Central Brazilian Synod for the states of Rio de Janeiro, Minas Gerais, São Paulo, and Espírito Santo were founded in 1911 and 1912, respectively. Already by 1900, ties were established to the Protestant senior church council (Oberkirchenrat), which sent a permanent representative to Brazil for the first time in 1911. In contrast to these organizations, the Evangelical Lutheran Synod of Santa Catarina, Paraná and Other Countries of South America, founded in 1905, received their pastor from the Lutheran church treasury associations. In addition, the rivalry with the Missouri Synod, started by German immigrants in the United States, was becoming apparent.[24]

In Argentina the share of Protestants among the Germans and ethnic Germans was estimated to be around 65 percent. From 1899 the majority were concentrated in the German Evangelical Synod of La Plata, which, along with fifteen listed parishes in Argentina, also included three parishes with various locations for services in Uruguay and Paraguay. The largest congregation was in Buenos Aires. Beyond this, some parishes existed in the provinces of Entre Ríos and Santa Fe and in the newly established settlements in the northern territories, where spiritual needs were usually met by itinerant preachers. Along with youth ministries and social services, evangelical churches maintained about thirty schools, primarily in the province of Entre Ríos. The Missouri Synod had been active in La Plata since 1905. They ran a theological college in Crespo.[25]

Another German Lutheran synod was founded in Latin America in 1906 in Chile, where about two-thirds of the Germans abroad were Protestants. In 1914 it comprised ten parishes. Besides the large urban parishes in Concepción, Valparaíso, and Santiago, there were further parishes in Temuco, Valdivia, Osorno, and Puerto Montt and near Lake Llanquihue. Due to the vast distances and a strong desire for self-sufficiency, closer relations did not develop among the parishes within the Chile Synod. At any rate, the "national" work in collaboration with the German heritage organizations was accorded great importance in all communities.[26]

The Catholic Church, by contrast, did not take a systematic approach to promoting the German heritage, although it was represented by the work of German orders in Latin America. The majority of the scattered Catholic Germans abroad were not served by German clergy but belonged to the respective Latin American parishes. This did not apply, however, to the southern states of Brazil, where there were larger, to some extent religiously segregated German settlements and about 40 percent of the Germans and ethnic Germans were Catholic. Of particular importance was the work of the Jesuits from German provinces, who were principally active in the school and community ministries in Rio Grande do Sul from 1842 onward. They also operated a seminary in São Leopoldo, where the language of instruction was nonetheless Portuguese. The Franciscans started to build up Brazilian ecclesiastical provinces again in 1891. Besides this, Benedictines, Salesians, and other German clerics and some diocesan priests were also active in Brazil.[27]

Similar to Brazil, the German Catholic Church's pastoral care to the Germans abroad in Argentina and Chile was tended to by various orders. By the nineteenth century, Jesuits, Redemptorists, and especially Divine Word missionaries were present in Argentina. Due to their efforts various communities were established, as in Buenos Aires (1911). For the most part, the fathers of the Divine Word served as teachers and operated a number of the various Catholic schools. From the turn of the century the Divine Word missionaries worked in Chile as pedagogues along with their missionary work through the Bavarian Capuchins. The children of the Latin American elites were also taught at their schools. Numerous conflicts arose in all countries due to the coexistence of Germans of different confessions.[28]

The Reich's leadership got involved in the effort to preserve the German heritage. Accordingly, the kaiser's navy periodically visited important Latin American ports and was celebrated by the Germans abroad. Already at this stage, these visits were intended to counteract the existing ideological and social conflicts and the differing interests of expatriate and ethnic Germans through an appeal to shared patriotism. Enthusiasm over the German naval power, especially among the Germans in Latin America, often led to the presence of naval detachments at the founding of naval associations, which then affiliated themselves with the central headquarters in Germany. Grand Admiral Alfred von Tirpitz consequently noted in hindsight that the navy had done more than the foreign office to cultivate "Germanness" overseas.[29]

One of the main instruments for government agencies and private organizations to promote "Germanness" were the so-called German international schools (*deutsche Auslandsschulen*). A secret memorandum by the education department of the foreign office, dated April 1914, laid out the current situation and the status of their development. Latin America's central importance in the report was obvious. According to a conservative estimate, there were a total of some 900 schools around the world, of which 734 were located in 12 Latin American countries; 600 schools were identified in Brazil alone. In terms of the total number of schools, Argentina came next with 70, and Chile with 40. Only then did Romania, a European state, follow with the fourth-highest number of schools at 26.[30]

Since the mid-nineteenth century and, more particularly, the beginning of the kaiser's "world politics," there was a steady increase in the number of German schools registered abroad. Many of the more important institutions in Latin America were founded in this period, including those in

Santiago (1891), Buenos Aires (the Belgranoschule, 1892), Asunción (1893), Caracas (1894), Mexico (1894), Havana (1898), Guatemala (1900), Porto Alegre (1901), Punta Arenas (1907), Lima (1910), and San Jose (1912). These and several of the existing older schools strove for closer cooperation with the German school system in order to help their students gain access to German universities. Indeed, prior to 1914 only three schools in Latin America (the Belgranoschule and the Germaniaschule in Buenos Aires, and the Deutsche Schule in Mexico) had the right to issue certificates for students to gain admittance to the one-year military service. The German government's interest in the foreign schools was demonstrated after the turn of the century by increased contributions from the Reich's schools fund, inspection trips and the official placement of teachers. All the same, regular criticism came from the Germans abroad about inadequate aid and their home country's disinterest.[31]

Since state support was generally denied to private German-speaking schools in Latin America, the issue of funding was a central concern. Even before the war, the majority of the costs were covered by tuition. In addition, the Germans abroad who were organized through school associations raised money by means of dues, school events, and donations. Further money came from the Reich's schools fund, which was allocated by the German foreign office according to significance, need, and the availability of resources.[32]

To sum up, despite efforts to promote a policy of "Germanness," a process of assimilation and acculturation was apparent even before the First World War. However, it was highly variable for the expatriate German groups in the different states, the diverse social strata and confessions, and in terms of its development over time. In the case of Chile, the process was first identified among the lower classes in the cities. Catholics were far more affected than Protestants. Germans abroad of the middle class were also able to quickly assimilate if they married into the nation's upper echelon. Other recognized paths toward assimilation were marrying into the local elite and the gradual abandonment of the native language, which often went hand in hand with enrolment in foreign-language schools.[33]

The Impact of World War I

When the war first broke out, all Latin American countries proclaimed their strict neutrality.[34] Initially the German minorities appeared to have no cause for concern. It was clear from the outset, however, that the conflict this time would not be limited to Europe but would also make its presence felt in Latin America. The Allies successfully implemented a new type of economic warfare with their naval blockade and the destruction of the German transoceanic cables. Contacts with Germany were already greatly restricted in September 1914.[35] For the many Germans actively involved in trade, this caused enormous disadvantages.

The Allies' most effective tool against German economic interests in Latin America proved to be the "blacklist" policy. It derived from the British Trading with the Enemy Act from December 1915. A blacklist was first published in February 1916 that contained the names of German, ethnic German, or German-friendly businesses and companies where German capital was invested. The ban, which restricted all Allied firms from conducting financial transactions with these companies, was enforced with the help of a comprehensive control and espionage system. This affected not only German and ethnic German companies but also their Latin American business partners.[36]

The aim of the blacklist was the long-term destruction of German overseas trade and German investments in Latin America. The measures had their intended effect. Purchasing raw materials, selling goods, applying for credit, and using services now all became a problem. Long-standing business relationships were dissolved. German employees at English and French companies were dismissed. At the same time, the cost of living increased. Many Germans abroad found their livelihoods severely threatened. Unemployment among the Germans contributed to significant social tensions. There were fewer and fewer neutral firms willing to cooperate since they, too, were fearful of appearing on the blacklist themselves.[37]

Besides the impact of the specific economic measures taken by the Allies, the interests of ethnic Germans were also affected by the anti-German sentiment. Pro-Ally propaganda organizations, for example in Brazil, had a hand in its cultivation. Commentary favoring the Allies predominated in the Argentine, Brazilian, and Chilean press. Only a few conservative newspapers such as the Chilean *Ilustrado Diario* sympathized with the Central Powers. Certainly the "wave of hatred for Germans" identified by some contemporaries at the beginning of the war was an exaggeration. Nonetheless, it pointed to the fact that Germany's reputation and, by extension, that of the Latin American German minorities had suffered considerably due to the invasion of neutral Belgium.[38] Even German commentators were forced to conclude that the press coverage accurately represented much of the public's opinion in Latin American. More precisely, it reflected the attitude of the dominant political and economic elites, who had developed stronger ties with France and England than with Germany due to cultural affinities and shared economic interests.[39] If the "Germans" in Latin America were often viewed as hardworking and industrious, they also had to contend with the stereotype of being arrogant and militaristic. The First World War had an obviously negative effect on the perception of many observers.

The twofold pressure emanating from the anti-German sentiment and the Allied economic war created new problems that had devastating consequences for the daily existence of the German minorities. It contributed to a "siege mentality" among the Germans abroad, which provoked defensive reactions and new strategies for survival.[40] Economically, the close ties to parts of the Latin American elites that had been traditionally good were maintained and strengthened. They were indispensable for camouflaging German goods through the use of the names of business partners. The domestic market and adjoining states increased in importance for the trade and direct investments of Germans abroad. Until April 1917, the United States was an important market and supplier of raw materials and goods. In general, the war years led to a withdrawal of national economies from the world market and a stronger focus on the region.[41]

In addition, the pressure from the economic war brought about the merger of various interest groups. German Argentine trading companies, for example, were organized as the Committee for the Freedom of Trade, which sought to influence policy through lobbying. In Brazil, German banks and leading businesses founded a special insurance company called Companhia Internacional de Seguros and thus made themselves independent from the Allied insurers but also from those of the Reich.[42] A direct response to the introduction of the blacklists was the founding of German chambers of commerce and trade associations in 1916. Chambers of commerce were established in Buenos Aires, Valparaíso, and Montevideo. In Rio de Janeiro, the association of German Brazilian companies was founded with local affiliates in São Paulo, Porto Alegre, Bahia, and Pernambuco. These organizations of trading companies, representatives of German industrial companies, and banks looked after their shared interests. They also supported the German propaganda efforts through donations to various Latin American newspapers and their involvement in the founding of a separate Spanish-language paper in Buenos Aires, La Unión.[43]

Besides the central economic aspect in the foundation of these interest groups in the main cities and ports, cultural and ethnic unity—that is,

the German identity—once again became an integration factor. The ethnic Germans in Latin America had also been infected by the nationalist
euphoria in the Reich. Many tried to make their way to Germany in order to actively join in the struggle. In several places, donations exceeded
expectations.[44]

The increasing pressure, however, meant that a stronger organizational
commitment was necessary. At first, charitable societies and press and in-
formational committees were created to address the most urgent problems.
The high point was the establishment of so-called Volksbünde. They as-
pired to unite all Germans and ethnic Germans under a national ideal and
give visible confirmation of the overseas truce in Argentina, Chile, and to a
lesser extent in Brazil.[45] The German Federation for Argentina (Deutscher
Volksbund für Argentinien; DVA) and the German-Chilean Association
(Deutsch-Chilenischer Bund; DCB) were established by 1916. A large proportion of the members were teachers, professors, journalists, and business leaders. The new foundations set the goal for themselves of becoming
umbrella organizations with local groups spread across the country. They
wanted to create a connection between the German nationals mostly living
in the cities and the ethnic Germans in the provinces, and they wanted to
reconcile the old conflicts between Catholics and Protestants.

The fact that this united front could be quite fragile, however, is shown
by the events in Chile. On the issue of membership, a compromise could
only be achieved after long negotiations. It provided for the inclusion of
ethnic Germans who, while lacking German-language skills, still reflected
the "German attitude." In 1916 the so-called Großbund aller deutschen
Feldgrauen (General Association of German Field Greys) was established
as a counterorganization.[46] Still, the DCB ultimately prevailed. In 1917 approximately one-fifth of Chile's ethnic Germans were organized in fifty local branches of the association. The DCB therefore had much greater success than the DVA. The members of these Volksbünde devoted themselves
in special committees to promoting German-language schools, nurturing
the German language and culture, counseling immigrants, and assisting
the unemployed and the needy as well as to propagandizing the war and
establishing ties with neighboring countries.[47]

A people's federation project was also initiated in Brazil, which was
nonetheless condemned to failure because of its utopian dimension and
the specific local conditions. From mid-1915 the Swiss pastor Gottlob Wilhelm Zimmerli campaigned on behalf of the German foreign office to set
up a Germanic Confederation for South America, which would eventually

comprise the entire subcontinent.[48] Early successes, such as the creation of local groups in Porto Alegre and Blumenau, could not belie the fundamental criticism raised by the German-Brazilian side against Zimmerli. Given the feelings of irritation toward the Germans, especially in Brazil, the mere idea of a "Germanic Confederation" gave rise to suspicions. The anti-German Brazilian newspapers and the British *Daily Mail*, in fact, were all too happy to accept the news as proof of German expansionism in Latin America. Since Zimmerli lost his official backing, the Germanic Confederation dissolved again in 1917.[49] The main reasons for the failure of these initiatives in Brazil were ultimately the rapidly growing tensions with the German Reich due to the U-boat warfare and the marked distrust before the war of the seemingly autonomous German communities in the southern states.

Anti-German Sentiments

The situation escalated even further with the United States' entry into the war in April 1917. The blacklists were greatly expanded, and their enforcement became much more effective. Thus, among other things, so-called gray lists were introduced that contained suspicious neutral companies. The "white lists," by the same token, verified the companies that were not under suspicion. As a result of the United States' war involvement, the year 1917 witnessed a severing of ties, and many Latin American countries entered the war on the side of the Allies.[50] In these countries, the German minorities' situation was sometimes very tense, whereas in some neutral states it remained undisturbed. The following examples show the range of responses of three different countries.

The reaction in Brazil was especially severe. Because of the sinking of Brazilian ships by German U-boats and other diplomatic incidents that were detailed in the pro-Allied press, tensions already ran high from the beginning of 1917. These coincided with attacks on German minority institutions. A few days after Brazil suspended its diplomatic relations with Berlin in April, anti-German riots were incited in Porto Alegre. Within three days, around three hundred houses were looted and destroyed. Soon after, the unrest spread to Pelotas. A second wave of mob action against German Brazilians came after the Brazilian declaration of war at the end of October, impacting such cities as Curitiba, Santos, and Rio de Janeiro.[51]

The anti-German press campaign and the reservations about the allegedly arrogant and even racist ethnic Germans were undoubtedly important factors in the outbreaks of violence. The Germans' lack of integration in the Brazilian commonwealth was now a cause for their blame. The massive mobilization of Brazilians points to the fact that there were a variety of anti-German stereotypes and emotions among the population, especially the sizable Italian communities, which could be tapped into relatively easily. This included a fear of an alleged German takeover, the proverbial "German threat." The spontaneity of the outbursts was put into question, however, for large companies and German newspapers were systematically attacked. It is thus likely that, along with the anti-German sentiment, bribes from the Allies also played a role.[52]

The Brazilian government was not in a position to effectively check the disorder. Be that as it may, various measures were implemented after the outbreak of war that made no distinction between German nationals and German Brazilians. As a consequence, all the publications and services in the German language were banned, a measure that hit the Protestant communities especially hard. A censorship office was set up, and the German schools were closed if they did not begin teaching lessons in Portuguese. Another set of laws was directed against the economic activity of the Germans. Among other things, the branches of the German banks were put under government control and the president was given the right to sell off German property. Finally, a state of emergency was proclaimed in the southern states, leading to the internment of several hundred Germans.[53]

The pressure increased considerably for the German minority in neutral Argentina, too. The campaign undertaken by entente-friendly organizations to break with the German Reich intensified after the entries of Brazil and the United States into the war. The sinking of Argentine ships by German U-boats was viewed by many Argentines as a provocation, and large anti-German rallies took place in April and June 1917. However, unlike in Brazil, there was also a vocal movement at this time of the so-called *neutralistas*, who recruited themselves from the ranks of military officers influenced by German training, Catholic priests, and other Conservatives. The climax of the anti-German riots followed a few months later in connection with a diplomatic incident known as the Luxburg Affair, in which the Argentine foreign minister was insulted by the German ambassador. As the German educator in Argentina Wilhelm Keiper put it, September 13, 1917 turned into a "black day" for Buenos Aires' German minority when their institutions were exposed to massive destruction and looting. Just as with the outbreaks of violence in Brazil, the violence in Argentina was hardly entirely spontaneous. The pro-Allied interest groups hired unemployed sailors to help facilitate the unrest.[54]

By contrast, the situation in Chile remained calm. No riots were carried out against the German minority, even though the vast majority of newspapers—especially the leading *El Mercurio*—made no secret of their pro-Allied stance. In Chile, it was primarily the external pressure of the Allied economic war that drove the Germans and ethnic Germans closer together.[55]

The growing strain caused the German minorities to respond by gradually adapting their survival strategies. For instance, the establishment and consolidation of the German-Chilean Confederation did not fail to cause concern. The pro-Allied Chilean press further evoked the phantom of the "German threat." The German-Chilean Confederation accordingly needed to take these attitudes into consideration with regard to its activities. In light of the anti-German riots, the German Federation for Argentina imposed even stronger restrictions. Outwardly, the German organizations in Chile and Argentina tried to attract as little attention as possible. In both cases, however, the German groups recognized the importance of maintaining informal links with leading politicians, business representatives, and opinion leaders in order to exert influence, even using corruption, as in Argentina.[56]

The most lasting change for the German minority occurred in Brazil. There harassment and hostility exacerbated their already existing tendency toward isolation. Rising unemployment caused economic difficulties. Numerous associations responded to the measures of the Brazilian government by dissolving themselves or by changing their names into Portuguese names. The example of João Becker—the German-born archbishop of Rio Grande do Sul who banned preaching in German—demonstrates the tendency to cooperate with the state. The life-threatening danger that at first seemed to emanate from the Brazilian legislation moderated over time because the regulations were not uniform in all states and were not always ruthlessly enforced.[57]

Conclusion

World War I confronted the heterogeneous German groups in Latin American countries with a completely new and unexpected situation. The external pressure was first manifested in the Allied economic war, which impacted almost all Germans and ethnic Germans with varying degrees of intensity. Another factor was the anti-German sentiment among the public, which was fueled by an entente-friendly press. From 1917 the situation for Germans abroad became considerably more precarious, especially in Brazil. First, anti-German legislation was an existential threat to the German minorities' social life, schools, churches, and associations. Even when compared to laws of the United States, these laws were unusually severe.[58] The scale of the violence against the Germans was also unprecedented. As motivating factors, the anti-German resentment and the perception of the Germans as a racist, marginalized, sectarian, and economically privileged group proved to be as important as the bribes from pro-Allied forces.

After the war, however, the escalation of violence was also quickly forgotten. Opinion about the Germans remained ambivalent. On the one hand, the Germans continued to be appreciated in the Latin American societies as industrious and valuable citizens; on the other hand, they were seen as a state within a state, and thus as a potential danger. Yet a gradual change was evident. During the war, but especially in the subsequent two decades and in the wake of growing nationalism, the Latin American states were no longer willing to grant the German minorities extensive cultural autonomy above and beyond other immigrant groups.

The Germans responded to this threat with a two-pronged approach: first, by intensifying relations with Latin American elites and, second, by attempting to reconstruct their national group identity on the basis of ethnic categories. The concept of a national association, which had resonated greatly during the war, indicated the revival of these ideas. Partly voluntarily and partly in response to external pressure, German Argentineans, German Chileans, and German Brazilians now defined themselves as Germans in a Latin American setting, while their awareness of being Argentineans, Chileans, or Brazilians with German ancestry faded into the background. Moreover, they were perceived by their environment in reference to the category of national difference, which also had an effect on their self-perception. In any event, the overseas truce proved to be fragile. There were already visible signs of deterioration in the final year of the war. When the largest German emigration wave to Latin America took place after the war and the Latin American countries intensified their nationalization efforts, it became clear that the aspect of ideological differences within the German groups outweighed the feelings of national solidarity.[59]

Notes

1. See *Statistik des Deutschen Reiches*, vol. 360, 229; Bernecker and Fischer, "Deutsche in Lateinamerika"; and Kellenbenz and Schneider, "La emigración alemana."

2. Penny, "German Polycentrism."

3. Oberkrome, "Geschichte, Volk und Theorie."

4. See Newton, *German Buenos Aires*, 26–29; Sauveur-Henn, *Un siècle*, 321–40; Roche, *La colonisation*, 482–86; Luebke, *Germans in Brazil*, 47–49; Young, *Germans in Chile*, 155–62; and Blancpain, *Les Allemands*, 596–602.

5. Blancpain, "Des visées pangermanistes"; and Kloosterhuis, "*Friedliche Imperialisten.*" Even before the founding of the Reich, the greater integration of ethnic Germans in the German national consciousness had been discussed; see Weidenfeller, *VDA*, 28–97.

6. Bilot, *Allemandes au Chili*.

7. This also applies, of course, to such terms as "German abroad," "German school," and so on. On this point, see Rinke, "*Der letzte freie Kontinent*," 337.

8. For Chile, see Young, *Germans in Chile*, 166–67.

9. In my distinction between the concepts "ethnic" and "national," I follow Hobsbawm, "Nation, State, Ethnicity, Religion," 38.

10. There is great need in this area of research for a comparative analysis on the history of German minorities in Latin America that is oriented to modern ethno- and sociohistorical issues. An important step in this direction has been made by Tobler and Waldmann, "German Colonies."

11. On this point, see Cohen, *Global Diasporas*, 68–76.

12. Osterhammel, *Die Verwandlung der Welt*, 175–76.

13. See, e.g., Lütge, Hoffmann, and Körner, *Geschichte*, 368–70. See also Rinke, "Export einer politischen Kultur," 353–80.

14. *Statistik des Deutschen Reiches*, 360:229; and Bernecker and Fischer, "Deutsche in Lateinamerika," 197–98.

15. Roche, *La colonisation*; and Oberacker and Ilg, "Die Deutschen in Brasilien." For Chile, see above all, plus Blancpain, *Les Allemands*. For Argentina, see Hoffmann, "Die Deutschen in Argentinien," 84–96 and 107.

16. Bernecker and Fischer, "Deutsche in Lateinamerika," 207–10.

17. Fischer, "Deutsche und schweizerische"; and Fiebig von Hase, *Lateinamerika*, 1:192–247. See also Hell, "Der Griff nach Südbrasilien"; and Kannapin, "Die deutsch-argentinischen Beziehungen," 74–86, 117–49 and 230–48.

18. Fiebig von Hase, *Lateinamerika*, 1:202–18; and Blancpain, "Des visées pangermanistes," 456–60. For more on the greater incorporation of ethnic Germans into the German national consciousness before the Reich's founding, see Weidenfeller, *VDA*, 28–97. On the question of citizenship, see ibid., 339–41.

19. The programmatic statements on this issue prior to 1914 are legion. On this point, see the bibliography in Fiebig von Hase, *Lateinamerika*, 2:1110–49; and Deutsches Auslands-Institut, ed., *Bibliographisches*.

20. Schaefer, *Deutsche Militärhilfe*.

21. Newton, *German Buenos Aires*, 26–29; Roche, *La colonisation*, 482–86; Luebke,

Germans in Brazil, 47–49; Young, *Germans in Chile*, 155–62; and Blancpain, *Les Allemands*, 596–602.

22. Blancpain, *Les Allemands*, 597; Roche, *La colonisation*, 483; and Newton, *German Buenos Aires*, 28. In 1929 Schreiber (*Das Auslanddeutschtum*, 305–7) counted a total of fourteen German hospitals in Argentina, Brazil, and Chile. The largest was in Buenos Aires, with two hundred beds and sixteen doctors.

23. Weidenfeller, *VDA*, 301–22 and 363.

24. Prien, *Evangelische Kirchwerdung*, 113–203. In summary form, see also, Prien, "Die 'Deutsch-evangelische Kirche.'"

25. Gabler, "Kirche und Schule," 119; Petersen et al., *Handwörterbuch*, 1:135–36; and Newton, *German Buenos Aires*, 25–26.

26. Politisches Archiv des Auswärtigen Amtes (PAAA), 79124, Gesandtschaft, *Die deutsche Kulturpropaganda*; Kohlsdorf, "Die deutsch-evangelische Kirche in Chile"; and Gabler, "Kirche und Schule," 120.

27. Kleinschmidt, *Das Auslandsdeutschtum*, 236–57; Luebke, *Germans in Brazil*, 38–39; and Brunn, *Deutschland und Brasilien*, 192–94.

28. Kleinschmidt, *Das Auslandsdeutschtum*, 230–35; Petersen et al., *Handwörterbuch*, 133–35; and Blancpain, *Les Allemands*, 602–13 and 751–82.

29. Von Tirpitz, *Erinnerungen*, 72; Brunn, *Deutschland und Brasilien*, 194–98; Newton, *German Buenos Aires*, 30; and Blancpain, "Des visées pangermanistes," 451. On the naval associations, see Ojeda-Ebert, *Deutsche Einwanderung*, 128; and Fiebig von Hase, *Lateinamerika*, 1:77.

30. The memoir has been published in Düwell, *Deutschlands auswärtige Kulturpolitik*, 268–370. See also Hell, "Griff nach Südbrasilien," 189–200 and 235–36.

31. Schmidt, "Grundlinien der geschichtlichen." On the expatriate German criticism, see Wilfert, *Die deutsche Auslandsschule*, 8–9.

32. Foreign office memorandum from April 1914, reprinted in Düwell, *Deutschlands auswärtige Kulturpolitik*, 307–14 and 333–70.

33. See the overview in Young, *Germans in Chile*, 166–67.

34. Worth consulting on the political attitudes in Latin America during World War I is Martin, *Latin America and the War*.

35. For a general discussion on the Allies' blockade, see Hardach, *Der Erste Weltkrieg*, 19–33.

36. Couyoumdjian, *Chile y Gran Bretaña*, 137–50. On the handling of the blacklists in Argentina, see Bundesarchiv Potsdam (BAP), Auswärtiges Amt (AA), 4732, Deutsche Handelskammer Buenos Aires, *Bericht über die Lage des deutschen Handels in Argentinien zu Anfang des Jahres 1919* (Buenos Aires, January 23, 1919). On Chile, see BAP, AA, 44813, Deutsche Handelskammer Valparaiso, *Bericht über die Lage des deutschen Handels in Chile zu Anfang 1918* (Valparaíso, December 14, 1918); and Hartwig, "Die Methoden des Handelskrieges."

37. Bundesarchiv Koblenz (BA), AA, 6674, Handelssachverständiger Bruchhausen, Generalkonsulat, to AA (Buenos Aires, May 22, 1916). On the problem of unemployment during the war, see Newton, *German Buenos Aires*, 38–45. Sauveur-Henn, *Un siècle*, 528. The problem was also encountered in Brazil: Luebke, *Germans in Brazil*, 196–99. On the effect of the blacklists in Brazil, see ibid, 113–14.

38. Gast, *Deutschland und Südamerika*, 9–10.

39. Sperber, "Die Haltung."

40. Luebke, *Germans in Brazil*, 92.

41. On trade with the United States, see BAP, Reichswirtschaftsministerium (RWM), 929, Konsul Rößler to AA (Rio Grande do Sul, September 24, 1915). According to a report from Chile, the terms of the blacklist were often bypassed by merchants from the Allied countries, who were able to secure lucrative deals in this way; BAP, AA, 44813, Erckert to AA (Santiago de Chile, April 26, 1920). On the efforts of German companies under the terms of the blacklists, see also Sheinin, "Diplomacy of Control," 175–76.

42. On the committees that were founded, see Gravil, *Anglo–Argentine Connection*, 137. On Companhia Internacional de Seguros, see Zimmermann, *Theodor Wille*, 157.

43. BAP, AA, 44674, Consul von der Heyde to AA (São Paulo, February 23, 1917); and Wahrhold Drascher, "Die deutschen Handelskammern in Südamerika," *Der Auslandsdeutsche* 7 (1924), 702–4. On La Unión, see PAAA (Politisches Archiv des Auswärtigen Amtes), 121902, Ambassador Luxburg to AA (Buenos Aires, April 25, 1916).

44. On the solidarity of the Germans in Latin America, see BAP, Deutsche Kolonialgesellschaft, 297, Deutsch-Südamerikanische Gesellschaft, "An die Deutsch-Südamerikaner und die Südamerikanischen Freunde Deutschlands" (August 1914); Gast, *Deutschland und Südamerika*, 37–39; Newton, *German Buenos Aires*, 32–51; and Sauveur-Henn, *Un siècle*, 529–30.

45. See, e.g., Luebke, *Germans in Brazil*; and Blancpain, *Les Allemands*, 831–61.

46. On Argentina, see Hayn, "Gründung und Kampfjahre," 133; "Die Tätigkeit des Deutschen Volksbundes"; and Newton, *German Buenos Aires*, 57–61. On Chile, see PAAA, Gesandtschaft Santiago de Chile, Schu 10 fl, DCB, Ambassador Erckert to Wilhelm Muennich (Santiago de Chile, December 1, 1917). See also the contemporary depiction of Kurt Bauer, "Die Chiledeutschen während des Weltkrieges," *Auslandsdeutsche Volksforschung* 2 (1938): 464–72; Blancpain, *Les Allemands*, 576–77 and 845–53; and Ojeda-Ebert, *Deutsche Einwanderung*, 130–34.

47. On the work of the DCB, see BA, Deutsches Ausland-Institut, Archiv (DAI-Archiv), Neu/1208, Paul Oestreich, "An das Deutschtum in Chile," *Proceedings of the DCB*, September 28–29, 1917 in Concepción. Santiago de Chile, 1917, 1–7; and BA, Deutsches Ausland-Institut, Archiv (DAI-Archiv), DCB, "Kurzgefasster Bericht ueber die Bundestaetigkeit seit der Gruendung bis zur letzten Tagung im Dezember 1925," Concepción 1930, 7–10.

48. PAAA, 20949, note for Under Secretary Zimmermann (Berlin, June 20, 1916); Luebke (*Germans in Brazil*, 107) correctly supposes that Zimmerli came to Brazil as an agent of the German government.

49. On Zimmerli's successes, see PAAA, 20949, Erckert to AA (Santiago de Chile, October 24, 1916). On the critique, see PAAA, 20948, Ambassador Pauli to AA (Petrópolis, February 22 and March 3, 1916); ibid., Ernst Rotermund to AA (São Leopoldo, February 18, 1916). On the anti-German propaganda, see PAAA, 20949, *Daily Mail* (September 14, 1916); PAAA, 60027, Counsellor Will, note (Berlin December 23, 1921).

50. Bailey, *Policy of the United States*, 306.

51. Luebke, *Germans in Brazil*, 119–46 and 162–74.

52. As ibid., 135, suggests.

53. Ibid., 164, 173–201. On the Brazilian war legislation, see Brasilianischer Chargé A. de Ipanema Moreira to Secretary of State Robert Lansing (Washington, November 9, 1918), Annex: Foreign Minister Nilo Peçanha to the Department of State, in supplement 2 of *Foreign Relations of the United States 93 (1918)*, 356–57. On the problems of the schools in particular, see also Koch, "Kriegsgeschichte der deutschen Schule."

54. For the perspective of an eyewitness, who nonetheless was already writing under the influence of the conditions of World War II, see Keiper, *Das Deutschtum*, 51–57. See also Newton, *German Buenos Aires*, 49–51. For the Argentine side, see Llairo and Siepe, *Argentina en Europa*, 17–33. For the Luxburg Affair, see above all, Doß, *Das deutsche Auswärtige Amt*, 46–65; and Kannapin, "Die Luxburg-Affäre."

55. The fiercest protests in Chile against the policy toward the Germans arose following the destruction of the German ships interned in Chilean ports in September 1918. Couyoumdjian, *Chile y Gran Bretaña*, 131–35.

56. For more on the bribery of influential politicians in Argentina, see Sheinin, *Diplomacy of Control*, 172–73. On the reactions of the Germans, see also Newton, *German Buenos Aires*, 47–48.

57. Luebke, *Germans in Brazil*, 180–99.

58. Ibid., 201.

59. On the 1920s, see Rinke, *"Der letzte freie Kontinent,"* 291–412; and Rinke, "Deutsche Lateinamerikapolitik."

7

In Search of Legitimacy

Chinese Immigrants and Latin American Nation Building

KATHLEEN LÓPEZ

There was not a single Chinese Cuban deserter; there was not a single Chinese Cuban traitor!

Gonzalo de Quesada, *Mi primera ofrenda*, 1892

Is it possible to believe that the barbarian Zulu or Inca Indian is more assimilable than people of the classical secular civilization of Asia?

Dora Mayer de Zulen, *La China, elocuente y silenciosa*, 1924

The yellow race, especially the Chinese race, is so distant from the Indo-Latin in civilization, in customs, in religion, and in political and moral ideals that the Chinese seem to us like beings from another world.

José Angel Espinoza, *El problema chino en México*, 1931

Beginning with the Haitian Revolution and the independence wars of the early nineteenth century, elite and popular sectors across Latin America and the Caribbean have engaged in complex discourses on race, citizenship, and nation. In the age of abolition, new flows of labor migrants entered the region to supplement or replace African slaves on plantations and to develop export economies and expand frontiers. They became a central component of debates on national culture and identity. Chinese immigrants, as one of the main sources of nonwhite labor, were simultaneously promoted as efficient workers for progress and prosperity and criticized as harmful to the physical and moral well-being of the nation. Through a comparative analysis of three countries with traditionally large Chinese populations—Cuba, Peru, and Mexico—this essay demonstrates the centrality of Chinese immigration to Latin American constructions of the nation. Each, in varying degrees, became a setting of anti-Chinese discrimination, policies, and violence, accompanied by public discourse on the suitability of the Chinese for national inclusion. The actions of Chinese migrants in defense of their claims to citizenship and belonging also subtly shaped the rhetoric of nation building. As Chinese became part of the fabric of these respective nations, they continually challenged discrimination and maintained their own ideas about inclusion in Latin American societies as well as Chinese diasporic communities.

Chinese Settlement Patterns in Latin America

While the broad patterns of Chinese migration were similar across Latin America and the Caribbean, their experiences diverged according to local political context, economic climate, and geographical settlement. As slavery came to an end over the course of the nineteenth century, planter and industrialist elites across the Americas faced the challenge of finding an adequate labor supply to fuel economic and territorial expansion. When attempts at bringing large, sustained numbers of white European workers to the region fell short, they turned to Asian indentured laborers. The British primarily imported East Indians for plantation labor in their Caribbean colonies (especially Guyana, Trinidad, and Jamaica) but also imported smaller numbers of Chinese, as did the French and Dutch. Central American republics such as Panama and Costa Rica also used Chinese for railroad construction.

The massive importations of Chinese to Cuba and Peru, however, drew the most criticism, prompting decades of international debate on "coolie" labor and the suitability of Asians for settlement in the New World.[1] Although South China had a long-standing tradition of emigration, new developments, including European incursions, overpopulation, natural disasters, and ethnic conflict, motivated Chinese to leave their villages beginning in the mid-nineteenth century. An antidynastic millenarian movement known as the Taiping Rebellion (1851–64) nearly toppled the Qing dynasty and further propelled migration, both internal and overseas. Displaced rebels escaped capture from officials by boarding ships bound for Southeast Asia, the Americas, and Hawaii. Local Qing authorities also used the coolie trade to rid themselves of hundreds of Taiping rebels.[2] In the Spanish colony of Cuba, tens of thousands of Chinese indentured laborers worked alongside slaves in the sugar, railroad, mining, and construction industries beginning in 1847, while in the newly independent republic of Peru they were concentrated on coastal sugar and cotton plantations and guano pits beginning in 1849. Planters and overseers blatantly disregarded the contract provisions, and Chinese were beaten, chained, deprived of food, and forced to work under inhuman conditions. The wages that supposedly distinguished immigrant contract laborers from African slaves were routinely withheld. Chinese experiences in the guano pits of Peru's Chincha Islands were among the most deplorable. Guano (seabird dung) was an effective fertilizer that became a highly profitable export for Peru. Gangs of coolies picked and loaded guano onto carts and shoveled it into boxcars or chutes leading to ships waiting below. The stench, toxic fumes, and extreme heat and humidity caused respiratory health problems and prompted suicides.[3]

An international investigation in 1874 led to the cessation of the traffic and the end of Chinese indenture in Cuba and Peru by the 1880s.[4] The coercion and brutality of the indenture system left little possibility for a Chinese laborer to return to China. Those who managed to survive indenture remigrated or settled into local societies as agricultural and urban workers, artisans, and labor contractors. By the 1880s and 1890s, they were followed by free laborers and small entrepreneurs. Additionally, Chinese merchants with capital and commercial networks in Hong Kong and San Francisco established branches of transnational firms for importing food and luxury goods from China and also engaged in the sale and distribution of local products.

Patterns of Chinese settlement differed significantly in Mexico, thereby contributing to a high degree of sustained anti-Chinese sentiment supported by official policies. Like Peru and the other Latin American republics, Mexico achieved independence from Spain in the early nineteenth century. Chinese began to settle its northern frontier regions during the 1860s and 1870s. After the passage of the U.S. Chinese Exclusion Act of 1882, more Chinese diverted their paths to Mexico, some with the intention of crossing into the United States legally or illegally. José de la Cruz Porfirio Díaz Mori, who ruled as dictator from 1884 to 1910, intensified efforts to bring in Chinese laborers for the development of farming and mining when Spanish immigration proved insufficient. Chinese merchants in Mexico monopolized the grocery and dry goods trade, bolstered by transnational linkages with U.S.-based Chinese wholesalers. Although the total numbers of Chinese in Mexico did not reach those of Cuba and Peru, by the early twentieth century they were a highly visible group, concentrated in the northern borderland regions and constituting the second-largest foreign community after the Spanish.[5]

Foreign Bodies and National Battlegrounds

In each of these three emerging nation-states, the Chinese played a pivotal role in major nationalist military struggles of the late nineteenth and early twentieth centuries. Whether as combatants, supporters, or targets, the experiences of the Chinese in battles for sovereignty and territory shaped images of them in the national imaginary and set the stage for their reception in the decades to come.

In Cuba, Chinese are known for their participation alongside former slaves in the nineteenth-century struggles for independence from Spain (1868–98). Cubans were forced to reconsider the relationship between race and the emerging nation, and the independence movement advocated the abolition of slavery and embraced Cubans of color. Intellectuals and activists of all socioracial backgrounds forged a conception of a raceless Cuban nationality as the ideological foundation of the movement.[6] Like African slaves, hundreds of Chinese indentured laborers followed their masters in supporting the insurgency, either as combatants or in auxiliary roles. The recent history of the Chinese as coolie laborers who had suffered the same atrocities as slaves made them a natural choice for the construction of a cross-racial discourse about Cuban revolutionary soldiers. Both slaves and coolies shared a common trajectory from bound laborers to *cimarrones* (runaways) to freedom fighters. Daily interactions with Cubans, participation in ethnic networks, and the making of legal claims facilitated the Chinese transition out of indenture. But it was their participation in the struggles for independence from Spain that enabled Chinese inclusion as an integral component in the public discourse on the Cuban nation. Nationalist writings on the role of the Chinese during Cuba's shift from colony to nation further cemented their position, at least on the surface. In particular, Cuban statesman Gonzalo de Quesada immortalized the patriotism and loyalty of Chinese freedom fighters in his 1892 work *Mi primera ofrenda*. It is often repeated that two Chinese veterans were eligible to serve as president of the first Cuban republic in 1902.[7]

Chinese in Peru were also pulled into an international dispute, the War of the Pacific (1879–83), fought between Chile, Peru, and Bolivia over boundaries and mineral-rich coastal territory. In contrast to Cuba, however, Peruvians came to know the Chinese as "traitors" who supported the enemy. Indentured laborers felt no loyalty to Peruvian landholder elites, whose continued wealth and privilege came at the expense of their own toil. When Chilean general Patrick Lynch entered the south in December 1880, about one thousand Chinese agricultural workers in the Cañete Valley joined his army. Armed Chinese with painted faces, charging in battle and sacking estates, generated a fearsome image among Peruvians. A Chilean popular song evokes the red-haired general liberating Chinese indentured laborers from Peruvian plantations: "The red prince freed the Chinese of Cerro Azul." While sympathetic toward the Chinese, the song perpetuates popular attitudes of Chinese as peculiar and savage, with their wartime shouts of: "Let's cut off their heads, let's eat their kidneys with chopsticks of ivory."[8] In a cruel twist, rather than being freed, many Chinese were forced by the Chilean army to return to work in nitrate mines and guano deposits, build roads, and bury the dead or care for wounded troops.

While the Cuban battleground provided an opening for Afro-Asian alliances against a common enemy, in Peru the popular classes turned their wrath against the Chinese. Chinese shopkeepers in Lima made sure to distance themselves from marauding bands of coolies by contributing to the public defense fund and forming a militia to defend the Peruvian capital. Still, the occupation of Lima exacerbated ethnic conflicts. On January 15, 1881, as the Chilean army advanced, Indians and mestizos sacked Chinese shops and killed some 70 or 80 merchants. In the following months, peasants in the countryside burned cane fields and attacked white landholders as well as hundreds of Chinese laborers (from 700 to 1,500 according to the British diplomat). Some Peruvian writers commented sympathetically on the massacres perpetrated against the Chinese amid the rioting and chaos. In his history of immigration to Peru, nineteenth-century scholar and diplomat Juan de Arona generally advocates for European laborers. But he portrays Chinese resistance during the February 1881 black uprising in the Cañete Valley in a positive light, describing it as "the most heroic and original action of our Chinese colony in those tragic days . . . that would remain forgotten if we do not bring it to light now. . . ."[9]

While Chinese in Mexico were mostly shopkeepers and merchants and did not join en masse in the revolutionary struggles of the early twentieth century, they served as highly visible targets of popular resentment. In the context of the antiforeignism and emerging nationalism of the Mexican Revolution of 1910, the concentration of Chinese made the northern regions especially conducive to anti-Chinese attitudes and policies. For two days in 1911 bands of soldiers associated with revolutionary leader Francisco Madero attacked Chinese residents in the town of Torreón, resulting in 303 deaths and extensive property damage. The incident marked one of the bloodiest anti-Chinese massacres in the Americas. Over the course of the

next decade, a growing xenophobia converged with revolutionary nationalism in Mexico, and Chinese continued to face attacks on their shops and
Sinophobic policies. General antiforeign sentiments and agitation among
the Mexican people became directed specifically against the Chinese.[10]

These prolonged battles—for independence in Cuba, for territorial and
economic sovereignty in Peru, and for revolution against the established
order in Mexico—were pivotal events in the construction of these nations. The involvement of a group of foreigners, therefore, could be used
to further a particular agenda for development, progress, and national
identity. Accounts of Chinese patriotism in Cuba and disloyalty in Peru
were surely exaggerated. Supporters of the Chinese in Cuba evoked their
unfailing loyalty during the struggles for independence, something un-
available to their counterparts in Peru, who were etched as traitors in Peruvian national memory. The wars also affected interethnic relations. In
Cuba, Chinese fought alongside Afro-Cubans and were at least nominally
incorporated into raceless nationhood. In Peru, however, racial and ethnic
divisions between Chinese, blacks, and indigenous peoples became sharper
as imported Chinese coolies were viewed as an instrument of the ruling
oligarchs. Landowning elites in Peru ultimately feared popular reaction
and ethnic disturbances more than the occupying Chilean army. Nationalist struggles had perhaps the deepest impact on the Chinese in Mexico.
The antiforeign attacks perpetuated during the revolutionary movement
in Mexico continued through the first half of the twentieth century and
included boycotts and discriminatory legislation, eventually culminating
in the most extreme outcome—the expulsion of the Chinese from Sonora
in 1931.

The Chinese, *Mestizaje,* and Latin American Nationalisms

Seeking political stability, economic prosperity, and international legitimacy, Latin American politicians and elites publicly debated how to
integrate the diverse populations of former colonial societies within the
territorial borders of the new nations. Theories of "scientific" racism prevalent in the late nineteenth century underpinned ideological arguments for
elimination of nonwhites from the national body. Eventually these yielded
to culturally based arguments that aimed for some version of *mestizaje* or
racial mixing as the foundation for the new nations and highlighted the
potential of native indigenous and African-descended populations.[11] At the
turn of the century the young Cuban republic, founded upon principles of a

raceless nationalism, attempted to come to terms with its African heritage. Decades later Peru and Mexico, with their larger indigenous populations, focused on the moral and educational uplift of Indians and mestizos.

Even while debating the place of the African and indigenous elements, Latin American nations consistently preferred European immigration as a key to whitening and progress. Proposals for nonwhite immigrants—especially black and Chinese—came under frequent attack. Official policies toward Chinese ranged from immigration restrictions and discouragement of permanent settlement to outright expulsion from the national territory, as in the case of Mexico. Popular opposition, while most extreme in Mexico, erupted into riots across the region. In the press, Chinese immigrants were uniformly described as clannish, corrupt, inassimilable, and unfair competition for natives. The same characteristics that made Chinese shops popular among local residents—offering low prices, extending credit, using family labor—became a source of resentment among the working classes.

The United States played a key role in shaping anti-Chinese attitudes and circulating ideas of "yellow peril" in the hemisphere. News of violent clashes between Chinese and labor movements and unflattering depictions of Chinese quarters spread beyond its shores. After the passage of the Chinese Exclusion Act in 1882, the United States sought to prevent Chinese and other undesirable immigrants from using Latin American and Caribbean seaports and border towns as a "stepping stone" for illegal entry. With the passage of Military Order No. 155 in 1902, the American occupation government directly imposed U.S. immigration law on the new Cuban nation, including a ban on the entry of Chinese laborers. Although not consistently enforced, it served as the official basis of Cuba's immigration policy through the first half of the twentieth century.[12]

At the outset of the Cuban republic, Chinese were nominally protected by a concept of nation and citizenship that embraced men of all races. The Cuban Constitution of 1901 granted universal manhood suffrage to former slaves and Chinese ex-coolies. However, despite recognition of the Chinese in the Cuban struggles for independence, and alongside their official inclusion in the nation, an alternate view developed in the press, in government and police reports, and in popular literature. Shortly after independence, tension between two seemingly opposite discourses took root: one imagining the Chinese as an essential part of the fabric of the Cuban nation, and the other portraying them as something exotic and alien (and in its more aggressive form, as something dangerous to the Cuban nation).[13]

Although influenced by U.S. policies, the nationalist focus on whitening throughout Latin America had its roots in Spanish colonialism and drew inspiration from European models of progress. In Cuba, the Law of Immigration and Colonization of 1906 allocated $1 million to promote white settlement, of which 80 percent was to be used toward bringing families from Europe, in particular the Canary Islands. The remaining $200,000 was designated for the importation of braceros, or day laborers, from Sweden, Norway, Denmark, and Northern Italy.[14]

Supporters of the legislation justified their promotion of white immigration with current racial theories in social science. Creole writer Ramón Meza y Suárez Inclán believed that "the vile shackle of a contract" lay behind Cuba's problems with Chinese, always associated with the atrocities of slave-like coolie trade, far from the desired image of modernity.[15] President of the Academy of Science Juan Santos Fernández supported the government's proposal for Spanish laborers as a means to achieve cultural progress and economic modernization. Santos contrasted Cuba's slow development to that of Germany and the United States, who paid attention to the physical characteristics of their populations. Cuba, in his view, had relied on inferior races from Africa, Yucatán, and Asia to fulfill its need for cheap agricultural labor. He attributed Cuba's low population density to the inability of its mixed races to reproduce. Echoing the arguments behind the caste system of colonial Spain, he claimed that the positive aspects of "purer" races mutated in mixed descendants, generating the "impulsive forces that produce the political crime of rebellion."[16] A major strand of thought within these debates linked Cuba's future to Spanish America even more so than to the United States. The bill's proponents noted the backwardness and poverty of fellow Latin American nations. However, they claimed, certain nations such as Mexico, Chile, Argentina, and Brazil "opened their doors to European immigration, which has begun to leave its benevolent influence on the progress of those peoples of our race."[17]

A state-sponsored project committing funds to the importation of white immigrants directly contradicted the multiracial vision of Cuba forged during the recent struggles for independence from Spain. Afro-Cuban leaders and their newspapers as well as the labor press denounced the proposal from different angles. Due to the efforts of prominent black congressmen, the final version of the law did not mention specific races to be excluded. However, by clarifying that the funding was earmarked for Canary Islanders and Northern Europeans, considered white, the language of the law excluded Afro-Caribbean and Chinese immigrants. The passage of the immigration law denied the viability of a native workforce, regardless of race.

Lillian Guerra comments that "a new Cuban nation would emerge, embodied by new Cubans: white, docile, and energetic servants of their masters' republican state."[18] The 1902 law officially excluded the Chinese, and the 1906 law reinforced the view that nonwhites were racially undesirable for settlement in the Cuban republic. In subsequent years, Creole intellectuals often juxtaposed Afro-Caribbeans and Asians, as in the essay "The Yellow Danger and the Black Danger" that appeared in the new cultural monthly magazine *Cuba Contemporánea*, and they pitted both groups against "Cuban solidarity."[19] Immigration policies translated into real numbers, and between 1900 and 1929, about 900,000 Spaniards entered Cuba.[20]

Anti-Chinese discourse rooted in ideologies of racial purity and nation building found even more tangible expression in Peru and Mexico. In May 1909 lower-class Peruvians burned and looted Chinese shops during what began as a Workers' Party rally in the streets of Lima. Cries of "Death to the Chinese!" and "Down with the Chinese!" were fueled by anger at the government for importing Chinese as cheap laborers. Just two days after the riot, the mayor of Lima ordered the destruction of the Callejón Otaiza, a group of buildings around a courtyard within which hundreds of Chinese lived and worked. The Chinese quarter had been a frequent target of criticism in the press and raids by sanitation authorities.[21] In Peru, where Chinese merchants dominated key sectors of industry, working classes used anti-Chinese portrayals to critique upper-class corruption and exploitation of the masses. Although the Chinese did not compete directly with many Peruvian trades, they were blamed for inflation in the shops and for unfair competition, "singled out more as a highly visible symbol than as a critical threat."[22] In 1917 members of a bakers' guild founded the Anti-Asian League (Liga Antiasiática) to protest competition from Chinese. At the Third Pan-American Scientific Congress in 1924, José Felix Cáceres of the Lima Geographical Society captured the anti-Chinese stereotypes that had been circulating for decades in his presentation of "The Racial Problem in Peru and Asian Immigration." He characterized Chinese as morally and physically inferior, "a constant obstacle to our psychic and physical well-being, due to the manifestation of their character, customs, temperament, and vices in repugnant excess," in particular brothels, gambling houses, and opium dens. While Chinese were clearly obstacles to progress, he claimed, the passive Indian population also resisted uplifting efforts. Like others of his time (and many among his Latin American audience), the solution for Cáceres was white immigration from Europe.[23]

In both Cuba and Peru a series of immigration restrictions excluded

Chinese during the first few decades of the twentieth century. The August 1909 visit of Chinese diplomat Wu Tingfang to Peru resulted in a voluntary suspension of Chinese emigration (similar to Japan's 1907 Gentleman's Agreement with the United States). However, the loosely enforced policies were no match for the market in false documents and failed to stop large numbers of Chinese from coming to Cuba or Peru, many with the aim of entering the United States.

The more extreme anti-Chinese sentiment in Mexico developed into a sustained, highly organized political campaign. The chief spokesman of the Mexican anti-Chinese movement was Sonoran schoolteacher and local political candidate José María Arana. In general, the campaign grounded itself in promotion of Mexican businesses and sanitation but also extended to support for a ban on intermarriage and residential segregation. Among the proliferation of ordinances were taxes; prohibitions on selling food, laundering clothes, and leasing land; demands for Chinese to hire more Mexican workers; and even a requirement that Chinese take public baths.[24] In the eyes of lower- and middle-class Mexican nationalists, wealthy Chinese merchants were another group of foreign capitalists, similar to the Americans and Europeans thought to be responsible for the economic exploitation of the Mexican people. Propaganda leader José Ángel Espinoza filled his anti-Chinese tracts with vile caricatures depicting disease and filth in Chinese-owned businesses and passages describing their supposed criminality and duplicity.[25] A proliferation of clubs and publications to disseminate the anti-Chinese message indicated a merging of middle-class and worker interests in defense of racial purity and patriotism. Altogether, 215 anti-Chinese organizations existed throughout the country by 1932.[26] As Evelyn Hu-DeHart notes, "Arana's lasting achievement was to change the mode of engagement with the Chinese from physical attacks on their properties and persons to a political campaign, using the law and political pressure to force them out of Mexico, in effect resorting to a different kind of violence."[27] *Antichinistas* even drew inspiration from the deportations of Mexicans by the United States to racially justify the expulsion of a particular group of foreigners.[28]

The Problem of Miscegenation

In each of these societies the question of the position of Chinese had arisen shortly after their arrival. Neither the Cuban nor the Peruvian governments intended for Chinese coolies, overwhelmingly single men, to settle, and forced recontracting became a common practice. After indenture, Chinese generally settled alongside local women of lower social strata, producing a second generation of "mixed" descendants. In Cuba Chinese entered into marriages or common-law unions with slaves and former slaves, and in coastal Peru, with Indians and to a lesser extent Afro-Peruvians.

During the late nineteenth century, Spanish officials formally classified Asians in Cuba as "white" for census purposes. Socially, however, they were viewed as nonwhite, and the mixed offspring of Chinese who blended into the local population were considered *de color* or mestizo.[29] Peruvians, on the other hand, resisted placing these mixed children within existing racial classification schemes. The young nation grappled with how to label the generation of new "foreigners" in its midst. Isabelle Lausent-Herrera notes the significance of debates over a racial category for mixed offspring of Chinese at this critical juncture in Peruvian history. Because they were not officially named, they were denied a place within Peruvian society. The local vernacular term *"injerto"* (transplant) came to be used for the offspring of Chinese men and indigenous women (but not Afro-Peruvian women). The use of this term suggests the extent to which Peruvian-born children with Asian features remained perpetual outsiders.[30]

The nationalist-inspired Sinophobia found throughout Latin America in the early decades of the twentieth century was highly gendered and focused on the debilitating effect that racial mixing with Chinese would have on a nation's purity. In general, elites came to consider miscegenation as a natural means to assimilate and integrate a nation's indigenous and African populations. But the same approach did not apply to Asians, and interracial mixing generated opposition to Chinese inclusion in the national body.

Pro-whitening elites in Cuba and Peru spoke of miscegenation with Chinese in terms of the degeneracy of society, with the children of such unions weakened physically and morally. In 1909, when a diplomatic representative petitioned for lifting restrictions on Chinese entry to Cuba, the commissioner of immigration cited "differences of language, religion, and customs that impeded the assimilation of the Chinese element" into Cuban society. Rather than assimilating, the Chinese clustered in the suburbs of major population centers, "forming colonies where they live a semi-savage existence, engaging in all kinds of vice, and constituting centers of infection." Furthermore, he emphasized, the Chinese that did form unions with blacks, *mulatos*, and even whites, "produce rickety descendants."[31] Likewise, images of Chinese Mexican children as racially degenerate and subhuman stemmed from a belief that the impure Chinese threatened

Mexican *mestizaje* and national identity. Against a backdrop of Mexican revolutionary nationalism, popular cartoons, poems, and songs (*corridos*) criticized Chinese Mexican unions. Proponents of the Sinophobic campaigns in Mexico took this linkage between miscegenation and nationalism even further by condemning Mexican women who married prosperous Chinese merchants as dirty, lazy, unpatriotic, and shameless. By law, Mexican women who married foreigners lost their Mexican nationality. In the eyes of ardent nationalists, then, these disloyal Mexican women became "Chinese" through the malleable constructs of race and citizenship. A typical cartoon depicts an imprisoned Mexican wife of a Chinese with her malformed offspring, accompanied by the caption: "Oh wretched one! You thought you would enjoy an easy life upon surrendering yourself to a Chinaman, and now you are a slave and the fruit of your error is a freak of nature."[32] Eventually, Chinese–Mexican intermarriage was banned in Sonora, as part of an attempt to translate into policy the unsuitability of Chinese and their offspring for membership in the postrevolutionary Mexican nation. Discourse also zeroed in on the damaging effect of Chinese immigrants who usurped "female" jobs and drove honest Mexican women into prostitution. In Mexican frontier society the Chinese had concentrated in work such as laundries and domestic service traditionally performed by Mexican women.

In Defense of Chinese Communities

In the face of anti-Chinese attacks, Chinese merchants across Latin America and the Caribbean launched a multipronged defense of their communities. They positively portrayed their contributions to the economic vitality of the nation and pointed out laws that (at least on paper) guaranteed equal treatment for all foreigners. Leaders of the Chinese communities in Cuba and Peru repeatedly called upon diplomats to protect their status as cosmopolitan merchants, seeking equal treatment to other foreigners. Beginning with the exclusion of Chinese laborers from Cuba in 1902, diplomats focused on the effect of immigration restrictions on transnational business activity. Chinese migrant elites in Peru similarly used economic achievement and progress as the basis for their claims to social legitimacy. In particular, they equated themselves with North American and European foreign merchants, considered by many of Peru's coastal elites to be an ideal model for the nation.[33] Despite severe obstacles, Chinese in Mexico also defended their community through ethnic associations and the legal system, even bringing claims before the Mexican Supreme Court. Robert Chao Romero details several cases in which they challenged the constitutionality and applicability of the anti-Chinese laws. They were not always successful, as in a 1930 decision upholding the ban on Chinese intermarriage with Mexicans. A federal legislator commented that the majority of the judges "consider Chinese immigration undesirable and pernicious for our nation."[34] Despite such defeats, through the act of petitioning, Chinese made claims to membership in Mexican society, whether as naturalized citizens or foreigners with rights.

Beyond seeking diplomatic and legal defense, the Chinese produced Spanish-language publications highlighting merchant community achievements, homeland politics, and integration into local society. At the core of these publications were claims to legitimacy as essential components of Cuban and Peruvian progress and national identity.

In Cuba, when a stricter immigration decree was passed in 1926, Chinese merchants demanded a change in policies. In an open letter to the Cuban president, the Association of the Chinese Colony of Cuba (Asociación de la Colonia China de Cuba) and the Chinese Chamber of Commerce of Cuba (Cámara de Comercio China de Cuba) described Chinese immigrants as model participants in the Cuban nation, "without violent occurrences, without intervening in the political struggles of China or this country."[35] A 1926 pamphlet titled "Legitimate Aspirations of the Chinese Colony of Cuba" invoked the history of Chinese participation in the Cuban wars for independence as a cornerstone of their claims to citizenship. The pamphlet stated: "many of our members lent their generous aid to the cause of Cuban independence, bravely fighting for the liberty of this nation, meriting what has been stated in books, pamphlets, diaries, discourses . . . from the Apostle of Independence José Martí to Gonzalo de Quesada."[36]

In 1924, the same year that a prominent Peruvian articulated a systematic anti-Chinese statement, the upper-strata Chinese in Peru distributed their own publication to members of congress. *The Chinese Colony in Peru: Representative Institutions and Men: Its Beneficial Action in National Life* paralleled other Chinese diasporic community publications with its biographies and celebratory advertisements of Chinese-owned firms. But essays on low rates of delinquency and begging among the Chinese revealed an intention "to convince congress of the importance of having a Chinese colony among us as an element of progress, as a factor of order, and as a stimulant of the national energies" through the employment of thousands of Peruvian workers in businesses and on plantations.[37] This approach dovetailed with the goals of the 1919 military coup in Peru that ushered in the second presidency of Augusto Leguía with his ambitions of Peruvian wealth and modernity, grounded in commerce, a rising middle class, and urban development. Adam McKeown describes this period as "a relatively golden age of influence and prestige for many of the Chinese merchants in Peru" who responded to Leguía's platform by portraying themselves as key to local development and international reputation.[38]

Besides upper-strata Chinese, some liberal intellectuals defended the Chinese presence within their respective Latin American nations. Support for the Chinese Revolution of 1911 and Sun Yat-sen's republican movement in China synchronized with the modernizing goals of Latin American nations. In Cuba, journalist Guillermo Tejeiro praised Chinese contributions to Cuban society and emphasized the revolutionary struggles for a modern nation shared by Chinese and Cubans.[39] Local supporters described Chinese immigrants as honorable and hardworking and at times reminded fellow Cubans of the maltreatment Chinese suffered during the coolie period. But in general the coolie period was relegated to the past, a vestige of the colonial era.[40]

One of the Peruvian Chinese community's most well-known defenders was the German-born Dora Mayer, who was educated in Peru as a young child and became an activist for the *indigenista* movement. In 1909 she cofounded the Pro-Indigenist Society (Asociación Pro-Indígena) along with Pedro Zulen, himself a Peruvian-born Chinese of mixed descent. The group sought to protect Indians from elite destruction in the name of reform and to study and preserve elements of native culture. Mayer also belonged to a group of intellectuals involved with the leftist, anti-imperialist American Popular Revolutionary Alliance that promoted Latin American unity and indigenous causes and drew inspiration from Sun Yat-sen's republican movement in China.[41] For the occasion of the centennial celebration of Peru's independence in 1924, Mayer published the book *China, Silent and Eloquent*, a celebration of the grandeur of Chinese civilization and history. One section focused specifically on the Chinese of Peru and their suitability for becoming proper Peruvian citizens, "a social element more useful than any other."[42] Mayer was impressed with the Chinese individuals or firms who owned or leased land on coastal haciendas, growing cotton, cane, rice, and corn and employing up to three hundred or four hundred Peruvian workers.[43] As Adam McKeown notes, this romanticized work marks a departure from Mayer's earlier pro-indigenist writings, in which she characterized Indians, blacks, and Asians as "the feet and the hands of the whites."[44] However, her newfound support for the Chinese as a solution for Peruvian economic and national development was a qualified one. She clearly distinguished the more educated and cultured recent arrivals from common laborers.

Mexican Chinese found few local defenders, with the exception of elite agriculturalists and industrialists who promoted inexpensive and efficient Chinese labor for the expansion of the tropical coastal regions and northern frontier. Rather than rallying Mexicans behind them, however, they drew the ire of the lower-middle classes and leaders of the anti-Chinese movement, who criticized these *chineros* as enemies of the nationalist cause.[45] As in Cuba and Peru, anti-Chinese attitudes and rioting were at times more an expression of class animosity than of sheer racism.

With the onset of the global depression and the formation of nativist movements in the 1930s, nationalization policies throughout Latin America targeted West Indians, Asians, and other foreigners. Across the region, late-nineteenth-century anti-Chinese discourses resurfaced and took on new forms. Although economic elites still deemed immigration necessary for industry and progress, a flurry of laws aimed to limit the Chinese in the workforce and prevent intermarriage with native women.[46] Many Chinese migrants returned to China after the onset of the global depression and the passage of restrictive laws. But the situation in Mexico diverged with the outright expulsion of Chinese. Chinese were deported from the northern state of Sonora in 1931, ostensibly for failure to comply with a law requiring that 80 percent of employees be Mexican. Some Chinese relocated to the capital and other regions of Mexico, some fled to the United States (where they faced Immigration and Naturalization Service interrogation), and some returned to China. By 1940 the Chinese population in Mexico dropped to less than five thousand, virtually eliminated in the northern regions.[47]

By contrast, in Cuba and Peru, we begin to see a degree of inclusion during the 1920s and 1930s, reinforced by multiple generations of locally born Chinese. At the height of nativist movements, established Chinese merchants launched new magazines to defend and promote their communities. In 1934 an association of Chinese merchants in Cuba founded the bilingual magazine *Fraternidad*, which specifically responded to issues of immigrant incorporation and generational differences.[48] With sections in Chinese and Spanish, the magazine was geared toward both Chinese and non-Chinese retailers, reflecting the Chinese community's desire for acceptance by the greater Cuban merchant community. The Chinese section included association business, homeland politics, and announcements relevant to the Chinese community while the Spanish section featured both prominent Chinese and Cubans in the society pages. Images and stories depicting the transnational Chinese merchant community in a favorable light filled the magazine's pages. Photos of weddings to Cuban women and baptisms of second-generation children underscored Chinese migrant integration into Cuban society and national culture. Even as they maintained transnational ties to China, merchants used the press to promote an image of the Chinese as an essential component of Cuban society and national identity since the independence struggles. Furthermore, the Spanish-language articles made the magazine accessible to the generation of Cuban-born Chinese who were unable to read Chinese characters.

Locally born Chinese, including those with Cuban or Peruvian mothers, also struggled for full inclusion both within the Chinese community and within larger society. Later generations were integral to defending the broader Chinese communities and to making claims for "cultural" citizenship in the respective nation-states. In Peru the locally born or *tusan* community developed strategies for acceptance within the traditional Chinese transnational merchant community. In 1931 two Peruvian-born Chinese founded the magazine *Oriental*, sponsored by Chinese and Peruvian wholesalers and focusing on Peruvian-born Chinese. The monthly magazine presented the *tusan* community as a counter to the Chinese-born merchants as the only "legitimate" stakeholders of and leaders of the established Chinese regional and political associations.[49]

In their defense of their communities, Chinese merchant elites distanced themselves from lower classes of laborers and store clerks and from the stigma of the earlier coolie period. They also subscribed to prevalent racial thinking, confident that their class position conferred an "honorary white" status upon them. In the case of Cuba, Fernando Ortiz's 1940 formulation of "transculturation" has been the basis for a conception of *cubanidad* or "Cubanness" that incorporates Europeans, Africans, and, to a lesser extent, Asians. Although this set of ideas offered a conceptual pathway toward an ideology of "belonging" to a transcultural Cuban nation, color continued to be pervasive for Chinese who continued to identify with white society and sought official recognition of their "mixed" children as *blanco* or white.[50] Peruvian Chinese similarly understood the socioracial hierarchy within which they operated and sought to claim a position as legitimate foreigners within the modernizing nation.[51]

World War II became a catalyst for Chinese migrants in the Americas when the fate of China during the Japanese occupation and praise for Chinese in the U.S. military fostered sympathy in public discourse. Unfortunately, the rise in status of Chinese in the Americas was accompanied by the demonization of Japanese in Latin America, whether immigrants or locally born. Japanese entry had followed on the heels of the Chinese through contract arrangements with Japanese emigration firms, a circumstance that offered them considerably more resources. Still, they were treated as a racial minority and suffered discriminatory attacks, especially in Peru (in an example of the "othering" of all Asians, Japanese merchants in Peru were called "chinos de la esquina" or street-corner Chinese). During World War II up to 1,800 Peruvian Japanese, along with 500 from other Latin American nations, were deported for incarceration in the United States, separated from their families, and stripped of their homes and businesses.[52] The Chinese magazines *Fraternidad* and *Oriental* advocated attacks and boycotts of Japanese businesses in Cuba and Peru. Chinese merchants seized the opportunity to further promote an image of their own community as an integral part of the nation. On a practical level, the wartime cooperation between allied governments led to the lifting of restrictions on Chinese entry into American ports. In the United States, men of Chinese descent enlisted with other Americans for battle, and the government repealed the long-standing Chinese Exclusion Act in 1943. Even before this landmark action, China and Cuba signed a reciprocity treaty in 1942 that eliminated immigration restrictions based on race or nationality and guaranteed the Chinese treatment equal to that of other foreigners in Cuba.[53]

During the postwar period, local histories and yearbooks began to celebrate the achievements of Chinese merchants. The time was ripe in Cuba for the appearance of Cuban journalist and historian Guillermo Tejeiro's illustrated book in commemoration of the centennial anniversary of the first arrival of the Chinese. This type of album is typical among Chinese overseas communities in the Americas. What makes it significant, however, is that it was published in Spanish by a non-Chinese author, intended primarily for consumption by Cuban audiences. Known for his advocacy of the Chinese community, Tejeiro had previously published an article in the Havana newspaper *El País* on the parallels between the Cuban and Chinese national heroes José Martí and Sun Yat-sen. Tejeiro reprinted the entire text of the 1942 treaty in his work commemorating the Chinese in Cuba, calling attention to its role in erasing the injustices of the previous four decades of Cuban immigration law. He highlighted the significance of the treaty for Sino-Cuban relations and for the development of the Chinese community in Cuba.[54] From the 1940s onward, a plethora of articles celebrating the history and customs of the Chinese in Cuba appeared in mainstream Cuban magazines such as *Bohemia* and *Revista Bimestre Cubana*.

The expulsion of the Chinese, which had devastating effects on Chinese Mexican families, also shaped conceptions of the Mexican nation. Julia Schiavone Camacho demonstrates how deported families moved beyond regional attachments as they developed strong national identities as Mexicans during their exile in the United States and in the Portuguese colony of Macau on the southeastern Chinese coast. Mexican women whose citizenship had been revoked after they married Chinese men mounted legal challenges to their status. From 1937 to 1938 the Mexican government granted permission for over four hundred Mexican women who had been in China to repatriate to Mexico with their children, a process that continued from the end of World War II through the 1960s. Their efforts to return home eventually compelled the Mexican government to expand its boundaries of citizenship and nation.[55] Likewise, Chinese merchants in Cuba sought to bring their wives and children from China as they demanded access to full protection under Cuban law and inclusion into Cuban national life.[56]

Conclusion

After the end of the abominable coolie trade, the Chinese who settled in Cuba encountered less discrimination than elsewhere in the Americas. Rather, they were officially incorporated into a conception of a raceless, classless citizenry beginning with the founding of the Cuban nation. Chinese participation in Cuba's liberation struggles and efforts at forming interracial marriages and other alliances were key to their earlier integration. The Cuban Revolution of 1959 further altered the Chinese community. On one hand, its promise to combat institutional racism offered a premise of equality for all racial and ethnic minorities. But the revolution devastated the foundation of the merchant class, and large numbers of Chinese left Cuba, especially after the nationalization of small businesses in 1968. With no substantial new migration, fewer than 150 native Chinese remain in Cuba today.

Yet through the middle of the twentieth century, the experiences of the Chinese in Cuba, Peru, and Mexico bore significant similarities. Anti-Chinese discourse portrayed them as "aliens" to be expunged rather than incorporated into the national body. In Cuba and Peru, campaigns and riots that focused on hygiene, morality, and labor competition targeted Chinese populations from time to time, especially during economic crises. Anti-Chinese attitudes reached an extreme in Mexico, caught up in the context of a revolutionary nationalism and anti-imperialism. The purge of Chinese from the northern Mexico in 1931 amounted to a full-blown attempt to cleanse the nation.

While historically Sinophobia can be found everywhere across Latin America and the Caribbean, perhaps more significant for the question of immigration and national belonging are the differences among anti-Chinese campaigns and the Chinese community's ability to mobilize a defense. In Cuba, anti-Chinese policies occurred alongside an official rhetoric that recognized Chinese participation in Cuban independence and the founding of the nation. Sinophobia never coagulated into a sustained, organized political movement, as it had in Mexico and to a much lesser extent in Peru. In Cuba and Peru, Chinese were deported in accordance with existing immigration policy but not en masse simply for being Chinese. Despite proposals for eliminating Havana's Barrio Chino in the 1920s, it grew to become the largest in all of the Americas by the 1940s.

While numbers were usually small in comparison to Afro-descended and indigenous populations in Latin America, the Chinese presence continually stirred nationalist imaginings. Exploring Chinese immigration is essential to understanding the development of hemispheric national identities. Scholarship on the region, however, has traditionally not reflected the significance of the Chinese to developing republics. Until recently, historians of Latin America focused on the study of European immigrants in industry and agriculture. Theorizing of race and identity has consequently been dominated by a concept of *mestizaje* primarily concerned with racial mixing of indigenous, African, and European populations.[57] Elite discourses on nation building concentrated on uplifting the African-descended population in Cuba and Indians in Peru and Mexico. Asians and Middle Easterners were viewed as beyond incorporation, due to perceived cultural differences, concentrated settlement patterns, and smaller numbers. The constant presence of anti-Chinese discourse reminds us of the significance of Chinese migration for constructions of national and cultural identity. Recent research with hemispheric, transnational, and borderland perspectives has begun to bring the Chinese presence from the margins to the center of academic debate in the study of migration, race, and citizenship in the Americas.[58]

Whereas Cuba's revolution halted significant new immigration, Peru and Mexico, like other Latin American countries, have continued to attract

Chinese migrants up to the present day. The new migrants, who differ from the more established Chinese merchants in regional dialect and class status, are generating new national discussions about foreign immigration and about China's geopolitical presence and economic role in Latin America and the Caribbean. Not surprisingly, much of this discourse echoes the anti-Chinese voices that filled newspapers and speeches across the region a century ago.

Notes

I am grateful to Nicola Foote and Michael Goebel for encouraging me to think comparatively and for their useful framework for conceptualizing immigration and national identity. I also thank Daniel Masterson and an anonymous reader for their comments and helpful suggestions for improving this chapter.

1. Accounting for deaths on the voyage, 124,873 Chinese arrived in Cuba from 1847 to 1874, and 92,130 arrived in Peru from 1849 to 1874. Scholars estimate even higher numbers than the official entries recorded at ports. Pérez de la Riva suggests a total of 150,000 to Cuba, including contraband and Chinese from California. Meagher calculates 109,146 arriving in Peru. Pérez de la Riva, *Los culíes*, 179; Rodríguez Pastor, *Hijos del Celeste Imperio*, 26; and Meagher, *Coolie Trade*, 222. For a recent comparative study of Chinese indentured labor in Latin America, see Narvaez, "Chinese Coolies." From final emancipation in 1838 until 1918, 429,623 migrants from India and 17,904 from China entered the British colonies, mostly British Guiana, Trinidad, and Jamaica. The last shipload of Chinese arrived in the British West Indies in 1884, while the importation and use of Indian laborers continued into the early twentieth century. Look Lai, *Indentured Labor*, 19.

2. Kuhn, *Chinese Among Others*, 39–40.

3. Meagher, *Coolie Trade*, 222–28.

4. Scholars have debated the experiences of Chinese indentured laborers in Cuba as nominally free workers in a slave society and as a step toward modernity and liberalism. As Lisa Yun notes, testimony from the Chinese themselves suggests a "counternarrative" to the interpretation of nineteenth-century Asian migrants to the Americas as voluntary and as representing a transition from slavery to wage labor. Yun, *Coolie Speaks*.

5. In 1926 the number of Spanish residing in Mexico reached 48,558, while that of Chinese reached 24,218, followed by Americans, Syro-Lebanese, Germans, and Canadians. Romero, *Chinese in Mexico*, 55–56.

6. For the development of this nationalist discourse and the contradictions within it, see Ferrer, *Insurgent Cuba*.

7. For the Chinese in the Cuban struggles for independence, see López, *Chinese Cubans*, ch. 4.

8. Bonilla, "War of the Pacific," 108. Jorge Inostroza popularized the song "Los chinos de Cerro Azul."

9. Arona, *La inmigración*, 49. Juan de Arona was the pseudonym for Pedro Paz Soldán y Unánue. For accounts of the Chinese in the War of the Pacific, see Bonilla, "War of the

Pacific"; Rodríguez Pastor, *Hijos del Celeste Imperio*, 231–32; and McKeown, *Chinese Migrant Networks*, 140–41.

10. See Hu-DeHart, "Immigrants"; Knight, "Racism, Revolution, and *Indigenismo*"; and Romero, *Chinese in Mexico*. For the role of the Chinese presence in shaping postrevolutionary regional and national identities in northern Mexico, see Rénique, "Race, Region, and Nation."

11. Graham, *Idea of Race*; and Appelbaum, Macpherson, and Rosemblatt, *Race and Nation*.

12. Corbitt, "Immigration in Cuba," 304–5. Sections 7 and 8 of the law excluded the Chinese, with the exception of those classified as merchants, students, diplomats, and tourists. Chinese workers who had resided in Cuba since April 14, 1899, were also exempt.

13. The discussion of the role of Chinese immigrants in constructions of Cuban national identity appears in different form in my book *Chinese Cubans*. Studies of race and nation-making in Cuba include Helg, *Our Rightful Share*; Ferrer, *Insurgent Cuba*; De la Fuente, *A Nation for All*.

14. "Expediente, en inglés y español, referente a la inmigración de braceros," Havana, July 11, 1906–March 13, 1908, exp. 82, leg. 121, Secretaría de la Presidencia, Archivo Nacional de Cuba.

15. Herrera Jerez and Castillo Santana, *De la memoria*, 25, citing Ramón Meza y Suárez Inclán, *La inmigración útil debe ser protegida* (Havana, 1906), 20–22. Meza delivered this paper at the Fifth National Conference on Social Services and Correction in Santiago de Cuba on April 16, 1906, in his capacity as delegate of the Sociedad Económico de los Amigos del País and president of the conference's immigration committee.

16. Guerra, *Myth of José Martí*, 147.

17. Ibid., 149.

18. Ibid., 150.

19. Pérez, "El peligro amarillo."

20. Helg, "Race in Argentina and Cuba." For racial gatekeeping policies, see Chomsky, "'Barbados or Canada?'"; and De la Fuente, *A Nation for All*.

21. Rodríguez Pastor, *Herederos del dragón*, 161–71; McKeown, *Chinese Migrant Networks*, 151–53; and Lausent-Herrera, "Chinatown in Peru," 75.

22. McKeown, *Chinese Migrant Networks*, 152.

23. The essay "El problema racial en el Perú y la inmigración asiática" appeared in the bulletin of the Lima Geographical Society. McKeown, *Chinese Migrant Networks*, 142–43.

24. Hu-DeHart, "Immigrants"; and Romero, *Chinese in Mexico*, ch. 6.

25. Espinoza, *El problema chino*; and Espinoza, *El ejemplo de Sonora*.

26. Romero, *Chinese in Mexico*, 163.

27. Hu-DeHart, "Indispensable Enemy," 81.

28. Schiavone Camacho, *Chinese Mexicans*.

29. Martínez-Alier, *Marriage, Class, and Colour*.

30. According to Lausent-Herrera, the term most likely originated among the rural population who were in contact with Chinese on the plantations, and it did not take on a pejorative connotation until its use by the press and official documents in the early twentieth century. The term was later supplanted by *"tusan"* (*tusheng*), usually reserved for Peruvian-born with two Chinese parents. After 1870 young female *injertas* were sought

after in marriage to other mixed Chinese or Chinese no longer under contract. Lausent-Herrera, "Tusans (*tusheng*)," 118.

31. "Expediente referente a la inmigración china," Havana, September 1, 1909–June 21, 1914, exp. 83, leg. 121, Secretaría de la Presidencia, Archivo Nacional de Cuba.

32. Schiavone Camacho, *Chinese Mexicans*, 45. For the gendered aspects of the anti-Chinese movement in Sonora and Chinese Mexican responses, see ibid., ch. 2.

33. McKeown, *Chinese Migrant Networks*, 137.

34. Romero, *Chinese in Mexico*, 169. For Chinese legal responses to anti-Chinese persecution, see ibid., 166–72. For an in-depth examination of Chinese merchant defensive strategies in Mexico during and after World War II, see González, "We Won't Be Bullied Anymore."

35. Chuffat Latour, *Apunte histórico*, 175.

36. Quoted in Eng Herrera and García Triana, *Martí en los chinos*, 11–12.

37. McKeown, *Chinese Migrant Networks*, 170; see also Lausent-Herrera, "Tusans (tusheng)," 125–26. The original Spanish title of the publication is "La Colonia china en el Perú. Instituciones y hombres representativos. Su actuación benéfica en la vida nacional."

38. McKeown, *Chinese Migrant Networks*, 163.

39. Tejeiro commemorated the life of Sun Yat-sen in an essay published on the anniversary of his death. Tejeiro, "Vida agitada."

40. Amid a national wave of anti-Chinese discourse, defenders of the Chinese community emerged in the provincial town of Cienfuegos. *El Comercio*, April 16, 1928, 1, 3.

41. The Alianza Popular Revolucionaria Americana was known locally as the Partido Aprista Peruano.

42. Mayer de Zulen, *La China*, 103.

43. Mayer included a chart of Chinese agriculturalists in Peru. Ibid., 178–80; and Rodríguez Pastor, *Herederos del dragón*, 200–201.

44. Mayer de Zulen, *La China*; and McKeown, *Chinese Migrant Networks*, 155, 171.

45. Romero, *Chinese in Mexico*, 175–78.

46. In *Radical Moves*, Lara Putnam presents a connective historical analysis of anti-immigration restrictions across the circum-Caribbean region, especially those that targeted black West Indians. A significant divergence from the pattern of anti-Asian restrictions across Latin America and the Caribbean occurred in dictator Rafael Trujillo's Dominican Republic, which shifted its policies in 1931. The nation became known for its open-door immigration policy that welcomed (with limitations) Jewish refugees from Europe, Spanish exiles from the Civil War, and Asians. However, only when European immigrants were found to be insufficient did Dominican elites turn to Chinese (and later Japanese) as a means to "whiten" society and to populate the border with Haiti.

47. Romero, *Chinese in Mexico*, 56.

48. The magazine (*Lianhe Yuekan*) was founded by the Union of Commercial Retailers of the Chinese Colony in Cuba (Unión de Detallistas del Comercio de la Colonia China en Cuba).

49. Lausent-Herrera, "Tusans (tusheng)," 126–30. The Chinese name of the magazine is *Tongfu Yipo* (Dongfang Yuebao in Mandarin).

50. In 1945, for example, José Wong Lam appealed the court in Cienfuegos, Cuba, to have his son's birth registry changed from mestizo (mixed) to *blanco* (white). "Rollo de

apelación en expediente sobre subsanación de error en la inscripción de nacimiento de José Wong Alonso" (1945), exp. 6652, Juzgado de Primera Instancia, Archivo Histórico Provincial de Cienfuegos.

51. McKeown, *Chinese Migrant Networks*, 175–77.

52. Lesser, *Negotiating National Identity*; and Takenaka, "Japanese in Peru." Michael Gonzales details Japanese experiences in agriculture from 1899 to 1923, when the Peruvian and Japanese governments ended the emigration agreement. Japanese protested over low wages and contract conditions, eventually joining forces with Peruvian peasants. See Gonzales, "Resistance among Asian Plantation Workers."

53. Corbitt, "Chinese Immigrants in Cuba," 130.

54. Ibid. The treaty was published in the *Gaceta Oficial de la República* on December 24, 1943, and is reproduced in Tejeiro, *Historia ilustrada*.

55. Schiavone Camacho, *Chinese Mexicans*; and Romero, *Chinese in Mexico*, 87.

56. See López, *Chinese Cubans*, ch. 7.

57. Hu-DeHart, "Multiculturalism." For studies that address non-European immigrants in Latin America, see Holloway, *Immigrants on the Land*; Lesser, *Negotiating National Identity*; and Alfaro-Velcamp, *So Far from Allah*.

58. Among this recent work are Siu, *Memories of a Future Home*; Lee, "Orientalisms in the Americas"; Hu-DeHart, "Indispensable Enemy"; Romero, *Chinese in Mexico*; Schiavone Camacho, *Chinese Mexicans*; Delgado, *Making the Chinese Mexican*; Chang, "Racial Alterity"; and Young, *Alien Nation*.

8

British Caribbean Migration and the Racialization of Latin American Nationalisms

NICOLA FOOTE

Immigration in Latin American nationalist discourses was associated overwhelmingly with whiteness and the ideal of social whitening. Elites influenced by scientific racism and social Darwinist intellectual currents that associated racial composition with modernity and progress sought immigrants who would "improve" their racial stock and bring cultural attributes that were perceived to be lacking in the existing population. As we have seen in this volume, this project was racked with contradictions: even the most "desirable" immigrant groups such as Germans or Italians could prove a focus of nationalist concern when they maintained their own cultural identities or provided economic competition, while Jewish and Middle Eastern immigrants prompted questions about how far the category of whiteness could be expanded. However, the tensions between immigration and whitening were brought into sharpest focus by British Caribbean migration—a group whose African descent made them the precise opposite of the whitening logic.[1] This group represented one of the largest immigrant flows to regions outside of the Southern Cone and played a critical role in the nation-building process. British Caribbean labor was essential to the construction of the transportation networks that facilitated the integration of national resources as well as to the development of the agro-export and mineral extraction industries that fueled the economic boom of the period 1880 to 1930. Yet the connection between immigration and whiteness was so powerful that these immigrants were not typically viewed as such. Considered highly undesirable by nationalist elites, British Caribbean immigrants were typically classified as temporary "contract workers" in customs logs and government data, thus distinguishing them from the European "settlers" and "colonists" who were seen to be the true, permanent, immigrant class.

This separation between British Caribbean migrants and the category of "immigrant" has fed into scholarly literature and affected our understanding of the relationship between West Indians and Latin American nation building. Although there has been a significant body of scholarship charting the essential contributions of British Caribbean migrants to regional economic development, Afro-Caribbean migrants have typically been omitted from comparative work on Latin American immigration while theoretical studies of Latin American race formation have rarely looked at black immigrants as case studies that can provide insight into broader racial currents.[2] This chapter addresses Aline Helg's call for a renewed focus on the connection between race formation and the transnational distribution of Afro-Caribbean workers in Latin America by examining the complex role West Indian migrants played in Latin American nationalisms in the late nineteenth and early twentieth century.[3] It assesses the racial discourses that surrounded black migrants and explores how their blackness came to symbolize the contradictions of nationalist development and came to be used as a shorthand for fears about neocolonialism and imperialism. It evaluates the relative weight that regional and international ideologies of blackness played in the exclusion of British Caribbean migrants and examines how intellectual currents translated into social realities and helped shape the lived experience of black immigrants. The chapter uses a broad comparative lens, evaluating the well-known case studies of Central America and Cuba as well as the often neglected migrations to the Andean and Amazonian regions of South America, and bringing migratory currents that predated the national period into conversation with those that emerged in the late nineteenth and twentieth century.

Nation Building, Modernity, and British Caribbean Immigration

Latin American modernization projects were intimately entwined with West Indian immigration. Almost every major infrastructural development across the continent—beginning with the first tropical railroad built in Panama in 1850 and ranging through the construction of roads, railways, and air bases in Costa Rica, El Salvador, Guatemala, Venezuela, Ecuador, Colombia, Peru, and Brazil—used West Indian labor to connect agricultural regions to coastal ports and create international networks. The size of migratory streams could range dramatically, from the 119 workers recruited for the expansion of the Valparaíso harbor in Chile to the 150,000 immigrants who worked in the construction of the Panama Canal.[4] The modernization of a transportation system in which exports had previously depended on mule paths and canoe was essential to national development and served to incorporate isolated and inaccessible areas more fully into the national patrimony, demarcating frontiers, facilitating the expansion of settlement in contested border regions, and creating a new range of agro-export investment opportunities.

As industrialization and urbanization in the United States and Europe stimulated demand for Latin American primary commodities, West Indians became a major workforce in the booming agro-export sector. Most significantly, they formed a primary labor force in the United Fruit Company's banana plantations in Central America and in the booming sugar plantations of early twentieth-century Cuba. West Indians also worked in the extraction of Amazonian rubber in Peru, Brazil, and Ecuador and in the collection of hardwoods in Mexico as well as for American sugar interests and fruit companies in Haiti.[5] British Caribbean migrants were also essential to mining and mineral extraction, working in gold and tin mining in Venezuela, Suriname, and Costa Rica; guano extraction in Colombia and the Galapagos Islands; and the booming oil industry in Venezuela. While men were more numerous in these migrations, women also were present; they were recruited for work as domestic servants, laundresses, and cooks, and they also worked autonomously as higglers and occasionally as prostitutes.

The centrality of British Caribbean immigrants to these infrastructural and agricultural development projects underscores the important yet ambivalent role they occupied within the nation-building process. West Indian workers transformed nonproductive regions into thriving parts of regional economies and were thus essential to economic modernization. But they also highlighted the limitations of modernization and the fact that it depended on foreign capital and foreign labor.

In some countries, the connection of West Indians to national integration was even more complicated. In the Miskito Coast of Nicaragua, the Colombian islands of San Andrés and Providencia and the Bay Islands of Honduras, black West Indian settlement predated the formation of the nation-state, and the key issue in terms of nationalist integration of territory was the assimilation of these spaces that were culturally and ethnically distinct and that did not identify with the new nations. In these regions the descendants of the enslaved laborers brought from the West Indies by eighteenth-century English privateering and land companies formed the basis of a black and mixed-race Creole population whose members traded chiefly with Jamaica and educated their children on the island. Their numbers were supplemented throughout the nineteenth century by the settlement of turtle fishermen from Jamaica and the Cayman Islands.[6] San Andrés and Providencia nominally became part of Colombia with independence in 1822 but remained economically and culturally isolated from the mainland. The British continued to formally hold the Miskito Coast and the Bay Islands into the 1850s, only ceding control to Nicaragua and Honduras in treaties under diplomatic pressure from the United States in 1859 and 1860.

Even after formal incorporation, English continued to be the dominant language and Protestantism the dominant religion, and cultural allegiances were more attuned to Britain and the United States than to Central America and South America. Assimilation thus became a nationalist priority. This took the most dramatic form in Nicaragua, where national troops invaded the Miskito Reserve in 1894.[7] In Colombia, the government assigned Catholic missionaries to San Andrés and Providencia to convert the West Indian–descended population and to teach them Spanish in an effort to "nationalize" the population.[8]

The presence of British Caribbean immigrants and their descendants was thus central to the creation of the physical space of the nation. Whether they were building the infrastructure necessary to ensure the integration of national resources or whether they themselves and the territory they inhabited were viewed as subjects for amalgamation and assimilation, the connection between West Indians and projects of integration and modernization raised profound questions of blackness and national belonging. These complex negotiations were influenced by regional and international racial discourses and can only be understood in the transnational context of U.S. economic penetration and expansion.

International Racial Discourses, Neocolonialism, and the Brutalities of the Black Immigrant Experience

Harsh working conditions, racial segregation, and often savage violence were staples of the West Indian experience in nineteenth- and early twentieth-century Latin America. The racism and violence British Caribbean migrants faced have typically been viewed by scholars as a function of U.S. norms and attitudes in American enclaves and have not been interpreted as symptomatic of broader currents. But while migrant experiences certainly underline U.S. racism, the most notable abuses occurred when official state actors—notably police officers and the armed forces—operated in collaboration with American corporate interests. While in part their collusion reflected the corruption and fragility of many Latin American states, it is also deeply revealing about racial attitudes at the regional level and how these intersected with international discourses.

The racial mechanisms of the labor control strategies employed by American companies were without doubt striking and important. U.S. corporations sought to impose the same kind of Jim Crow segregation on their labor force that prevailed in the American South. In the Panama Canal Zone, workers were assigned into gold and silver divisions according to race, with black "silver" workers paid in Panamanian silver as opposed to U.S. dollars, given barracks housing, and assigned more difficult and dangerous tasks; meanwhile, the United Fruit Company organized both tasks and amenities along racial lines.[9] A number of mechanisms were used by companies to avoid the practice of truly free wage labor. Payment to immigrant workers was often much lower than promised in recruiting contracts, and U.S. enterprises sometimes substituted cash wages for tokens redeemable only in company commissaries.

Practices of debt peonage were often applied to West Indian immigrants. Contracted fruit plantation workers in Nicaragua were not paid for their first two months of labor and were then told that the cost of the food they had been provided in the meantime, along with the provision of machetes and work boots, was to be withheld from their wages.[10] In the Peruvian Amazon, sex was apparently used as a tool to submit black male workers to the system of debt peonage. Arriving Barbadians were assigned Indian women by company officials to serve as their "temporary wives." The only place where workers could purchase the necessities to support their new "families" was in the company store, where prices were inflated 1,000 percent over cost.[11] Debt served to enhance the profit margins of international corporations by allowing them to cut labor costs at the same time as profiting from "wages" paid. It also reduced labor mobility and extended the labor cycle of workers—especially important in isolated areas where the cost of importing workers was high.

Working and living conditions for black migrants were often dire. Reports from the Panama Railroad in the 1850s told of men laboring in waist-deep water and simply slipping and falling to their deaths.[12] One letter of complaint from Jamaican railroad workers in Ecuador described the allocated sleeping quarters as "an open horse stable full of swamps and dirt" and asserted that conditions were so cramped it was impossible to lay down and that migrants had to "stand on their legs all the time," making it impossible to sleep.[13] In Colombia in 1891 twelve Jamaicans taken to the island of Roncador to load guano for the American-owned Colombia Guano and Phosphate Company were left stranded on a reef when their American ship departed without them. Seven escaped on a raft crafted out of coconut palms; the rest died of starvation, their decaying skeletons later uncovered by a British military command sent to investigate the accusations.[14]

Workers drew parallels with slavery in protesting their conditions. One Barbadian described migrants in Cuba as being "made to work like Galley slaves" and accused the Cuban government of "carrying on a slave trade."[15] In Peru, frightened workers wrote to the *Barbados Advocate* protesting the failure of the Peruvian Amazon Company to honor the terms of their contract, lamenting that "now we are Suffering day by day as slaves. We thought that we were going there as labourers but we found out afterwards there is Slaves where we are. We cannot get away because there is soldiers guarding us."[16]

Even when workers did not use the language of slavery, their treatment was reminiscent of the worst forms of unfree labor. Workers on the Veracruz Railroad in Mexico had to work under the control of guards armed with guns and were forced to go to bed at seven o'clock in the evening. Runaways were pursued by professional "hunters" with dogs and guns, and those captured were whipped, evoking clear echoes of slavery.[17] Likewise, the Ecuadorian police force were deployed to "hunt, capture and keep to forced labor men employed under forced contracts and deserting their work."[18] Captured deserters were tied with ropes in batches of nine or ten, and marched back to the railway works with armed soldiers on either side.[19] In Peru, British Caribbean rubber workers reported being tied up on cross poles, flogged, placed in the stocks, and marched through the rainforest chained by the neck for minor transgressions of company authority such as buying bread outside of the company store.[20]

Corporate officials sought to defend their actions by seeking to invoke two of the key racial stereotypes of blackness—laziness and criminality—in ways that resonated with nationalist public opinion. In a revealing article in the main Guayaquil newspaper, two journalists described how they had been invited by the Quito-Guayaquil Railway Company to take a guided tour of immigrant worker camps. When they met the superintendent of construction he read out an article to them from the Jamaican newspaper the *Daily Gleaner*, which he told them (and they duly relayed to readers) that the emigration of thousands of Jamaican day laborers to work on the railway in Ecuador had been a positive boon for the island because so many known criminals were included among their number.[21] This seems to have been a purposeful exaggeration of the meaning of the text in the original language. The article in question actually criticized the American recruitment company for rounding up any worker who would go, without consideration for their past experience or aptitude. The possibility that some convicted criminals may have been sent overseas was only one of the concerns, and was certainly not presented as a positive for Jamaica—quite the opposite—because it was feared this would undermine the success of the migration.[22] But the exaggeration seems to have had the desired effect. "After listening to this snippet which made our hair stand on end, we stayed by the Superintendent as if we were little old men and, unshockable, he said to us, pointing to his revolver—'don't worry.'" The rest of the article was then devoted to graphic accounts of the drunken antics of the workers (their visit had coincided with payday) and to emphatic repetitions of their gratitude for the protection of Americans with their guns from the terrifying blacks.[23]

The promise implicit in the *Grito del Pubelo* article that arms could be used to "protect" against black workers was frequently put into action. In addition to their own often brutal enforcement of labor discipline discussed above, American business officials frequently made use of government soldiers and police to defend their interests. Police were regularly called in to arrest workers who broke their contracts and took up positions with different companies, while the armed forces were routinely called in to break up strikes. In Cuba, estate owners frequently used state troops to drive away immigrants at the end of planting and harvest seasons in order to avoid paying wages owed.[24] State intervention was often violent. British Caribbean miners reported being beaten by Venezuelan police acting at the request of the El Callao Company when they tried to take up positions at a rival mine.[25] Police officers working at the bequest of the United Fruit Company in Costa Rica burned the houses of British Caribbean strikers to the ground and rooted up and destroyed their garden vegetable plots.[26]

An especially egregious state assault on British Caribbean immigrants occurred in Culebra, Panama, in 1885, when an attack by Colombian troops on a barracks where two hundred West Indian railroad workers were sleeping led to the deaths of twenty-five men and the serious injury of at least twenty others. Eyewitnesses testified that troops had blocked the doors to the barracks, preventing any escape, and hacked at fleeing men with swords and machetes. Troops then rifled through the trunks and possessions of the dead men, stealing their suitcases and personal belongings and removing watches and cash from the dead bodies.[27]

The Colombian government presented a narrative in which the troops were provoked by an attack on them by a "mob" of Caribbean immigrants, and argued that their actions were ultimately about keeping the peace and protecting the Colombian public. American interests in Panama accepted the position of the Colombian government wholesale. The *New York Times* wrote that "the individual ordinarily called 'the Jamaican nigger' . . . is without any exception the most insolent, lawless, brutal and offensive species of the human race" and insisted that the fact Colombian troops sustained no injuries from the alleged mob attack was "not the least a refutation of this story" since people within a mob were rarely good shots.[28]

Even after a joint British and French investigation found conclusively that Colombian troops were the unprovoked aggressors in the attack, the Colombian government continued to insist that the commanding officer, Captain Cobo, had done no more than "defend himself and attempt to pacify those who did not recognize his authority."[29] The more than fifty eyewitness reports were dismissed as unreliable because they were "Jamaicans, laborers, companions of the men who were killed"—their place of origin given as an explicit reason to discount their testimony. Nonblack testifiers, who admitted that they were not personal witnesses to the event, were granted more reliability as they painted a picture of an angry black mob capturing and torturing local villagers and firing weapons at troops.[30] After intensive British pressure, the Colombian Supreme Court demoted Cobo from the rank of captain, but officials expressed sympathy for his plight and were unhappy to see him punished, insisting that his conduct had "previously been irreproachable" and that "impudent zeal in the discharge of his military duties" had been his sole offense.[31] Although it is likely that military loyalties and offense at British meddling were also factors in official attitudes, the fact that the massacre of blacks could be discounted as "impudent zeal" that might be viewed as a mere blip of an otherwise successful career is telling about the depths of antiblack sentiment at the highest level of the Colombian government.

While the Culebra massacre was noteworthy for its scale, the murder of immigrants by police, armed forces, and company officials was far from uncommon. In Costa Rica a Limón worker wrote to his wife that seventeen workers had been shot by police in the plantation areas in one single week in 1910.[32] In Ecuador the shooting of Jamaicans seemed to have developed almost into a sport. One complaint lodged with the British Consulate pleaded, "They are shooting us like birds. An American called O'Brian is calling the people out of the camp and shooting them."[33]

Police shootings were especially widespread in Cuba at the height of the 1920s migratory boom. A Jamaican named Charles Sadler was shot in the back by a Cuban rural guard while his hands were tied behind his back. Another Jamaican man who summoned the police to report a crime was shot in the face by the Cuban police officer who arrived to investigate, losing an eye.[34] Oscar Taylor was shot dead from behind a closed door.[35] One Cuban Army officer was accused of the massacre of seventeen Jamaican workers in Camagüey, allegedly "ordering a machine gun trained on the defenseless men under the pretense of taking their photograph."[36] In several cases Cuban police officers were brought to trial for killing British Caribbean workers, but British Foreign Office documentation suggests that they were almost always acquitted of murder, either on grounds of self-defense or with the charge being downgraded to assault or "transgression of the law." The Cuban secretary of state stood by the judicial process and insisted there was no evidence of guilt on the part of any of the Cuban police, instead accusing West Indian immigrants of inciting trouble with their own violence and drunkenness.[37]

Women immigrants faced an additional layer of gendered vulnerability to official violence, with rape and sexual assault by police and company officials a common occurrence. The perpetrators were sometimes estate foremen and overseers who knew they would not be questioned by local law enforcement. In an especially tragic case in Puerto Rico, the manager of the hacienda Libre de Palma in Humacao raped Elizabeth Williams, the wife of a British Caribbean worker on the estate. Mr. Williams and some of his fellow migrant workers confronted the manager about the attack, whose response was to call in the civil guards. The men were arrested and imprisoned, and when Elizabeth and the other men's wives protested the arrest of their husbands, they were beaten by the guards and also taken to jail. The group was subsequently locked up without trial for over a year. Although Williams was found to be pregnant (it is unclear whether this was as a result of the rape), she was not released and later gave birth in jail, where her baby died.[38] The vulnerabilities of black women who sought retribution for sexual attack could hardly be more starkly apparent.

On other occasions the perpetrators of sexual violence were the police themselves. In Limón a Jamaican woman named Mrs. Francis Tait complained of being "molested" by police while imprisoned, while several Jamaican and Barbadian women in Guayaquil lodged reports of rape and sexual assault by the Ecuadorian police with the British consul.[39] A rape that took place in Honduras shows how police officers sometimes worked together in planning assaults. Emma Broomfield reported to the British consul how the deputy director of police came to her home with four fellow police officers and announced that they had orders to arrest her husband. When she told them her husband was not home, the deputy director entered her house, leaving the other officers outside the door, took off his coat, belt, and revolver, and forced her down on the bed. Her screams alerted a neighbor, who tried to see what was wrong, but he was refused entrance by the police officers, who said they were there "on authority." The consul did not investigate Broomfield's allegations, writing testily that the problems the West Indians had with the police were the result of their own failure to comply with police orders.[40] Yet the premeditated nature of the attack—the grouping of multiple officers, the stationing of officers outside the door—suggests that this was not an isolated incident and may well have been part of a more systematic pattern of sexual abuse.

The abuse of British Caribbean immigrants also could involve forcing them to serve as the perpetrators of assaults on other ethnic groups. Eastern Caribbean immigrants employed with the Peruvian Amazon Company were caught up in the notorious genocide in the Putumayo, forced, as investigating British Vice-Consul Sir Roger Casement wrote, "to act as armed bullies and terrorists over the surrounding native population," who were locked into a brutal system of forced labor and violence.[41] West Indian workers were used to conduct raids on Indian villages, capturing Indians and forcing them to work for the rubber companies. A Montserratian named John Brown, who escaped from the Putumayo, described how he had contracted to collect rubber with the Arana Company as part of a group of fifty West Indian men. On their arrival at the Putumayo River in April 1902, they were given guns and sent "into the forest to look for Indians, and to kill them. We refused, saying that we had not come to kill Indians but to do agricultural work." The migrants were told that if they would not kill Indians, they themselves would be killed. "They beat us with swords, they put us in guns (hands tied across knees with guns underneath knees), and did us all manner of wickedness. We cried for help but there was none . . . We tried to escape but there was no means of doing so—only one small steamer that belonged to the same company and they would not take us away." Even when their contracted term of labor ended after two years, the migrants were still not permitted to leave.[42]

The use of West Indian migrants to inflict terror on the Amazonian indigenous population became one of the central points of the international investigation into the system of slavery and forced labor as the Putumayo scandal broke following the publication of W. E. Hardenburg's journalistic reports in 1909 and 1910.[43] Sir Roger Casement, fresh from his investigation into the rubber genocide in the Congo, was sent to lead the British inquiry, and his official report, although it documented the terrible abuses Caribbean workers had themselves endured, was ultimately unsympathetic, describing them as "active agents" in a system of "armed extortion" and "brigandage."[44] The Peruvian government sought to allocate blame for the enslavement of Indians onto the black migrant overseers. The minister of foreign relations, for example, described the "Barbados negroes" as "the most implicit executors of every kind of order, no matter how infamous they might be. They were the real henchmen of the Putumayo, sowing horror and panic among the Indians."[45] At least two Barbadians were arrested and extradited in the American investigation into the atrocities.[46] Notably, after the 1912 scandal, despite two major international investigations, almost nothing was done to extricate the British Caribbean workers from the Amazon, many of whom remained trapped.

Stereotypes of blacks as savage and violent made claims of Barbadian culpability for genocide resonate with the wider public both locally and internationally. Indeed, it is likely that these stereotypes of blackness played a role in the assignment of blacks to the role of capturing and policing Indians in the first place. This reflects a broader reality: although in practice it was often West Indian immigrants who were the victims of crime and violence, they were framed in nationalist discourse as the dangerous carriers of such currents. Moreover, racial discourses were not just abstract ideas—they had real and practical consequences at the level of lived experience for British Caribbean immigrants. Thus it is essential to assess the ideological underpinnings of the brutal treatment British Caribbean workers received, and to examine how American ideas about black criminality, violence, and degradation intersected with those that already existed in Latin American society as a result of local histories of slavery as well as postemancipation racial hierarchies.

Crime, Disease, and Political Disruption: Antiblackness and the Discourse of Racial Danger

Throughout Latin America, British Caribbean migrants were consistently discussed by nationalist elites and intellectuals in terms that focused on their blackness as a source of "racial danger" and that characterized black immigrants as unhygienic, violent, and inherently criminal. These ideas had a remarkable consistency across time and space, with the same kinds of arguments articulated in Central America, South America, and Cuba, and as strongly in the late nineteenth and early twentieth century as in the 1930s and 1940s. As Lara Putnam notes in this volume, it took the re-configuration of economic and political realities and the rise to power of populist leaders for these discourses to move beyond the realm of exclu-sionary "racial fantasies" and to be translated into action through immigra-tion bans and deportations. However, the ideas forged in an earlier stage of British Caribbean immigration formed an important foundation of later antiblack nationalisms and are of critical importance in understanding their development.

At the heart of anti–West Indian discourse was the idea that Antillean immigrants imported delinquency and crime. British Caribbean migrants were perceived as prone to drunkenness and drug abuse, and were alleged to encourage these vices in the local population. In Ecuador, for example, the chief of police in Guayaquil blamed black immigration for a wave of drunkenness in the coastal provinces and argued that the behavior of Brit-ish Caribbean migrants threatened the integrity of Ecuadorian culture and society.[47] In a fascinating precursor of the War on Drugs, West Indians in the 1930s were accused of trafficking opium, cocaine, and morphine be-tween Colombia and the Caribbean islands and were blamed by Colom-bian elites for rising consumption of illegal drugs.[48] Black criminality was often seen as genetic and as an unshakeable reality of African lineage. In a 1906 essay that set the tone for nationalist thinking on race in the decade before Fernando Ortiz emerged as a founder of Afro-Cubanismo and an-tiracism, Ortiz argued that, in Cuba, black immigrants possessed inherent criminal tendencies that were a serious threat to Cuban society. Criminolo-gist Israel Castellanos labeled delinquency as "ethnically African."[49] Simi-larly, in Honduras, well-known writer Froylán Turcios denounced plans to import British Caribbean workers for the La Tela railroad, arguing that due to their "physiological makeup," blacks were "much more prone to violence and crime."[50]

Ideas about black criminality were often linked to Caribbean religious practices. Black migrants were routinely accused of practicing witchcraft and child sacrifice. In Costa Rica, the Pentecostal Union Baptist Society was described by the leading national newspaper as a "monstrous cult of undoubted affiliation with the devil," and sect leaders were accused of kidnapping children and drinking the blood of prepubescent girls.[51] In Venezuela it was a common belief that Antilleans sacrificed white children as a cure for sickness, and it was frequently rumored in the oil fields that white children in Maracaibo were disappearing, victims of black witch-craft.[52] These beliefs could have tragic consequences. In Cuba white crowds lynched a Jamaican man in 1919 after he was accused of planning to kidnap a white female child for a witchcraft ceremony while British Caribbeaners Edward Robinson and Bernard Hall were arrested in 1921 on the charge of stealing a Cuban child, who was later found to be asleep in her parents' house.[53] Aline Helg has discussed black religion as one of three "icons of fear" surrounding blackness in Cuba, and the experiences of British Caribbean migrants in Latin America as a whole demonstrates that this pathologization of African-derived religious practices had a pan-regional resonance that significantly impacted the experiences of black immigrants.[54]

Fear of black sexuality, another common trope in regional discourses of blackness, can also be seen clearly in the hysterical imagery of black men drinking the blood of white girls. Notably, however, it was the sexuality of Afro-Caribbean women, rather than men, that was seen as especially problematic in anti-immigration discourses, and women migrants were widely associated with prostitution and sexual promiscuity. Hortensia Lamar, the leader of an elite Cuban women's group, lamented that with the rise in black migration "prostitution . . . increased considerably and with inconceivable loathsomeness."[55] In Brazil Barbadian and Martiniquean women migrants were consistently referred to as prostitutes in contemporary discussions, despite the fact that most of them worked as laundresses or higglers.[56] Similarly, the arrival in Panama of a ship bringing 295 Martiniquean women immigrants to serve as domestic servants and laundresses scandalized American officials, who labeled them all as prostitutes. Although sexual relationships do seem to have been forged between some of the women and the Jamaican male laborers working on canal construction, only three cases of prostitution were officially documented, and a majority of the women were married and joined their husbands.[57] The panicked reaction from canal authorities reveals more about fears of black female sexuality than about immigrant realities.

Associating black women with prostitution also meant they were often blamed for the high rates of sexually transmitted diseases in migrant areas. This reflected a much broader correlation between British Caribbean immigrants and disease, which led to West Indians being constructed as a threat to national hygiene. Black immigrants were seen as having a particular predisposition to diseases such as tuberculosis, leprosy, syphilis, and even insanity, and were argued to be genetic carriers of diseases such as malaria, typhoid, intestinal parasites, and smallpox. This reflected high rates of disease stemming from poor conditions in West Indian labor camps as well as the tendency to label indigent migrants as insane and commit them to asylums. Emerging eugenic discourses were used to create a biological argument about disease and genetics that pathologized black migrants.[58]

These ideas were not just abstract but had real consequences at the level of lived experience. Concerns about black disease led to a Jamaican named Locksley Roye being shot dead in Cuba for refusing to take a dose of medicine prescribed to him at the quarantine station set up to screen incoming black migrants. As the *Daily Gleaner* recounted, "A doctor was not employed to persuade him, but a rural guard was sent for, and this worthy began his ministrations by having the man held down, opening his mouth, and forcibly inserting the medicine. Then, the Jamaican showing his objection violently to this mode of medical treatment, the rural guard shot him dead."[59] The British consul noted that "Roye was not ill, nor was he armed, and the necessity of an armed guard to administer medicine to immigrants is not easily explained."[60] The *Gleaner* suggested, tongue apparently in cheek, that "better dead than sick" might be the motto of the Cuban police, but it is highly likely that fear of black contagion was bound up in the police officer's action.[61]

British Caribbean migrants were not just viewed as a biological threat to the nation but also as a political threat. Many political leaders and intellectuals argued that British Caribbean migrants were a major contributor to regional political instability, owing to their alleged tendency toward violent uprising and their close association with U.S. imperialism. In Venezuela black migrants were perceived to be a significant factor in the civil wars of the nineteenth century. The Venezuelan minister of the interior expressed his concern about the arrival of blacks from Trinidad and Curaçao, "with the pretext of coming to work in Venezuela, but who . . . are very prejudicial to the tranquility of the territory," and voiced a suspicion that landowners were importing blacks specifically to serve in their personal armies, using the need for labor as a cover for political ambitions.[62] In Cuba the 1912 uprising by the Independent Party of Color (PIC) was attributed to black Caribbean migrants, with PIC leader Evaristo Estenoz rumored to be from the Dominican Republic or Jamaica (he was Cuban), and with Jamaican and Haitian immigrants said to have played a central role in the uprising (they did not).[63] In Central America the idea of an imminent armed black rebellion became a central feature of anti-immigrant agitation in the 1930s. The newspaper *Panama American* ran a series of articles alleging that blacks in the canal zone were on the edge of armed revolt in June 1933, while a petition in the same year by Costa Rican banana workers protesting the United Fruit Company hiring practices claimed that West Indians were taking up arms and predicted an imminent black "invasion" of the highlands.[64] In Honduras, British Caribbean migrants crossing the border with Belize to attend sporting events were assumed by the government to be smuggling weapons to rebel forces and were arrested and deported.[65]

In each of these cases historians have found little evidence to support contemporary arguments that West Indians were involved in armed uprisings. However, the perception of black immigrants as representing an armed threat and the way this perception was used to underline concerns about Antillean immigration are significant for its connection to deeper racial discourses regarding blackness and political violence. One of the dominant tropes of regional blackness was the idea of black predisposition to violence and militarism. This stemmed partly from colonial-era fears of slave rebellions and was accelerated by Afro-Latin American use of military service as a strategy for social advancement in the national period.[66] Ecuadorian historian Hans Heiman Guzmán encapsulated these ideas in his suggestion that the importation of African slaves had "disrupted the course of Ecuadorian history" because of the "bloody and warlike ways of blacks."[67] Similarly in Venezuela, economist Alberto Adriani insisted that "in our country they [blacks] have been the raw material of disorder, the element from which our armies have recruited almost all their revolutions."[68] This idea that blacks were the root of political disturbance was developed into arguments that blacks were simply incompatible with democracy. Venezuelan historian José Gil Fortoul drew on Herbert Spencer to argue that racial characteristics determined political practice and that the country's long history of authoritarianism was the result of racial demographics.[69] For Venezuela to have any chance to develop meaningful democratic institutions, Gil Fortoul argued, further black immigration had to be prevented.

The connection of British Caribbean migrants to U.S. expansion also contributed to characterizations of them as a threat to political stability. Cuban historian Emilio Roig de Leuchsenring, for example, argued that black migration was problematic because African-descended peoples, being a "weaker" race, were more susceptible to domination by U.S. capital.[70] This idea that the presence of blacks made nations vulnerable to U.S.

intervention had widespread resonance. Many Latin American intellectuals began to make the connection between racial demography and U.S. military intervention and to formulate this into a new measure of anti-blackness. Alberto Adriani, for example, argued that "the Americans have certain prejudices against the black race, and do not collaborate willingly even with their compatriots of that race. . . . The Americans will show themselves to be merciless with regions inhabited by races that they consider inferior, like the black." This is why the American preference for black labor was so dangerous—it brought in immigrants who not only did not contribute to "social progress" (whitening) but who also weakened the nation's international positioning.[71] The connection between West Indian immigrants and foreign powers thus became a self-reinforcing cycle, in which black migrants were both symbols of U.S. imperialism and perceived to be a risk factor for further domination.

Diaspora Nationalisms and West Indian Exclusion

It would be too simplistic to present British Caribbean migrants simply as passive foils for racial discourses. They also contributed to the xenophobia and nativism they encountered through their own ideas and actions, and British Caribbean diaspora nationalisms were an important factor in the othering of West Indian immigrants. Throughout the region, Antillean immigrants identified strongly and overtly as British and took pride in what they perceived as their Anglo-Saxon culture. British Caribbean migrants negotiated the dominant regional and international discourses of the time by rejecting ideas about black inferiority and emphasizing instead their connection to the cultural elements praised in scientific racial theory.

The travel narrative of British railway engineer Walter Wood provides a telling example of how fashion and language were used to project a sense of superiority among Trinidadian and Barbadian migrants in 1890s Venezuela. As he recounted, "It was most amusing to see several of them, within an hour of their arrival, dressed up, with a great display of shirt fronts, collars &c, and in good cloth suits, parading the streets and the Plaza, as if the whole place belonged to them and not hesitating to let it be known that they were '*English*.'"[72] While he found their efforts to claim a stake in Englishness amusing, they seemed to resonate in Maracaibo, and by the 1930s the term "ingles" had become synonymous with black immigrants from the British Caribbean, with whites from England itself designated as "un inglés blanco."[73]

British Caribbean pride in Anglo-Saxon culture could also lead to contempt for Latin American host societies. In Limón, black immigrants dismissed Spanish as "bird language" and regarded mestizo Costa Ricans as uneducated and backward peasants.[74] A petition by Hispanic banana workers to the Costa Rican National Assembly in 1941 complained, "For forty long years we Costa Ricans were displaced from the . . . Atlantic Zone by Negroes. . . . They think that they are superior to us. . . . They look down upon our language."[75] One second-generation Jamaican immigrant revealed that growing up in the 1930s and 1940s she was forbidden to date Hispanic men and was ostracized from her family when she started a relationship with a mestizo Costa Rican.[76]

Immigrants nurtured their British identity through the formation of clubs, churches, and mutual aid societies specifically for people from the British Caribbean. These institutions provided an important venue for saving and for community aid and played a critical role in cultural preservation and maintaining difference from the dominant community—celebrating important British and West Indian holidays with songs, dancing, and food brought over from the islands; teaching English to the children of migrants; and providing a space for community sporting events, most notably cricket. The Garveyist Universal Negro Improvement Association (UNIA) also formed an important element of the British Caribbean community infrastructure and strongly influenced cultural and political developments and race consciousness within the black immigrant community. The pan-Africanism that the UNIA promoted encouraged black immigrants to take pride in their blackness and gave migrants the tools to challenge the racism and oppression they faced, pitting them directly against the antiblack discourses of dominant nationalisms.

Garveyism intersected closely with pro-imperial British diaspora nationalisms. The Garveyist weekly newspaper the *Workman*, published in Panama by the West Indian Protective League and circulated throughout Latin America, took a "very pro-British" approach, emphasizing the significance of membership in the British Empire and praising British interventions on behalf of the West Indian community.[77] In general, West Indians in Central America and South America were committed to Empire, rallying round the war effort in World War I and World War II and promoting enthusiasm for British expansionism through their social institutions. A speech given at "Empire Night" in the West Indian Masonic Hall in Colón to celebrate what would have been the 102nd birthday of Queen Victoria typifies the way in which Britain was elevated by Caribbean migrants: "It will go forth from the Republic of Panama to the civilized world that the Britishers whose hearts are sincere have pledged their loyalty to the British Empire. If ever its sovereignty is threatened or its dignity assailed we will fly to the banner of defense. Take away the British Empire and we have nothing. I do not love the empire for its government, but for the principles on which the government rests. Those are what we fight for; those are what the nations of the world rest on."[78] Through the glorification of the British Empire, migrant commitment to a rival foreign power was clearly and unambiguously projected.

West Indian identification with Britain could have very real consequences in areas where territorial boundaries were under dispute. In Nicaragua, for example, Jamaican influence in the Mosquito Reserve was perceived as a major threat to national sovereignty. In 1875 the Nicaraguan government complained to the British Foreign Office about Jamaican interference in the reserve, suggesting that "certain natives of Jamaica" were "inciting" the king of the Mosquito to "infringe the Sovereign Rights of Nicaragua."[79] The governor of Jamaica dismissed the likelihood of black Jamaican influence on the reserve, stating that "nothing can be more unlikely than that the negroes of this Island should concern themselves with the affairs of a distant country; and if indeed some few individuals may have been induced to do so it is certain that their support is quite valueless."[80] Yet Jamaicans did play a significant role in the Bluefields uprising of 1909 and formed a major component of conservative general Juan José Estrada's U.S.-funded army, leading many Nicaraguan elites to hold them responsible for the subsequent invasion of U.S. marines.[81]

Similarly, in Venezuela the important gold mines of El Callao were in disputed territory claimed by the British as part of British Guiana in the nineteenth century. The majority of the workers in these mines were migrants from Trinidad, Barbados, and Jamaica who supported British claims and were enthusiastic about the military action that occurred in 1884 and 1895. As one American chronicler testified, "The miners . . . would very much prefer an English colonial government to Venezuelan rule. I have been told by dozens of men, Americans, Germans, native Venezuelans and representatives of other nations that if the question were submitted to the people the decision would be almost unanimously in favor of England."[82] In this context of border conflict, and with the enthusiasm they manifested for British colonial rule, West Indians could easily be interpreted as agents of Empire.

Certainly, the British Colonial Office was an important source of support for British Caribbean migrants, and however ambivalent British consular officials sometimes were about their responsibilities toward black Caribbean subjects, they could also provide an important source of protection. West Indian claims to British intervention were often interpreted as a manifestation of covert imperialism, pushing British ideas about the correct operation of the judicial system onto Latin American governments and allowing British Caribbean immigrants to sidestep the local rule of law. The Cuban secretary of state, for example, accused migrants of "committing acts of disrespect, misdemeanours and breaches of the law" but seeking "impunity" through British diplomatic attention.[83]

An intriguing example of the kinds of legal principles that were often at stake in British intervention can be seen in the case of Jerome Jackson, a British Caribbean immigrant in Brazil who was imprisoned for burglary in Rio Grande do Sul in 1902. The British consul investigated and became convinced that Jackson had been falsely imprisoned because his conviction was based on the confession of an Italian immigrant who worked with Jackson as a stevedore. The Italian later retracted his confession, claiming that it had been beaten out of him in a brutal police interrogation and that neither he nor Jackson knew anything of the crime. The consul believed that the conviction had not been overturned simply because the victim of the burglary was a prominent local judge and, convinced there had been a miscarriage of justice, requested the intervention of the British government.[84] A petition was presented to the Brazilian government in Jackson's favor, but officials insisted that there were no legal grounds for a retrial and that a presidential pardon was not a possibility in cases prosecuted at the provincial level. The Colonial Office insisted that since the issue was one of wrongful imprisonment, a solution must be found, and they continued to push for a clemency ruling. Although ultimately Jackson was not released, his case was extensively engaged by the British and Brazilian government. Leading British officials translated and pored over 160 pages of court proceedings. Specialists in Brazilian law were consulted. Arguments were made about what statements made under cross-examination were worth, how confessions should be extricated, and how guilt in a crime should be determined.[85] All of this represented an effort to institute British ideas about what constituted fair and impartial justice onto the Brazilian legal system with a West Indian immigrant at its center.

The Jackson case was not unique. In Puerto Rico the British government

intervened after six British Caribbean migrants working on a sugar plantation were imprisoned without trial and sentenced to labor in a chain gang
for resisting arrest following a dispute over management abuses. The consul
protested the fact they had not been informed of the charges against them
and had received no trial, and that their right to contact British authorities
for assistance had initially been denied.[86] British intervention was made
when Barbadian Adolphus Coulson was found guilty of the murder of his
wife in Panama and sentenced to death without a jury trial. While the Colonial Office felt that his case "need excite no pity" because he had confessed
to poisoning his wife, it was still important "for the sake of principle" to
raise an appeal based on the absence of a jury.[87] As the undersecretary
of state wrote: "It would appear . . . desirable to test the question on the
ground that there is a danger that injustice may be done to British Colonial
subjects, especially negroes, if they are liable to be tried for serious offenses
without a jury."[88] Compensation suits were also pursued by the British
government in many of the cases of police shootings and official violence
discussed earlier in this chapter, and were often successful. British Caribbean migrants played a decisive role in pushing these interventions—they
wrote letters, visited consular offices, and insisted upon support for their
rights. Such cases further entangled the relationship between migrants and
external powers and consolidated the association between West Indians,
neocolonialism, and outside intervention.

Inclusionary Nationalisms and the Limits of Assimilation

Migrant mutual aid networks, daily cultural practices, and efforts to benefit from Britain's international status did not preclude attempts to seek
national inclusion. Second- and third-generation British Caribbean immigrants began to engage more fully with Latin American politics from
the 1920s onward and to form organizations that articulated specifically
Latin American nationalisms. In Panama the National League of Criollos,
a second-generation political organization formed to gain rights for Panamanians of West Indian descent, fervently identified with the Panamanian
nation, stating that it would consider "all Antilles parents who try to in-
culcate in the minds of born Panamanians a different nationality, or [who]
try to bring to the child's mind a higher regard for institutions and ideas,
rather than teaching him those of his country of birth," as "enemies of the
soil and parasites on the Republic."[89] The strong language underlines their
frustration at the continued association of second- and third-generation

immigrants with Caribbean islands they had never visited, and their desperation to overturn the perception of Antilleans as agents of British and American imperialism and to project an image of loyalty and commitment. Their efforts were replicated in Costa Rica and Honduras as second- and third-generation Caribbean immigrants in enclave communities sought citizenship and national recognition.[90]

This new generation of West Indian community leaders promoted assimilation and became convinced that the struggles they experienced in their efforts to gain greater inclusion were jeopardized by problematic community-level cultural practices. As a result they sought the transformation of group customs. Sometimes leaders focused on the minutiae of everyday life. The "West Indian News" segment of the *Panama Star and Herald* ran a series of editorials railing against what it called the "boisterous and flippant practice" of engaging marching brass bands for funeral processions, a practice that the paper noted both Americans and Panamanians viewed as undignified and unserious.[91] In other instances, community leaders dwelt on more fundamental issues, such as family structure and patterns of religious worship. In Costa Rica, for example, community elites sought to stigmatize African-derived religious practices such as spirit possession and to vilify matriarchal family structures in which women served as heads of households.[92]

These efforts to gain national inclusion through community regulation often led to class-based fractures as community elites sought to police and control the behavior of other immigrants. Community leaders became convinced that it was the moral failings of lower-class blacks rather than the racism of dominant society that undermined their hopes of integration. This attitude perhaps reflects an internalization of the class discourses inherent within emerging ideologies of *mestizaje*, which appeared to hold out the promise of inclusion and mobility for those who met national cultural and behavioral standards regardless of race or ethnicity.

Yet British Caribbean efforts at acceptance ultimately failed. This can be seen most dramatically in Panama, where the 1941 constitution rendered those of British Caribbean descent born in Panama after 1928 ineligible for citizenship, casting those born after that date into what Michael Conniff described as a "nationality limbo" that severely impacted their ability to travel and find work and education. The British consul took up the issue of citizenship with President Arias, who acknowledged that tens of thousands of British Caribbean–descended people would become stateless. But he argued that he was in fact being generous, quipping in what appears to be a distasteful joke, albeit one that is deeply revealing about the depth of antiblack attitudes underlying the law: "At any rate, I will not do as the Nazis do: I will not shoot them."[93] That even second- and third-generation immigrants of British Caribbean descent were viewed as wholly foreign underlines the deep relationship between race, culture, and national identity.

Neither could inclusionary efforts stem the wave of deportations that proliferated in the 1930s and 1940s, fueled by the passing of highly restrictive immigration laws. Quota laws and immigration bans led to the forced repatriation of tens of thousands British Caribbean migrants, many of whom had left their islands of origins decades before and whose family ties were all in Latin America. Cases like that of Emma Patrie, a Jamaican widow in her sixties who was deported from Panama after twenty-nine years and returned to Jamaica almost blind and with no family in the island were not uncommon.[94] Deportations were often exceptionally brutal and undignified. In Venezuela armed police removed British Caribbean migrants from their homes and workplaces and took them to deportation camps, where they were forced to work unpaid for several months to "pay" for their return passage and were fed only bread and cheese. Deportees were placed in dugout canoes and sent up the Barima River to British Guiana, or forced at gunpoint to jump off into chest-deep water yards from the Trinidadian coast.[95]

Often deportations from legislation aimed at getting rid of recent British Caribbean immigrants in fact targeted members of the preexisting black Caribbean-descended community. In Honduras, any black, English-speaking person stopped without papers was deported to Belize during the 1930s. Many deportees appealed to the British consul afterward, insisting that they had been born in Honduras, not infrequently tracing their heritage back to the eighteenth-century settlement of the Bay Islands. People traveling back from athletic events in Belize and children who had been sent to go to school in Jamaica were often denied reentry to their homes, splitting up families and adding to the number of stateless blacks. The "repatriation" of Afro-Hondurans to Belize was also noted by British officials, who lamented that "this colony is in danger of having saddled on it, persons unconnected with it, who are not even British subjects."[96] However, the British government imagined that the Roatán Islanders deported to Belize were purposefully presenting themselves as British subjects in order to gain access to the wealth of the British Empire. In fact, as Glenn Anthony Chambers has argued, their "accidental" deportation was just the last in a long line of efforts to eradicate blackness from the national character.[97]

Even in countries where black immigrants were more successful in gaining nominal citizenship, their inclusion was far from absolute, and it was predicated on expanded state control over the British Caribbean community. West Indians and their descendants were granted Costa Rican citizenship in 1948 as a direct result of their support for José Figueres in the civil war. Yet this was followed by the massive penetration of the central state into Limón and a campaign to hispanicize the Afro-Caribbean population by eradicating English-language education and placing new restrictions on Protestant churches. Moreover, the white–mestizo Central Valley was still considered to represent the "real" Costa Rica and the ideal of racial homogeneity continued to be a center point of national identity.[98]

The unsuccessful struggles of British Caribbean immigrants to obtain national inclusion underline the limitations of an assimilationist framework for understanding Latin American realities. Immigrants were viewed positively only within a specific racial lens, and those who were of a race perceived to be problematic were stigmatized and rejected even when understood to be economically important. If hyphenated European identities did not emerge because Italian Brazilians and German Argentines were so quickly absorbed as national subjects, the inverse is true for black immigrants. There were no Jamaican Costa Ricans or Trinidadian Venezuelans because they were not accepted as such, remaining instead simply *jamaiquinos* and *antillanos*.

Conclusion

A comparative analysis of West Indian immigration has deep resonance for understanding the relationship between migration and nationalism in Latin America. British Caribbean immigrants were essential to processes of national integration. They played a critical role in building transportation infrastructure, extracting mineral wealth, and developing systems of plantation agriculture. Yet they were deeply problematic for analogous stages of nation-building—facilitating the spread of national consciousness and ensuring national sovereignty—because of the strongly held conviction that they were not suitable as permanent immigrants and could not become national citizens. In part, this was because of the immigrants' close relationship with dominant foreign powers and because of their minimal identification with their Latin American host nations. Yet it was also more fundamentally about their race, which was considered to disqualify British Caribbean immigrants from acquiring the status of nationals. Thus, the concerns of countries that had imported large numbers of West Indians for economic and infrastructural development projects became similar to those faced by countries with large West Indian-descended populations in geographically isolated places that preexisted the nation-state. The same type of "nationalizing" campaigns that were pursued in Nicaragua and Colombia in the nineteenth and early twentieth century were adopted by nations such as Panama, Costa Rica, and Venezuela in the 1930s and 1940s.

Exploring the intense racialization of these processes sheds new light on the positioning of blackness within Latin American nationalisms. Dominant theories of blackness and national identity in Latin America emphasize the exclusion of blackness from nationalist ideals of *mestizaje* but present this exclusion as a consequence of blacks' lack of cultural and legal distinctiveness as opposed to indigenous people, which led to them being discursively blended into the category of the masses.[99] A systematic analysis of British Caribbean immigration underlines that in fact the exclusion of blacks from national identity was intentional, systematic, and based on a fear of blackness as a source of danger and pollution. Antiblackness was deeply embedded within Latin American nationalisms and shaped the lived experience of black immigration in profound and sometimes traumatic ways.

Beatings, floggings, false imprisonment, shootings, rape—even massacres and lynchings—became almost routine in the British Caribbean diaspora. Black immigrants were vulnerable to abuses because of the ways in which American corporate ideas about appropriate mechanisms of racial discipline intersected with Latin American fears of imagined black criminality, violence, and poor hygiene. British Caribbean adaptation strategies and diaspora nationalisms only reinforced the problem by bolstering perceptions of them as unnational and outside of the citizenship base.

The role of international currents in shifting discourses of blackness is significant. British Caribbean migration was fostered partly by international elites and served as a reminder of how foreign influence was bound up in modernization projects and deeper concepts of modernity. American racial practices also contributed to and reinforced the stigma surrounding blackness. An analysis of British Caribbean migration thus reminds us of the ethnic underpinnings of national identity while also elucidating the transnational dynamics of identity formation and how nationalist ideas were shaped by international discourses.

Yet elite attacks on black immigrants were directed just as much at "indigenous" black populations—Afro-Latin American descendants of slavery, the Garifuna—as at British Caribbean people, and the attacks represented an effort to exclude blackness from national imaginaries. As notions of blackness were brought to the fore by British Caribbean immigration, their meaning was negotiated in a manner that reinforced conceptualizations of racial hierarchy and fueled the racialization of space. Preexisting fears of blackness mediated the migratory experience of British Caribbean people, but their migration also reshaped and reconstituted these images, reinscribing the exclusion of blackness ever more firmly into the racialization of national identity.

An exploration of the experiences of British Caribbean immigrants thus complicates our understanding of the positioning of immigrants within Latin American racial systems, further underlining the limitations of the conventional argument that "immigrant" was a privileged category related to nonblackness and non-Indianness. As Lesser and Rein point out in this volume, such a formulation is deeply problematic for many groups and does not take account of class and ethnic diversity within migratory streams. However, it is especially inapplicable to West Indians who were nonprivileged specifically because they *were* black. Excluding this reality from theoretical models of migration only serves to perpetuate the discursive separations promoted by Latin American nationalists who denied black migrants the status of immigrants because they did not comply with the logic of social whitening. A full assessment of the relationship between immigration and Latin American nationalism therefore must pay close attention to the racialization of distinct migrant streams and challenge the analytical binary between immigrant and blackness.

Notes

1. This chapter uses the term "British Caribbean" to refer to migrants who originated from the British West Indian islands and British Guiana. Migrants from this region often identified themselves as "West Indian"—a classification that has more typically been used in the scholarly literature—so this term is also employed here as a descriptor. Haitians were also sometimes part of the black immigrant stream, especially in the Caribbean islands of Cuba, Puerto Rico, and the Dominican Republic, and many of the racial discourses directed at British Caribbean migrants were also formed in relation to Haitian migration. However, since the realities and identities of Haitian migrants seem to have differed from those of migrants from the British Caribbean—most notably in the absence of a claim to British subjecthood—they do not form part of this chapter.

2. Well into the 1980s, surveys of migration to Latin America examined only European immigrants, with Middle Eastern and Jewish migration considered in very brief outline and West Indians completely omitted. See Bastos de Avila, *Immigration in Latin America*;

and Mörner, *Adventurers and Proletarians*. More recently, Baily and Miguez's comparative study of migration, while far more inclusive in its attention to non-European immigrants, reiterates the binary between blackness and immigration, suggesting that to understand the relationship between migration, race and ethnicity immigration we must ask "how did immigrants . . . react to and interact with blacks?" See Baily and Míguez, *Mass Migration*, 285. Comparative work in Latin American racial theory is just as notable for its lack of engagement with black immigrant realities. Applebaum et al.'s groundbreaking collection *Race and Nation*, for example, included no chapter on black immigrant communities although it did address European and Chinese migrants, while Dixon and Burdick's excellent recent volume, *Comparative Perspectives*, does not assess black immigration as a factor in shaping regional blackness.

3. Helg, "Aftermath of Slavery," 156.

4. West Indian immigration to Chile has been completely overlooked by historians. For British consular reflections on recruitment for Chile, see G. S. R. Archer, Recruitment Agent in Panama to W. L. C. Philips, Acting Colonial Secretary, August 14, 1913, National Archives, Kew, United Kingdom; Colonial Office (CO) 28/282/25.

5. British Caribbean immigration to Haiti has been so neglected that even a 2004 conference devoted to exploring Jamaica–Haiti connections did not examine the matter—the discussion instead centered on Haitian migrants in Jamaica. See University of the West Indies-Mona Latin America-Caribbean Center, *Haiti–Jamaica Connection*. Reports in the Jamaican press on Haitian efforts to restrict Jamaican immigration provide insights into the nature of the immigration stream and the challenges of immigrant realities. See *Daily Gleaner* July 9, 1930; October 23, 1930; March 11, 1931; June 1, 1931; October 31, 1931.

6. Jones and Glean, "English Speaking Communities"; Dawson, "Evacuation of the Mosquito Shore"; and Crawford, "Transnational World Fractured."

7. Gordon, *Disparate Diasporas*, 53–67.

8. Desir, *Between Loyalties*, 12, 112–15. It should also be noted that in each instance, policies of Hispanicization took hold at the exact moment that the boom in rubber and coconut exports led to the increased penetration of U.S. capital and the onset of a new wave of West Indian migration. Governments did little to distinguish between established black Creoles, black indigenous communities such as the Garifuna or Miskitu, and newer West Indian migrants, viewing them all as nonnational, and the renewed influx of black immigrants reignited concerns about the sovereignty of marginal regions.

9. Newton, *Silver Men*; and Bourgois, *Ethnicity at Work*.

10. *Daily Gleaner*, April 25, 1911.

11. Consul-General Casement to Sir Edward Grey, March 17, 1911, in Great Britain, Foreign Office, *Correspondence Respecting the Treatment of British Colonial Subjects*, 6.

12. Petras, *Jamaican Labor Migration*, 73.

13. Statement of David Burril, Alex White, Joseph Francis, Charles Goban, Jonh Letty, and George Gedis, in "Precis of Complaints Received from Labourers vs the MacDonald Company," CO 137/618/14477.

14. Neale Porter to W. R. Estes, May 6, 1892; The Custos of the Cayman Island to the Colonial Secretary, 18 June 1892; A. A. Weldon to H. M. S. Partridge, August 23, 1892. All in U.S. State Department General Records. Consular Despatches, Kingston, Jamaica. U.S. National Archives (USNA), Microcopy X 353.1 U58g T31, Reel 33.

15. *Barbados Weekly Herald*, June 8, 1929.

16. Quoted in Richardson, *Panama Money*, 110.

17. *Daily Gleaner*, March 4, 1908.

18. Colonial Secretary to Mr. J. Lanigan, March 20, 1900, in CO 137/618/14477.

19. "Report on the Condition of the Jamaican Labourers employed under contract with the government of Jamaica by James P. MacDonald on the construction of a railway from Guayaquil to Quito in the Republic of Ecuador," February 1901, in CO 137/618/14477.

20. Consul-General Casement to Sir Edward Grey, January 31, 1911, in United States Department of State, *Slavery in Peru*, 231–35.

21. *El Grito del Pueblo*, December 6, 1900.

22. *Daily Gleaner*, November 3, 1900.

23. *El Grito del Pueblo*, December 6, 1900.

24. Haggard to Cuban Secretary of State, January 3, 1924, in Great Britain, Foreign Office, and Cuba, Secretaría del Estado, *Correspondence between His Majesty's Government and the Cuban Government*, 5.

25. E. Gorst to the Foreign Office, March 25, 1907, in CO 295/443/10862.

26. Murray to Governor of Jamaica, May 29, 1919, in Great Britain, Foreign Office, *Correspondence Respecting the Treatment of British Colonial Subjects*.

27. See summary in Dickinson to the Marquis of Salisbury, February 6, 1887, in CO 137/533/6890.

28. "The Culebra Massacre: A Few Lawless Negroes Responsible for the Affair," *New York Times*, June 17, 1885, 3.

29. "Précis of the Official Report of the Proceedings against Captain Pedro Antonio Cabo for Exceeding His Duty in the Affair at Culebra," enclosure, Dickinson to Foreign Office, January 15, 1887, in CO 137/533/5194.

30. Text of Supreme Court of Justice Ruling, as printed in *Diario Oficial*, January 26, 1887; enclosure, Dickinson to the Marquis of Salisbury, February 6, 1887, in CO 137/533/6890.

31. Dickinson to the Marquis of Salisbury, February 6, 1887, in CO 137/533/6890.

32. Letter from the National Amalgamated Furnishing Trades Association on behalf of Mrs. J. Glaney, enclosed in Mallet to FO, November 18, 1910, FO 371/944/41616.

33. "Precis of Complaints Received from Labourers vs the MacDonald Company," CO 137/618/14477.

34. *Barbados Advocate*, October 27, 1924.

35. Haggard to Cuban Secretary of State, January 3, 1924, in Great Britain, Foreign Office, and Cuba, Secretaría del Estado, *Correspondence between His Majesty's Government and the Cuban Government*.

36. Wynter, *Jamaican Labor Migration*, 194.

37. Carlos Manuel de Cespedes to Charge d'Affaires, July 4, 1924, in Great Britain, Foreign Office, and Cuba, Secretaría del Estado, *Further Correspondence*, 37.

38. H. A. Cooper to the Colonial Office, March 1, 1873, in CO 318/270/5857. The assault was recorded by the British Consul as taking place on August 20, 1871.

39. Mallet to FO, December 2, 1911, in FO 288/125/565; and Beauclerk to FO, Lima, July 5, 1902, in CO 137/631/34768.

40. Young to FO, June 24, 1916, in FO 371/2643.

41. Consul-General Casement to Sir Edward Grey, January 31, 1911, in United States Department of State, *Slavery in Peru*, 226. For the wider literature on the rubber boom and genocide in the Putumayo, see Fernandez, "Upper Amazonian Rubber Boom"; Stanfield, *Red Rubber, Bleeding Trees*; and Taussig, *Shamanism, Colonialism and the Wild Man*.

42. John Brown to Commissioner of Montserrat, February 3, 1910, in CO 28/274/8.

43. Originally published as a series of articles in *Truth*, Hardenburg's report was published in book form following the interest attracted by U.S. and British government investigations. Hardenburg, *The Putumayo, the Devil's Paradise*.

44. Consul-General Casement to Sir Edward Grey, January 31, 1911, in United States Department of State, *Slavery in Peru*, 226. He was more sympathetic in his personal diary, noting that "they said they acted under fear, under compulsion, and I believed it." Mitchell, *Amazon Journal of Roger Casement*, 128.

45. Romuelo Paredes, Confidential Report, Ministry of Foreign Relations, Iquitos, September 30, 1911, in United States Department of State, *Slavery in Peru*, 149.

46. Consul Fuller to Secretary of State, Iquitos, August 5, 1912, in United States Department of State, *Slavery in Peru*, 42; Sir Edward Grey to Mr. des Graz, F. O., January 16, 1911, in United States Department of State, *Slavery in Peru*, 221.

47. Informe de la Intendente de Policía de Guayaquil al Ministro de lo Interior, *Mensajes e Informes*, 1900. Archivo Biblioteca de la Función Legislativa, Quito.

48. *Daily Gleaner*, September 10, 1932.

49. Ortiz, "Inmigración desde el punto," 54–56; and Amador, "Redeeming the Tropics," 88.

50. *El Nuevo Tiempo*, July 15, 1916.

51. *El Diario de Costa Rica*, September 20, 1936; *La Voz del Atlántico*, November 7, 1936; and *Atlantic Voice*, November 7, 1936.

52. Tinker Salas, *Enduring Legacy*, 134.

53. Helg, *Our Rightful Share*, 238–39; Enclosure No. 2, West Indian Labourers in Cuba, in Great Britain, Foreign Office, and Cuba, Secretaría del Estado, *Further Correspondence*, 4.

54. Helg, *Our Rightful Share*, 16–17.

55. Hortensia Lamar, "La lucha contra la prostitución y la trata de blancas," *Revista Bimestre Cubana* 18 (1923): 134.

56. Julio Nogueira, "A Madeira-Mamoré: A Bacia do Mamoré," *Jornal do Commercio*, January 31, 1913, 15.

57. *Daily Gleaner*, December 28, 1905.

58. See, for example, Le Roy Cassá, "Inmigración anti-sanitaria," 16–18.

59. *Daily Gleaner*, July 18, 1924.

60. Mr. G. Haggard to the Cuban Secretary of Foreign Affairs, January 3, 1924, in Great Britain, Foreign Office, and Cuba, Secretaría del Estado, *Correspondence between His Majesty's Government and the Cuban Government*, 5.

61. *Daily Gleaner*, July 18, 1924.

62. Cited in Torconis de Veracoechea, *El proceso de la inmigración en Venezuela*, 73.

63. See most notably Velasco, "El problema negro," 75, 79.

64. Conniff, *Black Labor on a White Canal*, 84; and Archivo Nacional de Costa Rica (ANCR), Serie Congreso, no. 16753.

65. Chambers, *Race, Nation and West Indian Immigration*, 130–31.

66. See Foote and Horst, *Military Struggle and Identity Formation*, especially chapters by Beattie, Foote, and Sanders.

67. Heiman Guzmán, *Los inmigrantes*, 50.

68. Adriani, "Venezuela," 88.

69. Gil Fortoul, *El hombre y la historia*, 13–14.

70. Roig de Leuchsenring, *Los problemas sociales*, 18.

71. Adriani, "Venezuela," 88–89.

72. Wood, *Venezuela*, 86.

73. Leonard, *Men of Maracaibo*, 106.

74. Purcell, *Banana Fallout*.

75. Quoted in Bourgois, "Black Diaspora in Costa Rica," 149.

76. Life story submitted by Dalia in *Autobiografías Campesinas*. Unpublished manuscript collection, Universidad Nacional Autónoma, Costa Rica.

77. Opie, *Black Labor Migration*, 87.

78. *Panama Star and Herald*, May 26, 1921.

79. Earl of Derby to the Colonial Office, April 1, 1875, in CO 137/480/36.

80. Sir William Grey to the Earl of Camararon, May 14, 1875, in CO 137/479/19.

81. "Jamaicans in the Nicaragua Revolution," *Daily Gleaner*, April 14, 1910.

82. Curtis, *Venezuela*, 242.

83. Cespedes to Charge d'Affaires, July 4, 1924, in Great Britain, Foreign Office, and Cuba, Secretaría del Estado, *Further Correspondence*, 37.

84. Hewitt to Marquess of Landsdowne, April 1, 1905, in CO 28/264/16186.

85. "Case of Jerome Jackson," in CO 28/269/5443.

86. Cooper to Colonial Office, March 1, 1873, in CO 318/270/5857.

87. CO 28/269/29756.

88. Under-Secretary of State, Colonial Office to the Foreign Office, August 19, 1907, in CO 28/269/29756.

89. *Panama Star and Herald*, October 8, 1926.

90. See Harpelle, "The Social and Political Integration of West Indians," 116; and Chambers, *Race, Nation and West Indian Immigration*.

91. *Panama Star and Herald*, October 11, 1926.

92. Foote, "Rethinking Race, Gender and Citizenship," 204–5.

93. Conniff, *Black Labor on a White Canal*, 98–99.

94. *Daily Gleaner*, May 1, 1939.

95. *Daily Gleaner*, July 13, 1939.

96. Collett to FO, July 10, 1938, in FO 369/126/28133.

97. Chambers, *Race, Nation and West Indian Immigration*, 70–77, 124–25.

98. Biesanz and Biesanz, *Costa Rican Life*.

99. Wade, *Race and Ethnicity*; and Whitten, *Black Frontiersmen*.

9

Italian Fascism and Diasporic Nationalisms in Argentina, Brazil, and Uruguay

MICHAEL GOEBEL

> And the bystanders, seven or eight merchants from Brazil, Uruguay, and Argentina, long emigrated from Italy, exclaimed in choir:
> "We are still Italians! We are still Italians!"
>
> Enrico Corradini, *La patria lontana* (1910)

The opening scene of the 1910 novel by the Italian nationalist Enrico Corradini, *La patria lontana* (The distant fatherland), confronts a patriotic Italian traveler on a visit to Brazil with a wine merchant of Italian origin from the Argentine province of Mendoza. The European visitor accuses the Italian Argentine businessman of having betrayed his fatherland by producing wine in Argentina, thereby contributing to the decline of Italian viticulture. Against these charges, several people of Italian origin from various South American countries vociferously protest their *italianità* (Italianness). But to no avail, as Corradini's readers learn. The patriotic visitor, surely an alter ego of Corradini, who when writing the novel had just returned from a long trip to South America, always prevails with his argument that emigrants to South America had long lost their true ethnic identity to a shapeless melting pot.[1] Emigration to South America, according to Corradini's message, sucked the blood out of Italy's veins and diluted the country's essences by scattering its people all over a world where they languished in servitude to other nations. A vigorous and youthful military expansionism, especially in Africa, was needed instead. Consistent with such views, Corradini's Nationalist Association would merge with the Italian Fascist Party in 1923. Benito Mussolini adopted a similar stance and in the 1920s sought to curb emigration, especially to Argentina, the country with the highest proportion of Italians outside Italy.

Corradini's opinion differed markedly from the vision outlined only ten years earlier by the liberal economist Luigi Einaudi in his book *Un principe mercante* (A merchant prince).[2] Here, Italian settlement in far-flung Argentina was portrayed as a peaceful conquest for the mutual socioeconomic benefit of brother peoples. Rather than decrying assimilation into the host society as a dilution of Italianness, Einaudi celebrated Italy's allegedly amicable diaspora and contrasted it to the belligerent imperialism of other European countries. The difference between Corradini's account and that of Einaudi betrayed much wider discrepancies in the appreciation of the value and purpose of emigration for Italy's national development. It also testified to a broader shift in which, around the turn of the century, ethnicity was increasingly privileged as the defining element of *italianità*.

Although the association of this shift with debates about emigration was perhaps especially intimate in Italy, such a nexus between ethnic nationalism and the diaspora developed in other European countries too. Ethnic nationalists in turn-of-the-century Germany invoked the German community in southern Brazil as a repository of a pristine Deutschtum untarnished by the perils of modernity, as Stefan Rinke's and Frederik Schulze's articles in this volume demonstrate.[3] Diasporas, in other words, fed the nationalist imagination at home. There was, however, a telling difference between the Italian and the German case. While German nationalists pointed to Brazil as an idyllic rural haven of the purest essences of "Germanness," they scorned the United States—where Germans formed a much larger proportion of the population than they did in Brazil—as an amorphous melting pot that in no time watered down the arrivals' national identity.[4] Italian nationalists, by contrast, singled out South America—particularly Argentina—as the place that through admixture most endangered the emigrants' identity. Although such nationalist discourses were in good measure projections, the difference between German and Italian appreciations of their diasporas also suggests that they were not entirely independent from the social experiences of overseas migrants on the ground.

By discussing different diasporic nationalisms among Italians in three Latin American countries, this chapter makes two contributions to the study of migration. First, as the comparison with the Germans indicates, it shows that the social history of migration and the political and intellectual history of diasporic nationalism are intimately connected to each other. This should go without saying, perhaps, but all too often the social history of migration and the intellectual history of various types of nationalism continue to be divorced. Second, the chapter demonstrates that, just as migrants themselves were not homogenous groups, their diasporic nationalisms were not either. In other words, there was more than one nationalism among the various Italian diasporas of Latin America and the different kinds often competed with each other. To tease out these two main arguments, the chapter adopts a comparative angle, examining fascism and diasporic nationalisms among Italians in Brazil, Uruguay, and Argentina during the period of the Italian kingdom.

It emerges that, contrary to Corradini's vision, Italian migrants were, in Emilio Franzina's words, "living agents" in the worldwide spread of nationalism.[5] Even though this was true for the nineteenth century, too, much of the historiography on Italian diaspora nationalism, whether in Latin America or elsewhere, has so far concentrated on one particular period, namely that of fascism. As this literature has shown, the identification of Italian emigrants with fascism was in many cases the outgrowth of a vague and much older identification with the homeland, now represented by the strongman Mussolini rather than a wholesale adherence to fascist ideology.[6] In many instances, joining local branches of the Fascist Party could thus be an expression of a much broader diasporic nationalism. Opponents of fascism, on the other hand, similarly drew on certain tropes allegedly embodying *italianità* to defend their political position. While fascism can therefore be treated as one instance of diasporic nationalism, there was no straightforward path from one to the other.

Comparing the different American countries in which many Italians settled, it has been argued that fascism kindled less support in Latin America than it did in the United States, where scholars have cast it as an instance of "defensive nationalism," a rallying behind Mussolini based on ethnic pride in reaction to discrimination by the receiving society.[7] With more specific regard to the cases under consideration here, João Fábio Bertonha has maintained that the Italian communities of the Rio de la Plata countries remained more immune to fascism than those in Brazil.[8] While this chapter supports this comparative argument in general terms, it adopts a more long-term perspective on various kinds of nationalism and patriotism among the Italian communities of the three countries in order to arrive at a better understanding of how the social, economic, and cultural features of these communities interacted with political developments over time. The chapter examines these variations counterchronologically, starting with some observations on the comparative weight of fascism in the Italian communities of Argentina, Uruguay, and Brazil.

Fascism and Italian Migrants

Mussolini's policy regarding emigration followed a two-pronged approach.[9] On the one hand, his regime viewed emigration to the Americas and Europe, if not to Africa, as a sign of national weakness that had to be assuaged. On the other hand, Mussolini saw Italians abroad as a promising bridgehead to buttress fascist foreign policy. The regime therefore sought to strengthen homeland ties among overseas Italian communities and harness them to the fascist state and its ideology either through the diplomatic corps or party organizations. Among the latter, the foremost vehicles for this purpose were the *fasci all'estero* or, a few years later, local branches of the leisure organization Opera Nazionale Dopolavoro, which Italian consuls and other public envoys were supposed to spread. By the 1930s Italian ambassadors and consuls were simultaneously the bosses of local branches of the Fascist Party.[10]

In Latin America, efforts at bringing Italians abroad into the fascist fold were most clearly directed toward Brazil and Argentina.[11] Not only did Italian foreign policymakers consider them to be the most influential Latin American nations (besides Mexico, which was still marred by internal conflicts). More significantly, they were also the two countries with by far the largest Italian populations in Latin America. Almost 1 million Italian citizens lived in Argentina at the eve of World War I, and roughly 560,000 in Brazil shortly after the war. Although absolute numbers were lower than those of Italians in the United States (approximately 1.6 million according to the 1920 census), the share of the Italian-born population in Latin America's principal destination countries of overseas migrants was much larger. Roughly one-third of all overseas immigrants in Argentina, Uruguay, and Brazil between 1850 and 1950 were Italians. Their proportion was highest in the Rio de la Plata countries of Argentina and Uruguay, particularly if the population of Italian origin is included in the count, not only—as was customary in Latin American censuses—those born in Italy. Just like immigrants as a whole, Italians clustered especially in large cities, first and foremost Buenos Aires and São Paulo, but also in the region's secondary cities, such as Montevideo, Rosario, and Porto Alegre (see figures 9.1 and 9.2).

The degree of success that crowned the fascist government's attempts to enthrall overseas Italians to the new regime in the homeland varied between countries as well as over time and within the communities. Initially

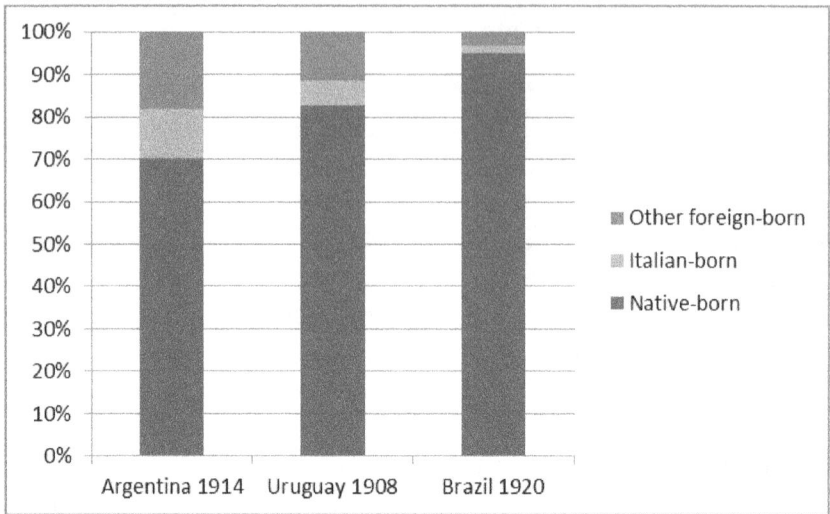

Figure 9.1. Chart depicting Italians as a percentage of total population in the nations of Argentina, Uruguay, and Brazil.

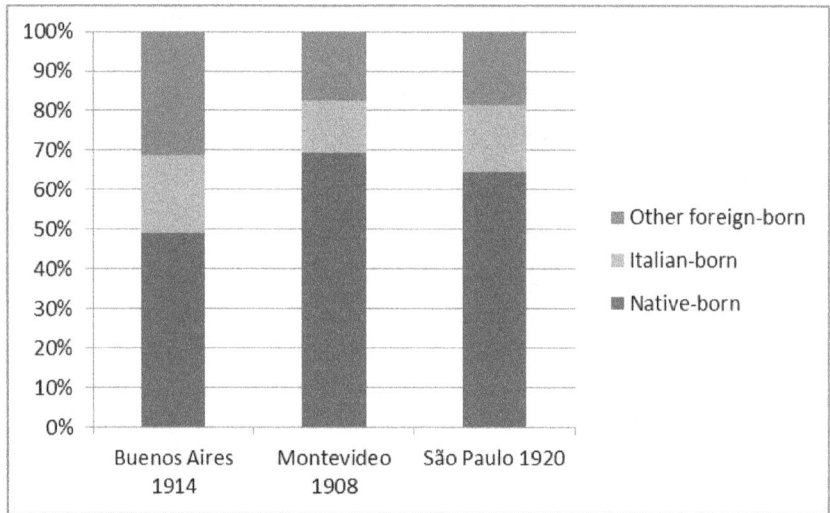

Figure 9.2. Chart depicting Italians as a percentage of total population in the cities of Buenos Aires, Montevideo, and São Paulo.

Italian World War I veterans, who had left Latin America for Europe to fight on Italy's side during the war and returned to Latin America there-after, played a crucial part in setting up local fascist branches, sometimes spontaneously and without previous approval from Italy. In many cases the Italian Fascist Party even withheld official recognition on the grounds that a local branch contained too many unreliable or undesirable members.[12] The fascist regime's intention of merging a broader sense of *italianità* with fascist ideology took time to sink in more deeply as the emigrants' daily dealings with Italian community organizations or diplomatic representatives brought them into closer touch with fascist imagery and ideas. The Italian–Ethiopian war of 1935 marked a highpoint of patriotic identification with the homeland as well as with the fascist regime.[13] Political conjunctures and government attitudes in the respective Latin American host countries either hampered or facilitated fascist efforts at proselytizing as well as antifascist activities. Organizational endeavors of whatever political couleur proved more arduous in rural areas than in urban settings. Historians have argued that the middle and upper social strata of Italian communities in Latin America were more receptive to the fascist message than workers were.[14]

While for all these reasons comparing the "success" of fascism among the Italian communities of various countries is difficult, most indicators suggest that Italians in the Rio de la Plata embraced fascism less enthusiastically than their compatriots in Brazil, let alone in the United States, did. The number of *fasci* that were founded in the early 1920s in the respective countries reflected this: by 1924–25 Brazil counted more than forty such branches, but only eight had been established in Argentina.[15] Whereas Brazil's major Italian newspaper, *Fanfulla* of São Paulo, wholeheartedly embraced fascism, its Argentine equivalent, *La Patria degli italiani*, did not.[16] Similarly, a memorandum about the influence of Italian fascism written by the French Foreign Ministry in 1938, worried about France's waning influence in intellectual circles in Latin America, confirmed this viewpoint, commenting at length on fascist influences in Brazil while noting that in Argentina, "in spite of the numerical importance of the Italian colony . . . we do not think that a very noticeable effort has been made by the fascist groups with a view of influencing the official actions of the Argentine government."[17]

Different approaches to Brazil and Argentina in fact harked back to earlier reports of fascist envoys to South America, which also confirmed the impression that fascism made greater inroads in Brazil than in the Rio de la Plata. In 1927 Amadeo Fani, a delegate of the secretary general of the *fasci all'estero*, Cornelio di Marzio, informed his boss that Argentina's nature as a materialist melting pot, in which social ascent meant everything, entailed that large parts of the Italian Argentine community had irrevocably lost their interest in the homeland and consequently did not identify with the fascist government. In Brazil, by contrast, Fani wrote with some surprise that Italian immigrants and even their descendants felt strongly Italian and that there were many ardent supporters of Mussolini among them. Fani explained that this was the case because Italians in Brazil were less assimilated than in Argentina. Consistent with Corradini's vision, Fani thus correlated assimilation in the host society with a lack of patriotic fervor and, by inference, with distance from the fascist regime.[18] Or, put differently, greater ethnic segregation equaled more nationalism, which equaled more fascism, according to Fani's reasoning.

While differences in the degree of support for the fascist regime seem to have been real enough, the underlying assumptions on the basis of which Fani and others accounted for this difference—namely, the correlation of ethnic segregation in the host society with both nationalism and fascism—merits two comments. First, the conflation of fascism with diasporic nationalism tout court requires qualification. Antifascist groups in the Italian diaspora, after all, also drew on a myriad of symbols of *italianità*. In particular, they sought to mobilize the symbols of the Risorgimento for their political purposes. For example, on the occasion of founding a periodical in Buenos Aires in 1929 with the title *Il Risorgimento*, the recently exiled Italian socialist Francesco Frola, who became a leading antifascist activist in various Latin American countries, explained that "the *risorgimento*, I note as an Italian, cannot be but anti-fascist: for liberty against violence, for justice against arbitrariness, for democracy against dictatorship."[19] Both the fascist regime in Italy and antifascists at home and abroad laid claims to being the rightful heirs of the nineteenth-century national hero Giuseppe Garibaldi.[20] The republican leader Giuseppe Mazzini also served as an emblem for antifascists, of whom many emerged from republican groups that in the nineteenth century had been Mazzinians.[21] Fascists and antifascists alike celebrated September 20, the date on which the Italian army captured Rome in 1870, marking the unification of Italy. The degree of support for fascism, in other words, was not simply a matter of how patriotic the various Italian communities felt but which political group proved more effective in appropriating a series of elements derived from nineteenth-century ideas about Italian national identity.

The second comment concerns the relationship between assimilation in the host society and attachment to fascism. It has been argued for the case of Italians in the United States that identification with the fascist regime indeed had to do with the migrants' low degree of assimilation. Cheering for Mussolini, so this argument holds, was a reaction against discrimination, segregation, and socioeconomic marginalization.[22] The comparison between the Rio de la Plata countries and the United States, where fascism struck a stronger chord among Italians, seems to bolster such an argument: on most of the usually applied yardsticks—such as socioeconomic standing and mobility in relation to the host society, marriage patterns, or residential segregation—Italian immigrants and their descendants appeared to be more "integrated" in Argentina and Uruguay than in the United States.[23] The argument does not work well, however, if one compares Brazil, in particular São Paulo, and the Rio de la Plata. To be sure, as Samuel Baily has shown, there were significant differences between the Italians of Buenos Aires and those of São Paulo in terms of community organizations. Associational life was more developed, organized, and effective among Italians in Buenos Aires than in São Paulo, an observation that speaks against Fani's and Corradini's view that Italians in Argentina lacked a sense of community.[24] But there is little evidence of substantial dissimilarities with regard to the overall socioeconomic standing, marriage patterns, residential integration, or discrimination. The level of ownership of industrial properties around the time of World War I, for instance, was roughly similar for Buenos Aires, Montevideo, and São Paulo.[25] Nonetheless, identification with the fascist regime seems to have been more widespread in São Paulo than in the River Plate.

Explaining Differences

There are several alternatives to the simple formula of "assimilation" in order to explain the greater support for fascism among Brazil's Italians compared to those in the River Plate countries. A first option, which scholars have rarely considered, has to do with the regional origins of migrants within Italy. After all, fascism found more adherents in some Italian regions than in others. As is well known, the proportion of southerners within the respective Italian communities of the Americas was much higher in the United States than in Latin America, where the immigrant stream was more evenly divided between northern Italians, who on average arrived earlier, and those from the Mezzogiorno. Moreover, among the American areas of settlement, São Paulo received a disproportionately high number of families from the Veneto who, after the abolition of slavery in 1888, arrived on subsidized tickets to work on coffee *fazendas*.[26] Variance in regional origins, however, does not serve well as an explanation in and of itself. If anything, by the early twenties Mussolini had more active supporters and voters in the north than in the south, which would make stronger adherence to fascism in the United States difficult to explain. As for Brazil, Veneto did not stand out as a "particularly fascist" region.[27] In a migratory context such as this, an explanation based exclusively on premigratory factors is not convincing.

The contemporary politics in the receiving countries at first glance appear to be a more persuasive explanatory factor. Italian antifascists, for example, often linked up with local socialists and other left-wing groups whose political power must have reflected back on the effectiveness of antifascist networks within the Italian communities and may by extension have hampered the prospects of fascist emissaries to inspire overseas Italians for the new regime in Rome.[28] Socialism had indeed taken deeper roots in Buenos Aires and Uruguay than in Brazil, which might have been a reason for the relative weakness of antifascism in the latter country. The issue could be broadened further. Citing the Brazilian government of Getúlio Vargas of 1930–45 and its anticommunist repression after 1935, Bertonha has even claimed that political culture in Brazil was generally more authoritarian and, hence, akin to Italian fascism than in Uruguay and Argentina. In his view, such affinities between Italian fascism and the political culture and the government in Brazil partially explain the greater resonance of fascism among Italians in that country.[29] Similarly, the aforecited French memorandum opined that, in contrast to Brazil, the reason for the more limited repercussions of fascism in Argentina was "that the great majority of the Argentine people has sincerely democratic sentiments."[30]

The relationship between Italian fascism and national politics in Latin America therefore deserves some closer scrutiny. Vargas' propaganda department signed an agreement of mutual cooperation with the Italians, from whose perspective it was designed to favor and sway public opinion in Brazil in Italy's favor. Brazilian newspapers often received cables from the Italian news agency Stefani, and Brazil was the only country in Latin America where a truly professional Italian radio, supervised by the fascist state, operated. Italian schools in southern Brazil and the Dante Alighieri Society, both designed to spread Italian culture abroad but supervised by the fascist government, served as vehicles for fascist indoctrination and propaganda among both Italian immigrants and native-born Brazilians.[31] Moreover, the extreme right-wing Brazilian Integralist Action (AIB), a party founded by Plínio Salgado in 1932 with generous borrowings from Italian fascist ideology and mobilization practices, operated freely until 1937. Including many first- and second-generation Italians who sympathized with Mussolini, the AIB was cofinanced by the Italian embassy in Rio de Janeiro and liaised with fascist foreign policymakers in Rome.[32] By the mid-thirties at least, in many ways the highpoint of fascist foreign propaganda, Brazil indeed appears to have offered a more hospitable climate for Mussolini's proselytizing.

There are numerous caveats to such a straightforward explanation, however. Even the more specific claim regarding the importance of socialism is problematic. After all, Mussolini himself was a former socialist and, with the exception of Piedmont, fascism initially found greater support in Italy precisely in those regions that also had an important socialist constituency.[33] The formula according to which more socialism equaled less fascism is therefore not especially convincing. Concerning the broader argument about political culture as a whole, there are even weightier problems. It would be difficult, for instance, to accommodate the case of Italians in the United States in such a model. Few historians would be prepared to argue that political culture in the United States was generally more authoritarian and akin to fascism than in Latin America. The political comparison between the three Latin American countries has serious pitfalls too. If we follow the above-cited report by Fani or the number of *fasci* as indicators, differences between Brazil and Argentina predated Vargas' rise to power and the foundation of the *integralistas*. The assertion that Argentina's political culture as a whole was more liberal than Brazil's is debatable too. As Federico Finchelstein has shown, Mussolini's message did find a positive echo among right-wing Argentine *nacionalistas*, whose movements were no less important than that of their Brazilian counterparts, the *integralistas*.[34] The case of Uruguay sits uncomfortably in this scheme. While some scholars have depicted Uruguayan political culture as distinctly liberal and democratic in comparison to Argentina, the right-wing Uruguayan government of Gabriel Terra (1931–38) maintained unusually cordial relations with Mussolini's Italy to the extent that the Italian envoy to Montevideo became something close to a Uruguayan government adviser. At the same time, Uruguay had a particularly active and internationally well-connected scene of antifascist Italian exiles.[35]

At any rate, Italian fascist cooperation with local right-wing nationalist groups such as the *nacionalistas* in Argentina and the *integralistas* proved to be a double-edged sword. As David Aliano has demonstrated for Argentina, Mussolini's geopolitical goals in South America provoked strong reactions and attempts to "nationalize" politics and curb fascist influence.[36] Right-wing nationalist movements in Latin America were torn between the attraction that fascism exerted on them and their rejection of foreign meddling. From the viewpoint of fascist foreign policy, too, cooperation with these movements could thus be a treacherous matter. Until the 1920s at least, as Jeane DeLaney's chapter in this volume reveals for the case of Argentina, these movements showed their nativist anti-immigrant roots, which mitigated their attractiveness from the perspective of both Italian foreign policy and Italian immigrants.[37] In the 1930s *nacionalistas* and *integralistas* gradually shed this nativism and became less elitist and more populist in what amounted to a growing ideological convergence with Italian fascism. These borrowings not only revealed how the rise of rightist nationalism in Europe fed into its Latin American counterparts but also recommended them as potential tools for fascist envoys in their attempts to influence politics in South America. Yet, instead of filling the ranks of local branches of the *fasci*, those descendants of Italian immigrants potentially attracted to fascism now joined these extreme right-wing Latin American movements in increasing numbers. This prompted new worries for Italian envoys in the host countries about the "Brazilianization" or "Argentinization" of "their" diaspora. For example, the Italian ambassador in Rio, Vincenzo Lojacono, reported to Rome in 1937 that he had heard of "specialists within the country [Brazil], some of whom are good Fascists, who speak of Integralism as the tomb of *italianità*."[38]

Similarly, although the Argentine army, in which *nacionalista* ideas spread during the 1930s, included many middle-ranking officers who sympathized with Mussolini's message (most famously the later president Juan Perón), the army was also a formidable vehicle for the social integration and ascent of Italian immigrants.[39] This, too, ran against Italian foreign policy designs of preserving the patriotic fervor of Italy's emigrants in order to draw on them as a bridgehead of fascist influence in the world, of which the Argentine army from another angle appeared to be a promising bridgehead. When Italian diplomats were forced to decide, geopolitical aims usually overrode their concerns about the emigrants losing their *italianità*. Lojacono thus chose to continue his backing of the *integralistas* and even pushed their plans to unseat the Vargas government through a military coup—a plan that backfired because Vargas outlawed the AIB and instituted the infamously authoritarian Estado Novo, which again drew some inspiration from the Italian fascist model.[40] In spite of, or because of, its borrowings from fascism, Vargas' various governments were in fact especially nationalist in their intolerance regarding any expression of ethnic particularity, especially in combination with foreign attempts to influence Brazilian politics. Well before the Estado Novo, Vargas had moved against Italian schools in southern Brazil. As is well known, his government joined World War II in 1942 on the side of the Allies, whereas the military regime of Argentina (1943–45), equally inspired by aspects of Mussolini's corporatism, remained neutral until March 1945, in good part because of its leaders' sympathies with the Axis Powers. For all these reasons, politics or the political culture in Brazil and Argentina cannot wholly account for the greater receptiveness for fascism of Italians in Brazil compared to those in Argentina. In short, even if one were to accept the problematic argument that a more illiberal political climate prevailed in Brazil in contrast to the River Plate countries, it is not clear whether this facilitated or undermined the spread of Italian fascism in Brazil.

This is not to say that origins in Italy and politics in the receiving societies played no role in determining the specific course that Italian diasporic nationalisms were to take in the respective countries. The problem is that isolating factors specific to origin from those relating to the receiving context makes little sense. It is in the history of the connection between places of origin and destination where the most convincing explanations can be found. One argument often mentioned but rarely spelled out in the historiography deserves particular attention here: it has been maintained that the previous resonance of liberal Mazzinian nationalism, greater in the Rio de la Plata and perhaps also southern Brazil than in São Paulo, hindered the later acceptance of fascism in Latin America's Italian communities.[41] The argument sounds odd at first because after all a liberal Risorgimento nationalism existed in Italy, too, without deterring Mussolini's rise to power. It is therefore not so much the emergence of an earlier nonfascist patriotism linked to nineteenth-century liberal republicanism that mattered per se; what mattered were the specific ways in which it related to the organizational development of community life and, crucially, to political elites in the host countries. Attention to these questions shifts emphasis away from the assumption that there was "more" or "less" diasporic nationalism among Italian communities of different countries, pointing instead to the importance of competing interpretations of Italianness. The argument ultimately accords greater importance to the issue of timing of the migratory process and, with this, generational matters, which proved pivotal.

Risorgimento Nationalism in the Rio de la Plata

In order to understand differences between Argentina, Uruguay, and Brazil in this respect, the long-term history of Italian migration to Latin America has to be considered in some more detail. Although statistical data relating to immigration in nineteenth-century Latin America are notoriously unreliable, sketchy, and problematic to compare, it is clear that Italian migration to the River Plate began much earlier than to Brazil, where it really took off on a larger scale only from the late 1880s (see figures 9.3, 9.4, and 9.5). This difference appears to be even greater if one bears in mind the size of the existing population by the mid-nineteenth century, which of course was much greater in Brazil than in Argentina, let alone Uruguay. In Uruguay, the proportion of Italians among the population as a whole was particularly large already by the middle of the nineteenth century, so scholars have spoken of "a case of precocious migration."[42] As early as the late eighteenth century there had been a significant migration of Ligurian traders to the Rio de la Plata, in particular via Cádiz. During the decades following Argentine independence these pioneers were joined by growing contingents from northwestern Italy, including political exiles of the Piedmontese insurrection of 1821.[43]

As Maurizio Isabella has shown for the case of Mexico, exiled Risorgimento activists were intimately involved in state- and nation-building attempts in Spanish America, not least because their undertakings at home had been so bound up with events in Spain in the first place.[44] In the Rio de la Plata, a close relationship between local political elites and Italian exiles

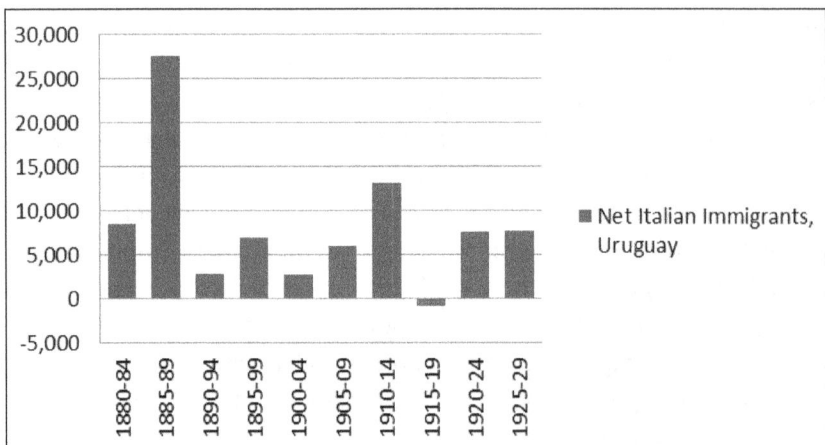

Figure 9.3. Chart depicting net number of Italian immigrants to Uruguay, 1880–1929.

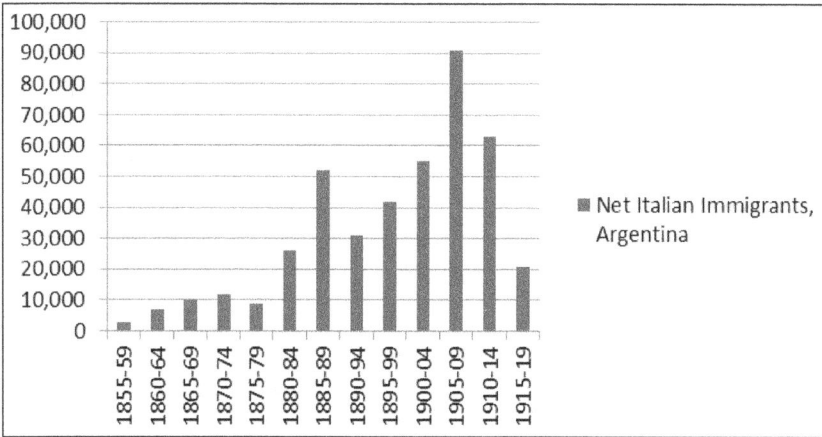

Figure 9.4. Chart depicting net number of Italian immigrants to Argentina, 1855–1919.

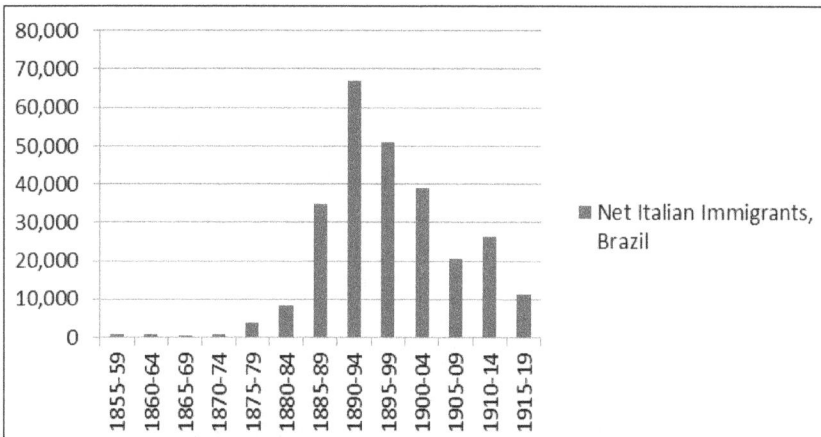

Figure 9.5. Chart depicting net number of Italian immigrants to Brazil, 1855–1919.

developed. Even though his roots do not seem to have played a central role for him, one of Argentina's founding fathers and foremost national heroes, Manuel Belgrano, was the son of a Ligurian merchant. The so-called Generation of 1837, from which the leading Argentine statesmen-writers during the period of "national organization" after 1852 hailed, borrowed heavily from the ideas of Giuseppe Mazzini and the Giovine Italia in general.[45] The most important mediator in this ideological exchange was the Ligurian Giovanni Battista Cuneo, who had left Italy after the failed uprising in Genoa in 1837 and then helped organize some of the leading Argentine intellectuals in Montevideo, where they were exiled during the dictatorship of Buenos Aires' governor Juan Manuel de Rosas. Even the arguably xenophobic Rosas himself could count on a prominent Risorgimento exile as a panegyrist, Pedro de Angelis.[46]

The most famous of these exiles was Garibaldi himself, whose extended stay in South America earned him the nickname "hero of two worlds" and, through the iconic gaucho attire he sported during his later military exploits in Italy, fed back into Italian popular culture. After being sentenced to death in Genoa, he set sail for Rio de Janeiro in 1835 but soon became entangled in the political and military strife that at the time was endemic in southern Brazil and the River Plate region. He first fought on the side of Rio Grande do Sul's republican *farrapos* against Brazil's imperial government in Rio de Janeiro and from 1842 joined the liberal *colorados* in Uruguay's civil war of 1839–51. With his Brazilian wife and remnants of Uruguay's "Italian legion," he returned to Italy in 1848, where he put the military expertise he had acquired in South America at the service of Italian unification. While Garibaldi unsurprisingly became a central national symbol for Italians in Latin America, memories of his adventures additionally lived on in local political traditions. In southern Brazil, republican regionalists often invoked Garibaldi as a hero, whereas in Uruguay he was frequently hailed by the *colorados*, who became the dominant political faction in the early twentieth century.[47]

Since Italian communities in the River Plate region reached a critical mass much earlier than they did in most of Brazil, ethnic associations flourished earlier too. Given their customary interests in the politics of the homeland, many such institutions were steeped in the liberal brand of unification nationalism espoused by figures such as Mazzini or Garibaldi. The most famous case is that of Buenos Aires' mutual-aid society Unione e Benevolenza, founded in 1858, whose success in bridging divisions between Italians of different regional origins in Italy even preceded the unification of Italy itself. As Samuel Baily and Andrea Scarli have underlined, the early development of such community organizations was crucial in bestowing a sense of identity on both settled migrants and, more importantly, new arrivals.[48] Arguably, the point could be made even more forcefully for Montevideo. In 1885, for instance, the director of Montevideo's Italian school wrote: "The Italian colony of Montevideo is perhaps, among all those of the Americas, the one that has most social clubs in relation to its size."[49] Due to the size and richness of the Italian immigrants' organizational life, the boundary between migrant community institutions and state-building efforts in Argentina and Uruguay became blurred. Mutual-aid societies or Italian hospitals, for example, were crucial in the general development of a public health sector. Around the turn of the century Argentina's most important Italian newspaper, *La Patria degli Italiani*, was the country's third-largest daily in terms of sold copies, and its editor-in-chief, Basilio Cittadini, was simultaneously vice president of the Argentine press association.[50] In short, Argentina's and Uruguay's Italian communities developed ethnic institutions at an early stage and in conjunction with the nation-building efforts of those countries' elites, with whom they held close ties during much of the nineteenth century.

This cordial relationship, to be sure, was challenged from the late nineteenth century onward, especially in Argentina, owing to a combination of factors. Parallel to the growing ethnicization of national identity in Europe, growing parts of Argentina's native elite turned away from the preceding liberal nation-building model and began to valorize authentic criollo cultural customs. As Lilia Ana Bertoni has observed, the Italian community, widely associated politically with the ideas of the Generation of 1837, was often singled out as a target in the arguments of the emergent cultural nationalists.[51] Even former advocates of immigration, such as Domingo Sarmiento, began to criticize the "Italianization" of Argentina as immigration reached a truly massive scale from the 1880s onward.[52] With a greater proportion of Italians now coming from the impoverished Mezzogiorno, even in Uruguay Italians, especially if they came from the south, began to suffer from prejudice.[53] Over time anti-immigrant attitudes were coupled with anxieties about working-class activism, leading to the Argentine law of residency that eased the expulsion of foreigners in 1902. In his 1909 book *La restauración nacionalista*, Argentine cultural nationalist Ricardo Rojas—discussed in some detail by Jeane DeLaney in this volume—complained about the existence of prominent statues of Mazzini and Garibaldi in central Buenos Aires. Garibaldi at best stood for a specific political tradition in the River Plate, Rojas argued, whereas Mazzini "as a thinker does not reach universal proportions. Our nationality does not owe this man anything," he concluded.[54] The same nativist elites, meanwhile, revalued the Spanish heritage and language as an element of national identity fanned by the Spanish–American war of 1898 and a rising anti-imperialism across Latin America, which pitted Anglo-Saxon "materialism" against Hispanic "spirituality." In Argentina this reconsideration culminated in the institutionalization of the pan-Hispanic festivity of the Día de la raza (October 12, when Columbus landed in the Americas) as a national holiday in 1917.[55]

However, as Rojas' musings on Garibaldi reveal, the rejection of Italian republican influences was targeted as much against Argentina's nineteenth-century political traditions associated with the Generation of 1837 as it was against liberal Italian nationalism. The problem, rather, was the extent to which the two strands had become merged in the eyes of posterior cultural nationalists in Argentina. Rojas' principal complaint was about "*our* cosmopolitan culture," which had led to prioritizing statues of Garibaldi and Mazzini in prominent places over those of homegrown national heroes. On other occasions Rojas highlighted Garibaldi's military skills and likened them to those of the native gauchos, who at the time were transformed into a prime marker of Argentine national identity.[56] The overriding point when comparing the River Plate countries to Brazil, therefore, is the lasting link between Mazzinian traditions and nation-building elites in mid-nineteenth century Argentina and Uruguay. As late as 1932, for instance, both Italian antifascists in Buenos Aires and the local press likened Garibaldi's political achievements to those of Argentina's liberator, José de San Martín.[57] That the drawing of such parallels was possible was the result of the early establishment of a sizeable Italian community with powerful organizations that developed in convergence with the politics of the host country and hence led to intimate political ties between Italian exiles and local political elites.

Longue-durée Paths

For several reasons, this was much less true for Italians in Brazil. First, the timing and nature of Italian immigration, especially in the principal area of settlement (São Paulo), was different. There were, quite simply, far fewer Italians in the region before 1890 than there were in the Rio de la Plata. When they arrived in larger numbers, most were initially poor Venetian families settling in the countryside with little access to Brazilian institutions. Such circumstances hindered the development of the kind of ties between an immigrant elite and the politics of the host country that had developed in Argentina and Uruguay. Second, the principal areas of settlement of Italians in Brazil, again in contrast to Argentina and Uruguay, were geographically removed from the center of national political power. Although the Brazilian capital, Rio de Janeiro, did have an Italian community, this was not nearly as important as that of Buenos Aires or Montevideo. Hence, if community leaders could establish close contacts with political elites in the host country, these ties were usually regional, not national. Third, even if the possibility of links with the national political elite had existed, Brazil's imperial decision makers would most probably have shown themselves far less enthusiastic about republican ideas, whether from Italy or elsewhere, than the political leaders of Spanish American countries. The endemic military troubles and the political fragmentation of nineteenth-century Spanish America arguably made politics in those countries more permeable for outsiders to begin with when compared to the elitist stability of imperial Brazil.

Such an overarching comparison between three national cases masks important variations within Brazil. Because, in contrast to immigration in Uruguay and Argentina, immigration in Brazil was primarily a regional, not a national, affair (and was perceived as such by contemporary observers), immigration as a marker of identity or as a fountainhead of political traditions was assimilated in differing ways by the political elites of different provinces (or states after 1889). Though not specifically related to Italians and their diaspora nationalism, *paulista* regionalists drew on their state's history of European immigration in order to distinguish a supposedly "white" São Paulo from the "dark" rest of the country.[58] The more pertinent example, however, is that of Rio Grande do Sul. In many respects, the area's social, economic, political, and cultural history as well as that of its Italian immigrants was more similar to that of the River Plate countries than to the rest of Brazil. It has even been argued that Rio de Grande do Sul should be considered historically as a part of a common "Platine" region.[59] Italian settlement in Rio Grande began much earlier, was more spontaneous than that of the initially state-sponsored immigration in São Paulo, and included a significant number of Risorgimento exiles. As Garibaldi's involvement with the *farrapos* testifies, Rio Grande do Sul's Italians, similarly to those of Uruguay, also became engaged in local politics. There emerged a lasting discursive link between Italian diaspora patriotism and gaucho (Riograndense) regionalism, as can be derived from the names of towns and hamlets in the "Italian zone" north of Porto Alegre, such as Farroupilha, Bento Gonçalves, or Garibaldi.

As one would expect on the basis of this argument, fascism indeed found fewer followers among the Italians of Rio Grande than it did in São Paulo, notwithstanding the common idealization of Rio Grande do Sul's immigrant enclaves as pristine rural repositories of authentic *italianità*—a trope similarly found in German nationalist literature by the turn of the century.[60] In part this difference can be attributed to the overwhelmingly rural character of Italian settlement in southern Brazil, which complicated organizational efforts of any kind. The parallel with Argentina and Uruguay, however, suggests that another factor also played a decisive role. Similarly to the River Plate countries, yet in contrast to São Paulo, the development of an organized Italian community with a crucial contingent of liberal professionals and political exiles had from early on allowed for a close overlap of local politics with that of the Italian diaspora. An early conflation of Italian national symbols with local ones made it subsequently more difficult for Italian fascism to construe an aggressive version of *italianità* in marked contradistinction to local identities.

The timing of the migratory process, in other words, appears to be the most crucial variable in explaining different trajectories of Italian diaspora nationalism and different receptions of fascism in the Americas. There is ultimately also a demographic component to this argument. Italians in Argentina and Uruguay, but also in Rio Grande do Sul, were older on average than those of São Paulo. Moreover, Argentina's and Uruguay's "Italian" communities naturally contained a much larger contingent of locally born people of Italian—and more often partial Italian—ancestry than in Brazil. Unsurprisingly, Italian-born younger generations were more likely to have direct ties with the politics of their home country as well as contact with consulates and other institutions of the Italian fascist state. As Robert Newton has observed for the case of Argentina, enthusiastic supporters of the fascist cause were disproportionately found among the younger cohorts of the Italian community.[61] Too often forgotten by the scholarship, this generational issue applied to Italy itself, where fascism was more warmly received among younger people than among the elderly.[62] The generational makeup of overseas Italian communities thus likely had an impact on their reception of fascism.

Conclusion

Contrary to the view of contemporary fascist observers, the prospects for the success of fascism among Italians in Latin America could not simply be reduced to the question of whether respective communities were more or less "assimilated" and whether they espoused more or less patriotic attachment to their homeland as a consequence. Nor could the reasons for the varying fate of diasporic nationalisms among Italians in Latin America be found unilaterally in either Italy or Latin America. Rather, it was the history of the transnational connection itself that shaped the experience of several generations of migrants and their relationship to both homeland and host country. These histories differed among the three cases examined in this chapter. As Fernando Devoto has put it in a catchy phrase, "everything in

Argentina seems Italian, but at the same time it is difficult to single out what really is [Italian]."[63] The statement could certainly be extended to Uruguay, and perhaps also to Rio Grande do Sul, but much less to the rest of Brazil. There was, in other words, not simply "more nationalism" and "less assimilation" among the "living agents" in the spread of nationalism and their descendants in one country than in another. Instead the political history of Italian immigrants in Latin America took varying paths over time stemming from the history of transatlantic ties between Europe and Latin America. There were different types of diasporic nationalisms, some of them competing, in different places and at different times. Just as Italians in Latin America were not a homogenous group, neither was their nationalism.

Notes

1. Corradini, *La patria lontana*.

2. Einaudi, *Un principe mercante*. For a similar juxtaposition between Corradini and Einaudi, see Choate, *Emigrant Nation*, 49–53 and 159–68; and Pagano, "From Diaspora to Empire."

3. Conrad, *Globalisierung und Nation*, 229–78.

4. Ermarth, "Hyphenation and Hyper-Americanization."

5. Franzina, *Gli italiani*, 15.

6. A concise global overview is de Caprariis, "'Fascism for Export'?" The most re-searched case has been that of the United States: Diggins, *Mussolini and Fascism*; Cannistraro, *Blackshirts in Little Italy*; and Luconi, *La "diplomazia parallela."* On Latin America, see Scarzanella, *Fascistas en América del sur*; and Bertonha, *O fascismo e os imigrantes*. On Paris, see Milza, "Le fascisme italien." On Australia, see Cresciani, *Italians in Australia*, 73–97. On Canada, see Principe, *Darkest Side*. On Tunisia, see Bessis, *La Méditerranée fasciste*.

7. Bertonha, "Italiani nel mondo anglofono," 24.

8. Bertonha, "Fascismo, antifascismo."

9. Cannistraro and Rosoli, "Fascist Emigration Policy" provides a concise overview.

10. "Memorandum confidentiel sur l'activité du fascisme . . . ," n.d. [1938], 8, Centre des Archives Diplomatiques (CAD), 6CPCOM39.

11. A useful overview is Mugnaini, *L'America Latina e Mussolini*.

12. Gentile, *Struggle for Modernity*, 145–60.

13. Bertonha, "A 'Foreign Legion'?"; Rodríguez Ayçaguer, *Un pequeño lugar*, 279–85; and Scarzanella, "Cuando la patria llama." A similar assessment about the slow inroads and the peak of fascism in "Memorandum . . . ," n.d. [1938], 1–2 and 12, CAD, 6CPCOM39.

14. From a Marxist perspective, this argument has been made especially for Rio Grande do Sul: Giron, *As sombras do littorio*. A critical discussion can be found in Bertonha, *O fascismo e os imigrantes*, 220–23, who nonetheless maintains this overall argument. A more nuanced discussion for Argentina is Newton, "Ducini, Prominenti, Antifascisti."

15. Caprariis, "'Fascism for Export'?," 158. More generally, see Trento, "I fasci in Brasile";

and Zanatta, "I fasci in Argentina negli anni trenta." As usual, information on Uruguay is hard to come by.

16. Trento, "L'identità dell'emigrato italiano"; and Bertagna, *La stampa italiana*, 9–10 and 57–60.

17. "Memorandum . . . ," n.d. [1938], 31, CAD, 6CPCOM39.

18. Sanfilippo, "Il fascismo"; and Sergi, "Fascismo e antifascismo."

19. Quoted in Bertagna, *La stampa italiana*, 56.

20. Fogu, "'To Make History'"; Bresciano, "El antifascismo," 96 and 103; and Cattarulla, "Orgoglio italiano."

21. Contu, "L'antifascismo italiano," 458.

22. A useful overview is Pretelli, "La risposta del fascismo."

23. Klein, "Integration"; Baily, *Immigrants*; and Goebel, "*Gauchos, Gringos* and *Gallegos*."

24. Baily, *Immigrants*, 228–31.

25. Alvim, *Brava gente!*, 141–42; Goebel, "*Gauchos, Gringos* and *Gallegos*," 216–21; and Beyhaut et al., "Los inmigrantes en el sistema ocupacional argentino." Rates of ethnic endogamy were remarkably low among Italians in Brazil: see Klein, "Social and Economic Integration," 325.

26. Holloway, "Creating the Reserve Army?"

27. Petersen, "Elettorato e base sociale," 644.

28. See, e.g., Cane, "'Unity for the Defense of Culture.'"

29. Bertonha, "Fascismo, antifascismo," 123.

30. "Memorandum . . . ," n.d. [1938], 1–2 and 12, CAD, 6CPCOM39.

31. Ibid., 2–3, 9, and 25–28.

32. On its membership, see Seitenfus, "Ideology and Diplomacy"; Bertonha, "Between Sigma and Fascio"; and Zega, "'Italiani alta la testa!,'" 88.

33. Petersen, "Elettorato e base sociale," 645.

34. Finchelstein, *Transatlantic Fascism*; and Deutsch, *Las Derechas*. The French "Memorandum . . . ," n.d. [1938], 29–30, CAD, 6CPCOM39, singled out the Legión Cívica Argentina, the Legión de Mayo, and the Asociación Nacionalista Argentina as the three Argentine groups closely cooperating with the Italian embassy.

35. Aldrighi, "Luigi Fabbri en Uruguay." On Terra and fascism, see Marocco, *Sull'altra sponda del Plata*, 89–125; and Oddone, "Serafino Mazzolini." See also "Memorandum . . . ," n.d. [1938], 28, CAD, 6CPCOM39. For a comparison of political culture in Argentina and Uruguay, see Spektorowski, "Nationalism and Democratic Construction."

36. Aliano, *Mussolini's National Project in Argentina*.

37. Deutsch, *Las Derechas*, 41–44 and 99–112.

38. Quoted in Seitenfus, "Ideology and Diplomacy," 521.

39. Nascimbene, "Assimilation of Italians."

40. Seitenfus, "Ideology and Diplomacy," 521–34.

41. From a global perspective, see Gabaccia and Ottanelli, *Italian Workers*, 1–20; and Franzina, *Gli italiani*, 369–71. On Latin America, see Bertonha, "O antifascismo," 23; Fanesi, "Italian Antifascism and the Garibaldine Tradition."

42. Devoto, "Un caso di migrazione precoce."

43. Devoto, *Historia de los italianos*, 48–54. On the influence of early Ligurian traders, see Brilli, "La diaspora commerciale."

44. Isabella, *Risorgimento in Exile*, 32–64.

45. Gallo, "Esteban Echeverría's Critique"; Myers, "Giuseppe Mazzini"; and Marani, *El ideario mazziniano*.

46. On Cuneo and de Angelis, see, generally, Scheidt, *Carbonários*.

47. Examples are Collor, *Garibaldi e a guerra*; and Pereda, *Garibaldi en el Uruguay*.

48. Baily and Scarli, "Las sociedades de ayuda mutua."

49. Bordoni, *Montevideo*, 163.

50. Baily, "Role of Two Newspapers," 327 and 329.

51. Bertoni, *Patriotas*.

52. Sarmiento, *Conflicto y armonía*.

53. Oddone, *Una perspectiva europea*, 83.

54. Rojas, *La restauración nacionalista*, 455.

55. On Argentine elite attitudes to Spanish and Italian immigrants in comparison, see, generally, Moya, *Cousins and Strangers*, 332–84.

56. Rojas, *Eurindia*, 214 and 216; Rojas, *Historia de la literatura Argentina*, 406.

57. Fanesi, "Italian Antifascism," 168.

58. Weinstein, "Racializing Regional Difference."

59. See, e.g., Jochims Reichel and Gutfreind, *As raízes históricas*.

60. Bertonha, *O fascismo e os imigrantes*, 218–26.

61. Newton, "Ducini, Prominenti, Antifascisti," 44–45.

62. See Wanrooij, "The Rise and Fall"; and Linz, "Some Notes toward a Comparative Study," 81.

63. Devoto, "Italiani in Argentina," 4.

10

"The Summit of Civilization"

Nationalisms among the Arabic-Speaking Colonies in Latin America

STEVEN HYLAND JR.

Arabic-speaking migrants from the eastern Mediterranean and residing in the Americas played a critical role in the formation, evolution, and diffusion of nationalist ideologies and national identities to their home societies during the first half of the twentieth century. The creation of layered identities and the formulation of ideas about the destiny of the old country was a contested process, producing dissolution and refashioning of the larger community and inspiring the creation of parochial institutions—all of which hardened lines of division within the émigré colonies. There were three critical geopolitical issues directly affecting this group of diverse people, namely, the 1908 Young Turk Revolution, the Ottoman Empire's entry into World War I on the side of the Central Powers, and the emergence and decline of the French and British mandates in Syria, Lebanon, and Palestine following the collapse of the Ottoman state. For the majority of these migrants living in the Americas, the question of the French in Syria and Lebanon was by far the most divisive and consequential concern for the community. The mandate provoked the continued and decisive fragmentation of the Arabic-speaking colonies across the Americas as lines of association were redrawn, complete with the promulgation of new institutions, emergence of new press organs, and the birth of new national identities. Migration and transnational processes, notwithstanding local considerations, forced these people to reformulate how they viewed themselves, the immigrant community to which they belonged, and how best to present it to the host society. At the collective level, local memory was constantly contested, readjusted, and rewritten based upon the contingencies of life and goals of various actors. Certainly, these immigrants were critical to the formation of modern national identities in Argentina, Brazil, and elsewhere in Latin America; however, this essay focuses on the formation and evolution of political identities linked to the old country. As such, to fully understand the long-distance nationalism of these migrants, scholars must assess the social relations among and makeup of Arabic-speaking immigrants to fully appreciate how distant political transformations influenced émigré communities and gave rise to national identities.

This essay highlights some of the key actions and expressions of various nationalist sentiments among Arabic-speaking populations in the Americas. Given the fact that a substantial portion of immigrants from the eastern Mediterranean likely did not associate with immigrant institutions, this discussion focuses on the colonies' intellectual and socioeconomic elites.[1] That said, it is likely that most immigrants would have shared in one or more of the sentiments and ideas circulating in the colonies' Arabic-language newspapers.[2] The essay uses signifiers such as "Syrian," "Lebanese," and "Palestinian" but situates the terms in their historical context. It is clear from the historical evidence that these typologies were never neutral signifiers but were contested spaces designed to create boundaries of inclusion and exclusion.

What's in a Name? Ottomans, Syrians, Lebanese, Syrian-Lebanese, Palestinians, and Arabs

The establishment of modern nation-states and, thus, hegemonic national identities in the Middle East happened in the context of massive emigration, imperial collapse, global war, European imperialism, and decolonization during yet another global war. As such, the states of Lebanon and Syria and territories populated by Palestinians, including present-day Israel, experienced severe political transformations directly affecting the urgencies of nation building, the creation, appropriation and refashioning of national symbols, and the self-identification of these polities. Immigrants from these lands residing in the Americas contributed material aid, clashed in ideologically charged debates regarding the destiny of their homelands, and helped formulate national identities of these newly formed states. At the same time, situations on the ground and the makeup of the community and its elite in the Americas also influenced a particular colony's approach to these national questions. Taken together, there was no single response to these national questions by immigrants across the continents and, importantly, religious identity did not predict necessarily one's political allegiance.

A majority of sojourners from Bilad al-Sham (present-day Syria, Lebanon, and Israel/Palestine) who lived abroad between 1880 and 1950 arrived before World War I carrying Ottoman documents. These travelers formed a part of the mass movement of people moving to the Americas. Many of the pioneer generation—those who arrived in the Americas prior to 1900—possessed better skills, had access to capital and information, and were overwhelmingly Christian. Most of these migrants elected commerce as the best way to achieve financial betterment, creating an intercontinental phenomenon of the Arab itinerant peddler.[3] As emigration became a more widespread phenomenon after 1900, the composition of the flow changed as poorer and less educated migrants moved, including many more Muslims.

Yet scholars rarely have produced thoughtful discussion about how these migrants possessed a number of competing loyalties and layered identities or why certain allegiances became more or less prominent over time. For many of these people, the terms "Syrian," "Lebanese," "Palestinian," and "Arab" metamorphosed in significance multiple times over the course of a couple of decades. Local issues, such as host society values, legal regimes, economic participation, stereotypes, and prejudices, influenced identity formation. Politics of the homeland and institution building by the migrants themselves did too. The creation of immigrant and national identities was a contested process having as much to do with the old country as with local, internal deliberations within these émigré colonies.

Authors have increasingly focused on the ethnicity of these migrants to better assess how these immigrants viewed and presented themselves privately and publicly, but this scholarship too has suffered from a disposition that there was something essential, an a priori element to a Lebanese, Syrian, or Palestinian identity. Yet focusing on ethnicization—the creation of an ethnic identity in relation to a perceived outside group—has been a critical contribution to the study of Arabic-speaking migrants in the Americas.[4] As Akram Khater has elegantly argued, Syrians became Syrians in the Americas, but this identity was constructed in direct relation with fellow immigrants elsewhere, in dialogue with intellectuals based in Beirut, Cairo, and Damascus and with the host society's social and moral values in mind.[5] Community institutions, particularly the press, served as the critical catalyst to this collective identity formation. Charting the development of these community institutions can assess the expression of competing, emergent, and novel identities and how they change over time.[6]

Ethnicity fundamentally refers to relationships and contacts between groups of people.[7] For ethnicity to materialize, groups of people must have a "minimum amount of contact" between each other and think about "ideas of each other as being culturally different from themselves."[8] It is, therefore, a feature of a relationship and not an innate or primordial quality of a certain group of people. Ethnic groups rely on cultural and historical artifacts to help create boundaries with those deemed different. People use symbols that evoke a certain meaning with which many from the group identify, fostering a perceived authentic and shared cultural heritage.[9] Hence, the construction in the Americas of Arab, Lebanese, Palestinian, and Syrian identities were sensitive to multiple forces, ideologies, and processes.

In the United States, for instance, immigrants did not possess equal economic rights as citizens. Residents there could lease property, but they could not purchase real estate unless they had at least applied for citizenship. Syrian immigrants debated among themselves the value of taking U.S. citizenship. After evaluating, an increasing number of Syrians pursued this option and thus had to prove before a court in places like New York and Atlanta their descent from the Caucasian race, as stipulated by the law. The urgency of creating a racial classification in the first decade of the twentieth century provoked a heated transnational debate among Arabic speakers, including such prominent intellectuals as Jurji Zaydan in Cairo and Muhammad Kurd Ali in Damascus, regarding the importance of defining a racialized identity.[10] This issue was simply not a concern for Syrian immigrants in Argentina, who had equal economic and civil rights as Argentines whether or not they naturalized. More broadly, the process of ethnicization of Arabic speakers would become increasingly associated with nationalist movements. Nationalism, the politicization of ethnic identity, shaped culture because "ethnic, linguistic, and racial differences, *hitherto politically inconsequential*, [acquired] an ideological force and institutional weight."[11] The idea of national culture had an integrative potential where in many cases elites embraced a shared identity and past with non-elites for the first time. Yet when nationalists appropriated symbols and attached a nationalist discourse to them, their meanings changed, necessarily including some and excluding others.[12]

For the Arabic-speaking communities in the Americas, the cultural and social elites of these immigrants spearheaded the formation of a hegemonic immigrant identity through the erection of community institutions and periodicals. Within the community and in the Arabic-language press published in the Americas prior to the collapse of the Ottoman Empire, the community referred to themselves as "*jāliyya suriyya*" and "*jāliyya 'uthmāniyya*" ("Syrian colony" and "Ottoman colony," respectively). In Spanish, they used "*colonia siria*," "*colectividad siria*," and "*colectividad sirio-otomana*." Latin American officials alternated between "*colonia siria*," "*turcos*," "*árabes*," and "*sirios*." Argentine officials standardized the use of Ottoman for their political identity in 1914, and Brazilian administrators did not start counting Syrians and Lebanese as separate recognized political identities until 1921.[13] This hegemonic immigrant identity went through a variety of transformations during World War I and later throughout the French and British colonial moment in Lebanon, Palestine, and Syria. After the collapse of the Ottoman state, immigrants in Latin America began to refer to themselves as Lebanese, Palestinians, Syrians, and Syrian-Lebanese. Which terms were used depended upon local consideration of the particular immigrant communities.

While there is a certain necessity and convenience in using these typologies, simply dividing these people into Syrians and Lebanese and Palestinians has obscured the alterations of the meanings of these terms wrought by intense political transformations in the old country and the corresponding debates and urgencies within the Arabic-speaking colonies in the Americas. Moreover, these terms, as used by most scholars of these communities, essentialize these identities into seemingly self-evident axioms, conflating nationality with ethnicity and obscuring internal dynamics and diversity.[14] And despite the current tendency to see ethnicity as "indissolubly linked to nationalism and race, to ideas about normative political systems and relations, and to ideas about descent and blood," scholars of immigrants and minorities must appreciate the fluidity and amorphous nature of cultural symbols and discourses and how internal and external processes transformed them.[15]

The Ottoman Empire and the Syrian Colonies in the Americas

The role of the Ottoman state and its émigré communities in the lives and destiny of each other is remarkably understudied. Part of this problem stems from a general acceptance on the part of scholars to propagate or accept certain myths about the emigrants. The Syrian colonies throughout the Americas forged a saga of fleeing religious persecution from their Ottoman Muslim overlords.[16] The truth is less dramatic. Changes in the regional economy of Bilad al-Sham created an environment where an increasing number of Syrians, who benefited from increased access to education and information, sought adventure, economic relief, and vast riches by moving into the *mahjar* (land of emigration). As the local economies expanded and greater wealth circulated even among peasants of Mount Lebanon, the Ansariya Mountains and the Valley of the Christians, a cultural shift placed emigration as an acceptable life choice and recognized social practice. While emigration from Ottoman domains was technically illegal until 1900, state officials and diplomats could do little to stem the tide.[17]

Once in the *mahjar*, relations among the migrants and with the Ottoman state were complex, featuring a variety of issues, demands, fears, and expectations. As early as 1890 Syrian immigrants in Buenos Aires began requesting the Ottoman state to establish formal diplomatic relations with Argentina.[18] Brazil and the United States had forged agreements earlier in the nineteenth century. Outside of these formal channels, immigrants certainly kept in touch with family and friends by using the standardized international mail service, remitting between 20 million and 35 million French francs back to the old country via wire transfer and subscribing to periodicals and journals published in Cairo, Beirut, Jerusalem, New York City, Rio de Janeiro, and Buenos Aires.[19] The Young Turk Revolution (July 24, 1908) and the Ottoman entrance into World War I on the side of the Central Powers (August 2, 1914) were two historical events in the old country that proved consequential to immigrants abroad. These incidents intersected with local issues confronting immigrants in the Americas, such as naturalization.[20] For a great number of Arabic speakers abroad, the political destiny of the old country prompted a great deal of anxiety, distress, mobilization, and confrontation.

In broad terms, Syrian immigrants in the Americas desired to remain a part of the Ottoman Empire prior to World War I.[21] In response to a New York–based Arabic-language newspaper support in 1904 for naturalization, Naʿum Labaki, a Christian from Mount Lebanon based in São Paulo, argued in his paper *al-Munāẓir* that Syrians must "remain loyal to Ottomanism and committed to Syrian patriotism [*wataniyya*] so they can return to Syria."[22] The expressed opinions were as diverse as the composition of immigrants, and in spite of "antagonistic attitudes on the part of certain groups of politically motivated intellectuals," the Arabic-speaking communities in the Americas possessed "close and friendly contact" with Istanbul.[23] Hence, it was not contradictory for Palestinians in Chile to establish the Sociedad Otomana de Beneficencia in 1904 or Maronites from Mount Lebanon in Tucumán to organize the Sociedad Turco-Argentina in 1898.[24]

When the Young Turks seized power in July 1908 and reinstated constitutional rule, the Syrian émigré colonies embraced them. People across the hemisphere held celebrations commemorating the heroes of the revolution and the shared commitment to reform within the empire. In Buenos Aires, the colony organized an event at the posh theatre house Casa Suiza featuring a performing ensemble of young girls, Ottoman flags, Chinese lanterns, a portrait of Midhat Paşa (author of the Ottoman Constitution) and a rendition of Argentine and Ottoman anthems.[25] In New York, the Young Turks, the Armenian Revolutionary Federation, and the Hunchakist Society hosted a raucous celebration at Carnegie Hall comprising "Turks, Armenians, Syrians, Albanians and even some former Greek subjects of the Sultan."[26] Under banners written in Armenian, Turkish, and French declaring "Hurrah for the Young Turks," "Hurrah for the Armenian Revolutionary Federation," and "Liberty, Equality and Fraternity," Ottoman Chargé d'Affaires Munji Bey noted the mutual suffering of the Sublime Porte's subjects under the despot Sultan ʿAbd al-Ḥamīd and called for a common purpose, declaring, "But we must be friends and brothers now. We must respect justice. If we use this force which God has given us we shall be strong and we will fight for liberty without blood."[27] In November 1912 Tanus Shahin Abi Dagher, writing as "an Ottoman from Mount Lebanon" and supposedly on behalf of the three thousand Syrians in Venezuela, dispatched a letter to the Grand Vizier Kamil Paşa declaring the ability to muster twenty thousand émigrés in Latin America to return and battle the Balkan separatists and defend the "Great Ottoman state."[28] In Brazil, Nami Jafet, a former schoolteacher in Mount Lebanon, the most respected Syrian intellectual in South America and likely the wealthiest immigrant too, offered public and full-fledged support for the Ottoman Constitution and the Young Turk government on the fourth anniversary of the revolution, concluding with a rousing "Long live the Constitution! Long live the Ottoman homeland!"[29]

Notions of liberty and constitutional rule served as the critical elements for the celebrations in Argentina, Brazil, and the United States. Despite the proscribed nature of democratic practices in these countries, the perception of liberty, the opportunity to purchase property and pursue economic betterment combined to influence how Arabic speakers understood their place in local society and how they interpreted the events in the old country. Arabic-speaking émigrés attempted to identify with their host countries through the liberal discourse of guaranteed individual rights and national leaders responded in kind. For instance, Syrians in Buenos Aires celebrated the empire's entrance into the pantheon of free nations, while the distinguished Socialist legislator for the capital, Alfredo Palacios, dispatched a letter reminding local Syrians that one must fight for liberty. Nami Jafet persistently cited Brazil as a "land of freedom and equality, the country of democracy." At the event in Carnegie Hall, U.S. assistant secretary of the treasury James B. Reynolds read a letter from President Theodore Roosevelt pronouncing that all men who believe in liberal government should take great interest in the events taking place in the Ottoman Empire. Congressman Herbert Parsons spoke on behalf of "young America" in congratulating the restoration of the constitution and welcoming the "newer torch bearers of liberty."[30]

The excitement of revolution collided with the inertia of institutional change. As the Young Turks, in the form of the Committee on Union Progress, implemented a series of policies perceived to be pro-Turkish, many politically active Syrians began pondering what the particular arrangement should be within the larger imperial superstructure, initiating an intercontinental debate.[31] On the whole, Syrian communities in the Americas supported greater autonomy (expressed as "administrative decentralization") and equality of representation within the Ottoman bureaucracy. This was best exemplified by Syrian émigrés' participation in and support of the First Arab Congress, held in Paris, France, in June 1913. The month before the meeting, the Cairo-based Ottoman Administrative Decentralization Party sent letters to editors of Arabic-language periodicals in the Americas requesting opinions regarding the pace and depth of reform.[32] As the congress convened, delegates from New York and a Paris-based envoy for the Syrian colonies in Mexico attended. At the event's conclusion, the participants produced eleven resolutions and three appendices to be delivered to the Ottoman ambassador stationed in Paris. The most important ones focused on the guarantee of political rights, Arabic as an official state language, improved representation in the Ottoman bureaucracy, and greater local rule via administrative decentralization. These declarations inspired Syrian colonies as far afield as Waynoka, Oklahoma, and Rio de Janeiro to wire congratulatory telegrams to Paris.[33] Yet as it became clear in October 1913 that the Ottoman state would not implement these reforms, communities in Brazil and the United States, as part of a coordinated strategy with activists in Europe, the empire and Egypt, sent telegrams to Istanbul demanding implementation.[34] Despite this increased agitation for greater autonomy and reform within the empire, broad swathes of Syrians abroad continued to celebrate the constitution and the Ottoman state on the eve of global war.[35]

The Ottoman Empire's entrance into World War I as part of the Central Powers provoked great consternation on part of many in the various Syrian colonies and inspired critics of the regime's stalled reforms and advocates of independence to intensify their claims and demands. Indeed, the calls for Lebanese and Armenian independence reached critical mass and led to direct, and at times violent, altercations within the colonies in São Paulo and Buenos Aires. During the war the Syrian communities moved toward a definitive break between the Ottoman state and Greater Syria while simultaneously formulating new and at times confused ethnic and racialized identities: Lebanese, Syrian, and Arab. At the same time, new questions emerged orbiting around whether Mount Lebanon formed a part of an independent Syrian state and whether France should serve as a guarantor and mentor in the transition to independence. In an effort to secure support for French designs in the Levant, the Paris-based and French-funded Syrian Central Committee dispatched Dr. Cesar Lakah and Jamil Mardam Bey to Latin America to raise money and volunteers for the Légion d'Orient, a fighting force folded within the French military. The committee envisioned this group comprised of Syrian volunteers helping to fight for the independence of Lebanon and Syria. This Lakah-Mardam mission met varying success depending on which community they visited.[36]

In Argentina, after an initial push of support for the Ottoman war effort, those who were politically committed divided along three axes: pro-Independent Lebanon, independent Syria including Lebanon under the aegis of France, and the establishment of an Arab-led Islamic empire with Husayn, the sharīf of Mecca, as its head. Disagreements between these compatriots became so heated that violence manifested multiple times, provoking the expulsion of Ottoman sympathizers (diminished though never extinguished during the war) from the Barrio Turco, located in the downtown Socorro district radiating out from Tres Sargentos Street, as well as the murder of a Syrian Armenian at the hands of a Syrian Muslim in the La Boca neighborhood.[37] While most of the intellectuals advocating French policy in the Levant were Maronites, early on it was not solely them. Alejandro Schamún, a Maronite Catholic writing January 21, 1919, in *La Nación*, argued that Syria included Lebanon and needed French support, while the Lebanese Union in Buenos Aires, a largely Maronite organization, demanded a Lebanon free from European influence. Emir Emin Arslan, a Druze from Mount Lebanon and former Ottoman consul general in Buenos Aires, publicly supported the goals of the Syrian Central Committee, including in an open letter to President Woodrow Wilson.[38] In Brazil leading members of the colony also struggled to find common ground and consensus. As the war progressed the Lebanese Renaissance Society, which was established in 1912, dedicated itself to the independence of Mount Lebanon. In Rio de Janeiro, émigrés established the Syrian-Lebanese Patriotic Society with Nami Jafet as its president. This organization advocated the independence of Syria (including Lebanon) under the aegis of the French, and contributed men and money to the Syrian Central Committee, which raised volunteers for the French Legion d'Orient.[39] Yet friction between activists in Brazil boiled over into homicide, as Ilyas Masarra, a journalist for the pro-French Arabic-language periodical *al-Brazīl*, murdered Salim Labaki, editor of a rival, pro-Ottoman journal.[40] In the United States, the Lebanon League of Progress, led by Naoum Mokarzel, advocated for Lebanese independence. His group clashed with the Syria-Mount Lebanon League of Liberation, which included important intellectuals such as Kahlil Gibran, Ameen Rihani, and Mikha'il Na'ima. This group called for the independence of Syria and Lebanon but did not speculate or advocate on how the arrangement between the two entities should be manifest.[41]

The end of World War I produced a brief moment of Syrian self-rule. In June 1919 the Syrian National Congress convened, composed of delegates from the former Ottoman administrative districts of Syria, Beirut, Aleppo, Mount Lebanon, and Jerusalem. The congress pronounced Faisal al-Hashemi, son of the sharīf of Mecca, king of the Syrian Arab Kingdom on March 8, 1920.[42] This constitutional monarchy lasted just four months but produced divisions among the émigrés in the Americas. For instance, the Lebanon-Syria Commission in Montevideo telegrammed French prime minister Alexandre Millerand to protest the "pretensions" of Faisal and reaffirmed their request of Lebanon and Syria's independence with France as guarantor.[43] Groups in Argentina and Paraguay dispatched similar cablegrams. At the same time, Dr. George Sawaya, prominent physician and intellectual, articulated clearly to the French embassy that the destiny of an Arab kingdom lay in the hands of the Allied powers. Following the fall of Faisal in the summer of 1920, Sawaya's newly founded Arab Patriotic Party organized meetings and sent telegrams to local diplomatic missions and the League of Nations condemning France and Britain.[44]

The French and British Mandates and the Lebanese and Syrian Colonies

The Early Mandate

The beginning of the new decade witnessed the collapse and partition of the Ottoman Empire and fall of King Faisal in Damascus and the granting by the League of Nations to France of a mandate over Syria and Lebanon. For Arab nationalists, the short-lived monarchy of Faisal I in Damascus was the realization of their dreams and political activities. France's forceful deposing of Faisal in July 1920 and the subsequent creation of the State of Greater Lebanon, which would become the French-dependent Republic of Lebanon in 1926, were critical events for Lebanese nationalists. For advocates of a Greater Syria, many viewed the mandate with great anticipation. In the midst of the maelstrom of competing nationalisms, some intellectuals moved to form groups advocating cultural politics. For instance, young intellectuals established the Shabība Mutahīda (United Youth) in San Miguel de Tucumán, Argentina, on June 4, 1921. This group held public events, published a newspaper, staged plays, and used the printing press to further its mission of fashioning an Arab fellowship. In January 1922 the organization launched the monthly literary review *al-Hadiqa* (the garden). In the opening editorial, the directors declared that the surge of competing views expressed in the Arabic press in the Americas on politics and national destinies resulted from poor national education. The editors announced they would use novels to help foster love for the nation, avoid divisive politics, and move Arabic speakers along the path "to reach the summit of civilization."[45]

Yet this vision of a cultural pan-Arabism for the colonies proved futile. A group of activists in Buenos Aires united and formed the Syrian-Lebanese Committee, featuring the leading intellectuals and some of the colony's wealthier members. These men began organizing a public event scheduled for July 1922 designed to remonstrate France's imposition of colonial rule. The scheduled demonstration caused grave concern for supporters of French rule, in particular the Maronite priests resident in Buenos Aires. The superior of the Lebanese missionaries, the order of Maronite priests, convinced the French minister in Argentina to meet with the Buenos Aires chief of police, municipal leaders, and the undersecretary of state at the offices of the Argentine foreign ministry. The diplomat requested state intervention to prevent the demonstration from taking place; however, the

Argentines refused to intercede. Some 250 people took to the streets in protest of France's presence in the Levant. In the aftermath, Gen. Henri Gouraud, the high commissioner of the French Republic in Syria and Lebanon, sent a letter to the Argentine president requesting his help in managing the efforts of "a fanatical party of the Lebanese-Syrian colony in Argentina" that had been spreading lies about the mandatory powers. The communication seemingly carried great weight. After the reception of this letter, Argentine officials collaborated with their French counterparts to quiet the dissidents and prevent public criticism of France.[46] The actions of the Argentine government in support of the French demonstrated that anti-imperialism equated with anti-American sentiment.

Similar to Argentina, Syrian and Lebanese émigrés in Brazil advocated a variety of positions and ethnonational identities through the creation of new institutions, the Arabic press, and the occasional public demonstration. France's decision to create Greater Lebanon heartened pro-French Lebanese in São Paulo and Rio de Janeiro and provoked others. Khalil Saadeh, now resident in Brazil, used his newspaper, al-Jarīda, as the mouthpiece of his new National Democratic Party (Hizb al-Dīmuqrātī al-Watanī), an organization that demanded full independence of Lebanon, Palestine, and Syria under the leadership of locals and the move toward true secular, democratic governance. These aims compared with Asad Bishara's Syrian National Party (Hizb al-Watanī al-Surī). Yet a strong pro-French current was channeled through the Lebanese Renaissance Party (al-Nahda al-Lubnānī) and the periodicals al-Brazīl, al-Qalam al-Hadīd, and Fatāt Lubnān.[47] The creation of Greater Lebanon also inspired some immigrant institutions in Latin America to transform themselves to fit new realities and identities. For instance, the Sociedad Sirio-Libanesa in Durazno, Uruguay, changed its name to the Comité Patriótico Libanés.[48]

The Great Syrian Revolt (1925–1927)

The news of the rebellion in Jebel Druze and Damascus in August 1925, known as the Great Syrian Revolt, provoked a variety of opinions and actions by Syrians and Lebanese in the Americas. In Argentina, the press related French actions as "particularly odious and barbaric," thus intensifying opposition toward the French Mandate and prompting a public relations campaign across Argentina. Even the pro-mandate institutions began to see support for France among their membership dissolve. The communities in Rosario and Mendoza raised money for the victims of the Damascus shelling. The colony in Mendoza held a large protest demonstration during which Syrian and Lebanese merchants shuttered their shops and conducted a procession of mourning complete with black flags. The French worked assiduously with Argentine officials to prevent similar events. At the same time, the French Chargé d'Affaires partnered with the president of the Club Libanés in Mendoza to publish a note declaring that the public protest did not have the support of the majority of Mendoza's Lebanese. A whisper campaign ensued suggesting there was an assassination attempt on the French consul.[49]

In Buenos Aires intellectuals mobilized with great purpose, organizing street demonstrations, demanding—via telegrams to the League of Nations—that France quit its mandate, and pursuing the support of Argentina's representative to the League's Office of Intellectual Cooperation. The Círculo de Damas Siro-Argentinas invited Syrians and Lebanese to the Casa Suiza on November 8, 1925, for a wake mourning the lost lives in the outbreak of violence. The ladies stressed this was an apolitical event. Emir Emin Arslan led the anti-mandate charge with a series of articles in *La Nación*, including a confession of his previous error in supporting the French presence in Syria and Lebanon. Habib Estéfano, former Maronite priest and partisan and official for King Faisal's short rein in Damascus, gave public conferences in the most important venues in Buenos Aires and elsewhere in Argentina; even President Marcelo T. de Alvear attended an event. French diplomats asked Argentine officials to intervene and secured a promise from the Argentine press to refrain from printing the articles of Arslan and the speeches of Estéfano. The French, fearing a public relations debacle, even asked the consul in Mendoza to seek state help in muzzling Estéfano in that Andean province.[50]

Yet certain Lebanese and Syrians in Argentina continued to support the French, especially the Maronite priests. Pro-mandate groups dispatched letters of support to the League of Nations and raised ten thousand francs for the communities afflicted by the violence. In October 1926 Estéfano gave a public lecture in Tucumán's prestigious Sarmiento Society excoriating the French mandate in Syria and Lebanon. Naguib Bacclini, a noted Lebanese intellectual in the province, published an editorial in his newspaper *Sada al-Sharq* (Echo of the east) berating Estéfano as "a renegade Ex-Maronite priest" who suffered from a "Bedouin mentality." Bacclini then argued that France was the right partner for Lebanon as it was the paladin of culture and democratic governance.[51]

The criticism of the French for the repression and shelling of Damascus seemingly was more muted elsewhere in the Americas. Pro-French organizations in Uruguay never wavered in their support. In January 1926 the Liga Patriótica Libanesa in Montevideo circulated a statement declaring that the rebels "came to rob, steal and persecute the Christians." The Liga then sent a telegram to the League of Nations condemning the foreign campaign against "dear" France and demanding the continuation of the mandate in Syria and Lebanon. The Club Libanés, which historically kept some distance from the French legation, split. A group dispatched a telegram in the name of the organization to the League of Nations criticizing French actions, provoking another group to declare anew their organization's attachment to France. In Paraguay, after two members from the Unión Líbano-Siria in Concepción failed to establish a separate organization protesting the bombing of Damascus, the Buenos Aires–based Antiochian Greek Orthodox bishop Ignatius Aburrus, during a trip to visit his flock, used the pulpit to express the "loyalty to France" by all Syrians and Lebanese in attendance, regardless of confessional identity.[52]

The large Syrian and Lebanese communities in Brazil split over how to respond to the October bombing of Damascus by the French, during which more than one thousand civilians perished. Khalil Saadeh sent a cablegram to the League of Nations condemning France's "cruel behavior." Rashid Atiyeh, publisher of the pro-French *Fatat Lubnan*, organized a meeting of the colonies' leading members to advocate for open condemnation of the French. Consensus was elusive as several members desired to focus on the crime—not the mandate itself—and push humanitarian efforts. The Antiochian Greek Orthodox communities in Brazil raised and dispatched sixty thousand French francs to their patriarch in Damascus, an activity mirrored by several other Syrian and Lebanese organizations there.[53]

Lebanese and Syrian émigré colonies in the United States also raised large sums of money to aid the bombing victims of the French. The community there also divided over how to respond to the violence. Some individuals, speaking in the name of all Syrians and Lebanese in the United States, wired telegrams to the League of Nations to protest France. These actions provoked the American-Syrian Federation, the "representative organization of the Syrians in the United States, [with] affiliated organizations throughout the country," to clarify that no such protest by the institution or its constituents had been lodged. Naoum Mokarzel, president of the Lebanon League of Progress, went so far as to say that the rebellion against the French was simply cover for "murdering the native Christians" and razing and pillaging Christian villages and towns. Hence, the French departure was tantamount to an existential threat for Levantine Christians.[54] This declaration provoked a response from fellow Christian Habib Katibah, a New York-based member of the Palestine National League and the Syrian National Society, to point out that the "leaders of the Syrian Nationalist movement" had agreed to the Maronite demand that the French remain in Greater Lebanon provided that they quit the rest of Syria. The French, for Katibah, used the protection of the Christian populations as a pretext for its "lusty colonial ambitions."[55] Yet, as the violence continued unabated into the next year, the Syrian Convention, another body said to represent Syrian-Americans and Syrians in the United States, met in Detroit and formally asked for help from the U.S. government to "give Syria her rights as befits her culture, her capacity and her aspirations."[56]

Of the nations with large numbers of Levantine immigrants, Argentina stands out as possessing the most vocal critics of the French presence in Lebanon and Syria. Two primary factors may account for this characteristic. First, the Arabic-speaking colonies in Argentina numbered 160,000 by 1928, with more than half coming from Syria. This compares to the overwhelming majority of Lebanese Christians in Brazil and Uruguay and Palestinians in Chile. Second, the presence of Emir Emin Arslan and brothers Wadi and Alejandro Schamún likely played a critical role. Each came from a prominent family from Mount Lebanon, had close relatives active in anti-French politics in the homeland, and possessed great respect from both the Syrian-Lebanese colonies in Argentina and Argentine government officials. Arslan and the Schamúns each published their own periodicals that demanded self-determination of their homelands. Finally, Muslims accounted for one-third of the immigrant population from the Levant. This vibrant community was especially active in the industrial city of Rosario and Buenos Aires, and it enacted a variety of strategies to challenge French rule and support political and educational initiatives in the old country.

The High Era of the Mandate

Despite the stalling of the Great Syrian Revolt in 1927, an active campaign against the mandate persisted in Syria and the Americas, especially after the French dissolved the Syrian assembly following an impasse relating to specific articles for inclusion in a Syrian Constitution. This placed the French, in the eyes of its critics, as an imperialist power. The Unión Libanesa continued its demand for complete independence and its criticism of the French. Estéfano perdured, lecturing throughout Argentina and, in the eyes of French diplomats, spreading "his harmful venom." Yet there was apparently a noticeable waning of support among some actors and the Argentine public due to the schisms plaguing the executive committee of the Syrian-Palestinian Congress based in Cairo and the revolutionaries in Transjordan and Syria.[57] Even some Maronite priests, hearty supporters of the mandate, expressed occasional disagreement with French policy in Lebanon and Syria.[58]

At the end of the 1920s several Syrian revolutionaries emigrated to South America, in particular to Argentina. Upon their arrival they sought the support of Emir Emin Arslan, George Sawaya, and Habib Estéfano. Arslan, who was disillusioned at this point with the events in Syria and the politics that the Damascene Muslims had toward the Druze, rejected the overtures for financial support by Assad al-Bakri, nephew of the prominent Syrian nationalist Nasib al-Bakri. Further, Sawaya and Arslan asserted that al-Bakri did not leave Syria to work on behalf of the revolution but rather to *hacer la América*. With this rumor circulating, the fundraising for al-Bakri stopped and only Estéfano contributed to the drive. With these meager funds, al-Bakri moved on to visit the Syrian and Lebanese colonies in Chile.[59] But efforts on behalf of the revolution continued in Argentina. In April 1932 the editor of the Buenos Aires Arabic-language weekly *al-Watan* (The homeland) published a letter from the leader of the Syrian Revolutionary Forces, Sultan Paşa al-Atrash, acknowledging receipt of the most recent remittance of funds and thanking the "generous almsgiving" (*al-muhsin al-karīm*) from the Arabic-speaking colonies in Argentina. He urged these people to continue giving material aid and emotional support against the "politics of colonialism" (*siyāsat al-istʿamār*), a call many immigrants heeded.[60] The same edition contained a letter from Yusef al-ʿIssa, a Palestinian Christian based in Amman who was part of the Arab nationalist intelligentsia. Al-ʿIssa emphasized the continued struggle of the freedom fighters (*mujāhidīn*) against the French, proudly announcing that various Syrian political parties had met in Egypt and had agreed to unify in common cause in support of the fighters.[61]

The resistance benefited from an organized transnational network that exchanged letters and moral support, collected and transferred money to pay for the fight against European colonialism, and debated the future of the homeland. Suleiman Najm al-Bikfāni, a fundraiser for the Syrian revolutionaries, was in constant communication with the leaders of the resistance, including Sultan al-Atrash and leading Arab nationalist figures in South America. In Argentina al-Bikfāni traveled to large cities and small towns where Arabic-speaking immigrants worked and lived, collecting donations for the resistance. In addition to securing funds for remittance, al-Bikfāni, who self-identified as a "volunteer freedom fighter," also published the names of the donors and the amounts they gave.

Nevertheless, a firmer sense of a Lebanese national identity among those in Argentina continued to develop at the expense of a collective Syrian or Arab fellowship and with consequences at the institutional level. For instance, activists designed the Centro Libanés in Tucumán specifically as a political association catering to immigrants from Lebanon and the morphing sense of identification with a Lebanese nation. The controversy surrounding this group spread throughout the Syrian and Lebanese colonies in Argentina in early 1931. In explaining the reason for establishing this institution, the members of the Lebanese Center rejected the notion that Syrians and Lebanese were united by "indissoluble bonds" as a "false conventionality." Furthermore, the founders proclaimed "the children of two distinct states [Syria and Lebanon] could never work jointly in good of the interests of their homeland."[62] In Santiago, Chile, the Club Sirio and Centro Libanés emerged in 1934, spurring a massive wave of institution building within the colonies there.[63]

Nineteen-thirty-six was a critical year for Syria, Lebanon, Palestine, and their émigrés in the Americas. The rise of Lebanese president Émile Eddé in January 1936, his partial restoration of the constitution, and his push for parliamentary elections led pro-mandate and anti-mandate Lebanese to close ranks under the banner of an independent Lebanon. This year also witnessed the completion and ratification of the French-Lebanese Treaty (November 13); a protocol of agreement for the French-Syrian Treaty (September 9); the creation of the Phalanges Libanaises by Maronite Pierre Gemayel; the establishment of the Syrian Popular Party by Antun Saadeh, an ardent Syrian nationalist from a Christian Lebanese family who lived for years in Argentina and Brazil; and the claim over Antakya by Turkey. The Syrian Congress enthusiastically ratified the French-Syrian Treaty on December 27, but the French parliament refused, creating another political impasse.[64]

These events were seminal in galvanizing immigrants from Lebanon in Argentina behind the push for independence while at the same time proved decisive in hardening the final split between Syrian and Lebanese émigrés. In August 1936 Maronite priest Miguel Latuf Inderi invited Lebanese of all faiths to an event at the Colegio San Marón in the Retiro neighborhood in downtown Buenos Aires to unite all behind the idea of protecting the independence and integrity of Greater Lebanon. On August 28 a Lebanese delegation led by Domingo Kairuz (president of the Unión Libanesa),

Nami Fares, and the Maronite superior presented a letter to the French ambassador for the French government requesting that the mandatory powers ensure the territorial integrity of Lebanon and support the efforts of Lebanese President Eddé and the Maronite patriarch. These activities inspired the creation of the Asociación Patriótica Libanesa on October 18, 1936, its headquarters at the Colegio San Marón. The organization brought together old supporters of the French in Lebanon and some of the anti-mandate Lebanese. Rachid Rustom, a delegate of the *asociación*, arrived in Tucumán and established a branch office the following August, which was rebranded Asociación Libanesa de Socorros Mutuos in 1938. The Tucumán-based organization's leadership included prominent merchants and public intellectuals who embraced the goal of an independent Lebanon free from French control.[65] At this point, the internal split of the Syrian-Lebanese colony in Tucumán and beyond was complete; the product of national identities hardened in the crucible of European colonialism. The idea of a Lebanon folded within a nation with Syria was now a nonstarter.

It was in this context that the Syrian Social Nationalist Party (SSNP) leader Antun Saadeh arrived in Argentina in 1939. To a hero's welcome, Saadeh relocated to Tucumán in 1939 at the invitation of Yubran Massuh, a local Syrian intellectual. The colony's wealthiest merchants and youth leaders met him at the train station, and later held a huge party in his honor at the home of Camel Auad, a prominent wholesaler. At this event, local members of the Syrian-Lebanese colony organized a political party committed to the independence of Syria.[66] Antun Saadeh advocated a Syrian nationalism. For this movement, the past and future Syria included contemporary Syria, Lebanon, Jordan, historical Palestine, the Sinai Peninsula, and the island of Cyprus. These lands possessed natural borders and an assortment of people that over time formed one nation. As a result, Saadeh and his disciples eschewed Arab nationalism, asserting that it was "a surrender of Syria's uniqueness, and an acceptance by its gifted people of an inferior status." This emphasis on a Syrian national identity attracted many "among the educated urban population" in Syria and Lebanon.[67]

As Saadeh settled into his new environs, Yubran Massuh escorted and introduced Saadeh to the various Syrian-Lebanese colonies in Argentina, and soon the two established a periodical, *al-Zawbaʻa* (The cyclone) with Massuh as editor and chief propagandist. It was in Tucumán that Antun Saadeh set out to mobilize the immigrant colonies and create branches of the SSNP across Latin America. He initially encountered strong support from a broad cross-section of these communities in the Americas. Active groups emerged in Argentina, Chile, and Mexico, who published articles in *al-Zawba'a* and produced their own local publications. In Tucumán, Saadeh's arrival inspired intense action at the cultural level as immigrants formed theatrical troupes, organized meetings, and produced plays and poetry about the homeland. A strong SSNP branch in Mexico published a periodical in Spanish, and the young Aniceto Schain, the son of an immigrant from Homs, Syria, living in Santiago, Chile, became a regular contributor to *al-Zawba'a*.[68] The Syrian nationalist cause also featured a dispersed set of financial supporters. For instance, Syrian-Lebanese merchants located on the island of Fernando Pó, Spanish Guinea, raised and wired eleven thousand Spanish pesetas (two hundred British pounds sterling).[69] These transnational connections were simply a continuation of a long-held practice by Arabic-speaking immigrants in the Americas, who used communication and transportation technologies to maintain contact, carry on debates, share news, and remit money to support revolutionary movements and assist relatives in the old country.

Yet this early surge in support encountered heavy resistance from many established immigrants who were advocating an independent Lebanon, thus stoking controversy over who spoke for the community. For Saadeh and his adherents, a Syrian identity surmounted all other identities, and divisions along confessional lines were viewed as an impediment to the nationalist project. While others within the Syrian-Lebanese colony also viewed the tragedy of religious divisions and its impact on the community, Saadeh venomously attacked all competitors and enemies, real and perceived.[70] The most infamous case involved a six-month, thirty-six-part rhetorical assault on the dean of Arabic-language poets in the Americas, Rashīd al-Khuri, also known as al-Shā'ir al-Qarawī (Village Poet), who was based in São Paulo. The feud aired for so long that prominent Arab intellectuals residing in New York intervened on behalf of al-Qarawī.[71] This pugilistic attitude toward some of the most esteemed members of the Syrian and Lebanese lettered class abroad and the criticism directed at the supporters and fans of these poets surely undercut support for Saadeh. Shortly after the series concluded, the SSNP in Mexico published two older articles desperately showing that even the most famous Lebanese in the Americas supported a unified Syria.[72] As Saadeh's perceived influence waned, funding for *al-Zawba'a* must have suffered either from cancelled subscriptions or weak fundraising, or both, because by late 1944 the editors began publishing infrequently. For their part, the French never considered Saadeh or his movement in Argentina to be much of a threat.[73]

Meanwhile, Arab nationalists residing in the Americas met in Buenos Aires in early 1941 to discuss the status of the homeland. Emir Emin Arslan served as president of the First Pan-Arab Congress in America (al-Muʿtamar al-ʾArabī al-awwal fī Amīrikā), announcing Shakib Arslan, Emin's cousin, as the official representative before governments and international bodies. The participants included Sunni Muslims and Christians, such as the Zaki and Elias Qonsol, brothers from Nabk, Syria. The attendees agreed on and published a set of principles, the second declaring Syria consisted of "Lebanon, Palestine, and East Jordan," and together this territory made up the Arab land (*quṭr ʿarabī*). The subsequent principle rejected the legitimacy of the French and British Mandates and denied a Jewish national home (*al-waṭan al-qawmī al-sahyūnī*) in "Southern Syria (Palestine)."[74]

Nevertheless, for both Saadeh and the delegates of the pan-Arab Congress, the goal of a united Syria on the scale imagined was simply an unattainable dream. The majority of Syrians and Lebanese in Argentina stayed away from the pan-Arab and pan-Syrian advocates and propagandists. In addition, the treaties signed by France and the political figures in Lebanon and Syria provided a clear path to the end of mandatory rule and eventual independence. As a result, most émigrés in Latin America moved their support to these initiatives, despite the fact that implementation was years in the offing.

Conclusion

The independence of Syria (1946) and Lebanon (1943) signaled the end of a long pursuit for self-determination and struggle against French colonialism by people in the Levant and their compatriots abroad. Yet the establishment of the new nation-states still had consequences in the Americas. For instance, independence provoked problems in relations between émigrés now from distinct countries. It also created strife in many of the mutual aid societies, cultural associations, and other clubs in Brazil founded in an era where the dominant immigrant identity was Syrian as partisans initiated legal proceedings to break apart institutions established in this era.[75] Actions such as these helped mark the conclusion of nationalist activities by Lebanese and Syrians trying to create barriers of distinction or programs of inclusion. The reality was that Lebanese and Syrians were now politically distinct peoples with separate national governments with which to identify. The course of the first half of the twentieth century witnessed a

variety of nationalist sentiments and ideologies emerge. As political transformation and economic collapse, war and famine, colonialism and revolution gripped the old country, Lebanese and Syrians articulated, debated,
and grasped at ideologies and arrangements they thought would best serve
their homelands. These competing nationalisms added layers to these immigrant identities that on many occasions resulted in internecine violence
and sparked contested claims over who spoke in the name of the community. In many cases homeland politics was as much about the local composition of the immigrant colony as it was about securing independence.
At the same time, the advocates of these novel national identities were in
continual contact with their peers, competitors, and family who remained
in the Levant. These émigré communities marshaled resources, mustered
volunteers and combatants, wired letter after letter to the League of Nations and international politicians advocating various positions regarding
the Levant, and communicated with officials from the host society. Indeed,
Arabic-speaking émigrés were critical in the formation of Lebanese and
Syrian national identities and nationalist ideologies, both in the old country and abroad. Appreciation of these processes and changes allow for a
more subtle understanding of immigrant lives and the evolution of community life amid profound political transformation during the first half of
the twentieth century.

Notes

1. Jeffrey Lesser and Raanan Rein make this point regarding Jewish populations in
Latin America, challenging scholars to study "unaffiliated ethnics" too (see also chapter
5 of this volume). I eschew the challenge in this particular essay but certainly recognize
the importance of incorporating immigrants who did not associate with the community
or its institutions in studies. See Lesser and Rein, "New Approaches to Ethnicity," 31–32.

2. Abdeluahed Akmir asserts that the Arabic press in Argentina reflected "faithfully
the life, aspirations and values of the Arab community." Akmir, "La prensa árabe en Argentina," 294.

3. For North America, see Khater, *Inventing Home*, 74–75; for Mexico, consult Alfaro-
Velcamp, *So Far from Allah*, 29–30; for Brazil, review Lesser, *Negotiating National Identity*,
50–51; and for Nicaragua, see González, *Dollar, Dove, and Eagle*, 70–71, 81–82.

4. The concept of ethnicization has been a staple of studies on immigrant communities in the United States; however, little of the scholarship examines how these groups
fashioned identities in relation with those in the homeland. See, for instance, Conzen et
al., "Invention of Ethnicity."

5. See Gualtieri, *Between Arab and White*, 81–112; Khater, *Inventing Home*, 71–107; and
Khater, "Becoming 'Syrian.'"

6. For North America, see Khater "Becoming 'Syrian,'" 302; and Gualtieri, *Between Arab and White*.

7. For recent reviews of the concept and scholarship, see Eriksen, *Ethnicity and Nationalism*; and Banks, *Ethnicity*.

8. Eriksen, *Ethnicity and Nationalism*, 12.

9. Certainly, ethnic identities are lived identities; however, the ascription of ethnicity by observers cannot be overlooked. The individual or group constructs ethnicity and boundaries as much as the observer does. Banks, *Ethnicity*, 190.

10. Gualtieri, *Between Arab and White*, 65–73.

11. Jusdanis, *Necessary Nation*, 19.

12. Eriksen, *Ethnicity and Nationalism*, 98–103; and Jusdanis, *Necessary Nation*, 39–43.

13. See República Argentina, *Tercer Censo*, vol. 2; and *Boletim do Departamento Estadual do Trabalho* 16, no. 58, first trimester of 1927.

14. For examples of this tendency, see Valverde, "Integration and Identity in Argentina"; Klich and Lesser, *Arab and Jewish Immigrants*; and Khatlab, *Mahjar*.

15. Banks, *Ethnicity*, 189.

16. Khater, "Becoming 'Syrian,'" 303–4.

17. Khater, *Inventing Home*, 52–55.

18. "Arribo del Cónsul Otomano," *La Nación* (Buenos Aires), October 30, 1910.

19. Archivo, Biblioteca y Museo de la Diplomacia (ABMD), Box 1210, Folder 42, Arturo de Luciano to Argentina's Minister of Foreign Affairs Victoriano de la Plaza, November 22, 1910; and Ruppin, *Syrien als Wirtschaftsgebiet*, 24–25.

20. Naturalization for Syrian émigrés in the United States was more important than it was for the colonies in Latin America. Immigrants in Argentina, for instance, had equal economic rights as citizens whereas foreign nationals were prohibited by federal law from purchasing real estate in the United States. Hence, there was greater incentive to naturalize in North America, and a correspondingly larger percentage of Syrians pursued U.S. citizenship than elsewhere in the Americas. See Gualtieri, *Between Arab and White*, 52–80.

21. Prior to the pioneering works of Akram Khater and Sarah Gualtieri, most scholars subscribed to the notion that Syrian émigrés departed the Levant primarily due to Ottoman oppression, a rhetorical device deployed by emigrants themselves. This trope also colored the scholarship on Ottoman state and Arab society relations in Syria, Lebanon, and Palestine in the late Ottoman period, which Hasan Kayalı convincingly dispels. See Khater, *Inventing Home*, 48–70; Gualtieri, *Between Arab and White*, 21–51; and Kayalı, *Arabs and Young Turks*, 17–143.

22. Quoted in Gualtieri, *Between Arab and White*, 86.

23. Karpat, "Ottoman Emigration," 193.

24. Olguín Tenorio and Peña González, *La inmigración árabe*, 122; and "Solicitada," *El Orden* (San Miguel de Tucumán), June 10, 1898.

25. "La constitución otomana," *La Nación* (Buenos Aires), September 9, 1908.

26. The Armenian Revolutionary Federation (ARF) and the Hunchakist Society were Marxist-influenced movements established by Armenians from the Russian Empire in the late nineteenth century that advocated for the independence of Armenians in the Ottoman Empire. In the lead-up to the Young Turk Revolution, ARF partnered with the Committee on Union and Progress—the civil-military secret society that led the coup

against the Sultan—until 1913 in the Second Constitutional era (1908-18). Four ARF and two Hunchakist members won election to the Ottoman parliament in 1908. See Davison, "Armenian Crisis"; and Nalbandian, *Armenian Revolutionary Movement*, 30–131, 151–78. In New York the elements of the Hunchakist Society apparently operated as a mafia outfit led by the Armenian archbishop, extorting and assassinating members of the Armenian colony in the city. See "Evolution of the Armenian Hunchakist," *New York Times*, August 4, 1907.

27. "Roosevelt Hails Freedom in Turkey," *New York Times*, September 7, 1908.

28. The Balkan Wars of 1912 and 1913 were led by and then fought between the Balkan League, composed of Bulgaria, Serbia, Greece, and Montenegro, which sought independence and to wrest additional lands, such as Macedonia, from the Ottomans. Hall, *Balkan Wars*; and Necati Kutlu, "Ottoman Subjects," 242–44.

29. Jafet, *Ensaios e Discursos*, 233–47; for Jafet's business concerns, consult Dean, *Industrialization of São Paulo*, 31–32, 113; and Tofik Karam, *Another Arabesque*, 25–29.

30. "La constitución otomana," *La Nación* (Buenos Aires), September 9, 1908; a facsimile of Palacios' July 1909 note to Schamún is found in Akmir, "La inmigración árabe," 820; and Jafet, *Ensaios e Discursos*.

31. Hasan Kayalı criticizes the Turkification trope prevalent in the scholarship as overplayed. See Kayalı, *Arabs and Young Turks*, 82–96.

32. See the letter to Alejandro Schamún, editor of the Buenos Aires-based *al-Salam* newspaper, dated May 6, 1913, from the Ottoman Administrative Decentralization Party. Akmir, "La inmigración árabe," 795–96.

33. Tauber, *Emergence of the Arab Movements*, 178–97; and Ḥizb al-Lā-Markazīyah bi-Miṣr, *al-Mu'tamar al-'Arabī al-Awwal*, 185–86, 207–10.

34. Tauber, *Emergence of the Arab Movements*, 204–5.

35. See, for instance, the massive banquet in São Paulo held on the sixth anniversary of the Young Turk Revolution featuring the elite of the Syrian colony, the local director of the London Bank, and the Ottoman consul, Emir Sami Arslan. "Constituição Ottomana," *O Estado de São Paulo*, July 24, 1914.

36. See "O Banquete a Colónia Siria a Dois Membros do Grande Comite Syrio de Paris," *O Estado de São Paulo*, August 20, 1917; and Tauber, *Arab Movements in World War I*, 212–14.

37. Ikmīr, *al-'Arab*, 142–43.

38. Klich, "Argentine–Ottoman Relations," 177–205; and Brégain, *Syriens et Libanais*, 149.

39. "O Brasil na Guerra," *O Estado de São Paulo*, December 4, 1917; and Tauber, *Arab Movements in World War I*, 214.

40. Logroño Narbona, "Development of Nationalist Identities," 67–69.

41. Tauber, *Arab Movements in World War I*, 226–27; E. G. Tabet, "The French in Syria," *New York Times*, May 4, 1919; and Logroño Narbona, "Development of Nationalist Identities," 102–3.

42. Matthews, *Confronting an Empire*, 24–25.

43. "A Independencia do Libano," *O Estado de São Paulo*, March 19, 1920. See also the telegrams to Millerand from various Arabic-speaking colonies in the Americas that

challenged Faisal's claim; located in Archives Diplomatiques La Courneuve, Série E, Box 44, Folder 313.

44. Brégain, *Syriens et Libanais*, 148–50; and Logroño Narbona, "Development of Nationalist Identities," 105–6.

45. "Kalimatunā al-Aūla," *al-Hadīqa* (San Miguel de Tucumán), January 3, 1922.

46. "Pro Independencia de Siria," *La Razón* (Buenos Aires, Argentina), July 24, 1922; quoted in Brégain, *Syriens et Libanais*, 151–53; and Logroño Narbona, "Development of Nationalist Identities," 110–11.

47. Logroño Narbona, "Development of Nationalist Identities," 72, 108–10.

48. Brégain, *Syriens et Libanais*, 149; and Logroño Narbona, "Development of Nationalist Identities," 109–10.

49. Brégain, *Syriens et Libanais*, 154–56; and Logroño Narbona, "Development of Nationalist Identities," 115–16.

50. Brégain, *Syriens et Libanais*, 156–58; and Logroño Narbona, "Development of Nationalist Identities," 116–18.

51. Brégain, *Syriens et Libanais*, 158; and "Habib Estéfano o Estofán," *Eco de Oriente*, October 30, 1926.

52. Brégain, *Syriens et Libanais*, 154–55.

53. Logroño Narbona, "Development of Nationalist Identities," 114–15.

54. Naoum A. Mokarzel, "Syria a Religious Problem," *New York Times*, November 29, 1925.

55. H. I. Katibah, "Islam and Christians in Syria," *New York Times*, December 6, 1925.

56. A. M. Shakpa, "Pleads for Aid to Syria," *New York Times*, January 25, 1926.

57. The Syrian-Palestinian Congress was called to session in 1921 in Geneva, producing a demand for independence and territorial integrity (folding Lebanon and Palestine into a larger Syria) and delivering it to the League of Nations. In Geneva, the congress elected an executive committee and relocated its headquarters to Cairo. The committee was composed of two primary groups. The former was led by Michel Lutfallah, scion of a fabulously wealthy Christian Lebanese family based in Egypt, and Abd al-Rahman Shahbandar, a physician from a middle-class merchant family in Damascus. Both men were Western-educated and supported a secular nationalism. Shakib Arslan, Rashid Rida, and members of the Istiqlal (Independence) Party led the latter group. Arslan and Rida supported an Islamic-influenced nationalism while the Istiqlalists were battle-hardened pan-Arabists who brooked no compromise with the British or French and were based in Amman. Personal rivalries and recriminations of compromise and corruption led to a schism among these camps as the Great Syrian Revolt stalled in 1927. See Khoury, "Factionalism"; and Matthews, *Confronting an Empire*, 75–81.

58. Brégain, *Syriens et Libanais*, 159.

59. Ibid., 159–60.

60. "Jawāb Sulṭān Bāshā al-Aṭrash ʿan al-Irsāliyya al-Māliyya al-Akhīra," ("Response of Sultan Paşa al-Atrash to the latest financial remittance"), *al-Waṭan* (Buenos Aires), April 28, 1932. "Istʿamār" translates into English as both imperialism and colonialism. See Wehr, *Dictionary of Modern Written Arabic*, 644.

61. "Min murābidh al-mujāhidīn ila al-waṭiniyyin fi al-jumhūriyya al-fadhiyya," *al-Waṭan* (Buenos Aires), April 28, 1932.

62. "El Centro Libanés. Causas de su fundación," *al-Hurrīyya* (San Miguel de Tucumán), February 3, 1931.

63. Olguín Tenorio and Peña González, *La inmigración árabe*, 126; and Mattar, *Guía Social*, 191–92.

64. Classic accounts include Hourani, *Syria and Lebanon*, 199–229; and Khoury, *Syria and the French Mandate*. See also Brégain, *Syriens et Libanais*, 167.

65. Mario N. Turbay, "Asociación Libanesa de Socorros Mutuos. Una parte importante de su historia," *La Casa* (San Miguel de Tucumán), November 1993, 48; Ponsati, *Aportes para una reseña*, 31; and Brégain, *Syriens et Libanais*, 166–67.

66. "Awal Mars fī Tūkūmān," *al-Zawba'a*, July 15, 1943. *Al-Zawba'a* was edited in Tucumán and published in Buenos Aires.

67. Dawisha, *Arab Nationalism*, 97–98.

68. See, among others, Aniceto Schain, "Inquietud Siria," *al-Zawba'a*, April 15, 1942; and Mattar, *Guía Social*, 317.

69. "Mabarra Qawmīya," *al-Zawba'a*, April 1, 1942. Fernando Pó is now known as the island of Bioko, where Malabo, the capital of Equatorial Guinea, is located.

70. "al-Bunyān al-Marsūs," *al-Zawba'a*, August 15, 1941; "World War: Middle Eastern Theater: Mixed Show," *Time*, June 23, 1941. The series against al-Qarawi ran in *al-Zawba'a* from October 15, 1941 to May 1, 1942. See also Maatouk, "Saadeh's Views on Literature."

71. The series ran in *al-Zawba'a* from October 15, 1941, to May 1, 1942. See also Maatouk, "Saadeh's Views on Literature."

72. "El Apocrifo Nacionalismo 'Libanés,'" *al-Zawba'a*, September 15, 1942.

73. Brégain, *Syriens et Libanais*, 169–70; Schumann, "Nationalism"; Dawisha, *Arab Nationalism*, 98.

74. al-Mu'tamar al-'Arabī al-Awwal, *al-Kitāb al-akhḍar*, 44; and "al-Kitāb al-akhḍar al-thānī," *al-Fiṭra al-Islāmīyya* (Buenos Aires), July 14, 1944. Brégain incorrectly notes that Rachid Rustom was the lone Christian at the congress. See Brégain, *Syriens et Libanais*, 170–73.

75. Khatlab, *Mahjar*, 34.

Conclusion

Writing Latin American Nations
from Their Borders

Bringing Nationalism and Immigration Histories into Dialogue

NICOLA FOOTE

How does replacing a nation-state or "groupist" perspective on immigration with a comparative, pan-continental approach reshape our knowledge of the process and significance of migrations in Latin America?[1] How are understandings of Latin American nation building and national identity formation advanced by a focus on immigration? And how does bringing migration into explicit communication with nationalism contribute to theory building in both fields? This conclusion synthesizes the findings that emerged from the three interlocking questions posed by contributors to this volume. It uses the themes of assimilation, race formation, and transnationalism to explore how the development of regional nation-states was inextricably entwined with global migratory currents.

Inserting Latin America into the Global Historiography of Migration

This volume shows that an in-depth and comparative study of immigration to Latin America can make multiple important contributions to the global historiography of migration. The questions posed by the contributors directly engage several of the research priorities laid out in the most recent "state of the field" overview in the *International Migration Review*. The essays collated here examine and contextualize immigrant transnationalism and assess the role of immigrants in the formation of economic, sociocultural, and political institutions by looking at states and state systems in cross-national comparative perspective—issues labeled as the most pressing concerns for the field by Alejandro Portes and Josh DeWind.[2]

The book underlines the importance of Latin America as a receiving destination for immigrants, and demonstrates that migration played a transformational role in regional nation-building processes. Full consideration of Latin America as a migratory destination challenges the U.S.-centric paradigms that have imagined transatlantic migratory flows as a North American phenomenon. Just as Atlantic migration has been prioritized by researchers to the point where the Pacific and trans-Asian and African migrations that were part of same global processes have been marginalized within global historiographies and models, understandings of Atlantic migrations themselves have been skewed by the focus on the United States at the expense of Latin America.[3] This volume examines the ways in which Latin America formed part of an integrated and interlocking transatlantic migratory circuit, and reinforces the argument that migration and nation formation throughout the Americas as a whole should be viewed as entangled and inseparable processes.

Lara Putnam's chapter makes this case most strongly through her conceptualization of the "entangled histories" through which Caribbean nation formation emerged out of events and developments spanning the anglophone, francophone, and Spanish-speaking Antilles and the Atlantic coasts of Central America and South America. This entanglement operated both at the level of legislation and of identity formation. Anti-Chinese laws passed in the Greater Caribbean, for example, were influenced by those in the United States and Canada enacted in the 1880s, which were themselves informed by debates surrounding the experiences of indentured Asian workers in Cuba, Trinidad, and Guyana beginning in the 1840s. Similarly, British West Indian nativism was fueled by black exclusion in the migratory circuits of the Latin American rimlands while the racialization of East Indians, Chinese, and Syrians within British Caribbean nationalisms was shaped by the racial discourses of Spanish America and the strong associations between race and national identity that had structured the experiences of black migrants. Several other chapters also highlight how migratory currents were entwined with global geopolitics. Stefan Rinke shows that German immigration to the Southern Cone cannot be understood outside of German histories of empire and expansion, and was profoundly shaped by the international alliances of World War I. Likewise, Steven Hyland reveals how the identities of Arab immigrants were forged in relationship to the shifts in the Ottoman Empire resulting from the Young Turk Revolution and World War I, and he highlights how Middle Eastern histories were profoundly shaped by transnational intellectual and political networks in Rio de Janeiro and Buenos Aries.

The breadth and depth of transnational associations is a common theme throughout the volume. Kathleen López shows how Chinese merchants in Peru, Cuba, and Mexico were part of transnational commercial networks that circulated merchandise imported from China via ethnic entrepreneurs in California. In the same manner, Jürgen Buchenau examines the close economic ties between Japanese immigrants in Mexican Pacific Port cities and their counterparts on the West Coast of the United States. Both authors depict frequent border crossings by migrants, with the U.S.–Mexico border being the site of a surprisingly large amount of back-and-forth Chinese and Middle Eastern migration. This transnational circulation was not limited to Asian migrants. My chapter demonstrates that British Caribbean migrants circulated through a far greater range of spaces than has typically been acknowledged in the historiography, with migratory networks expanding down the Amazon and up into the Andes, and incorporating ties and linkages made in an earlier wave of migration that began in the eighteenth century. Both Michael Goebel and Jeane DeLaney touch on the famous European *golondrinas* (back-and-forth migrants), while Goebel elucidates the range of secondary migrations through which Italian immigrants moved across national borders in the Southern Cone. As such, the volume definitively dismisses the idea of migration as a one-way flow from point A to point B, and addresses José Moya's call for Latin Americanists to treat migration "as a series of movements that include temporary and permanent settlement, return, back-and-forth traveling between sending and receiving societies, and relocation from one destination to another outside the point of origin."[4]

In addition to broadening the geographies of Latin American migration, the book also expands our perception of its chronological reach. In conventional periodizations of migration, 1914 has been seen as an effective cutoff point, with the outbreak of the Great War seen to mark the end of mass global movement. Adam McKeown has challenged this received wisdom and argues that it applies only to Germany and Italy as sending destinations and the United States as a receiving destination.[5] This interpretation is borne out by this volume. Jürgen Buchenau shows that immigration to Mexico in fact increased during the 1920s—precisely as a result of exclusionary laws in the United States that diverted immigrant streams—while in the 1930s Mexico became an important destination for Spanish refugees fleeing Francoism. Lara Putnam's chapter demonstrates that migration to Cuba hit a high point after World War I as sugar prices soared while Haitian migration to the Dominican Republic surged in the same period. Similarly, the Venezuelan oil boom between 1920 and 1935 prompted a pronounced wave of British Caribbean migration. Even in the "classic" immigration case studies of the Southern Cone, the idea of 1914 marking a period of decline does not entirely hold. Michael Goebel's chapter provides evidence that although the numbers of Italian immigrants to Uruguay crashed during and immediately after World War I, they began to rebuild steadily in the 1920s. Frederik Schulze attests that Japanese migration to Brazil boomed in the interwar period, while Jeffrey Lesser and Raanan Rein show that Eastern European and Jewish immigration to Brazil and Argentina grew significantly through the 1920s and '30s, with Jewish immigration hitting a peak in 1938.

The idea of World War I ushering in a new era of anti-immigration legislation does not quite hold up in these case studies either. Our volume again builds on McKeown's arguments by demonstrating that the hardening of borders and the rise of government regulation over immigration was part of a cumulative process in place since at least the 1870s.[6] Multiple chapters establish that restrictions on black and Asian immigration were the norm throughout South America from the late nineteenth century onward, even if they were rarely enforced. Only in Central America and the Caribbean, where U.S. economic penetration was most acute and national elites had to contend more directly with the preferences of foreign capital, was immigration regulation a new phenomenon after 1914. A comparative focus on Latin American migration thus questions the assumption that World War I marked a definitive shift in either the numbers or the legal underpinnings of transatlantic migration.

Immigrant and Nation in Latin America

The contribution of Latin American case studies to the global historiography of migration can be seen even more clearly when the process of nation formation becomes the central unit of analysis. As Michael Goebel argues, when the study of migration and nationalism are examined in conjunction, new insight is presented into each field. In probing the relationship between immigrants and nation formation, the contributors in this volume advance debates around core questions in migration theory, including assimilation, transnationalism, and diaspora, while also contributing to regional understandings of nationalism by suggesting that in Latin America nation building occurred in fairly substantial part *through* immigration.

At the simplest level of nation formation, the unprecedented expansion of population brought by immigration wrought a demographic revolution. Small populations in marginal countries that had been on the edge of the Spanish Empire were radically transformed by the absorption of huge numbers of migrants. Argentina received some four million immigrants in the years between 1870 and 1930 while 1.2 million immigrants arrived in Brazil in the space of the single decade of the 1890s. Even where the raw number of immigrants was relatively small in the greater scheme of transcontinental immigration systems, the presence of immigrants could have truly profound implications for national demographics. The example of Uruguay where three hundred thousand immigrants contributed to a sevenfold increase in the local population is especially revealing, but one of the insights of the volume is that parts of the Caribbean experienced similar migratory patterns to the classic immigration case studies of the Southern Cone. Lara Putnam shows how territories like British Guiana and Trinidad, which were less developed prior to emancipation, became such important destinations for mass immigration (mainly from India) that by 1930 almost a quarter of the population had been born overseas. In some of the Caribbean rimland towns of Central America, immigrants quickly came to outnumber nationals. According to the 1927 census, Limón, for example, had 1.5 foreigners (mostly from the British Caribbean) for each native-born Costa Rican.[7]

Expanding the population base was essential to economic development as well as to staking territorial claims. Juan Bautista Alberdi's insistence that "to govern is to populate" dominated modernization plans across the continent. Immigrant workers developed the roads, railways, and airbases that served to integrate national resources and were the primary labor force in the agro-export and mining industries that brought marginal spaces in tropical lowland regions into the global economy. Immigrant colonization helped to form national boundaries and consolidate nationalist land claims. Schulze's chapter, for example, explores how European settlement in the southernmost Brazilian provinces of Rio Grande do Sul, Santa Catarina, and Paraná solidified national ownership of territory also claimed by Argentina.

The relationship between immigrants and territorial claims was sometimes unexpected. My chapter addresses the genocide of indigenous peoples in the Peruvian Amazon during the rubber boom, and points out that this was blamed on Barbadian migrants. The international scandal the genocide created ironically helped Peru to assert its regional claims. The Putumayo region where the devastating abuses occurred had also been claimed by Colombia and Ecuador, but it was Peru that was labeled as responsible for the region by international investigators. As the scandal broke, Ecuador and Colombia were only too happy to drop their claims in order to avoid any censure, leaving Peru temporarily embarrassed but ultimately with control of the rubber-rich region. Migrants in this context were not only the agents who made the nation's claim to control meaningful, but they also provided a convenient scapegoat who could be blamed for actions that threatened the nation's international reputation.

The role of immigrants in the mapping of national spaces can also be seen through their role in urbanization. Immigrants in most of the case studies reviewed here formed overwhelmingly urban populations, flowing into expanding cities whose massive growth was also supplemented by internal migration from the countryside. Urbanization represented an important form of nation building that heralded the creation of new sites of national power.

Both urban and rural immigrants pushed forward economic transformations that strengthened the national treasury and expanded the administrative reach of the state. Skilled and unskilled immigrants brought the raw manpower and technical expertise needed to bring about industrial development. Immigrant peddlers and merchants played a crucial role in developing regional consumer culture by extending networks of credit and providing popular access to industrial goods.[8] Immigrants also contributed to agricultural advancements. López details the centrality of Chinese immigrants to the continuation of plantation production systems following the abolition of the slave trade; Lara Putnam and I demonstrate the critical contribution of British Caribbean immigrants to the agro-export sector; and Schulze shows how German immigrants in Brazil helped develop the coffee industry. Immigrants also contributed to enhanced agricultural production as peasant subsistent producers, with European and Japanese colonists granted land rights in exchange for bringing agricultural development to sparsely populated rural areas. Lesser and Rein show that the correlation between immigrants and agrarian development was so powerful that it became the lynchpin of immigrant nationalisms, with the most common trope of immigrant museums across the continent being that immigrants had "made the land bloom."

The pattern described here did not hold everywhere. In Mexico these same economic transformations were achieved through the use of foreign capital without recourse to expansive immigrant labor. The same was true in the Andes. These differences may have related to population patterns: areas that were heartlands of pre-Columbian indigenous civilizations had access to reserves of labor that other nations did not, and thus were not as economically dependent on immigration, even if the "racial fantasies" of elites who desired social whitening manifested parallels at times. Yet it remains the case that in many parts of the region the physical transformations of nation building occurred in significant part through immigration.

If immigrants helped shape the expansion of national territories and economies, they were also essential to imaginings of nationhood, both at the elite and popular level. National identities were constantly changing and being remade in this period, and the experiences of immigrants provide a useful window for tracing how ideas of nation shifted from the nineteenth-century idea of a political association based on civic ideals to the early-twentieth-century ethnocultural formulation predicated on the idea of a national "race" forged through *mestizaje*. Immigrants were inextricably entwined with nationalist visions of modernity—symbols first of the promise (and later of the failings) of the U.S.–driven technocratic model of development elaborated, as DeLaney details, by the Argentine generation of 1837 and adopted continentwide in an effort to sweep away the legacies of Spanish colonialism and allow Latin America to emerge as a global economic leader.[9] The presence of immigrants also served to make the nation tangible and meaningful for ordinary people, and in the populist protests and xenophobic riots catalogued throughout this volume we see that, at least for the urban mestizo working classes, interactions with immigrants contributed to their own imaginings of what it meant to be part of the nation.

Two important themes to come out of the case studies presented here are the role of intellectual discourse on immigration in shaping nationalism, and the way in which representations of migrants contributed to the imagining of national boundaries of inclusion and exclusion. The significance of intellectual discourse for understanding the realities of Latin American immigration has sometimes been questioned by historians. José Moya has pointed to the immigration histories of Mexico, the Andes, and Guatemala to argue that elite whitening and civilizing rhetoric had more to do with "the intellectual history of the region's elites . . . than with the demographic and sociocultural history of its peoples," suggesting that "political rhetoric, like bananas, is sometimes just that, and migration clearly obeyed mightier laws than those produced in national legislatures."[10] That immigration could not be determined by nationalist desire is unarguably true, but the intellectual discourses produced by elites were more than just bananas—or, at least as tangible as them in some senses. Discourses could not determine *whether* immigrants arrived, but they could mediate the experiences of them once they were present on national soil. Several of the chapters emphasize how intellectual discourses shaped immigrant lives. DeLaney explores the way in which nationalist debates over immigration affected immigrants' own perceptions of whether they could be a Protestant or a Jew, or could conserve their Spanish or Italian heritage, and still become an "Argentine." My chapter suggests that intellectual discourses could in some instances be a matter of life or death, arguing that representations of black migrants as savage, violent, and disease-ridden led some police and army officers to feel so afraid (or, alternatively, contemptuous) of West Indian immigrants that they used armed force against them with few qualms.

Recognition of the role of intellectuals in shaping nationalisms does not distract from the significance of other agents and institutions. The volume also accentuates the importance of the state as a central staging ground for the negotiation of national identity. The state appears as a weak actor in many of the case studies presented, with state capacities often lagging behind the visions of nationalist projects. The fragility and especially the financial weakness of the state in many areas meant that day-to-day immigration decisions about who was admitted to the national territory were not always controlled by state officials, and legislation was often sidestepped and ignored. Local officials worked in collaboration with foreign corporations and sometimes took autonomous actions. Yet, despite its weaknesses, the state served as a crucial touchstone in the allocation of citizenship, serving as a critical space in which immigrants and those who supported and opposed them negotiated access to civil, political, and social rights. Multiple chapters show that ideas about citizenship and national belonging were played out and made real through state constitutions, immigration codes, labor and education policy, and the regulation of military service. In focusing on citizenship and the state as areas where social and political power was distributed, the volume points to the role of the state in shaping ideas of nationhood, and advances recent calls by political scientists for the incorporation of rights as a legal and institutional variable into the analysis of international migration.[11]

Negotiating National Inclusion: Assimilation, Pluralism, and Citizenship

Evaluating inclusion and exclusion regarding immigrants inevitably means looking at issues of assimilation and integration. This volume moves beyond the traditional assumption that immigrants were more quickly and successfully integrated into Latin American societies than was the case in the United States, an argument that has effectively associated the absence of hyphenated identities with integration.[12] Contributors document profound and often violent hostility toward many groups of immigrants, and show that xenophobia had broad pan-regional and cross-chronological resonance. Race riots protesting the presence of various groups were frequent. The Chinese seemed to be the most common targets of such outbursts, with chapters by Putnam, Buchenau, and López documenting popular anti-Chinese uprisings and massacres in Peru in 1881 and 1909, Mexico in 1911, and Jamaica in 1918. As Lara Putnam demonstrated, members of trading diasporas were particularly convenient scapegoats in times of economic depression, and popular hostilities toward such groups were encouraged by elites because they distracted anger and attention away from the deeper causes of economic hardship, such as unequal landholding structures and exclusionary political systems. Yet it was not only mercantile communities who were the victims of xenophobic violence. Fears about divided German loyalties culminated in a wave of anti-German riots during World War I, Afro-Antilleans were the subjects of systematic deportations and sustained violent abuses including lynching and massacres, and even in Argentina—typically held up as the classic case study of easy assimilation—the rise of right-wing nationalism targeted Jewish immigrants, and anti-Semitism also rose in Brazil in the aftermath of the Great Depression. All of this suggests that the received wisdom that Latin America was somehow less xenophobic than other receiving destinations cannot be upheld.

As such, this volume significantly advances our understandings of processes of assimilation in Latin American. As Michael Goebel notes in the introduction, the recent shifts in migration theory that have complicated the conventional opposition between assimilation and pluralism have not found their way into the historiography of Latin America. The case studies presented here bring the region more firmly into conversation with contemporary migration theory, and view assimilation as a complex, multilayered process that also involved the transformation of the mainstream.

DeLaney's chapter in particular helps to turn the conventional question about assimilation on its head. She argues that European immigrants to Argentina were successful in integrating precisely because assimilation was not expected of them. Immigrants were seen as bearers of superior cultural values who would sweep away the dusty Spanish colonial heritage and help forge a new, more modern national culture. Thus, the measure of their success was not how well they fit into the mainstream but whether they could sufficiently change the mainstream and create a more "civilized" culture. In effect, then, it was pluralism itself that fueled immigrant assimilation. Where immigrants felt at home in a society they had reshaped to partially reflect their image, ethnic identity markers were no longer necessary.

The idea of immigration as central to nation formation did not hold the same resonance everywhere. This in turn impacted upon processes of assimilation. In Mexico, where immigration was regarded with more caution in the nineteenth century because of the association between the presence of foreigners, war, and loss of territory, the onus was on immigrants to adapt to a national identity; there was no expectation that Mexican society would adapt to immigrant culture. As a result, separations and distinctions remained entrenched. Indeed, Buchenau sees the absence of the hyphen—the typical indicator of the success of assimilation—as a barrier to immigrant integration, suggesting that without a hyphenated identity to ease the transition between "Mexican" and "foreigner," many immigrants elected to remain in the latter camp.

Levels of integration and assimilation also varied by ethnic group and depended on the kinds of social and economic capital immigrants brought with them. Where immigrants started on the social and economic "ladder" mediated their relationship with the mainstream significantly. Because of their whiteness, European migrants brought enormous social capital regardless of their economic resources, which meant they were seen as "improving" the demographic composition of the nation. Jewish, Middle Eastern, and to a lesser extent Japanese (and some Chinese) immigrants possessed substantial economic capital and were perceived to bring wealth and industrial or agricultural knowledge that would advance national economic development. This in turn provided them with the opportunity to expand their social capital by making claims to whiteness (discussed in more detail later). As a result, these groups were granted a greater chance to achieve inclusion and assimilation.

However, not all who had the chance to assimilate took the opportunity. Incentives and motivations mattered, and some immigrants appear to have concluded that they could gain more from staying within ethnic economies and seeking the support and protection of their ethnic peers than they would in joining the mainstream. This was true for some members of trading diasporas, but it was an especially noteworthy tendency among diaspora communities composed solely of sojourning economic elites. This can be seen most strikingly in the case of the American, French, German, and Spanish immigrants in Mexico City, discussed by Buchenau, who formed "enclave" societies behind high gated walls. It was also true of the American and British corporate officials who appear in my chapter as the abusers of West Indian workers, and who are rarely considered as immigrants in the scholarly literature. Similarly, where assimilation was perceived to lead to marginalization, it was rejected, and British Caribbean migrants on balance preferred to reject an ethnic minority status and instead seek a claim to racial superiority by emphasizing their Anglo-Saxon heritage and insisting on their distinctiveness from their host societies.[13] In that sense, then, the Latin American case studies presented here reinforce Alba and Nee's argument that patterns of assimilation can be explained by looking at incentives from the dominant society, but they also stress the role of immigrant's own evaluation of how these should be weighed.[14]

Conceptualizing Diaspora Nationalisms

Certainly, to fully understand the relationship between immigrants and nation formation, it is essential to examine the issue of inclusion and exclusion from the perspective of immigrants themselves and to evaluate their own identities, desires, and perceptions. If the presence of immigrants made the idea of the nation tangible to many ordinary Latin Americans, the concept of nation also became real to most immigrants through their experience of migration. However, it was not always the Latin American host nation with which they came to affiliate: there were always competing loyalties for immigrants, and whether they adopted Latin American identities depended not only on what host nations and elites wanted but also on broader transnational processes. Any discussion of assimilation and integration therefore cannot proceed in isolation from the evaluation of diaspora nationalisms.

It is clear that many immigrants (or at least their home governments and ethnic community leaders) had very different ideas about what contribution they would make to their host nation than did the nationalist elites recruiting them. Both Schulze and Rinke suggest that German immigration could be characterized as an imperial diaspora, and they show how the preservation of the language and culture of the emigrants was explicitly viewed after 1871 as a tool for expanding German economic interests and informal empire. While Latin American governments viewed German immigration as a means to racial and national improvement and assumed and desired that assimilation would take place, many German actors saw migration as a way to strengthen the German nation and to expand and preserve German language and culture. German elites both at home and in Latin America sought to fight off de-Germanization, which they equated with racial degeneration. Similar views were held by the governments of other migrating groups. The Italian state prior to the emergence of fascism saw immigration to Latin America as representing a form of "peaceful conquest" while the Japanese government perceived immigration to Brazil as a means of expanding their international influence.

In such cases, emigrant state policy could prove an essential component in shaping diaspora identities. The German government provided funding for German-language schools and for the support of institutions such as the Association for Germanness Abroad. The Japanese government likewise gave financial support to schools and immigrant societies. In other cases the immigrants themselves called on their states of origin to recognize and support the maintenance of their identities. Hyland shows how Syrian ethnic leaders pushed the Ottoman state to establish diplomatic ties with Argentina so that they could open official lines of communication, while British Caribbean subjects agitated for the British government to intervene in legal and economic disputes on their behalf, in the process insisting on their right to a British identity. Immigrants who escaped persecution could make no claims on their originating state but formed institutions that fueled chain migrations and helped to shape cohesive diaspora identities, such as the Jewish Colonization Association that helped fund agricultural settlement for Jewish migrants in Argentina and Brazil. These negotiations remind us that, as Green and Weil have insisted, emigration and immigration must be viewed in conjunction, as mutually constitutive realities.[15]

Immigrants also forged distinct ethnic and political identities through the rich associational lives they created. Virtually all of the groups considered here forged and sustained "multi-stranded social relations that link[ed] together their societies of origin and settlement."[16] They sent remittances home, operated small cross-national businesses, invested their savings in their home countries, and established social services, recreational activities, clubs, hospitals, schools, and churches that catered specifically to their own ethnic group. These institutions were as much about the maintenance of day-to-day cultural practices and the need for mutual support as they were about patriotic fervor. Yet the institutions created were the means through which migrants became transnational actors, expanding their networks and connections overseas while also retaining a presence in their original societies. It was also through these institutions and networks that many immigrants began to develop national identities that would not necessarily have resonated with them prior to immigration. Goebel points out how Italian migrants gained a sense of themselves as unified "Italians" rather than as people of distinct regional origins through the experience of migration, while the eastern Mediterranean immigrants discussed by Hyland, who became passionate advocates and shapers of Syrian and Lebanese nationhood from within Brazil and Argentina, are classic examples of groups gaining their national identity in the diaspora. Similarly, Putnam shows how Hindus and Muslims in Trinidad consolidated as "Indians" in the face of racial discrimination, sharing among themselves religious and cultural symbols that would have separated them in India.

This is not to suggest that diaspora nationalisms were uniform or unvaried. This volume also draws our attention to the local specificities that shaped the expression of diaspora nationalisms. Immigrant groups were never homogenous, and immigrants from the same nation of origin could manifest distinct identities and political loyalties depending on factors such as their specific region of origin, when migration occurred, and the political and religious orientation of the founding members of an individual diaspora community. Goebel's chapter shows how differential support for fascism among Italian immigrants in the Southern Cone can only be explained through intimate organizational processes occurring at the level of distinct individual communities—not by broad-brush categorizations about degree of ethnic segregation or host nation political leanings, as has previously been argued. Such insights further emphasize the necessity of bringing social histories of migration and intellectual histories of nationalism into closer dialogue.

Immigration, Ethnicity, and Latin American Race Formation

In the discussion of both assimilation and diaspora nationalisms, the fusing and unfusing of distinct ethnic identities was one of the primary issues at stake. The categorization and conceptualization of race and ethnicity were absolutely critical to immigrant experiences, and it is not possible to fully evaluate the relationship between nation and immigration without discussing race. This volume directly advances Samuel Baily's call for the prioritization of research on the relationship between race and immigration, and demonstrates conclusively that an analysis of immigration can provide critical new insight into Latin American race formation.[17] Immigration has largely been marginal to Latin American racial theory. Despite the wave of research on race, gender, and nation over the last two decades, few historical studies of race and national identity have used a comparative lens, and most have focused on indigenous groups or Afro–Latin Americans—rarely on immigrants or their descendants. Yet race was absolutely central to the history of immigration to Latin America. Immigration policy and legislation was founded on a racial logic that borrowed heavily from the biological discourses of scientific racism and eugenics; the problems immigration posed to national polities were often expressed in terms of racialized difference, while ultimately assimilation was often determined by how and where immigrants fitted into preexisting racial categories and hierarchies.

Migratory patterns were driven in part by changing racial demographics. In coastal plantation regions, most notably Brazil, Cuba, and other parts of the Caribbean, mass immigration was prompted by the shift in labor relations generated by the abolition of slavery and the slave trade. Immigration was also shaped by the dispossession of indigenous peoples. In the Southern Cone success in attracting European immigrants was prompted in part by the genocide of indigenous peoples. In Mexico the few successful instances of immigrant colonization were prompted by liberal land reform, notably the Law of Fallow Land discussed by Buchenau, which allocated private investors title to indigenous communal lands.

As several chapters in this volume pointed out, the idea of whitening dominated discourses of immigration and immigration policy was always predicated on acquiring the "right" type of immigrant. These ideas were woven into immigration codes, and legislation governed entrance and the acquisition of rights prioritizing Europeans. Asian and African-descended people were often formally barred from entrance, and legal barriers were erected to their acquisition of citizenship rights that were not applied to Europeans. In Ecuador, for example, European immigrants could apply for citizenship after just two years of residency, but black and Chinese immigrants were ineligible for citizenship regardless of their length of residence.[18] In Panama, as my chapter showed, even second- and third-generation black immigrants were excluded from rights of citizenship in the 1941 constitution.

But this volume also suggests that the concept of whitening itself is in need of a deeper interrogation than it has previously been allocated, and that the category of "whiteness" on which it was predicated was far from stable. Questions have been raised in U.S. immigration history over the way in which the whiteness of certain categories of European immigrants was contested, and attention has been drawn to how labels such as "Celtic," "Hebrew," "Latin," "Slav," "Iberic," and "Mediterranean" operated as racial terms, designed to mediate access to power.[19] Yet the whiteness of immigrants to Latin American has largely been taken for granted.[20] However, the flexibility and inclusivity of whiteness as a category during the era of mass immigration was extremely significant and provides an important partial explanation for some of the differences between immigrant experiences and socioeconomic mobility in Latin America as opposed to the United States. Critically considering whiteness also advances a deeper understanding of the racial underpinnings of *mestizaje* in Latin America.

In marked contrast to the United States, most Jewish and Middle Eastern immigrants to Latin America, and even some Japanese and Chinese, were officially classified as "white." As noted earlier, this was fundamentally related to class positioning. Immigrants who brought financial capital or business skills and aptitudes that could tangibly contribute to economic development were able to tap into the class dynamics that underpinned discourses of whitening and gain social status as groups pushing forward modernization, industrialization, and development.

Yet the flexibility of whiteness does not suggest that white supremacy was any less powerful within Latin America. The admittance of preferred immigrant groups to the category did not undermine whiteness; rather, it reinforced and reconstructed it as the apex of social prestige and political and economic power. The inclusive negotiation of whiteness also served to reconstruct the negation of blackness within national identities. Lesser and Rein, for example, suggest here that Jewish claims to whiteness in Brazil were mediated through nonblackness. In the inverse of the one-drop rule in the United States, because Jewish immigrants were not black, they could become white through cultural action. They achieved this by rejecting work associated with blacks as sharecroppers on large plantations (work that had at one point been fulfilled by non-Jewish German immigrants whose racial status was less ambiguous).

Interestingly, some of the most obviously "white" immigrant groups seemed to reject inclusion in Latin American racial categories of any kind, with the British, French, German, and American ethnic enclaves in Mexico, and to a lesser extent German immigrants in Argentina and Brazil, preferring to remain separate from mainstream Latin American society—a decision that, regarding Mexico, Buchenau attributes to ethnic enclaves' conviction of their own Anglo-Saxon superiority. It was precisely their efforts to negotiate the international discourses that shaped such attitudes that made Latin American national elites so keen to extend the category of whiteness to a broader cross-sector of immigrants. The idea that the logic of social whitening could be fulfilled by classifying non-European groups as white was consistent with emerging racial nationalisms based on *mestizaje*, which engaged dominant scientific racisms by negotiating them and insisting that the (unquestioned) inferiority of black and indigenous groups could be overcome through mixture with "more civilized" groups.

Mestizaje seems to have provided an important platform through which immigrants could engage local nationalisms. Lesser and Rein demonstrate how immigrants explicitly laid claim to *mestizaje* by creating fictive historical links to allow them to make a claim to the core ethnic underpinnings of national identity. Jewish immigrants used histories of crypto-Jews in the colonial period to make a claim to a deeper rooted presence in Latin America than their nineteenth- and twentieth-century migrations would otherwise allow. Some Asian immigrants used phenotypic similarities with indigenous peoples to make claims to indigenity. Japanese ethnic leaders in Peru posited the idea that the Incas were a lost tribe of Japanese while Chinese immigrants in Mexico claimed that the founders of the Aztec Empire were shipwrecked Chinese.

Although both whiteness and *mestizaje* were flexible discourses, there were limits to their expansiveness, and these served as important brakes on immigrant inclusion. Notably, groups who were not seen as potentially "meltable" into the imagined national white–mestizo race were rejected as antinational. The dynamics of inclusion and exclusion centered around ideas of miscegenation and exclusionary currents applied most strongly to black and Chinese immigrants.

Both whitening and *mestizaje* were at their core about racial mixture: improving the national racial stock through cultural and biological blending. The painting by Modesto Brocos that depicts German immigrants "saving" Afro-Brazilians from the curse of Han illustrates this point powerfully (see Frederik Schulze's chapter). Blacks were saved in this formulation through the eradication of blackness, just as the nation would be saved through the same means. That miscegenation was viewed as a tool to whiten existing populations meant that the presence of nonwhites in the immigrant stream was very problematic since it defeated the whole premise of immigration as a civilizing tool. The biological discourses underpinning social constructions of race meant that in the whitening formulation, cultural transformation would be demonstrated through physical shifts in phenotype. Thus, any group (including Jews, Japanese, and Arabs) that arrived with phenotypic characteristics associated with "Caucasians"—light skin, straight nose, and straight hair—could play the whitening role because they would lend these physical attributes (perceived to be an extension of cultural and intellectual assets) to the national population. Conversely, miscegenation with Chinese and black immigrants was a source of tremendous nationalist concern. Both my chapter and Putnam's demonstrate that black immigrants were characterized as a source of racial danger, and trace how the fear that black fecundity would overwhelm the national population base reached almost hysterical proportions in certain contexts. Similarly, López explores the horror with which intermixing between Chinese immigrants and the local population was viewed. In Peru the children of Chinese and indigenous women were classified as *injerto* (transplant) while the offspring of Afro-Peruvians and Chinese were shunned still further, the denial of an official label a clear signal that they were not supposed to exist. Miscegenation that mixed local populations with whites was seen as strengthening the nation while mixing with nonwhites was seen as a path toward degeneration.

The exclusion of blacks and Chinese from discourses of *mestizaje* calls attention to the importance of race as a category for understanding assimilation. In Alba and Nee's definition, assimilation is a form of ethnic change that occurs as result of changes taking place on either side of an ethnic boundary.[21] The case studies presented here show that some boundaries were more malleable than others, and that racialized imaginings of biological heredity operated as a critical factor in determining their porousness. National identities could be inclusive of ethnic diversity, but attitudes toward racial difference were much more unyielding. This suggests that some of the classic arguments about differential assimilation made by Warner and Srole back in 1945 have some validity. While their argument that it would take dark-skinned Europeans like Armenians and Sicilians eight generations to assimilate, and that the integration of African Americans would prove almost impossible was patently incorrect, their basic idea that phenotype and perceived racial identities shape the ability to assimilate seem to have some resonance, at least within the Latin American context.[22]

The relationship between phenotype and national identity can also be

298 · Nicola Foote

seen in attitudes toward near-neighbor migrations. Putnam shows how migrants from neighboring territories went largely unremarked in political debates, despite their significant numbers. Only when ethnic divisions between neighbors were racialized did nativist tensions take form, and then they often spilled over into violence. The genocide of Haitian migrants in the Dominican Republic in 1937 was the ultimate example of this; it stemmed in significant measure from the pathologization of blackness. A core part of Dominican efforts to construct a "white" national identity entailed the classification of black Haitian migrants as different and antinational, and the perception of this difference as threatening to national integrity led to extreme measures to extirpate this threat.[23]

That blackness and Chineseness were profoundly racialized categories certainly contributed to the violence black and Chinese immigrants experienced. While xenophobic violence and rioting was directed against Germans and Middle Eastern immigrants as well as against blacks and Chinese in the case studies presented here, it was only the latter group who were subject to large-scale massacres and for whom violent deaths at the hands of state officials were common. The nature of these racializations seems to relate to international racial discourses. Attitudes toward Chinese immigrants were shaped by the U.S.-projected discourse of the threat posed by a "yellow peril." Likewise, blackness was characterized as especially problematic within scientific racism, and blacks inevitably appeared at the bottom of imagined racial hierarchies, regardless of how these were specifically construed. The force of this discursive negativity combined with economic and strategic concerns—fear of Chinese competition among the urban middle-classes, and the association of black demography with U.S. domination—may have made it harder for these categories to be renegotiated in a more inclusive manner.

Conversely, in the British Caribbean, blackness informed national identity in precisely the opposite manner. Emerging protonational identities coalesced *around* blackness and largely excluded East Indian and other Asian immigrants. Putnam argues that this was in direct response to the racialization of nativisms in Latin America: returning British Caribbean migrants developed their own nationalisms in a mirror image form, encouraged by regional elites who saw anti-Asian agitation as a convenient distraction from white power.

Immigration, then, brings ethnicity to the fore of a discussion of Latin American race formation. Jeffrey Lesser has insisted elsewhere that the value of immigration to racial theory is its introduction of ethnicity as a category and the way this pushes us to move beyond the idea presented in nationalist ideologies that Latin America was a society fused from the collision of these three original races and to thus expand our understanding of who participated in the formation of mestizo nations.[24] Yet the clear significance of ethnicity for understanding racial categories does not mean that race and ethnicity can be blurred together. Racialization operated in tandem with ethnicity, and sometimes through it, but race and ethnicity were processes that produced distinct and separate outcomes. This volume makes clear that certain ethnic groups become associated with particular racial distinctions such that group characteristics were imputed to heredity while others were viewed through lenses that were more mutable and changeable. This in turn impacted processes of assimilation and shaped the racialization of existing populations as much as it did immigrants themselves.

Gendering Immigration Histories

Both immigration and race formation are profoundly gendered phenomenon, and assessing their interrelationship also helps us understand the gendering of the nation.[25] Gender is at best a secondary theme in most of the chapters because—as Lesser and Rein point out in their contribution—far too little of the existing scholarship on Latin American immigration currently examines gender, sexuality, or the specific experiences of women and children. This makes it difficult for synthetic overview pieces such as those collected here to fully engage with such issues. Yet there are many clearly gendered currents that underpin the case studies that speak to the need for additional research in this field.

As with race, gender fundamentally impacted who was counted as an immigrant. Men dominated migratory streams, and this fed into immigration legislation. In Argentina, for example, both the constitution of 1853 and the 1876 law of immigration and colonization defined "immigrant" as a "male head of household."[26] Such definitions put single and unaccompanied women immigrants at a distinct disadvantage, making it more difficult for them to gain labor contracts or obtain government support.

Women immigrants occupied a problematic positioning within nationalist imaginaries and immigrant women were singled out in many of the anti-immigrant discourses that the chapters assess. In the very act of migration, women challenged dominant gender ideologies that associated women with domesticity and the home. The preference for women to migrate as part of families calls attention to the threat that single female immigrants were perceived to pose to patriarchal structures of authority. As Anne McClintock has famously pointed out, women's role in nationalist discourses was typically as upholders of the past, as the people in and by whom tradition was inculcated.[27] In migrating, women were taking on a more typically male role of striving for the modern. This was as troubling for elites in Latin American receiving nations as it was for those in countries of emigration. Women migrants were seen as morally suspect and were frequently characterized as vectors for prostitution and insanity. The argument that Afro-Caribbean women were responsible for the spread of prostitution in areas of high West Indian immigration was mirrored in the well-known hand-wringing over "white slavery" in Argentina.[28] The representation of immigrant women as sexually immoral could have tragic consequences at the level of lived experience and was likely a factor in the violent rapes and sexual assaults of British Caribbean women migrants discussed in my chapter. More research is urgently needed to uncover whether these kinds of attacks were part of the experiences of immigrant women from other ethnic groups.

The sexual stereotyping of immigrants affected men as well as women. López shows how Chinese male sexuality was seen as a moral threat in Peru, where Chinese men were characterized as addicted to prostitutes and blamed for the spread of brothels. In Mexico this was take a step further with Chinese men characterized as driving Mexican women into prostitution by taking on traditionally "female" jobs such as laundry work and domestic service. Putnam reveals that the spark for the 1918 anti-Chinese riot in Jamaica was the shooting of an Afro-Jamaican man by a Chinese immigrant in a fight over a love triangle. Fears about black male sexuality were often the spark for violence against British Caribbean migrants, as happened most notably in Cuba where several black male immigrants were lynched for allegedly abducting white children.

Discourses and policies surrounding miscegenation reveal the role sexuality played in shaping ethnic boundaries. As discussed earlier, European miscegenation was seen as strengthening the nation while black and Chinese miscegenation was viewed as a source of racial pollution and national degradation. Positive and negative incentives for miscegenation were created through the regulation of women's sexuality. Social and sometimes legal sanctions were placed on local women who forged relationships with "the wrong kinds" of immigrants. Prior to 1936, Mexican women who married foreigners lost their right to Mexican citizenship—a way to ensure that the children of immigrants were not granted the rights of jus solis. Special steps were taken to prevent miscegenation with Chinese immigrants, and in the state of Sonora marriages between Mexican women and Chinese men were legally banned. Conversely, Buchenau shows how Mexican efforts to encourage foreigners to assimilate in the 1930s proceeded through legislation waiving immigration restrictions for those who married Mexican women. Notably, immigrant women who married Mexican men were not included in this legislation, thus reconstituting the association between "immigrant" and "male." The same formulation is present in the Brazilian painting *The Redemption of Ham*, in which a male European immigrant is depicted as "improving" the national race through his relationship with an Afro-Brazilian woman. Such policies and discourse underscore the way in which women's bodies served to demarcate ethnic boundaries.

Given the importance of marriage to processes of ethnicization, racialization, and assimilation, more research is needed on topics such as the agency of immigrant women within marital decisions, the way in which patriarchal values in certain immigrant cultures shaped endogamy rates and patterns of ethnic entrepreneurship, and the way in which claims to whiteness shaped marriage patterns. Did high rates of endogamy reflect efforts by immigrant men to control and restrict the access of native men to immigrant women (as was likely the case for the East Indians in the Greater Caribbean discussed by Putnam)? Were male migrants who brought wives from home more able to direct the labor of women and children toward family businesses than those who married locally, and did this affect the economic strategies they pursued? Was there a relationship between social positioning and endogamy? Were decisions made by Arab and Japanese immigrants to send home for wives an effort to maintain their class prestige by avoiding intermarriage with local mestizo, black, or indigenous populations that might jeopardize their claims to whiteness? Answering these questions will provide a new perspective on regional understandings of the relationships between race, gender, and nation.

Concluding Remarks

In using the comparative method pioneered by Samuel Baily, this volume has broken through the methodological nationalisms that have impeded the study of Latin American migrations, and offers a foundation for a more integrated history of Latin American immigration.[29] The broad comparative and trasnational lens reveals the complexity and interrelatedness of migratory currents and allows us to see the intersections of global, regional, and local forces in Latin American nation formation. The approach also challenges exceptionalist arguments that have held that certain immigrant experiences, whether in particular places (the United States or Argentina) or of distinct groups (Jews or Italians) were somehow unique, and this approach underlines that, although each immigrant group and receiving destination had their own special particularities, there are many meaningful points of comparison.

The volume presents significant insight into Latin American nation building, providing new angles on the role of intellectuals and the state in the forging of national identity; complicating debates on *mestizaje*; centering miscegenation as a window into gender and nation; and underlining the fluidity and multi-citedness of identity formation. In drawing attention to the international currents that shaped Latin American nationalisms and to the entangled networks that structured state formation, the case studies presented here historicize the workings of transnationalism in a region in which the phenomenon is typically associated only with the contemporary wave of out-migration, and allow us to pinpoint the deep-rooted transnational processes out of which Latin American nation-states were forged. While many of the chapters focus on elite discourses and government policy, they nevertheless provide an important reminder of the importance of subaltern agency to nation building. The decisions made by ordinary people at the individual and household level to move somewhere new and strive to improve their socioeconomic circumstances completely reshaped not just their personal lives but the configuration of Latin American economies, polities, and societies—often in ways not envisaged or intended by the elites who encouraged and incentivized their migration.

This volume is by no means a complete study of immigration and nation in Latin America. The massive internal migration that led huge numbers of Andean peoples to move to costal plantations and cities and the displacement of Mesoamerican and Patagonian indigenous peoples, for example, are beyond its remit, and the focus is purely on international immigration, which formed just one part of an interlocking process of shifting demographic boundaries in the period under consideration. Even within this framework, some groups and regions are given less attention than others. Yet it is hoped that the volume helps to reposition Latin America within the global historiography of migration, stimulate new research into the relationship between nationalism and immigration, and make a contribution toward halting the region's marginalization within theoretical models.

Notes

1. The title is adapted from Donna Gabaccia's suggestion that "We can write the story of nations from their borders." Cited in Green and Weil, *Citizenship*, 8.

2. Portes and DeWind, "Cross-Atlantic Dialogue," 829–30.

3. The exclusion of Latin America has been perpetuated even within efforts to challenge U.S.-centricity. The recent edited collection by Dirk Hoerder and Nora Faires, for example, seeks to explore how the processes of migration and state formation in North America—defined as Canada, the United States, Mexico, and the Caribbean islands—were integrated and interlocking, yet it sidesteps the fact that, as Lara Putnam points out in this volume, the relationship between Caribbean migration and state formation cannot be understood without consideration of Central and South American processes. See Hoerder and Faires, *Migrants and Migration*.

4. Moya, "Continent of Immigrants," 3.

5. McKeown, "Global Migration," 172.

6. McKeown, *Melancholy Order*.

7. Dirección General de Estadística y Censo, *Censo de población de Costa Rica*, 63.

8. This point is also made by Moya, "Continent of Immigrants," 23.

9. Miller, *Reinventing Modernity*, 16–18.

10. Moya, "Continent of Immigrants," 3. This builds on arguments Moya has made elsewhere, notably in *Cousins and Strangers*.

11. Hollifield, "Politics of International Migration."

12. See, for example, Míguez, "Introduction," xxii.

13. This parallels the argument Rajagopalan Radhakrishnan makes regarding East Indian migrants in the United States, who, on naturalizing and accepting an American identity, simultaneously minoritize their identity by becoming American—but an ethnic minority American. See Radhakrishnan, "Ethnicity in an Age of Diaspora," 121.

14. Alba and Nee, *Remaking the American Mainstream*.

15. Green and Weil, *Citizenship*.

16. Quote taken from a classic definition of "transnationalism" provided in Basch, Glick Schiller, and Szanton Blanc, *Nations Unbound*, 7.

17. Baily, "Conclusion," 285.

18. Foote, "Race, State and Nation," 264.

19. Jacobsen, *Whiteness*; and Roediger, *Wages of Whiteness*.

20. For a major exception in the Latin American literature, see Lesser, *Negotiating National Identity*.

21. Alba and Nee, *Remaking the American Mainstream*, 11.

22. Warner and Srole, *Social Systems*.

23. See Howard, *Coloring the Nation*; and Derby and Turits, "Historias de terror." This interpretation also reflects recent arguments made by anthropologist Jorge Duany about how the ethnicity of Haitian migrants in the Dominican Republic and of Dominican migrants in Puerto Rico has been racialized as black, leading to their exclusion. Duany, "Racializing Ethnicity."

24. Lesser, *Negotiating National Identity*, 11.

25. Donato et al., "A Glass Half Full?"

26. Cook-Martín, "Soldiers and Wayward Women," 576.

27. McClintock, "No Longer in a Future Heaven," 105.

28. See Guy, *Sex and Danger*.

29. Baily, "Adjustment of Italian Immigrants"; Baily, *Immigrants in the Lands of Promise*; and Baily and Miguez, *Mass Migration*.

Bibliography

ABBREVIATIONS

ABMD	Archivo, Biblioteca y Museo de la Diplomacia, Buenos Aires, Argentina
ANC	Archivo Nacional de Cuba, Havana, Cuba
ANCR	Archivo Nacional de Costa Rica, San José, Costa Rica
BA	Bundesarchiv Koblenz, Germany
BAP	Bundesarchiv Potsdam, Germany
CAD	Centre des Archives Diplomatiques, La Courneuve, France
CO	National Archives, Kew, United Kingdom; Colonial Office
FAPECFT	Fideicomiso Archivos Plutarco Elías Calles y Fernando Torreblanca, Mexico City
FO	National Archives, Kew, United Kingdom; Foreign Office
PAAA	Politisches Archiv des Auswärtigen Amtes, Berlin, Germany
USNA	United States National Archives

PRIMARY SOURCES

Unpublished Archival Sources

Archivo Biblioteca de la Función Legislativa, Quito, Ecuador
    Mensajes e Informes 1900
Archivo, Biblioteca y Museo de la Diplomacia, Buenos Aires, Argentina
    Box 1210, Folder 42
Archivo Nacional de Costa Rica, San José, Costa Rica.
    Serie Congreso, no. 16753
Archivo Nacional de Cuba, Havana, Cuba.
    exp. 82, leg. 121
Bundesarchiv Koblenz, Germany.
    AA 6674
    Archive of the Deutsches Ausland-Institut (DAI-Archiv): Neu/1208
Bundesarchiv Potsdam, Germany.
    AA 4732
    AA 44674

AA 44813

RWM, 929

Centre des Archives Diplomatiques, La Courneuve, France.

6CPCOM39

Fideicomiso Archivos Plutarco Elías Calles y Fernando Torreblanca, Mexico City (FAPECFT).

Archivo Plutarco Elías Calles, Fondo Plutarco Elías Calles, serie 0204, gav. 86, exp. 56, inv. 1082.

National Archives, Kew, United Kingdom; Colonial Office.

28/264/16186

28/269/5443

28/269/29756

28/274/8

28/282/25

137/479/19

137/480/36

137/533/5194

137/533/6890

137/618/14477

137/631/34768

295/443/10862

295/596/17

318/270/5857

318/406/1

950/44

National Archives, Kew, United Kingdom; Foreign Office.

288/125/565

369/126/28133

371/2643

371/944/41616

Politisches Archiv des Auswärtigen Amtes, Berlin, Germany.

20948

20949

60027

121902

Schu 10 fl, DCB

U.S. National Archives

State Department General Records. Consular Despatches, Kingston, Jamaica
Microcopy X 353.1 U58g T31, Reel 33

PERIODICALS

al-Fiṭra al-Islāmīyya (Buenos Aires, Argentina), 1941.

al-Hadīqa (San Miguel de Tucumán, Argentina), 1922.

al-Hurrīyya (San Miguel de Tucumán, Argentina), 1931.

al-Watan (Buenos Aires, Argentina), 1932.

al-Zawba'a (San Miguel de Tucumán and Buenos Aires, Argentina), 1941–43.

Atlantic Voice (Limón, Costa Rica), 1936

Barbados Advocate (Bridgetown, Barbados), 1924.

Barbados Weekly Herald (Bridgetown, Barbados), 1929.

Boletim do Departamento Estadual do Trabalho (São Paulo, Brazil), 1927.

Daily Gleaner (Kingston, Jamaica), 1905–39.

Der Bund (Santiago de Chile) 1918.

El Comercio (Quito, Ecuador), 1928.

El Diario de Costa Rica (San José, Costa Rica), 1936.

Deutsches Volksblatt (Porto Alegre, Brazil), 1914.

Eco de Oriente (San Miguel de Tucumán, Argentina), 1926.

O Estado de São Paulo (São Paulo, Brazil), 1914–20.

El Fígaro (Havana, Cuba), 1926.

Foreign Relations of the United States (Washington, DC), 1918.

Forjando (Buenos Aires, Argentina), 1940–42.

Fraternidad (Havana, Cuba), 1939.

El Grito del Pueblo (Guayaquil, Ecuador), 1900.

Jornal do Commercio (Rio de Janeiro, Brazil), 1913.

Limón Searchlight (Limón, Costa Rica), 1931.

Mitteilungen des südamerikanischen Instituts (Cologne, Germany), 1916.

La Nación (Buenos Aires, Argentina), 1908–10.

New York Times (New York), 1885–2013.

El Nuevo Tiempo (Tegucigalpa), 1916.

El Orden (San Miguel de Tucumán, Argentina), 1898.

Panama American (Panama City, Panama), 1926–27.

Panama Star and Herald (Panama City, Panama), 1921.

Plural JAI (Buenos Aires, Argentina), 2012.

Port of Spain Daily Mirror (Port of Spain, Trinidad), 1904.

Port of Spain Weekly Guardian (Port of Spain, Trinidad), 1920.

La Razón (Buenos Aires, Argentina), 1922.

Revista Bimestre Cubana (Havana, Cuba), 1923.

La Voz del Atlántico (Limón, Costa Rica), 1936.

The West Indian (St. George's, Grenada), 1915.

PUBLISHED BOOKS AND JOURNAL ARTICLES

Adriani, Alberto. *Labor Venezolanista*, 6th ed. Caracas: Academia Nacional de Ciencias Económicas, 1989.

———. "Venezuela y los problemas de inmigración." *Cultura Venezolana: Revista Mensual* 9 (1926): 83–92.

Agar, Lorenzo, ed. *Contribuciones árabes a las identidades iberoamericanas*. Madrid: Edición Karim Hauser y Daniel Gil, 2009.

Akmir, Abdeluahed. "La inmigración árabe en Argentina (1880–1980)." PhD diss., Universidad Complutense de Madrid, 1991.

———. "La prensa árabe en Argentina." In *Huellas comunes y miradas cruzadas: Mundos árabe, ibérico e iberoamericano*, edited by Mohammed Salhi, 291–305. Rabat, Mor.: Universidad Mohamed V, 1995.

———. *Los árabes en América Latina: Historia de una emigración*. Madrid: Siglo XXI, 2009.

Alba, Richard, and Victor Nee. *Remaking the American Mainstream: Assimilation and Contemporary Immigration*. Cambridge, MA: Harvard University Press, 2003.

Albaladejo, Christophe. "Les descendants des Allemands de la Volga dans la Pampa: La résistance comme culture." In *Une pampa en mosaïque: Des communautés locales à l'épreuve de l'ajustement en Argentine*, edited by Jean-Christian Tulet, 113–44. Paris: L'Harmattan, 2001.

Alberdi, Juan Bautista. *Bases y puntos de partida para la organización política de la República Argentina: Derivados de la ley que preside al desarrollo de la civilización en la América del Sud*. Barcelona: Linkgua, 2007.

Aldrighi, Clara. "Luigi Fabbri en Uruguay, 1929–1935." *Estudios Migratorios Latinoamericanos* 12, no. 37 (1997): 389–422.

Alfaro-Velcamp, Theresa. "Immigrant Positioning in Twentieth-Century Mexico: Middle Easterners, Foreign Citizens, and Multiculturalism." *Hispanic American Historical Review* 86, no. 1 (2006): 61–92.

———. *So Far from Allah, So Close to the United States: Middle Eastern Immigrants in Modern Mexico*. Austin: University of Texas Press, 2007.

Aliano, David. *Mussolini's National Project in Argentina*. Madison, NJ: Fairleigh Dickinson University Press, 2012.

al-Muʿtamar al-ʿArabī al-Awwal fī Amrīkā, *al-Kitāb al-akhḍar al-thānī fī masāʾil Lubnān wa-Sūrīya wa-Filasṭīn*. Buenos Aires: al-Lajna al-Tanfīdhīya al-Dāʾima, 1944.

Álvarez, Alejandro. "Latin America and International Law." *American Journal of International Law* 3, no. 2 (1909): 269–353.

Alvim, Zuleika M. F. *Brava gente! Os italianos em São Paulo, 1870–1920*. São Paulo: Brasiliense, 1986.

Amador, José. "Redeeming the Tropics: Public Health and National Identity in Cuba, Puerto Rico and Brazil, 1890–1940." PhD diss., University of Michigan, 2008.

Anderson, Benedict. *Imagined Communities: Reflections on the Origin and Spread of Nationalism*. 2nd ed. London: Verso, 1991.

Anderson, Wanni W., and Robert G. Lee, eds. *Displacements and Diasporas: Asians in the Americas*. New Brunswick, NJ: Rutgers University Press, 2005.

Andrews, George Reid. "Brazilian Racial Democracy, 1900–1990: An American Counterpoint." *Journal of Contemporary History* 31, no. 3 (1996): 483–507.

Anuario Estadístico de la República Oriental del Uruguay 21, no. 8 (1907–1908), part 3. Montevideo, 1911.

Appelbaum, Nancy P., Anne S. Macpherson, and Karin Alejandra Rosemblatt, eds. *Race and Nation in Modern Latin America*. Chapel Hill: University of North Carolina Press, 2003.

Arona, Juan de. *La inmigración en el Perú*. Lima, 1891.

Asdrúbal Silva, Hernán, ed. *Inmigración y estadísticas en el Cono Sur de América: Argentina–Brasil–Chile*. Mexico City: Instituto Panamericano de Geografía e Historia, 1990.

Avé-Lallemant, Robert. *Reise durch Süd-Brasilien im Jahre 1858*. Leipzig: Brockhaus, 1859.

Avni, Haim. "Antisemitism in Argentina: The Dimensions of Danger." In *Approaches to Antisemitism: Context and Curriculum*, edited by Michael Brown, 57–77. New York: American Jewish Committee, 1994.

———. *Argentina and the Jews: A History of Jewish Immigration*. Tuscaloosa: University of Alabama Press, 1991.

———. *Argentina y las migraciones judías*. Buenos Aires: Milá, 2005.

Bailey, John, and Sibila Seibert. "Inmigración y relaciones étnicas: Los ingleses en la Argentina." *Desarrollo Económico* 18, no. 72 (1979): 539–58.

Bailey, Thomas A. *The Policy of the United States toward the Neutrals, 1917–1918*. New York: Ayer Publishing, 1979.

Baily, Samuel L. "The Adjustment of Italian Immigrants in Buenos Aires and New York, 1870–1914." *American Historical Review* 88, no. 2 (1983): 281–305.

———. "Conclusion: Common Themes and Future Directions." In *Mass Migration to Modern Latin America*, edited by Samuel L. Baily and Eduardo José Miguez, 279–88. Wilmington, DE: SR Books, 2003.

———. *Immigrants in the Lands of Promise: Italians in Buenos Aires and New York City, 1870 to 1914*. Ithaca, NY: Cornell University Press, 1999.

———. *Labor, Nationalism, and Politics in Argentina*. New Brunswick, NJ: Rutgers University Press, 1967.

———. "The Role of Two Newspapers in the Assimilation of Italians in Buenos Aires and São Paulo, 1893–1913." *International Migration Review* 12, no. 3 (1978): 321–40.

Baily, Samuel L., and Eduardo José Míguez, eds. *Mass Migration to Modern Latin America*. Wilmington, DE: SR Books, 2003.

Baily, Samuel L., and Andrea Scarli. "Las sociedades de ayuda mutua y el desarrollo de una comunidad italiana en Buenos Aires, 1858–1918." *Desarrollo Económico* 21, no. 84 (1982): 485–514.

Banks, Marcus. *Ethnicity: Anthropological Constructions*. London: Routledge, 1996.

Bar-Gil, S. *We Started with a Dream: Graduates of Latin American Youth Movements in the Kibbutz Movement 1946–1967* (in Hebrew). Jerusalem: Machon Ben Guiron, 2005.

Bartelt, Dawid. "Fünfte Kolonne ohne Plan: Die Auslandsorganisation der NSDAP in Brasilien, 1931–1939." *Ibero-Amerikanisches Archiv* 19, no. 1–2 (1993): 3–35.

Barth, Fredrik, ed. *Ethnic Groups and Boundaries: The Social Organization of Culture Difference*. Prospect Heights, IL: Waveland Press, 1998.

Basch, Linda, Nina Glick Schiller, and Cristina Szanton Blanc, *Nations Unbound: Transnational Projects, Postcolonial Predicaments, and Deterritorialized Nation-States*. Amsterdam: Gordon and Breach Publishers, 1994.

Basdeo, Sahadeo. "Indian Participation in Labour Politics in Trinidad, 1919–1939." *Caribbean Quarterly* 32, no. 3–4 (1986): 50–65.

Bastos de Avila, Fernando. *Immigration in Latin America*. Washington, DC: Pan American Union, 1964.

Bauböck, Rainer, and Thomas Faist, eds. *Diaspora and Transnationalism: Concepts, Theories and Methods*. Amsterdam: Amsterdam University Press, 2010.

Bauer, Kurt. "Die Chiledeutschen während des Weltkrieges." *Auslandsdeutsche Volksforschung* 2 (1938): 464–72.

Bayly, Christopher, and Eugenio F. Biagini, eds. *Giuseppe Mazzini and the Globalization of Democratic Nationalism, 1830–1920*. Oxford: Oxford University Press, 2008.

Bejarano, Margalit. "La inmigración a Cuba y la política migratoria de los EE.UU. (1903–1933)." *Estudios Interdisciplinarios de América Latina y el Caribe* 4, no. 2 (1993): 113–28.

Bejarano, Margalit, and Edna Aizenberg, eds. *Contemporary Sephardic Identity in the Americas: A Collection of interdisciplinary Studies*. Syracuse, NY: Syracuse University Press, 2012.

Benchimol, Samuel. *Eretz Amazônia: Os judeos na Amazônia*. Manaus: Valer, 1998.

Benjamin, Thomas. *A Rich Land, a Poor People: Politics and Society in Modern Chiapas*. Albuquerque: University of New Mexico Press, 1989.

Benson, Nettie Lee. "Territorial Integrity in Mexican Politics, 1821–1833." In *The Independence of Mexico and the Creation of the New Nation*, edited by Jaime E. Rodríguez O., 275–307. Los Angeles: University of California, Los Angeles, Latin American Center, 1989.

Berger, Stefan. "Germany: Ethnic Nationalism par excellence?" In *What Is a Nation? Europe 1789–1914*, edited by Timothy Baycroft and Mark Hewitson, 42–60. Oxford: Oxford University Press, 2006.

Bernasconi, Alicia, and Owaldo Truzzi. "Política imigratória no Brasil e na Argentina nos anos de 1930: aproximações e diferenças." In *Políticas migratórias: América Latina, Brasil e brasileiros no exterior*, edited by Teresa Sales and Maria do Rosário R. Salles, 111–37. São Carlos: Editora UDSCar, 2002.

Bernecker, Walther. *Die Handelskonquistadoren: Europäische Interessen und mexikanischer Staat im 19. Jahrhundert*. Stuttgart, Ger.: Steiner Verlag, 1988.

Bernecker, Walther L., and Thomas Fischer, "Deutsche in Lateinamerika." In *Deutsche im Ausland—Fremde in Deutschland: Migration in Geschichte und Gegenwart*, edited by Klaus J. Bade, 197–214. Munich: C. H. Beck, 1992.

Berninger, George D. *La inmigración en México, 1821–1857*. Mexico City: Secretaría de Educación Pública, 1974.

Bertagna, Federica. *La stampa italiana in Argentina*. Rome: Donzelli, 2009.

Bertonha, João Fábio. "Between Sigma and Fascio: An Analysis of the Relationship between Italian Fascism and Brazilian Integralism." *Luzo-Brazilian Review* 37, no. 1 (2000): 93–105.

———. "Fascismo, antifascismo y las comunidades italianas en Brasil, Argentina y Uruguay: Un perspectiva comparada." *Estudios Migratorios Latinoamericanos* 14, no. 42 (1999): 111–33.

———. "A 'Foreign Legion' for Mussolini? A Transnational Experience of Fascist Volunteers During the Ethiopian War." Paper presented at the Third European Congress on World and Global History, London, 2011.

———. "Italiani nel mondo anglofono, latino e germanico. Diverse prospettive sul fascismo italiano?" *Altreitalie* 26 (2003): 40–64.

———. "O antifascismo no mundo da diaspora italiana: Elementos para uma analise comparativa a partir do caso brasileiro." *Altreitalie* 17 (1998): 16–32.

———. *O fascismo e os imigrantes italianos no Brasil*. Porto Alegre: EDIPUCRS, 2001.

Bertoni, Lilia Ana. *Patriotas, cosmopolitas y nacionalistas: La construcción de la nacionalidad argentina a fines del siglo XIX*. Buenos Aires: Fondo de Cultura Económica, 2001.

Bessis, Juliette. *La Méditerranée fasciste: L'Italie mussolinienne et la Tunisie.* Paris: Karthala, 1981.

Bethell, Leslie. *The Abolition of the Brazilian Slave Trade: Britain, Brazil and the Slave Trade Question 1807–1869.* Cambridge: Cambridge University Press, 1970.

Beyhaut, Gustavo, Roberto Cortés Conde, Haydée Gorostegui, and Susana Torrado. "Los inmigrantes en el sistema ocupacional argentino." In *Argentina, sociedad de masas,* 3rd ed., edited by Torcuato S. Di Tella, Gino Germani, and Jorge Graciarena, 85–123. Buenos Aires: EUDEBA, 1966.

Biesanz, John Berry, and Mavis Hiltunen Biesanz. *Costa Rican Life.* New York: Columbia University Press, 1944.

Bilot, Pauline. *Allemandes au Chili.* Rennes, France: Presses Universitaires de Rennes, 2010.

Blancpain, Jean-Pierre. "Des visées pangermanistes au noyautage hitlérien: Le nationalisme allemand et l'Amérique Latine (1890–1945)." *Revue Historique* 281 (1989): 433–60.

———. *Les Allemands au Chili, 1816–1945.* Cologne: Böhlau, 1974.

Blumenbach, Johann Friedrich. *Über die natürlichen Verschiedenheiten im Menschengeschlechte.* Leipzig: Breitkopf and Härtel, 1798.

Bodian, M. *Dying in the Law of Moses: Crypto-Jewish Martyrdom in the Iberian World.* Bloomington: Indiana University Press, 2007.

Bockelman, Brian. "Between the Gaucho and the Tango: Popular Songs and the Shifting Landscape of Argentine Identity, 1895–1915." *American Historical Review* 116, no. 3 (2011): 577–601.

Bolland, O. Nigel. "Labor Protests, Rebellions, and the Rise of Nationalism during Depression and War." In *The Caribbean: A History of the Region and Its Peoples,* edited by Stephan Palmié and Francisco Scarano, 459–74. Chicago: University of Chicago Press, 2011.

———. *The Politics of Labour in the British Caribbean: The Social Origins of Authoritarianism and Democracy in the Labour Movement.* Kingston, Jam.: Ian Randle, 2001.

Bonilla, Heraclio. "The War of the Pacific and the National and Colonial Problem in Peru." *Past and Present* 81 (1978): 92–118.

Borchard, Hermann. *Die deutsche evangelische Diaspora: Erstes Heft; Australien, Südafrika, Südamerika.* Gotha: Perthes, 1890.

Bordoni, Giosuè. *Montevideo e la repubblica dell'Uruguay.* Milan, 1885.

Bosch, Beatriz. "La colonización de los alemanes del Volga en Entre Ríos, 1878–1888." *Investigaciones y Ensayos* 23 (1977): 295–310.

Bouknight-Davis, Gail. "Chinese Economic Development and Ethnic Identity Formation in Jamaica." In *The Chinese in the Caribbean,* edited by Andrew Wilson, 69–92. Princeton, NJ: Markus Weiner, 2004.

Bourdé, Guy. *Urbanisation et immigration en Amérique latine: Buenos Aires XIXe et XXe siècles.* Paris: Montaigne, 1974.

Bourgois, Phillipe. "The Black Diaspora in Costa Rica: Upward Mobility in Costa Rica." *New West Indian Guide* 60, no. 3–4 (1986): 149–65.

———. *Ethnicity at Work: Divided Labor on a Central American Banana Plantation.* Baltimore: Johns Hopkins University Press, 1989.

Brack, Gene M. *Mexico Views Manifest Destiny, 1821–1846: An Essay on the Origins of the Mexican War*. Albuquerque: University of New Mexico Press, 1975.

Brading, David A. "Creole Nationalism and Mexican Liberalism." *Journal of Interamerican Studies and World Affairs* 15 (1973): 139–90.

———. *Los orígenes del nacionalismo mexicano*. Mexico City: El Colegio de México, 1979.

Brégain, Gildas. *Syriens et Libanais d'Amérique du sud (1918–1945)*. Paris: L'Harmattan, 2008.

Brepohl de Magalhães, Marionhilde. *Pangermanismo e nazismo: A trajetória alemão rumo ao Brasil*. Campinas: UNICAMP, 1998.

Brereton, Bridget. "'All ah we is not one': Historical and Ethnic Narratives in Pluralist Trinidad." *Global South* 4, no. 2 (2010): 218–38.

———. *A History of Modern Trinidad, 1783–1962*. Port of Spain and London: Heinemann, 1981.

Bresciano, Juan Andrés. "El antifascismo ítalo-uruguayo en el contexto de la segunda guerra mundial." *Deportate, esuli, profughe* 11 (2009): 94–111.

Brilli, Catia. "La diaspora commerciale ligure nel sistema atlantico iberico: Da Cadice a Buenos Aires, 1750–1830." PhD diss., Università degli Studi di Pisa, 2008.

Brodsky, Adriana M., "'Miss Sefaradí' and 'Queen Esther': Sephardim, Zionism, and Ethnic and National Identities in Argentina, 1933–1971," *Estudios Interdisciplinarios de América Latina y el Caribe* 23, no. 1 (2012): 35–60.

Brown, Jonathan C. "Foreign and Native-Born Workers in Porfirian Mexico." *American Historical Review* 98 (1993): 786–818.

———. *Oil and Revolution in Mexico*. Berkeley: University of California Press, 1993.

Browne, George P. "Government Immigration Policy in Imperial Brazil, 1822–1870." PhD diss., Catholic University of America, 1972.

Brubaker, Rogers. *Citizenship and Nationhood in France and Germany*. Cambridge, MA: Harvard University Press, 1992.

———. "The 'Diaspora' Diaspora." *Ethnic and Racial Studies* 28, no. 1 (2005): 1–19.

———. "Ethnicity, Race, and Nationalism." *Annual Review of Sociology* 35 (2009): 21–42.

———. "Ethnicity without Groups." *Archives Européennes de Sociologie* 43, no. 2 (2002): 163–89.

———. "The Manichean Myth: Rethinking the Distinction between 'Civic' and 'Ethnic' Nationalism." In *Nation and National Identity: The European Experience in Perspective*, edited by Hanspeter Kriesi, Klaus Armingeon, Hannes Siegrist, and Andreas Wimmer, 55–71. Zurich: Rüegger, 1999.

———. "The Return of Assimilation? Changing Perspectives on Immigration and Its Sequels in France, Germany, and the United States." *Ethnic and Racial Studies* 24, no. 4 (2001): 531–48.

Bruckmayr, Philipp. "Syro-Lebanese Migration to Colombia, Venezuela and Curacão: From Mainly Christian to Predominantly Muslim Phenomenon." *European Journal of Economic and Political Studies* 3, Special Issue: Transnational Islam (2010): 151–78.

Brunn, Gerhard. *Deutschland und Brasilien (1889–1914)*. Cologne: Böhlau, 1971.

Buarque de Holanda, Sérgio. *Raizes do Brasil*. Rio de Janeiro: Olympio, 1936.

Buchenau, Jürgen. *In the Shadow of the Giant: The Making of Mexico's Central America Policy, 1876–1930*. Tuscaloosa: University of Alabama Press, 1996.

———. *Plutarco Elías Calles and the Mexican Revolution*. Lanham, MD: Rowman and Littlefield, 2007.

———. "Small Numbers, Great Impact: Mexico and Its Immigrants, 1821–1973." *Journal of American Ethnic History* 20, no. 3 (2001): 23–49.

———. *Tools of Progress: A German Merchant Family in Mexico City, 1865–Present*. Albuquerque: University of New Mexico Press, 2004.

Buchrucker, Cristian. *Nacionalismo y peronismo: La Argentina en la crisis ideológica mundial (1927–1955)*. Buenos Aires: Editorial Sudamericana, 1987.

Burkholder, Mark. *Spaniards in the Colonial Empire: Creoles Vs. Peninsulars?* Chichester, U.K.: Wiley Blackwell, 2012.

Burns, E. Bradford. *Nationalism in Brazil: A Historical Survey*. New York: Praeger, 1968.

Calhoun, Craig. *Nationalism*. Minneapolis: University of Minnesota Press, 1997.

Camposortega Cruz, Sergio. "Análisis demográfico de las corrientes migratorias a México desde finales del siglo XIX." In *Destino México: Un estudio de las migraciones asiáticas a México, siglos XIX y XX*, edited by María Elena Ota Mishima, 23–53. Mexico City: El Colegio de México, 1997.

Cane, James. "'Unity for the Defense of Culture': The AIAPE and the Cultural Politics of Argentine Antifascism, 1935–1943." *Hispanic American Historical Review* 77, no. 3 (1997): 443–82.

Cannistraro, Philip V. *Blackshirts in Little Italy: Italian Americans and Fascism 1921–1929*. West Lafayette, IN: Bordighera Press, 1999.

Cannistraro, Philip V., and Gianfausto Rosoli. "Fascist Emigration Policy in the 1920s: An Interpretive Framework." *International Migration Review* 13, no. 4 (1979): 673–92.

Caprariis, Luca de. "'Fascism for Export'? The Rise and Eclipse of the Fasci Italiani all'Estero." *Journal of Contemporary History* 35, no. 2 (2000): 151–83.

Carneiro, Maria Luiza Tucci, and Marcia Yumi Takeuchi, eds. *Imigrantes japoneses no Brasil: Trajetória, imaginário e memória*. São Paulo: Edusp, 2010.

Carnegie, James. *Some Aspects of Jamaica's Politics, 1918–1938*. Kingston: Institute of Jamaica, 1973.

Carr, Barry. "Identity, Class, and Nation: Black Immigrant Workers, Cuban Communism, and the Sugar Insurgency, 1925–1934." *Hispanic American Historical Review* 78, no. 1 (1998): 83–116.

Casey, Matthew. "Haitian Migrants in Cuba, 1902–1940." PhD diss., University of Pittsburgh, 2012.

Cattarulla, Camilla. "Orgoglio italiano: La propaganda fascista in Argentina attraverso il Risorgimento." *Studi Latinoamericani* 3 (2007): 301–16.

Chambers, Anthony. *Race, Nation and West Indian Immigration to Honduras*. Baton Rouge: Louisiana State University Press, 2010.

Chang, Jason Oliver. "Racial Alterity in the Mestizo Nation." *Journal of Asian American Studies* 14, no. 3 (2011): 331–59.

Charlton, Audrey. "'Cat Born in Oven Is not Bread': Jamaican and Barbadian Immigrants in Cuba between 1900 and 1959." PhD diss., Columbia University, 2005.

Cherjovsky, Iván, "La faz ideológica del conflicto colonos/JCA: el discurso del ideal agrario en las memorias de Colonia Mauricio." In *Marginados y consagrados: Nuevos estudios sobre la vida judía en la Argentina*, edited by Emmanuel Kahan, Laura Schenquer, Damián Setton, and Alejandro Dujovne, 47–66. Buenos Aires: Lumiere, 2011.

Chickering, Roger. *We Men Who Feel Most German: A Cultural Study of the Pan-German League, 1886–1914*. Boston: Allen and Unwin, 1984.

Chinea, Jorge L. "Race, Colonial Exploitation and West Indian Immigration in Nine-teenth-Century Puerto Rico, 1800–1850." *Americas* 52, no. 4 (1996): 495–519.

Choate, Mark I. *Emigrant Nation: The Making of Italy Abroad*. Cambridge, MA: Harvard University Press, 2008.

Chomsky, Aviva. "'Barbados or Canada?' Race, Immigration, and Nation in Early Twen-tieth-Century Cuba." *Hispanic American Historical Review* 80, no. 3 (2000): 415–62.

Chuffat Latour, Antonio. *Apunte histórico de los chinos en Cuba*. Havana: Molina y Cia., 1927.

Cimet, Adina. *Ashkenazi Jews in Mexico: Ideologies in the Structuring of a Community*. Albany: State University of New York Press, 1997.

Cinel, Dino. *From Italy to San Francisco: The Immigrant Experience*. Stanford, CA: Stan-ford University Press, 1982.

Coaracy, Vivaldo. *Problemas nacionais*. São Paulo: Sociedade Impressora Paulista, 1930.

Cohen, Martin A. *The Martyr: Luis de Carvajal, a Secret Jew in Sixteeen-Century Mexico*. Albuquerque: University of New Mexico Press, 2001.

Cohen, Robin. *Global Diasporas: An Introduction*. 2nd ed. London: Routledge, 2008.

Cohen, Steven Martin. *American Assimilation or Jewish Revival?* Bloomington: Indiana University Press, 1988.

Colby, Jason M. *The Business of Empire: United Fruit, Race, and U.S. Expansion in Central America*. Ithaca, NY: Cornell University Press, 2011.

Collado Herrera, María del Carmen. *Empresarios y políticos: Entre la Restauración y la Revolución*. Mexico City: Instituto Nacional de Estudios Históricos de la Revolución Mexicana, 1996.

Collor, Lindolfo. *Garibaldi e a guerra dos farrapos*. Rio de Janeiro: José Olympio, 1938.

Colom González, Francisco. "La imaginación nacional en América Latina." *Historia Mexi-cana* 53, no. 2 (2003): 313–39.

Conniff, Michael Jr. *Black Labor on a White Canal: Panama, 1904–1981*. Pittsburgh: Uni-versity of Pittsburgh Press, 1985.

Conrad, Sebastian. *Globalisierung und Nation im deutschen Kaiserreich*. Munich: C. H. Beck, 2006.

Constituição da República dos Estados Unidos do Brasil. Rio de Janeiro: Imprensa Nacional, 1934.

Contraloría General de la República, Dirección del Censo. *Memoria y cuadros del Censo de 1928*. Bogotá: Editorial Librería Nueva, 1930.

Contu, Martino. "L'antifascismo italiano in Argentina tra la fine degli anni Venti e i primi anni Trenta del Novecento: Il caso degli antifascisti sardi e della Lega Sarda d'Azione 'Sardegna Avanti.'" *Rivista dell'Istituto di Storia dell'Europa Mediterranea*, no. 6 (2011): 447–502.

Conzen, Kathleen Neils, David A. Gerber, Ewa Morawska, George E. Pozzetta, and Ru-dolph J. Vecoli. "The Invention of Ethnicity: A Perspective from the USA." *Journal of American Ethnic History* 12, no. 1 (1992): 3–41.

Cook-Martín, David. "Soldiers and Wayward Women: Gendered Citizenship, and Migration Policy in Argentina, Italy, and Spain since 1850." *Citizenship Studies* 10, no. 5 (2006): 571–90.

Corbitt, Duvon Clough. "Immigration in Cuba." *Hispanic American Historical Review* 22, no. 2 (1942): 280–308.

Corradini, Enrico. *La patria lontana*. Rome: Vecchiarelli, 1989.

Costanzo, Gabriela. *Los indeseables: Las Leyes de Residencia y Defensa Social*. Buenos Aires: Madreselva, 2009.

Costa Rica. *Base de datos del Censo de 1927*. http://ccp.ucr.ac.cr/censos.

Couyoumdjian, Juan Ricardo. *Chile y Gran Bretaña durante la primera guerra mundial y la postguerra, 1914–1921*. Santiago de Chile: Andres Bello, 1986.

Crawford, Sharika. "A Transnational World Fractured but Not Forgotten: British West Indian Migration to the Colombian Islands of San Andres and Providence." *New West Indian Guide* 85, no. 1–2 (2011): 31–52.

Cresciani, Gianfranco. *The Italians in Australia*. Cambridge: Cambridge University Press, 2003.

Crosby, Alfred. *Ecological Imperialism: The Biological Expansion of Europe, 900–1900*. Cambridge: Cambridge University Press, 1986.

Cuba, Dirección General del Censo. *Censo de 1943*. Habana: P. Fernández y cía., 1945.

Cuba, Comité Estatal de Estadísticas. *Memorias inéditas del Censo de 1931*. Habana: Editorial de Ciencias Sociales, 1978.

Cudjoe, Selwyn R. "Multiculturalism and Its Challenges in Trinidad and Tobago." *Society* 48, no. 4 (2011): 330–41.

Curtis, James R. "Mexicali's Chinatown." *Geographical Review* 85, no. 3 (1995): 335–48.

Curtis, William Eleroy. *Venezuela: A Land Where It's Always Summer*. New York: Harper and Bros., 1896.

Davis, Ethelyn C. "The American Colony in Mexico City." PhD diss., University of Missouri, 1942.

Davison, Roderic H. "The Armenian Crisis, 1912–1914." *American Historical Review* 53, no. 3 (1948): 481–505.

Dawisha, Adeed. *Arab Nationalism in the Twentieth Century: From Triumph to Despair*. Princeton, NJ: Princeton University Press, 2003.

Dawson, Frank Griffith. "The Evacuation of the Mosquito Shore and the English Who Stayed Behind." *Americas* 55, no. 1 (1998): 63–89.

Dean, Warren. *The Industrialization of São Paulo, 1880–1945*. Austin: University of Texas Press, 1969.

Debenedetti, Salvador. "Sobre la formación de una raza argentina." *Revista de Filosofía* 1, no. 2 (1917): 416–17.

De la Fuente, Alejandro. *A Nation for All: Race, Inequality, and Politics in Twentieth Century Cuba*. Chapel Hill: University of North Carolina Press, 2001.

DeLaney, Jeane. "Making Sense of Modernity: Changing Attitudes toward the Immigrant and the Gaucho in Turn-of-the-Century Argentina." *Comparative Studies in Society and History* 38, no. 3 (1996): 434–59.

Delgado, Grace Peña. *Making the Chinese Mexican: Global Migration, Localism, and Exclusion in the U.S.–Mexico Borderlands*. Stanford, CA: Stanford University Press, 2012.

Della Pergola, Sergio. "Demographic Trends of Latin American Jewry." In *The Jewish Presence in Latin America*, edited by Judith Laikin Elkin and Gilbert W. Merkx, 85–133. Boston: Allen and Unwin, 1987.

Delpar, Helen. *The Enormous Vogue of Things Mexican*. Tuscaloosa: University of Alabama Press, 1992.

Departamento de la Estadística Nacional, *Censo general de habitantes*. Mexico City: Talleres Gráficos de la Nación, 1925.

Derby, Lauren. "Haitians, Magic, and Money: Raza and Society in the Haitian-Dominican Borderlands, 1900 to 1937." *Comparative Studies in Society and History* 36, no. 3 (1994): 488–526.

Derby, Lauren, and Richard Turits. "Historias de terror y los terrores de historia: La masacre haitiana de 1937 en la Republica Dominicana." *Estudios Sociales* 92 (1993): 65–76.

Desir, Lucia. "Between Loyalties: Racial, Ethnic and 'National' Identity in Providencia, Colombia." PhD diss., Johns Hopkins University, 1989.

Deutsch, Sandra McGee. *Crossing Borders, Claiming a Nation: A History of Argentine Jewish Women, 1880–1955*. Durham, NC: Duke University Press, 2010.

———. *Las Derechas: The Extreme Right in Argentina, Brazil, and Chile, 1890–1939*. Stanford, CA: Stanford University Press, 1999.

Deutsches Auslands-Institut, ed. *Bibliographisches Handbuch des Auslandsdeutschtums*. Stuttgart: Ausland und Heimat, 1932 et seqq.

Devoto, Fernando J. "El revés de la trama: Políticas migratorias y practicas administrativas en la Argentina (1919–1949)." *Desarrollo Económico* 41, no. 162 (2001): 281–304.

———. *Historia de la inmigración en la Argentina*. Buenos Aires: Sudamericana, 2003.

———. *Historia de los italianos en la Argentina*. Buenos Aires: Biblos, 2006.

———. "Italiani in Argentina: Ieri e Oggi." *Altreitalie* 27 (2003): 4–17.

———. "Un caso di migrazione precoce: gli italiani in Uruguay nel secolo XIX." In *L'emigrazione italiana e la formazione dell'Uruguay moderno*, edited by Fernando J. Devodo, 1–36. Turin: Fondazione Agnelli, 1993.

Dezem, Rogério. "Hi-no-maru manchado de sangue: A Shindo Renmei e o DEOPS/SP." In *Imigrantes japoneses no Brasil: Trajetória, imaginário e memória*, ed. Maria Luiza Tucci Carneiro and Marcia Yumi Takeuchi, 243–72 (São Paulo: Edusp, 2010).

———. *Matizes do "amarelo": A gênese dos discursos sobre os orientais no Brasil (1878–1908)*. São Paulo: Associação Editorial Humanitas, 2005.

Dickmann, Adolfo. *Nacionalismo y socialismo: El socialismo y el principio de nacionalidad; Los argentinos naturalizados en la política*. Buenos Aires: Talleres gráficos Porter hnos., 1933.

Die Arbeit unter den Evangelischen Deutschen in Brasilien: Fünfter Bericht des Comité für die protestantischen Deutschen in Brasilien; Erstattet im Januar 1874. Barmen: Wiemann und Steinhaus, 1874.

"Die Tätigkeit des Deutschen Volksbundes für Argentinien im zweiten Bundesjahre." *Der Bund* 1 (1918): 3–7.

Dietrich, Ana Maria. *Caça às suásticas: O Partido Nazista em São Paulo sob a mira da Polícia Política*. São Paulo: Associação Editorial Humanitas and Imprensa Oficial do Estado de São Paulo, 2007.

Diggins, John P. *Mussolini and Fascism: The View from America*. Princeton, NJ: Princeton University Press, 1972.

Dirección General de Estadística y Censo, *Censo de población de Costa Rica, 11 de mayo 1927*. San Jose: Ministerio de Economía y Hacienda, 1960.

Dixon, Kwame, and John Burdick, eds. *Comparative Perspectives on Afro-Latin America*. Gainesville: University Press of Florida, 2012.

Dobry, Hernán. *Operación Israel: El rearme argentino durante la dictadura (1976–1983)*. Buenos Aires: Lumiere, 2011.

Dockterman, Daniel. "Hispanics of Mexican Origin in the United States, 2009." *Pew Research Hispanic Trends Project*, May 26, 2011. http://www.pewhispanic.org/2011/05/26/hispanics-of-mexican-origin-in-the-united-states-2009/.

Donato, Katherine M., Donna Gabaccia, Jennifer Holdaway, Martin Manalansan IV, and Patricia R. Pessar. "A Glass Half Full? Gender in Migration Studies." *International Migration Review* 40, no.1 (2006): 3–26.

Doß, Kurt. *Das deutsche Auswärtige Amt im Übergang vom Kaiserreich zur Weimarer Republik: Die Schülersche Reform*. Düsseldorf: Droste, 1977.

Drascher, Wahrhold. "Die deutschen Handelskammern in Südamerika." *Der Auslanddeutsche* 7 (1924): 702–4.

Dreher, Martin. *Kirche und Deutschtum in der Entwicklung der Evangelischen Kirche Lutherischen Bekenntnisses in Brasilien*. Göttingen: Vandenhoeck & Ruprecht, 1978.

Duany, Jorge. "Racializing Ethnicity in the Spanish-Speaking Caribbean: A Comparison of Haitians in the Dominican Republic and Dominicans in Puerto Rico." *Latin American and Caribbean Ethnic Studies* 1, no. 2 (2006): 231–48.

Duara, Prasenjit. "Historicizing National Identity, or Who Imagines What and When." In *Becoming National: A Reader*, edited by Goeff Eley and Ronald Grigor Suny, 151–74. Oxford: Oxford University Press, 1996.

———. "Transnationalism and the Predicament of Sovereignty: China, 1900–1945." *American Historical Review* 102, no. 4 (1997): 1030–51.

Düwell, Kurt. *Deutschlands auswärtige Kulturpolitik 1918–1932: Grundlinien und Dokumente*. Cologne: Böhlau, 1976.

Edelman, Marc. "A Central American Genocide: Rubber, Slavery, Nationalism, and the Destruction of the Guatusos-Malekus." *Comparative Studies in Society and History* 40, no. 2 (1998): 356–90.

Einaudi, Luigi. *Un principe mercante: Studio sulla espansione coloniale italiana*. Turin: Fratelli Bocca, 1900.

Eng Herrera, Pedro J., and Mauro G. García Triana. *Martí en los chinos, los chinos en Martí*. Havana: Grupo Promotor del Barrio Chino de La Habana, 2003.

Epp, Franz. *Rio Grande do Sul oder Neudeutschland*. Mannheim: Franz Bender, 1864.

Eriksen, Thomas Hylland. *Ethnicity and Nationalism: Anthropological Perspectives*, 2nd ed. London: Pluto Press, 2002.

Ermarth, Michael. "Hyphenation and Hyper-Americanization: Germans of the Wilhelmine Reich View German-Americans, 1890–1914." *Journal of American Ethnic History* 21, no. 2 (2002): 33–58.

Espagne, Michel. "Sur les limites du comparatisme en histoire culturelle." *Genèses* 17 (1994): 256–79.

Espinoza, José Angel. *El ejemplo de Sonora*. Mexico City, 1932.

———. *El problema chino en México*. Mexico City, 1931.

Fabri, Friedrich. *Bedarf Deutschland der Colonien? Eine politisch-ökonomische Betrachtung*. Gotha: Perthes, 1879.

Fahrmeir, Andreas. *Citizenship: The Rise and Fall of a Modern Concept*. New Haven, CT: Yale University Press, 2007.

Falcoff, Mark, and Frederick B. Pike. *The Spanish Civil War, 1936–1939: American Hemispheric Perspectives*. Lincoln: University of Nebraska Press, 1982.

Fanesi, Pietro Rinaldo. "Italian Antifascism and the Garibaldine Tradition in Latin America." In *Italian Workers of the World: Labor Migration and the Formation of Multiethnic States*, edited by Donna R. Gabaccia and Fraser M. Ottanelli, 163–77. Urbana-Champaign: University of Illinois Press, 2001.

Farcau, Bruce W. *The Chaco War: Bolivia and Paraguay, 1932–1935*. New York: Praeger, 1996.

Fausto, Boris, ed. *Fazer a América: A imigração em massa para a América Latina*. São Paulo: Editora da Universidade de São Paulo, 1999.

Ferenczi, Imre, and Walter Willcox, eds. *International Migrations*. Vol. 1, *Statistics*. New York: National Bureau of Economic Research, 1929.

Fernandez, Ingrid. "The Upper Amazonian Rubber Boom and Indigenous Rights, 1900–1925." *Selected Annual Proceedings of the Florida Conference of Historians* 15 (2008): 41–50.

Ferreira Perazzo, Priscila. *Prisioneiros da Guerra: os "súditos do Eixo" nos campos de concentração brasileiros (1942–1945)*. São Paulo: Associação Editorial Humanitas and Imprensa Oficial do Estado de São Paulo, 2009.

Ferrer, Ada. *Insurgent Cuba: Race, Nation, and Revolution, 1868–1898*. Chapel Hill: University of North Carolina Press, 1999.

Fiebig von Hase, Ragnhild. *Lateinamerika als Konfliktherd der deutsch-amerikanischen Beziehungen 1890–1903: Vom Beginn der Panamerikapolitik bis zur Venezuelakrise von 1902/03*. Göttingen: Vandenhoeck & Ruprecht, 1986.

Finchelstein, Federico. "The Anti-Freudian Politics of Argentine Fascism: Anti-Semitism, Catholicism, and the Internal Enemy, 1932–1945." *Hispanic American Historical Review* 87, no. 1 (2007): 77–110.

———. *Transatlantic Fascism: Ideology, Violence, and the Sacred in Argentina and Italy, 1919–1945*. Durham, NC: Duke University Press, 2010.

Fischer, Thomas. "Deutsche und schweizerische Massenauswanderung nach Lateinamerika, 1819–1914." In *Nord und Süd: Gegensätze–Gemeinsamkeiten–Europäischer Hintergrund*, vol. 1, edited by Wolfgang Reinhard and Peter Waldmann, 284–92. Freiburg: Rombach, 1992.

Fishman, Sylvia Barack. *Double or Nothing: Jewish Families and Mixed Marriage*. Waltham, MA: Brandeis University Press, 2004.

Flier, Patricia Graciela. "Historia y memoria de la colonización judía agraria en en Entre Ríos: La experiencia de Colonia Clara, 1890–1950." PhD diss., Universidad Nacional de La Plata, 2011.

Florentino, Manolo, and Cacilda Machado. "Ensaio sobre a imigração portuguesa e os padrões de miscingenação no Brasil (séculos XIX e XX)." *Portuguese Studies Review* 10, no. 1 (2002): 58–84.

Flores Caballero, Romeo. *Counterrevolution: The Role of the Spaniards in the Independence of Mexico, 1804–1838*. Translated by Jaime E. Rodríguez O. Lincoln: University of Nebraska Press, 1974.

Fogu, Claudio. "'To Make History': Garibaldianism and the Formation of a Fascist Historic Imagery." In *Making and Remaking Italy: The Cultivation of National Identity around the Risorgimento*, edited by Albert Russell Ascoli and Krystyna Von Henneberg, 203–40. Oxford: Berg, 2001.

Font, Mauricio. *Coffee and Transformation in São Paulo, Brazil*. Lanham, MD: Lexington Books, 2010.

Foote, Nicola. "Race, State and Nation in Early Twentieth Century Ecuador." *Nations and Nationalism* 12, no. 2 (2006): 261–78.

———. "Rethinking Race, Gender and Citizenship: Black West Indian Women in Costa Rica, 1920–1940." *Bulletin of Latin American Research* 23, no. 2 (2004): 198–212.

Foote, Nicola, and René D. Harder Horst, eds. *Military Struggle and Identity Formation in Latin America: Race, Nation, and Community During the Liberal Period*. Gainsville: University Press of Florida, 2010.

Foroohar, Manzar. "Palestinians in Central America: From Temporary Emigrants to a Permanent Diaspora." *Journal of Palestine Studies* 40, no. 3 (2011): 6–22.

Franzina, Emilio. *Gli italiani al nuovo mondo: L'emigrazione italiana in America, 1492–1942*. Milan: A. Mondadori, 1995.

———. *L'America gringa: Storie italiane d'immigrazione tra Argentina e Brasile*. Reggio Emilia: Diabasis, 2008.

Freidenberg, Judith Noemí. *The Invention of the Jewish Gaucho: Villa Clara and the Construction of Argentine Identity*. Austin: University of Texas Press, 2009.

Freyre, Gilberto. "Discurso inaugural." In *I Colóquio de Estudos Teuto-Brasileiros: Reazilado em Pôrto Alegre, de 24 a 30 de julho de 1963, sob os auspicious do Centro de Estudos Sociais da Faculdade de Filosofia da Universidade Federal do Rio Grande do Sul*, 17–20 (Porto Alegre: UFRGS 1966).

———. *The Masters and the Slaves: A Study in the Development of Brazilian Civilization*. 1933. New York: Alfred A. Knopf, 1946.

———. *New World in the Tropics: The Culture of Modern Brazil*. New York: Alfred A. Knopf, 1959.

Gabaccia, Donna. *Italy's Many Diasporas*. London: University College London Press, 2000.

Gabaccia, Donna R., and Fraser M. Ottanelli, eds. *Italian Workers of the World: Labor Migration and the Formation of Multiethnic States*. Urbana-Champaign: University of Illinois Press, 2001.

Gabler, Felix. "Kirche und Schule bei den Deutschen in Südamerika." *Die evangelische Diaspora* 8 (1926): 118–22.

Gal, Allon, Athena S. Leoussi, and Anthony D. Smith, eds. *The Call of the Homeland: Diaspora Nationalisms, Past and Present*. Leiden: Brill, 2010.

Gallo, Klaus. "Esteban Echeverría's Critique of Universal Suffrage: The Traumatic Development of Democracy in Argentina, 1821–52." In *Giuseppe Mazzini and the Globaliza-*

tion of Democratic Nationalism, 1830–1920, edited by Christopher Bayly and Eugenio F. Biagini, 299–310. Oxford: Oxford University Press, 2008.

Gálvez, Manuel. *En el mundo de los seres ficticios*. Buenos Aires: Librería Hachette, 1961.

———. *El solar de la raza*. 1913. Buenos Aires: Editorial Tor, 1936.

Gamio, Manuel. *Consideraciones sobre el problema indígena*. Mexico City: Instituto Indigenista Interamericano, 1948.

———. *Forjando Patria (pro nacionalismo)*. Mexico City: Manuel Porrúa, 1916.

Gandolfo, Romolo. "Inmigrantes y política en Argentina: La Revolución de 1890 y la campaña en favor de la naturalización automática de residentes extranjeras." *Estudios Migratorios Latinoamericanos* 6, no. 17 (1991): 23–55.

Gans, Herbert. "Toward a Reconciliation of 'Assimilation' and 'Pluralism': The Interplay of Acculturation and Ethnic Retention." *International Migration Review* 31, no. 4 (1997): 875–92.

Gans, Magda Roswita. *Presença teuta em Porto Alegre no século XIX (1850–1889)*. Porto Alegre: Editora da UFRGS and ANPUH/RS, 2004.

García, Alicia, and Ricardo E. Rodríguez Molas. *Textos y documentos: El autoritarismo y los argentinos; la hora de la espada, 1924–1946*. Buenos Aires: Centro Editor de América Latina, 1988.

Gast, Paul. *Deutschland und Südamerika*. Stuttgart: Deutsche Verlags-Anstalt, 1915.

Gellner, Ernest. *Nations and Nationalism*. Oxford: Blackwell, 1983.

Gentile, Emilio. *The Struggle for Modernity: Nationalism, Futurism, and Fascism*. Westport, CT: Praeger, 2003.

Gerchunoff, Alberto. *The Jewish Gauchos of the Pampas*. Translated by Prudencio de Pereda. Albuquerque: University of New Mexico Press, 1998.

Gertz, René. *O fascismo no sul do Brasil: Germanismo, nazismo, integralismo*. Porto Alegre: Mercado Aberto, 1987.

———. *O perigo alemão*. Porto Alegre: Editora da Universidade Federal do Rio Grande do Sul, 1991.

Gil Fortoul, José. *El hombre y la historia*. Madrid: Editorial América, 1916.

Giron, Loraine Slomp. *As sombras do littorio: O fascismo no Rio Grande do Sul*. Porto Alegre: Parlenda, 1994.

Glazer, Nathan, and Daniel Patrick Moynihan. *Beyond the Melting Pot: The Negroes, Puerto Ricans, Jews, Italians, and Irish of New York City*. Cambridge, MA: MIT Press, 1963.

Goebel, Michael. "Decentring the German Spirit: The Weimar Republic's Cultural Relations with Latin America." *Journal of Contemporary History* 44, no. 2 (2009): 221–45.

———. "Gauchos, Gringos and Gallegos: The Assimilation of Italian and Spanish Immigrants in the Making of Modern Uruguay 1880–1930." *Past and Present*, no. 208 (2010): 191–229.

———. "Von der *hispanidad* zum Panarabismus: Globale Verflechtungen in Argentiniens Nationalismen." *Geschichte und Gesellschaft* 34, no. 4 (2011): 523–58.

Goldberg, Florinda, and Iosef Rozen. *Los latinoamericanos en Israel: Antología de una aliá*. Buenos Aires: Editorial Contexto, 1988.

Gómez, Carlos. *Contribución al estudio de la inmigración en Venezuela*. Caracas: Universidad Central de Venezuela, 1906.

González, Fredy. "We Won't Be Bullied Anymore: Chinese-Mexican Relations and the Chinese Community in Mexico, 1931–1971." PhD diss., Yale University, 2013.

Gonzales, Michael J. "Resistance among Asian Plantation Workers in Peru 1870–1920." In *From Chattel Slaves to Wage Slaves: The Dynamics of Labour Bargaining in the Americas*, edited by Mary Turner, 201–23. Bloomington: Indiana University Press, 1995.

González, Nancie L. *Dollar, Dove, and Eagle: One Hundred Years of Palestinian Migration to Honduras*. Ann Arbor: University of Michigan Press, 1992.

González Cuevas, Pedro Carlos. *Maeztu: Biografía de un nacionalista español*. Madrid: Marcial Pons, 2003.

González Martínez, Elda. *La inmigración esperada: La política migratoria brasileña desde João VI hasta Getúlio Vargas*. Madrid: Consejo Superior de Investigaciones Científicas, 2003.

González Navarro, Moisés. *Los extranjeros en México y los mexicanos en el extranjero, 1821–1970*. Mexico City: El Colegio de México, 1993.

———. *Población y sociedad en México, 1900–1970*. 2 vols. Mexico City: Universidad Nacional Autónoma de México, 1974.

Gordon, Edmund. *Disparate Diasporas: Identity and Politics in an African Nicaraguan Community*. Austin: University of Texas Press, 1998.

Gordon, Milton. *Assimilation in American Life: The Role of Race, Religion, and National Origins*. New York: Oxford University Press, 1964.

Graham, Richard, ed. *The Idea of Race in Latin America, 1870–1940*. Austin: University of Texas Press, 1990.

Gravil, Roger. *The Anglo–Argentine Connection, 1900–1939*. Boulder: Westview Press, 1985.

Great Britain, Foreign Office. *Correspondence Respecting the Treatment of British Colonial Subjects and Native Indians Employed in the Collection of Rubber in the Putumayo District*. London: Harrison and Sons, 1912.

Great Britain, Foreign Office, and Cuba, Secretaría del Estado. *Correspondence between His Majesty's Government and the Cuban Government Respecting the Ill-Treatment of British West Indians in Cuba*. London: H. M. Stationary Office, 1924.

———. *Further Correspondence between His Majesty's Government and the Cuban Government Respecting the Ill-Treatment of British West Indians in Cuba*. London: H. M. Stationary Office, 1924.

Green, Nancy L. "L'histoire comparative et le champ d'études migratoires." *Annales* 45, no. 6 (1990): 1335–50.

Green, Nancy L., and François Weil, eds. *Citizenship and Those Who Leave: The Politics of Emigration and Expatriation*. Urbana: University of Illinois Press, 2007.

Greenfield, Sidney M. "Barbadians in the Brazilian Amazon." *Luso-Brazilian Review* 20, no. 1 (1983): 44–64.

Gualtieri, Sarah. *Between Arab and White: Race and Ethnicity in the Early Syrian American Diaspora*. Berkeley: University of California Press, 2009.

Guatemala, Ministerio de Fomento, Dirección General de Estadística. *Censo de la población de la república, 1921*, vol. 1. Guatemala: Talleres Gutenberg, 1924.

Guerin-González, Camille. "Repatriación de familias inmigrantes mexicanas durante la gran depresión." *Historia Mexicana* 25 (1985): 241–74.

Guerra, François-Xavier. *Le Mexique de l'Ancien Régime à la Révolution.* 2 vols. Paris: L'Harmattan, 1986.

Guerra, Lillian. *The Myth of José Martí: Conflicting Nationalisms in Early Twentieth-Century Cuba.* Chapel Hill: University of North Carolina Press, 2005.

Guy, Donna. *Sex and Danger in Buenos Aries: Prostitution, Family, Nation in Argentina.* Lincoln: University of Nebraska Press, 1991.

Guzmán, Roberto Marín. *A Century of Palestinian Immigration into Central America: A Study of their Economic and Cultural Contributions.* San José: Editorial Universidad de Costa Rica, 2000.

Hall, Michael. *The Balkan Wars, 1912–1913: Prelude to the First World War.* London: Routledge, 2000.

Halperín Donghi, Tulio. "¿Para qué la inmigración? Ideología y política inmigratoria y aceleración del proceso modernizador: El caso argentino (1810–1914)." *Jahrbuch Für Geschichte Von Staat, Wirtschaft und Gesellschaft Lateinamerikas,* no. 13 (1976): 437–89.

Handa, Tomoo. *O imigrante japonês: História de sua vida no Brasil.* São Paulo: T. A. Queiroz and Centro de Estudos Nipo-Brasileiros, 1987.

Hardach, Gerd. *Der Erste Weltkrieg, 1914–1918.* Munich: DTV, 1973.

Hardenburg, W. E. *The Putumayo, the Devil's Paradise: Travels in the Peruvian Amazon Region and an Account of the Atrocities Committed upon the Indians Therein.* London: T. F. Unwin, 1912.

Harms-Baltzer, Käte. *Die Nationalisierung der deutschen Einwanderer und ihrer Nachkommen in Brasilien als Problem der deutsch-brasilianischen Beziehungen 1930–1938.* Berlin: Colloquium-Verlag, 1970.

Harpelle, Ronald N. "Cross Currents in the Western Caribbean: Marcus Garvey and the UNIA in Central America." *Caribbean Studies* 31, no. 3 (2003): 35–73.

———. "The Social and Political Integration of West Indians in Costa Rica, 1930–1950." *Journal of Latin American Studies* 25, no. 1 (1993): 103–20.

Hart, John M. *Revolutionary Mexico: The Coming and Process of the Mexican Revolution,* 2nd ed. Berkeley: University of California Press, 1997.

Hartwig, Alfredo. "Die Methoden des Handelskrieges der Alliierten gegen Deutschland an der Westküste Südamerikas." *Deutsche Rundschau* 184 (1920): 1–21.

Hayn, Emil. "Gründung und Kampfjahre des Deutschen Volksbundes für Argentinien." *Jahrbuch des Deutschen Volksbundes für Argentinien* (1938): 133.

Heiman Guzmán, Hanns. *Los inmigrantes en el Ecuador: Un estudio histórico.* Quito: Casa Editora Liebmann, 1942.

Helg, Aline. "The Aftermath of Slavery in the Spanish Speaking Caribbean: Historiography and Methodology." In *Beyond Fragmentation: Perspectives on Caribbean History,* edited by Juanita de Barros, Audra A. Diptee, and David V. Trotman. Princeton, NJ: Markus Weiner, 2005.

———. *Our Rightful Share: The Afro-Cuban Struggle for Equality, 1886–1912.* Chapel Hill: University of North Carolina Press, 1995.

———. "Race in Argentina and Cuba, 1880–1930: Theories, Policies, and Popular Reaction." In *The Idea of Race in Latin America, 1870–1940,* edited by Richard Graham, 37–69. Austin: University of Texas Press, 1990.

Hell, Jürgen. "Der Griff nach Südbrasilien: Die Politik des Deutschen Reichs zur Umwandlung der drei brasilianischen Südstaaten in ein überseeisches Neudeutschland." PhD diss., University of Rostock, 1966.

Herman, Donald L. *The Latin-American Community of Israel*. New York: Praeger, 1984.

Herrera Jerez, Miriam, and Mario Castillo Santana. *De la memoria a la vida pública: Identidades, espacios y jerarquías de los chinos en La Habana republicana (1902–1968)*. La Habana: Centro de Investigación y Desarrollo de la Cultura Cubana Juan Marinello, 2003.

Herrero, Pérez. "Algunas hipótesis de trabajo sobre la inmigración española a México: Los comerciantes." In *Tres aspectos de la presencia española en México durante el porfiriato*, edited by Manuel Miño Grijalva, Pedro Pérez Herrero, and María Teresa Jarquín, 103–44. Mexico City: El Colegio de México, 1981.

Herskovits, Melville, Robert Redfield, and Ralph Linton. "Memorandum for the Study of Acculturation." *American Anthropologist* 38, no. 1 (1936): 149–52.

Hill, Robert A. "Boundaries of Belonging: Essay on Comparative Caribbean Garveyism." *Caribbean Studies* 31, no. 3 (2003): 10–33.

———, ed. *The Marcus Garvey and Universal Negro Improvement Association Papers*. Vol. 11, *The Caribbean Diaspora, 1910–1920*. Durham, NC: Duke University Press, 2011.

Ḥizb al-Lā-Markazīyah bi-Miṣr, *Al Muʾtamar al-ʿArabī al-Awwal: Al-munʿaqid fī al-qāʿah al-kubrá lil-Jamʿīyah al-Jughrāfīyah bi Shāriʿ San Jarmin fī Pārīs min yawm al-Arbiʿāʾ 13 Rajab sanat 1331/18 Ḥazīrān sanat 1913 ilá yawm al-ithnayn 18 Rajab sanat 1331/23 Ḥazīrān sanat 1913*. Cairo: Maṭbʿat al-Būsfūr, 1913.

Hobsbawm, Eric J. "Nation, State, Ethnicity, Religion: Transformations of Identity." In *Nationalism in Europe Past and Present*, vol. 1, edited by Justo G. Ramón Beramendi, Xosé M. Máiz and Núñez, 33–46. Santiago de Compostela: Universidade de Santiago de Compostella, 1994.

———. "Nationalism and National Identity in Latin America." In *Pour une histoire économique et sociale internationale*, edited by Bouda Etemad, Jean Baton, and Thomas David, 313–23. Geneva: Editions Passé Présent, 1995.

———. *Nations and Nationalism Since 1780: Programme, Myth, Reality*. Cambridge: Cambridge University Press, 1990.

Hobsbawm, Eric J., and Terence Ranger, eds. *The Invention of Tradition*. Cambridge: Cambridge University Press, 1983.

Hoerder, Dirk, and Nora Faires, eds. *Migrants and Migration in Modern North America: Cross-Border Lives, Labor Markets, and Politics*. Durham, NC: Duke University Press, 2011.

Hoffmann, Werner. "Die Deutschen in Argentinien." In *Die Deutschen in Lateinamerika: Schicksal und Leistung*, edited by Hartmut Fröschle, 40–145. Tübingen, Ger.: Horst Erdmann Verlag, 1979.

Hollifield, James. "The Politics of International Migration: How Can We 'Bring the State Back In'?" In *Migration Theory: Talking across Disciplines*, edited by Caroline B. Brettell and James F. Hollifield, 137–86. New York: Routledge, 2008.

Holloway, Thomas H. "Creating the Reserve Army? The Immigration Program of São Paulo, 1886–1930." *International Migration Review* 12 (1978): 187–209.

———. *Immigrants on the Land: Coffee and Society in Sao Paulo, 1886–1934*. Chapel Hill: University of North Carolina Press, 1980.

Honduras, Dirección General de Estadística. *Resumen del censo general de población, levantado el 29 de junio de 1930*. Tegucigalpa: Tipografía nacional, 1932.

Hourani, Albert. *Syria and Lebanon: A Political Essay*. London: Oxford University Press, 1946.

Howard, David. *Coloring the Nation: Race and Ethnicity in the Dominican Republic*. Boulder, CO: Lynne Reiner Books, 2001.

Hu-DeHart, Evelyn. "Immigrants to a Developing Society: The Chinese in Northern Mexico, 1875–1932." *Journal of Arizona History* 21 (1980): 274–312.

———. "Indispensable Enemy or Convenient Scapegoat? A Critical Examination of Sinophobia in Latin America and the Caribbean, 1870s to 1930s." *Journal of Chinese Overseas* 5 (2009): 55–90.

———. "Multiculturalism in Latin American Studies: Locating the 'Asian' Immigrant; or, Where Are the *Chinos* and *Turcos*?" *Latin American Research Review* 44, no. 2 (2009): 235–42.

———. "Racism and Anti-Chinese Persecution in Sonora, Mexico, 1876–1932." *Amerasia Journal* 9, no. 2 (1982): 1–28.

Hughes, Matthew. "Logistics and the Chaco War: Bolivia versus Paraguay, 1932–35." *Journal of Military History* 69, no. 2 (2005): 411–37.

Ikmīr, ʿAbd al-Wahed. *Al-ʿArab fī al-Arjuntīn*. Beirut: Markaz Dirasāt al-Wahda al-ʿArabiyya, 2000.

Irazusta, Julio, ed. *El pensamiento político nacionalista*. Buenos Aires: Obligado Editora, 1975.

Isabella, Maurizio. *Risorgimento in Exile: Italian Émigrés and the Liberal International in the Post-Napoleonic Era*. Oxford: Oxford University Press, 2009.

Jacobsen, Matthew Frye. *Whiteness of a Different Color: European Immigrants and the Alchemy of Race*. Cambridge, MA: Harvard University Press, 1998.

Jacobson, Shary. "Modernity, Conservative Religious Movements, and the Female Subject: Newly Ultraorthodox Sephardi Women in Buenos Aires." *American Anthropologist* 108, no. 2 (2006): 336–46.

Jafet, Nami. *Ensaios e discursos*. São Paulo: São Paulo Editora S/A, 1947.

Jauretche, Arturo. *FORJA y la década infame*. Buenos Aires: Peña Lillo Editor, 1984.

Jmelnizky, Adrián, and Ezequiel Erdei. *La población judía de Buenos Aires*. Buenos Aires: AMIA, 2005.

Jochims Reichel, Heloísa, and Ieda Gutfreind. *As raízes históricas do Mercosul: A Região Platina colonial*. São Leopoldo: Unisinos, 1996.

Johnson, Howard. "The Anti-Chinese Riots of 1918 in Jamaica." *Caribbean Quarterly* 28, no. 3 (1982): 19–32.

Jones, David, and Carlyle Glean. "The English Speaking Communities of Honduras and Nicaragua." *Caribbean Quarterly* 17, no. 1 (1971): 50–61.

Jusdanis, Gregory. *The Necessary Nation*. Princeton, NJ: Princeton University Press, 2001.

Kagan, Richard L., and Philip D. Morgan, eds. *Atlantic Diasporas: Jews, Conversos, and Crypto-Jews in the Age of Mercantilism, 1500–1800*. Baltimore: Johns Hopkins University Press, 2009.

Kahan, Emmanuel, Laura Schenquer, Damián Setton, and Alejandro Dujovne, eds. *Margi-*

nados y consagrados: Nuevos estudios sobre la vida judía en la Argentina. Buenos Aires: Lumiere, 2011.

Kannapin, Klaus. "Die deutsch-argentinischen Beziehungen von 1871 bis 1914 unter besonderer Berücksichtigung der Handels- und Wirtschaftsbeziehungen und der Auswanderungspolitik." PhD diss., Humboldt University Berlin, 1968.

———. "Die Luxburg-Affäre: Ein Beitrag zur Geschichte der Beziehungen zwischen Deutschland und Argentinien während des Ersten Weltkrieges." *Wissenschaftliche Zeitschrift der Humboldt-Universität Berlin* 13 (1964): 875–91.

Karam, John. *Another Arabesque: Syrian-Lebanese Ethnicity in Neoliberal Brazil.* Philadelphia: Temple University Press, 2007.

Karlen, Stefan, and Andreas Wimmer. *"Integration und Transformation": Ethnische Gemeinschaften, Staat und Weltwirtschaft in Lateinamerika seit ca. 1850.* Stuttgart: Heinz, 1996.

Karol, Jorge, and Fernando Moiguer. *Cultura de la diversidad: Argentina 2001–2004 y la comunidad judía.* Buenos Aires: B'nei B'rith Argentina, 2006.

Karpat, Kemal H. "The Ottoman Emigration to America, 1860–1914." *International Journal of Middle Eastern Studies* 17 (1985): 175–209.

Karush, Matthew. "The Melodramatic Nation: Integration and Polarization in the Argentine Cinema of the 1930s." *Hispanic American Historical Review* 87, no. 2 (2007): 293–326.

Katz, Friedrich. "Liberal Republic and Porfiriato." In *Mexico since Independence*, edited by Leslie Bethell, 49–124. Cambridge, MA: Cambridge University Press, 1991.

———. *The Secret War in Mexico: Europe, the United States and the Mexican Revolution.* Chicago: University of Chicago Press, 1981.

Kayalı, Hasan. *Arabs and Young Turks: Ottomanism, Arabism, and Islamism in the Ottoman Empire, 1908–1918.* Berkeley: University of California Press, 1997.

Kazal, Russell A. "Revisiting Assimilation: The Rise, Fall, and Reappraisal of a Concept in American Ethnic History." *American Historical Review* 100, no. 2 (1995): 437–71.

Kedourie, Elie. *Nationalism in Asia and Africa.* London: Weidenfeld and Nicholson, 1971.

Keiper, Wilhelm. *Das Deutschtum in Argentinien während des Weltkriegs 1914–1918.* Hamburg: Christians, 1942.

Kellenbenz, Hermann, and Jürgen Schneider. "La emigración alemana a América Latina, 1821–1931." *Jahrbuch für Geschichte Lateinamerikas* 13 (1976): 386–403.

Kelly, Helen. *Irish 'Ingleses': The Irish Immigrant Experience in Argentina, 1840–1920.* Dublin: Irish Academic Press, 2009.

Khan, Aisha. *Callaloo Nation: Metaphors of Race and Religious Identity among South Asians in Trinidad.* Durham, NC: Duke University Press, 2004.

———. "Journey to the Center of the Earth: The Caribbean as Master Symbol." *Cultural Anthropology* 16, no. 3 (2001): 271–302.

Khater, Akram. "Becoming 'Syrian' in America: A Global Geography of Ethnicity and Nation." *Diaspora* 14, no. 2–3 (2005): 299–331.

———. *Inventing Home: Emigration, Gender, and the Middle Class in Lebanon, 1870–1920.* Berkeley: University of California Press, 2001.

Khatlab, Roberto. *Mahjar: Saga Libanese no Brasil; Sociologia Iconografica.* Zaika, Leb.: Editorial Mokhtarat, 2002.

Khoury, Philip S. "Factionalism among Syrian Nationalists during the French Mandate." *International Journal of Middle East Studies* 13, no. 4 (1981): 441–69.

——. *Syria and the French Mandate: The Politics of Arab Nationalism, 1920–1945*. London: I. B. Tauris, 1987.

Kleber da Silva, Haike, and Isabel Arendt. *Representações do discurso teuto-católico e a construção de identidades*. Porto Alegre: EST, 2000.

Klein, Herbert S. "The Integration of Italian Immigrants into the United States and Argentina: A Comparative Analysis." *American Historical Review* 88, no. 2 (1983): 306–29.

——. "The Social and Economic Integration of Portuguese Immigrants in Brazil in the Late Nineteenth and Early Twentieth Centuries." *Journal of Latin American Studies* 23, no. 2 (1991): 309–37.

Kleinschmidt, Beda. *Das Auslandsdeutschtum in Übersee und die katholische Missionsbewegung*. Münster: Aschendorff, 1926.

Klich, Ignacio, ed. *Árabes y judíos en América Latina: Historia, representaciones y desafíos*. Buenos Aires: Siglo XXI, 2006.

——. "Argentine–Ottoman Relations and Their Impact on Immigrants from the Middle East: A History of Unfulfilled Expectations, 1910–1915." *Americas* 50, no. 2 (1993): 177–205.

Klich, Ignacio, and Jeffrey Lesser, eds. *Arab and Jewish Immigrants in Latin America: Images and Realities*. London: Frank Cass, 1998.

——. "Introduction: 'Turco' Immigrants in Latin America." *Americas* 50, no. 2 (1993): 1–14.

——. "'Turco' Immigrants in Latin America." *Americas* 53, no. 1 (1996): 1–14.

Kloosterhuis, Jürgen. *"Friedliche Imperialisten": Deutsche Auslandsvereine und auswärtige Kulturpolitik, 1906–1918*. Frankfurt: Lang, 1994.

Klor, Sebastian. "The Aliyah from Argentina to the State of Israel, 1948–1967." PhD diss., University of Haifa, 2012.

Knight, Alan. "Cardenismo: Juggernaut or Jalopy?" *Journal of Latin American Studies* 26 (1994): 73–107.

——. "Racism, Revolution, and *Indigenismo*: Mexico, 1910–1940." In *The Idea of Race in Latin America, 1870–1940*, edited by Richard Graham, 71–113. Austin: University of Texas Press, 1990.

——. "The United States and the Mexican Peasantry, c. 1880–1940." In *Rural Revolt in Mexico and U.S. Intervention*, edited by Daniel Nugent, 25–60. La Jolla: Center for U.S.–Mexican Studies, University of California, San Diego, 1988.

——. *U.S.–Mexican Relations, 1910–1940: An Interpretation*. La Jolla: Center for U.S.–Mexican Studies, University of California, San Diego, 1987.

Koch, Herbert. "Kriegsgeschichte der deutschen Schule in Santa Catharina." *Die Deutsche Schule im Ausland* 15 (1923): 136–42.

Kocka, Jürgen. "Comparison and Beyond." *History and Theory* 42 (2003): 39–44.

Kohlsdorf, "Die deutsch-evangelische Kirche in Chile," *Die evangelische Diaspora* 4 (1922): 70–74.

Kuczynski, R. R. *Demographic Survey of the British Colonial Empire*. Vol. 3, *West Indian and American Territories*. London: Oxford University Press, 1953.

Kuhn, Philip A. *Chinese among Others: Emigration in Modern Times*. Lanham, MD: Rowman and Littlefield, 2008.

Kunert, August. "Aus der deutschen Kolonie in Rio Grande do Sul." *Der deutsche Ansiedler* 37, no. 2 (1899): 13.

Lafaye, Jacques. *Quetzalcóatl and Guadalupe: The Formation of Mexican National Consciousness, 1531–1813*. Translated by Benjamin Keen. Chicago: University of Chicago Press, 1976.

Lake, Marilyn, and Henry Reynolds. *Drawing the Global Colour Line: White Men's Countries and the International Challenge of Racial Equality*. Cambridge: Cambridge University Press, 2008.

Lamar, Hortensia. "La lucha contra la prostitución y la trata de blancas." *Revista Bimestre Cubana* 18 (1923): 134.

Lanyon, Anna. *Fire and Song: The Story of Luis de Carvajal and the Mexican Inquisition*. Crows Nest, Aus.: Allen and Unwin, 2012.

Laurence, K. O. "The Importation of Labour and the Contract Systems." In *General History of the Caribbean*. Vol. 4, *The Long Nineteenth Century: Nineteenth-Century Transformations*, edited by Laurence and Ibarra Cuesta, 196–99. Paris: UNESCO, 2011.

Lausent-Herrera, Isabelle. "The Chinatown in Peru and the Changing Peruvian Chinese Community(ies)." *Journal of Chinese Overseas* 7 (2011): 69–113.

———. "Tusans (*tusheng*) and the Changing Chinese Community in Peru." *Journal of Chinese Overseas* 5, no. 1 (2009): 115–52.

Lee, Erika. "Orientalisms in the Americas: A Hemispheric Approach to Asian American History." *Journal of Asian American Studies* 8, no. 3 (2005): 235–56.

———. "The 'Yellow Peril' and Asian Exclusion in the Americas." *Pacific Historical Review* 76, no. 4 (2007): 537–62.

Leonard, Jonathan Norton. *Men of Maracaibo*. New York: G. P. Putnam and Sons, 1933.

Le Roy Cassá, Jorge. "Inmigración anti-sanitaria." Paper presented at La Academia de Ciencias Médicas, Fisicas, y Naturales de la Habana, Sesión del 14 de diciembre de 1923. Dorrbecker: La Habana, 1929.

Lesser, Jeffrey. *Immigration, Ethnicity and National Identity in Brazil, 1808 to Present*. New York: Cambridge University Press, 2012.

———. "Japanese, Brazilians, Nikkei: A Short History of Identity Building and Homemaking." In *Searching for Home Abroad: Japanese-Brazilians and Transnationalism*, edited by Jeffrey Lesser, 5–19. Durham, NC: Duke University Press, 2003.

———. *Negotiating National Identity: Immigrants, Minorities, and the Struggle for Ethnicity in Brazil*. Durham, NC: Duke University Press, 1999.

———. "(Re)Creating Ethnicity: Middle Eastern Immigration to Brazil." *Americas* 53, no. 1 (1996): 45–65.

———, ed. *Searching for Home Abroad: Japanese-Brazilians and Transnationalism*. Durham, NC: Duke University Press, 2003.

———. *Welcoming the Undesirables: Brazil and the Jewish Question*. Berkeley: University of California Press, 1994.

Lesser, Jeffrey, and Raanan Rein. "Challenging Particularity: Jews as a Lens for Ethnicity in Latin America." *Latin American and Caribbean Ethnic Studies* 1, no. 2 (2006): 249–63.

———. "New Approaches to Ethnicity and Diaspora in Twentieth-Century Latin America." In *Rethinking Jewish-Latin Americans*, edited by Jeffrey Lesser and Raanan Rein, 23–40. Albuquerque: University of New Mexico Press, 2008.

———, eds. *Rethinking Jewish-Latin Americans*. Albuquerque: University of New Mexico Press, 2008.

Levitt, Peggy, and Nina Glick Schiller. "Conceptualizing Simultaneity: A Transnational Social Field Perspective." *International Migration Review* 38, no. 3 (2004): 1002–39.

Levy, Maria Stella Ferreira. "O papel da migração internacional na evolução da população brasileira (1872 a 1972)." *Revista de Saúde Pública* 8 (1974): 71–73.

Lewis, Rupert. *Marcus Garvey: Anti-Colonial Champion*. London: Karia Press, 1987.

Lewis, W. Arthur. *Labour in the West Indies: The Birth of a Workers' Movement*. 1938. London: New Beacon Books, 1977.

Lida, Clara F. "Los españoles en México: Población, cultura, y sociedad." In *Simbiosis de culturas: Los inmigrantes en México y su cultura*, edited by Guillermo Bonfil Batalla, 425–54. Mexico City: Secretaría de Educación Pública, 1993.

Lima Câmara, Aristoteles de, and Arthur Hehl Neiva. "Colonizações nipônica e germânica no sul do Brasil." *Revista de Imigração e Colonização* 2, no. 1 (1941): 39–119.

Linz, Juan. "Some Notes toward a Comparative Study of Fascism in Sociological Historical Perspective." In *Fascism, A Reader's Guide: Analyses, Interpretations, Bibliography*, edited by Walter Laqueur, 3–121. Berkeley: University of California Press, 1976.

Llairo, Maria Monserrat, and Raimundo Siepe. *Argentina en Europa: Yrigoyen y la Sociedad de las Naciones, 1918–1920*. Buenos Aires: Ediciones Macchi, 1997.

Logroño Narbona, M. "The Development of Nationalist Identities in French Syria and Lebanon: A Transnational Dialogue with Arab Immigrants to Argentina and Brazil, 1915–1929." PhD diss., University of California, Santa Barbara, 2007.

Lone, Stewart. *The Japanese Community in Brazil: Between Samurai and Carnival, 1908–1940*. New York: Palgrave, 2001.

Look Lai, Walton. *Indentured Labor, Caribbean Sugar: Chinese and Indian Migrants to the British West Indies, 1838–1918*. Baltimore: Johns Hopkins University Press, 1993.

López, Kathleen. *Chinese Cubans: A Transnational History*. Chapel Hill: University of North Carolina Press, 2013.

Luconi, Stefano. *From Paesani to White Ethnics: The Italian Experience in Philadelphia*. Albany: State University of New York Press, 2001.

———. *La "diplomazia parallela": Il regime fascista e la mobilitazione politica degli italo-americani*. Milan: Franco Angeli, 2000.

Luebke, Frederic C. *Germans in Brazil: A Comparative History of Cultural Conflict During World War I*. Baton Rouge: Lousiana State University Press, 1987.

Lum, Yansheng Ma, and Raymond Mun Kong Lum. *Sun Yat-sen in Hawaii: Activities and Supporters*. Honolulu: University of Hawai'i Press, 1999.

Lütge, Wilhelm, Werner Hoffmann, and Karl Wilhelm Körner. *Geschichte des Deutschtums in Argentinien*. Buenos Aires: Deutscher Klub, 1955.

Lvovich, Daniel. "Argentina: Entre las puertas abiertas y el rechazo a los indeseables." In *Nación y extranjería: La exclusión racial en las políticas migratorias de Argentina, Brasil, Cuba y México*, edited by Pablo Yankelevich, 23–58. Mexico City: Universidad Nacional Autónoma de México, 2009.

———. *Nacionalismo y antisemitismo en la Argentina*. Barcelona: Javier Vergara, 2003.

Maeyama, Takashi. "Ancestor, Emperor, and Immigrant: Religion and Group Identification of the Japanese in Rural Brazil (1908–1950)." *Journal of Interamerican Studies and World Affairs* 14, no. 2 (1972): 151–82.

Maffia, Marta. "La migración caboverdeana hacia la Argentina: Análisis de una alternativa." *Trabalhos de Antropologia e Etnologia* 26 (1986): 191–207.

Mallea, Eduardo. *Historia de una pasión argentina*. Buenos Aires: Editorial Sudamericana, 1986.

Marani, Alma Novella. *El ideario mazziniano en el Río de La Plata*. La Plata: Universidad Nacional de la Plata, 1985.

Marocco, Gianni. *Sull'altra sponda del Plata: Gli italiani in Uruguay*. Milan: Franco Angeli, 1986.

Martin, Percy A. *Latin America and the War*. Gloucester, MA: Peter Smith, 1967.

Martin, Tony. *Race First: The Ideological and Organizational Struggles of Marcus Garvey and the Universal Negro Improvement Association*. Dover, MA: Majority Press, 1976.

Martínez-Alier, Verena. *Marriage, Class, and Colour in Nineteenth-Century Cuba: A Study of Racial Attitudes and Sexual Values in a Slave Society*. Cambridge: Cambridge University Press, 1974.

Masterson, Daniel M., and Sayaka Funada-Classen. *The Japanese in Latin America*. Urbana: University of Illinois Press, 2004.

Más y Pi, Juan. "El arte en la Argentina," *Renacimiento* 2, no. 6 (1911): 307.

Mattar, Ahmed Hassan. *Guía Social de la Colonia Arabe en Chile*. Santiago: Imprenta "Ahues Hnos.," 1941.

Matthews, Weldon C. *Confronting an Empire, Constructing a Nation: Arab Nationalists and Popular in Mandate Palestine*. London: I. B. Tauris, 2006.

Mayer de Zulen, Dora. *La China, elocuente y silenciosa: Homenaje de la colonia china al Perú con motivo de las fiestas centenarias de su independencia, 28 de Julio de 1921–9 de diciembre de 1924*. Lima: Editorial Renovación, 1924.

McClintock, Anne. "'No Longer in a Future Heaven': Women and Nationalism in South Africa." *Transition* 15 (1991): 104–23.

McGillivray, Gillian. *Blazing Cane: Sugar Communities, Class, and State Formation in Cuba, 1868–1959*. Durham, NC: Duke University Press, 2009.

McGuinness, Aims. *Path of Empire: Panama and the California Gold Rush*. Ithaca, NY: Cornell University Press, 2009.

McKeown, Adam. *Chinese Migrant Networks and Cultural Change: Peru, Chicago, Hawaii, 1900–1936*. Chicago: University of Chicago Press, 2001.

———. "Conceptualizing Chinese Diasporas, 1842–1949." *Journal of Asian Studies* 58, no. 2 (1999): 306–37.

———. "Global Migration, 1846–1940." *Journal of World History* 15, no. 2 (2004): 155–89.

———. *Melancholy Order: Asian Migration and the Globalization of Borders*. New York: Columbia University Press, 2008.

McLeod, Marc C. "Undesirable Aliens: Race, Ethnicity, and Nationalism in the Comparison of Haitian and British West Indian Immigrant Workers in Cuba, 1912–1939." *Journal of Social History* 31, no. 3 (1998): 599–623.

Meagher, Arnold J. *The Coolie Trade: The Traffic in Chinese Laborers to Latin America 1847–1874*. Bloomington, IN: Xlibris, 2008.

Merrick, Thomas W., and Douglas H. Graham. *Population and Economic Development in Brazil: 1800 to the Present*. Baltimore: Johns Hopkins University Press, 1979.

Meyer, Jean. "Les français au Mexique au XIXème siècle." *Cahiers des Amériques Latines* 9–10 (1974): 44–71.

Meyer, Lorenzo. *Su majestad británica y la Revolución Mexicana, 1900–1940*. Mexico City: Colegio de México, 1990.

Míguez, Eduardo José. "Introduction: Foreign Mass Migration to Latin America in the Nineteenth and Twentieth Centuries—An Overview." In *Mass Migration*, edited by Samuel L. Baily and Eduardo José Míguez, xiii–xxv. Wilmington, DE: SR Books, 2003.

Miller, Nicola. "The Historiography of Nationalism and National Identity in Latin America." *Nations and Nationalism* 12, no. 2 (2006): 201–21.

———. *In the Shadow of the State: Intellectuals and the Quest for National Identity in Twentieth-Century Spanish America*. London: Verso, 1999.

———. *Reinventing Modernity in Latin America: Intellectuals Imagine the Future, 1900–1930*. New York: Palgrave MacMillan, 2008.

Milza, Pierre. "Le fascisme italien à Paris." *Revue d'histoire moderne et contemporaine* 30, no. 3 (1983): 420–52.

Mitchell, Angus, ed. *The Amazon Journal of Roger Casement*. London: Anaconda Editions, 1997.

Mirelman, Victor A. *Jewish Buenos Aires, 1890–1930: In Search of an Identity*. Detroit: Wayne State University Press, 1990.

Mitchell, Nancy. *The Danger of Dreams: German and American Imperialism in Latin America*. Chapel Hill: University of North Carolina Press, 1999.

Mohammed, Patricia. "The Asian Other in the Caribbean." *Small Axe* 13, no. 2 (2009): 57–71.

Molina Enríquez, Andrés. *Los grandes problemas nacionales*. Mexico City: Imprenta de A. Carranza e hijos, 1909.

Mongia, Radhika. "Race, Nationality, Mobility: History of the Passport." *Public Culture* 11, no. 3 (1999): 527–55.

Monsiváis, Carlos. "Tantos millones de hombres no hablaremos inglés? (La cultura norteamericana y México)." In *Simbiosis de culturas: Los inmigrantes en México y su cultura*, edited by Guillermo Bonfil Batalla, 500–13. Mexico City: Secretaría de Educación Pública, 1993.

Moreira Leite, Dante. *O caráter nacional brasileiro: História de uma ideologia*. São Paulo: Editora UNESP, 2007.

Mori, Koichi. "Identity Transformations among Okinawans and Their Descendants in Brazil." In *Searching for Home Abroad: Japanese-Brazilians and Transnationalism*, edited by Jeffrey Lesser, 47–66. Durham, NC: Duke University Press, 2003.

Mörner, Magnus. *Adventurers and Proletarians: The Story of Migrants in Latin America*. Paris: UNESCO; Pittsburgh: University of Pittsburgh Press, 1985.

Morris-Suzuki, Tessa. *Re-Inventing Japan: Time, Space, Nation*. Armonk: M. E. Sharpe, 1998.

Maatouk, Mohamed. "Saadeh's Views on Literature and Literary Renovation." In *Antun*

Saadeh: The Man, His Thought; an Anthology, edited by Adel Beshara, 463–506. Reading, UK: Ithaca Press, 2007.

Moya, José C. "A Continent of Immigrants: Postcolonial Shifts in the Western Hemisphere." *Hispanic American Historical Review* 86, no. 1 (2006): 1–28.

———. *Cousins and Strangers: Spanish Immigrants in Buenos Aires, 1850–1930*. Berkeley: University of California Press, 1998.

———. "Spanish Emigration to Cuba and Argentina." In *Mass Migration to Modern Latin America*, edited by Samuel L. Baily and Eduardo José Míguez, 9–28. Wilmington, DE: SR Books, 2003.

Mugnaini, Marco. *L'America Latina e Mussolini: Brasile e Argentina nella politica estera dell'Italia, 1919–1943*. Milan: Franco Angeli, 2008.

Müller, Jürgen. *Nationalsozialismus in Lateinamerika: Die Auslandsorganisation der NS-DAP in Argentinien, Brasilien, Chile und Mexiko, 1931–1945*. Stuttgart: Heinz, 1997.

Munasinghe, Viranjini. *Callalloo or Tossed Salad? East Indians and the Cultural Politics of Identity in Trinidad*. Ithaca, NY: Cornell University Press, 2001.

Myers, Jorge. "Giuseppe Mazzini and the Emergence of Liberal Nationalism in the River Plate and Chile, 1835–60." In *Giuseppe Mazzini and the Globalization of Democratic Nationalism, 1830–1920*, edited by Christopher Bayly and Eugenio F. Biagini, 323–46. Oxford: Oxford University Press, 2008.

———. "Language, History, and Politics in Argentine Identity, 1840–1880." In *Nationalism in the New World*, edited by Don H. Doyle and Marco Antonio Pamplona, 117–42. Athens: University of George Press, 2006.

Nalbandian, Louise. *The Armenian Revolutionary Movement: The Development of Armenian Political Parties through the Nineteenth Century*. Berkeley: University of California Press, 1963.

Nállim, Jorge. *Transformations and Crisis of Liberalism in Argentina, 1930–1955*. Pittsburgh: University of Pittsburgh Press, 2012.

Narvaez, Benjamin Nicolas. "Chinese Coolies in Cuba and Peru: Race, Labor, and Immigration, 1839–1886." PhD diss., University of Texas at Austin, 2010.

Nascimbene, Mario. "The Assimilation of Italians and their Descendants in Argentine Society (1880–1925)." *Studi emigrazione* 33, no. 123 (1996): 412–47.

Necati Kutlu, Mehmet. "Ottoman Subjects in Latin America: An Archive Document and Some Reflections on the Probable Causes of their Immigration." *Archivum Ottomanicum* 25 (2008): 233–44.

Neulander, Judith S. "Crypto-Jews of the Southwest: An Imagined Community." *Jewish Folklore and Ethnology Review* 16, no. 1 (1994): 64–68.

Newton, Ronald C. "Ducini, Prominenti, Antifascisti: Italian Fascism and the Italo-Argentine Collectivity, 1922–1945." *Americas* 51, no. 1 (1994): 41–66.

———. *German Buenos Aires, 1900–1933: Social Change and Cultural Crisis*. Austin: University of Texas Press, 1977.

———. *The "Nazi Menace" in Argentina, 1931–1947*. Stanford, CA: Stanford University Press, 1992.

Newton, Velma. *The Silver Men: West Indian Labour Migration to Panama, 1850–1914*. Kingston: Institute of Social and Economic Research, University of the West Indies, 1984.

Ngai, Mae. *Impossible Subjects: Illegal Immigrants and the Making of Modern America.* Princeton, NJ: Princeton University Press, 2004.

Niblo, Stephen R. *War, Diplomacy, and Development: The United States and Mexico, 1938–1954.* Wilmington, DE: Scholarly Resources, 1995.

Nicaragua. *Censo General de 1920.* Managua: Tipografía nacional, n.d.

Niemeyer, E. Victor, Jr. *Revolution at Querétaro: The Mexican Constitutional Convention of 1916–1917.* Austin: University of Texas Press, 1979.

Nouwen, Mollie Lewis, and Ranaan Rein. "Cultural Zionism as a Contact Zone: Sephardic and Askenazi Jews Bridge the Gap on the Pages of the Argentine Newspaper *Israel.*" In *Contemporary Sephardic Identity in the Americas: A Collection of interdisciplinary Studies,* edited by Margalit Bejarano and Edna Aizenberg, 69–87. Syracuse, NY: Syracuse University Press, 2012.

Novak, Michael. *The Rise of the Unmeltable Ethnics: Politics and Culture in the Seventies.* New York: Macmillan, 1971.

Nucci, Priscila. "O perigo japonês." *História Social,* no. 12 (2006): 133–49.

Nugent, Walter. *Crossings: The Great Transatlantic Migrations, 1870–1914.* Bloomington: Indiana University Press, 1992.

Oberacker, Karl H., and Karl Ilg. "Die Deutschen in Brasilien." In *Die Deutschen in Lateinamerika: Schicksal und Leistung,* edited by Hartmut Fröschle, 184–224. Tübingen, Ger.: Horst Erdmann Verlag, 1979.

Oberkrome, Willi. "Geschichte, Volk und Theorie: Das 'Handwörterbuch des Grenz- und Auslandsdeutschtums.'" In *Geschichtsschreibung als Legitimationswissenschaft, 1918–1945.* 2nd ed., edited by Peter Schöttler, 104–27. Frankfurt: Suhrkamp, 1999.

Oddone, Juan Antonio. "La politica e le immagini dell'emigrazione italiana in Uruguay, 1830–1930." In *L'emigrazione italiana e la formazione dell'Uruguay moderno,* edited by Fernando J. Devoto, 77–119. Turin: Fondazione Agnelli, 1993.

———. "Serafino Mazzolini: Un misionario del fascismo en Uruguay, 1933–1937." *Estudios Migratorios Latinoamericanos* 12, no. 37 (1997): 375–87.

———. *Una perspectiva europea del Uruguay: Los informes diplomáticos y consulares italianos 1862–1914.* Montevideo: Universidad de la República, 1965.

Oeste de Bopp, Marianne. "Die Deutschen in Mexiko." In *Die Deutschen in Lateinamerika: Schicksal und Leistung,* edited by Hartmut Fröschle, 475–564. Tübingen, Ger.: Horst Erdmann Verlag, 1979.

Ojeda-Ebert, Gerardo Jorge. *Deutsche Einwanderung und Herausbildung der chilenischen Nation, 1846–1920.* Munich: Fink, 1984.

Olguín Tenorio, Myriam, and Patricia Peña González. *La inmigración árabe en Chile.* Santiago: Ediciones Instituto Chileno Arabe de Cultura, 1990.

Oliveira Botelho, José de. *A immigração japoneza.* Rio de Janeiro: Typographia Coelho, 1925.

Olliff, Donathon C. *Reforma Mexico and the United States: The Search for Alternatives to Annexation.* Tuscaloosa: University of Alabama Press, 1981.

Opie, Frederick Douglass. *Black Labor Migration in Caribbean Guatemala, 1882–1923.* Gainesville: University Press of Florida, 2009.

Ortiz, Fernando. "Inmigración desde el punto de vista criminológico." *Derecho y soci-*

ología, jurisprudencia, antropología, historia, filosofía, etica, economía política 1, no. 5 (1906): 54–64.

Osterhammel, Jürgen. *Die Verwandlung der Welt: Eine Geschichte des 19. Jahrhunderts.* Munich: C.H. Beck, 2009.

Ottley, Roi. *New World A'Coming: Inside Black America.* Boston: Houghton Mifflin, 1943.

Pacecca, María Inés. "El fantasma en la maquina: La praxis politíca de los extranjeros." In *Los contornos de la ciudadanía: Nacionales y extranjeros en la argentina del centenario,* edited by Susana Villavicencio, 111–30. Buenos Aires: EUDEBA, 2003.

Pagano, Tullio. "From Diaspora to Empire: Enrico Corradini's Nationalist Novels." *MLN* 119, no. 1 (2004): 67–83.

Palacio, Ernesto. *La historia falsificada.* Buenos Aires: Difusion, 1939.

Palma Mora, María Dolores Mónica. "Inmigrantes extranjeros en México, 1950–1980." PhD diss., Universidad Nacional Autónoma de México, 1999.

Palmer, Steven. "Racismo intelectual en Costa Rica y Guatemala, 1870–1920." *Mesoamérica* 31 (1996): 99–121.

Panamá, Secretaría de Agricultura y Obras Públicas, Dirección General del Censo. *1930 Censo Demográfico,* vol. 1. Panamá: Imprenta Nacional, 1931.

Park, Robert E., and Ernest Burgess. *Introduction to the Science of Sociology.* Chicago: Chicago University Press, 1921.

Park, Robert E., and Herbert A. Miller. *Old World Traits Transplanted.* New York: Harper, 1921.

Patel, Kiran Klaus. "Transatlantische Perspektiven transnationaler Geschichte." *Geschichte und Gesellschaft* 29 (2003): 625–47.

Paz, María Elena. *Strategy, Security, and Spies: The U.S. and Mexico as Allies in World War II.* University Park: Penn State University Press, 1997.

Pellegrino, Adela. *Historia de la inmigración en Venezuela siglos XIX y XX.* Vol. 1, Caracas: Academia Nacional de Ciencias Económicas, 1989.

Penny, H. Glenn. "German Polycentrism and the Writing of History." *German History* 30, no. 2 (2012): 265–82.

Pereda, Setembrino Ezequiel. *Garibaldi en el Uruguay.* Montevideo: El Siglo Ilustrado, 1914.

Pérez, Pelayo. "El peligro amarillo y el peligro negro." *Cuba Contemporánea* 9 (1915): 250–59.

Pérez de la Riva, Juan. *Los culíes chinos en Cuba (1847–1880): Contribución al estudio de la inmigración contratada en el Caribe.* Havana: Editorial de Ciencias Sociales, 2000.

Pérez Herrero, Pedro, and Nuria Tabanera, eds. *España-América Latina: Un siglo de políticas culturales.* Madrid: Aieti/Síntesis, 1993.

Perón, Juan D. "Mensaje del Señor Presidente de la República." *Diario de Sesiones, Cámara de Diputados* 1 (June 4, 1946): 39–41.

Persons, Stow. *Ethnic Studies at Chicago, 1905–45.* Urbana: University of Illinois Press, 1987.

Petersen, Carl, Paul Hermann Ruth, Otto Scheel, and Hans Schwalm. *Handwörterbuch des Grenz- und Auslandsdeutschtums.* Breslau: Hirt, 1933.

Petersen, Jens. "Elettorato e base sociale del fascismo italiano negli anni venti." *Studi Storici* 16, no. 3 (1975): 627–69.

Petras, Elizabeth MacLean. *Jamaican Labor Migration: White Capital and Black Labor, 1850–1930*. Boulder, CO: Westview Press, 1988.

Plotkin, Mariano Ben. *Mañana es San Perón: A Cultural History of Perón's Argentina*. Wilmington, DE: Scholarly Resources, 2002.

Plummer, Brenda Gayle. "Race, Nationality, and Trade in the Caribbean: The Syrians in Haiti, 1903–1934." *International History Review* 3, no. 4 (1981): 517–39.

Pomeranz, Kenneth. *The Great Divergence: China, Europe, and the Making of the Modern World Economy*. Princeton, NJ: Princeton University Press, 2000.

Ponsati, Hugo Luis. *Aportes para una reseña de la Colectividad Árabe Tucumana*. Tucumán, Arg.: Editorial e Imprenta Kalco, 1975.

Portes, Alejandro, and Josh DeWind. "A Cross-Atlantic Dialogue: The Progress of Research and Theory in the Study of International Migration." *International Migration Review* 38, no. 3 (2004): 828–51.

Portes, Alejandro, and Rubén G. Rumbaut. *Immigrant America: A Portrait*. Berkeley: University of California Press, 2006.

Portes, Alejandro, and Min Zhou. "The New Second Generation: Segmented Assimilation and Its Variants." *Annals of the American Academy of Political and Social Science* 530, no. 1 (1993): 74–96.

Post, Ken. *Arise Ye Starvelings: The Jamaican Labour Rebellion of 1938 and Its Aftermath*. The Hague: Martinus Nijhoff, 1978.

Pretelli, Matteo. "La risposta del fascismo agli stereotipi degli italiani all'estero." *Altreitalie* 28 (2004): 48–65.

Prien, Hans-Jürgen. "Die 'Deutsch-evangelische Kirche' in Brasilien im Spannungsbogen von nationaler Wende (1933) und Kirchenkampf." *Jahrbuch für Geschichte Lateinamerikas* 25 (1988): 517–18.

———. *Evangelische Kirchwerdung in Brasilien: Von den deutsch-evangelischen Einwanderergemeinden zur Evangelischen Kirche Lutherischen Bekenntnisses in Brasilien*. Gütersloh: Mohn, 1989.

Prieto, Adolfo. *El discurso criollista en la formación de la Argentina moderna*. Buenos Aires: Editorial Sudamericana, 1988.

Principe, Angelo. *The Darkest Side of the Fascist Years: The Italian-Canadian Press, 1920–1942*. Toronto: Guernica, 1999.

Proal, Maurice, and Pierre Martin Charpenel. *Los barcelonnettes en México*. Mexico City: Clío, 1998.

Purcell, Trevor W. *Banana Fallout: Class, Color, and Culture among West Indians in Costa Rica*. Los Angeles: University of California Press, 1993.

Putnam, Lara. *The Company They Kept: Migrants and the Politics of Gender in Caribbean Costa Rica, 1870–1960*. Chapel Hill: University of North Carolina Press, 2002.

———. "Eventually Alien: The Multigenerational Saga of British West Indians in Central America and Beyond, 1880–1940." In *Blacks and Blackness in Central America: Between Race and Place*, edited by Lowell Gudmundson and Justin Wolfe, 278–306. Durham, NC: Duke University Press, 2010.

———. *Radical Moves: Caribbean Migrants and the Politics of Race in the Jazz Age*. Chapel Hill: University of North Carolina Press, 2013.

———. "Unspoken Exclusions: Race, Nation, and Empire in the Immigration Restrictions of the 1920s in North America and the Greater Caribbean." In *Workers across the Americas*, edited by Leon Fink, 267–93. New York: Oxford University Press, 2011.

Quesada, Gonzalo de. *Mi primera ofrenda*. New York: Imprenta de El Porvenir, 1892.

Quijada, Mónica. "Latinos y Anglosajones: El 98 en el fin de siglo sudamericano." *Hispania* 57, no. 2 (1997): 589–609.

———. "El paradigma de la homogeneidad." In *Homogeneidad y nación con un estudio de caso: Argentina, siglos XIX y XX*, edited by Mónica Quijada, Carmen Bernand and Arnd Schneider, 15–47. Madrid: Consejo Superior de Investigaciones Científicas, 2000.

Quirós, Ronald Soto. "Inmigración e identidad nacional: Los 'otros' reafirman el 'nosotros.'" Licenciatura thesis, Escuela de Historia, Universidad de Costa Rica, 1998.

Raat, W. Dirk. *El positivismo durante el porfiriato*. Mexico City: El Colegio de México, 1975.

———. "Ideas and Society in Don Porfirio's Mexico." *Americas* 30 (1973): 32–53.

Radhakrishnan, Rajagopalan. "Ethnicity in an Age of Diaspora." In *Theorizing Diaspora: A Reader*, edited by Jana Evans Braziel and Anita Mannur, 119<n31. Malden, MA: Blackwell Publishing, 2003.

Reichl, Christopher. "Stages in the Historical Process of Ethnicity: The Japanese in Brazil, 1908–1988." *Ethnohistory* 42, no. 1 (1995): 31–62.

Rein, Raanan, ed. *Árabes y judíos en Iberoamérica: Similitudes, diferencias y tensiones sobre el trasfondo de las tres culturas*. Sevilla: Fundación Tres Culturas, 2008.

———. *Argentine Jews or Jewish Argentines? Essays on Ethnicity, Identity, and Diaspora*. Boston: Brill, 2010.

———, ed. *Más allá del medio oriente: Las diásporas judía y árabe en América Latina*. Granada: Editorial Universidad de Granada, 2012.

Reis, João José. *Slave Rebellion in Brazil: The Muslim Uprising of 1835 in Bahia*. Baltimore: Johns Hopkins University Press, 1993.

Rénique, Gerardo. "Race, Region, and Nation: Sonora's anti-Chinese Racism and Mexico's Postrevolutionary Nationalism, 1920s–1930s." In *Race and Nation in Modern Latin America*, eds. Nancy P. Appelbaum, Anne S. MacPherson, and Karin Alejandra Rosemblatt, 211–35. Chapel Hill: University of North Carolina Press, 2003.

Report of the Proceedings of the Fourth Congress of the Pan-American Federation of Labor. Conference held in Mexico City, Mexico, December 3–9, 1924.

República Argentina. *Tercer Censo Nacional levantado el 1º de Junio de 1914*. Buenos Aires: Talleres Gráficos de L. J. Rosso y Cía, 1916.

República Dominicana. Dirección General de Estadística Nacional, Sección del Censo. *Población de la República Dominicana distribuida por nacionalidades. Cifras del censo nacional de 1935*. Ciudad Trujillo: Sección de Publicaciones de la Dirección General de Estadística, 1937.

Richardson, Bonham. *Panama Money in Barbados*. Knoxville: University of Tennessee Press, 1985.

Rinke, Stefan. *"Der letzte freie Kontinent": Deutsche Lateinamerikapolitik im Zeichen transnationaler Beziehungen, 1918–1933*. Stuttgart: Heinz, 1996.

———. "Deutsche Lateinamerikapolitik, 1918–1933: Modernisierungsansätze im Zeichen transnationaler Beziehungen." *Jahrbuch für Geschichte von Staat, Wirtschaft und Gesellschaft Lateinamerikas* 34 (1997): 355–83.

———. "Export einer politischen Kultur: Auslandsdeutsche in Lateinamerika und die

Weimarer Republik." In *"Integration und Transformation": Ethnische Gemeinschaften, Staat und Weltwirtschaft in Lateinamerika seit ca. 1850*, edited by Stefan Karlen and Andreas Wimmer, 353–80. Stuttgart: Heinz, 1996.

Roberts, G. W. *The Population of Jamaica*. London: Conservation Foundation at the Cambridge University Press, 1957.

Roberts, G. W., and J. Byrne. "Summary Statistics on Indenture and Associated Migration Affecting the West Indies, 1834–1918." *Population Studies* 20, no. 1 (1966): 125–34.

Roche, Jean. *La colonisation allemande et le Rio Grande do Sul*. Paris: Institut des hautes etudes de l'Amérique latine, 1959.

Rock, David. *Argentina, 1516-1987: From Spanish Colonization to the Falklands War*. Berkeley: University of California Press, 1985.

———. *Authoritarian Argentina: The Nationalist Movement, Its History and Its Impact*. Berkeley: University of California Press, 1995.

Rodríguez Ayçaguer, Ana María. *Un pequeño lugar bajo el sol: Mussolini, la conquista de Etiopía y la diplomacia uruguaya, 1935–1938*. Montevideo: Ediciones de la Banda Oriental, 2009.

Rodríguez Pastor, Humberto. *Herederos del dragón: Historia de la comunidad china en el Perú*. Lima: Fondo Editorial del Congreso, 2000.

———. *Hijos del Celeste Imperio en el Perú*. Lima: Instituto de Apoyo Agrario, 1989.

Roediger, David R. *The Wages of Whiteness: Race and the Making of the American Working Class*. London: Verso, 1991.

Roig de Leuchsenring, Emilio. *Los problemas sociales en Cuba*. Havana: Federación Nacional de Torcedores de Cuba, 1927.

Rojas, Ricardo. *Eurindia: Ensayo de estética sobre las culturas americanas*. 1922–24. Buenos Aires: Losada, 1951.

———. *Historia de la literatura Argentina: Ensayo filosófico sobre la evolución de la cultura en El Plata*. Vol. 1, *Los gauchescos*. Buenos Aires: Imprenta de Coni Hermanos, 1917.

———. *Los gauchescos*, Vol. 1 of *La literatura Argentina: Ensayo filosófico sobre la evolución de la cultura en El Plata*. Buenos Aires: Imprenta de Coni Hermanos, 1917.

———. *La restauración nacionalista: Informe sobre educación*. Buenos Aires: Ministerio de Justicia e Instrucción Pública, 1909.

Romero, Robert Chao. *The Chinese in Mexico, 1882–1940*. Tucson: University of Arizona Press, 2010.

Romero, Sílvio. "O allemanismo no sul do Brasil." In *Provocações e debates*. Porto: Livraria Chardron, 1910.

Roniger, Luis, and Deby Babis. "Latin American Israelis: The Collective Identity of an Invisible Community." In *Identities in an Era of Globalization and Multiculturalism: Latin America in the Jewish World*, edited by Judit Bokser Liwerant, Eliezer Ben-Rafael, Yossi Gorny, and Raanan Rein, 297–320. Boston: Brill, 2008.

Ruppin, Arthur. *Syrien als Wirtschaftsgebiet*. Berlin: Benjamin Harz, 1920.

Sábato, Hilda. *The Many and the Few: Political Participation in Republican Buenos Aires*. Palo Alto, CA: Stanford University Press, 2001.

Sábato, Hilda, and Juan Carlos Korol. *¿Cómo fue la inmigración irlandesa en Argentina?* Buenos Aires: Plus Ultra, 1981.

Saito, Hiroshi, and Takashi Maeyama, eds. *Assimilação e integração dos japoneses no Brasil*. Petrópolis and São Paulo: Vozes and Editora da USP, 1973.

Sakurai, Célia. "Imigração japonesa para o Brasil: Um exemplo de imigração tutelada (1908–1941)." In *Fazer a América: A imigração em massa para a América Latina*, edited by Boris Fausto, 201–38. São Paulo: Editora da Universidade de São Paulo, 1999.

Salazar Anaya, Deli. *La población extranjera en México (1895–1990): Un recuento con base en los Censos Generales de la Población*. Mexico City: INAH, 1996.

———. "Migration: To Mexico." In *Encyclopedia of Mexico: History, Society, and Culture*, edited by Michael S. Werner, 883–84. Chicago: Fitzroy Dearborn, 1997.

———, ed. *Xenofobia y xenofilia en la historia de México siglos XIX y XX*. Mexico City: Secretaría de Gobernación, 2006.

Salgado Guimarães, Manoel Luís. "Nação e civilização nos trópicos: O Instituto Histórico e Geográfico Brasileiro e o projeto de uma história nacional." *Estudos Históricos*, no. 1 (1988): 5–27.

Samaroo, Brinsley. "The Indian Connection: The Influence of Indian Thought and Ideas on East Indians in the Caribbean." In *India in the Caribbean*, edited by David Dabydeen and Brinsely Samaroo, 43–60. Hertford, UK: Hansib/University of Warwick Centre for Caribbean Studies, 1987.

Sánchez Albornoz, Nicolás. "The Population of Latin America, 1850–1930." In *The Cambridge History of Latin America*. Vol. 4, *c. 1870 to 1930*, edited by Leslie Bethell, 121–52. Cambridge, MA: Cambridge University Press, 1986.

Sandoval García, Carlos. *Otros amenazantes: Los nicaragüenses y la formación de identidades nacionales en Costa Rica*. San José: Universidad de Costa Rica, 2002.

Sanfilippo, Matteo. "Il fascismo, gli emigranti italiani e l'America Latina." *Studi Emigrazione/Migration Studies* 43 (2006): 759–61.

Sarmiento, Domingo Faustino. *Conflicto y armonía de las razas en América*. 1882. Mexico City: Universidad Nacional Autónoma de México, 1978.

Sauveur-Henn, Anne Saint. *Un siècle d'émigration allemande vers l'Argentine 1853–1945*. Cologne: Böhlau, 1995.

Scalabrini Ortiz, Raúl, Alejandro Cattaruzza, Fernando D. Rodríguez, and Sylvia Saítta. *El hombre que está solo y espera: Una biblia porteña*. Buenos Aires: Biblos, 2005.

Scanlon, Arlene Patricia. *Un enclave cultural: Poder y etnicidad en el contexto de una escuela norteamericana en México*. Mexico City: CIESAS, 1984.

Scarzanella, Eugenia. "Cuando la patria llama: Italia en guerra y los inmigrantes italianos en Argentina: identidad étnica y nacionalismo (1936–1945)." *Nuevo Mundo–Mundos Nuevos* 7 (2007): 1–9. http://nuevomundo.revues.org/3735.

———, ed. *Fascistas en América del sur*. Buenos Aires: Fondo de Cultura Económica, 2007.

Schaefer, Jürgen. *Deutsche Militärhilfe an Südamerika: Militär und Rüstungsinteressen in Argentinien, Bolivien und Chile vor 1914*. Düsseldorf: Bertelsmann, 1974.

Scheidt, Eduardo. *Carbonários no Rio da Prata: Jornalistas italianos e a circulação de idéias na Região Platina (1727–1860)*. Rio de Janeiro: Apicuri, 2008.

Schiavone Camacho, Julia María. *Chinese Mexicans: Transpacific Migration and the Search for a Homeland, 1910–1960*. Chapel Hill: University of North Carolina Press, 2012.

Schiller, Nina Glick. "Long-Distance Nationalism." In *Encyclopedia of Diasporas: Immi-*

grant and Refugee Cultures around the World, edited by Melvin Ember, Carol R. Ember, and Ian Skoggard, 570–80. New York: Springer, 2005.

Schmidt, Franz. "Grundlinien der geschichtlichen Entwicklung der deutschen Bildungsarbeit im Ausland." In *Aus deutscher Bildungsarbeit*, vol. 1, edited by Franz Schmidt and Otto Boelitz, 22–30. Langensalza: Beltz, 1927.

Schmidt, Henry C. *The Roots of "Lo Mexicano": Self and Society in Mexican Thought, 1900–1934*. College Station: Texas A&M University Press, 1978.

Schneider, A. *Futures Lost: Nostalgia and Identity among Italian Immigrants in Argentina*. New York: P. Lang, 2000.

Schreiber, George. *Das Auslandsdeutschtum als Kulturfrage*. Münster: Aschendorff, 1929.

Schulze, Frederik. "O discurso protestante sobre a germanidade no Brasil: observações baseadas no periódico Der deutsche Ansiedler, 1864–1908." *Espaço Plural* 9, no. 19 (2008): 21–28.

Schumann, Christoph. "Nationalism, Diaspora and 'Civilizational' Mission: The Case of Syrian Nationalism in Latin America between World War I and World War II." *Nations and Nationalism* 10, no. 4 (2004): 599–617.

Schwarcz, Lilia Moritz. *The Spectacle of the Races: Scientists, Institutions, and the Race Question in Brazil, 1870–1930*. New York: Hill and Wang, 1999.

Scott, Rebecca. *Slave Emancipation in Cuba: The Transition to Free Labor, 1860–1899*. Pittsburgh: University of Pittsburgh Press, 2000.

Secretaría de Gobernación. *Quinto censo de población*, vol. 1: *Resumen General* (Mexico City: Dirección General de Estadística, 1934).

Seigel, Micol. "Beyond Compare: Comparative Method after the Transnational Turn." *Radical History Review* 91 (2005): 62–90.

———. "Cocoliche's Romp: Fun with Nationalism at Argentina's Carnival." *TDR: The Drama Review* 44, no. 2 (2000): 56–83.

Seitenfus, Ricardo. "Ideology and Diplomacy: Italian Fascism and Brazil." *Hispanic American Historical Review* 64, no. 3 (1984): 503–34.

Senkman, Leonardo. *Argentina, la Segunda Guerra Mundial y los refigiados indeseables, 1933–1945*. Buenos Aires: Grupo Editor Latinoamericano, 1991.

———. "Etnicidad e inmigración durante el primer peronismo." *Estudios Interdisciplinarios de América Latina y el Caribe* 3, no. 2 (1992). http://www1.tau.ac.il/eial/index.php?option=com_content&task=view&id=781&Itemid=272.

———. "Nacionalismo e inmigración: La cuestión étnica en las elites liberales e intelectuales argentinas: 1919–1940." *Estudios Interdisciplinarios de América Latina y el Caribe* 1, no. 1 (1990). http://www1.tau.ac.il/eial/index.php?option=com_content&task=view&id=809&Itemid=258.

Sergi, Pantaleone. "Fascismo e antifascismo nella stampa italiana in Argentina: Così fu spenta 'La Patria degli Italiani.'" *Altreitalie* 35 (2007): 4–43.

Seyferth, Giralda. "A colonização alemã no Brasil: Etnicidade e conflito." In *Fazer a América: A imigração em massa para a América Latina*, edited by Boris Fausto, 273–313. São Paulo: Editora da Universidade de São Paulo, 1999.

———. "Colonização e política imigratória no Brasil imperial." In *Políticas migratórias: América Latina, Brasil e brasileiros no exterior*, edited by Teresa Sales and Maria do Rosário R. Salles, 79–110. São Carlos: Editora UDSCar, 2002.

————. "German Immigration and Brazil's Colonization Policy." In *Mass Migration*, edited by Samuel L. Baily and Eduardo José Míguez, 227–44. Wilmington, DE: SR Books, 2003.

————. "Imigração e (re)construção de identidades étnicas." In *Cruzando fronteiras disciplinares: Um panorama dos estudos migratórios*, edited by Helion Póvoa Neto and Ademir Pacelli Ferreira, 17–34. Rio de Janeiro: Revan, 2005.

————. *Nacionalismo e identidade étnica: A ideologia germanista e o grupo étnico teutobrasileiro numa comunidade do vale do Itajaí*. Florianópolis: Fundação Catarinense de Cultura, 1981.

————. "Os imigrantes e a campanha de nacionalização do Estado Novo." In *Repensando o Estado Novo*, edited by Dulce Pandolfi, 199–228. Rio de Janeiro: Editora FGV, 1999.

Sheinin, David Matthew K. "The Diplomacy of Control: United States-Argentine Relations, 1910–1928." PhD diss., University of Connecticut, 1989.

Shepherd, Verene A. "The Dynamics of Afro-Jamaican–East Indian Relations in Jamaica, 1845–1945: A Preliminary Analysis." *Caribbean Quarterly* 32, no. 3–4 (1986): 14–26.

Silva Py, Aurélio da. *A 5ª coluna no Brasil: A conspiração nazi no Rio Grande do Sul*. Porto Alegre: Livraria do Globo, 1942.

Sims, Harold D. *The Expulsion of Mexico's Spaniards, 1821–1936*. Pittsburgh: University of Pittsburgh Press, 1990.

Singh, Kelvin. "Conflict and Collaboration: Tradition and Modernizing Indo-Trinidadian Elites (1917–56)." *New West Indian Guide* 70, no. 3–4 (1996): 229–53.

Siu, Lok C. D. *Memories of a Future Home: Diasporic Citizenship of Chinese in Panama*. Stanford, CA: Stanford University Press, 2005.

Skidmore, Thomas E. *Black into White: Race and Nationality in Brazilian Thought*. Durham, NC: Duke University Press, 1993.

Smith, Anthony. *National Identity*. Harmondsworth, UK: Penguin, 1991.

Sociedade Brasileira de Cultura Japonesa. *Uma epopéia moderna: 80 anos da imigração japonesa no Brasil*. São Paulo: Editora Hucitec, 1992.

Sofer, Eugene. *From Pale to Pampa: A Social History of the Jews of Buenos Aires*. New York: Holmes and Meier, 1982.

Solberg, Carl E. *Immigration and Nationalism, Argentina and Chile, 1890–1914*. Austin: University of Texas Press, 1970.

————. "Mass Migrations in Argentina." In *Human Migration: Patterns and Policies*, edited by William McNeill and Ruth Adams, 146–59. Bloomington: Indiana University Press, 1978.

Soluri, John. *Banana Cultures: Agriculture, Consumption, and Environmental Change in Honduras and the United States*. Austin: University of Texas Press, 2005.

Sorj, Bernardo. "Brazilian Non-Anti-Semite Sociability and Jewish Identity." In *Identities in an Era of Globalization and Multiculturalism: Latin America in the Jewish World*, edited by Judit Bokser Liwerant, Eliezer Ben-Rafael, Yossi Gorny, and Raanan Rein, 151–70. Boston: Brill, 2008.

Spektorowski, Alberto. "Nationalism and Democratic Construction: The Origins of Argentina and Uruguay's Political Cultures in Comparative Perspective." *Bulletin of Latin American Research* 19, no. 1 (2000): 81–99.

Sperber, O. "Die Haltung der südamerikanischen Presse im Weltkrieg." *Mitteilungen des Deutsch-Südamerikanischen Instituts* 4 (1916): 162–65.

Spliesgart, Roland. *"Verbrasilianerung" und Akkulturation: Deutsche Protestanten im brasilianischen Kaiserreich am Beispiel der Gemeinden in Rio de Janeiro und Minas Gerais (1822–1889).* Wiesbaden: Harrassowitz, 2006.

Stanfield, Michael Edward. *Red Rubber, Bleeding Trees: Violence, Slavery, and Empire in Northwest Amazonia, 1850–1933.* Albuquerque: University of New Mexico Press, 1998.

Statistik des Deutschen Reiches. Vol. 360, *Die Bewegung der Bevölkerung in den Jahren 1925 bis 1927.* Berlin: Statistisches Reichsamt, 1930.

Stearns, Peter N. "Nationalisms: An Invitation to Comparative Analysis." *Journal of World History* 8, no. 1 (1997): 57–74.

Stepan, Nancy Leys. *"The Hour of Eugenics": Race, Gender, and Nation in Latin America.* Ithaca, NY: Cornell University Press, 1991.

Stoddard, Lothrop. *The Rising Tide of Color against White World Supremacy.* New York: Charles Scribner's Sons, 1920.

Suter, Jan. "'Pernicious Aliens' and the *Mestizo* Nation: Ethnicity and the Shaping of Collective Identities in El Salvador before the Second World War." *Immigrants & Minorities* 20, no. 2 (2001): 26–57.

Takenaka, Ayumi. "The Japanese in Peru: History of Immigration, Settlement, and Racialization." *Latin American Perspectives* 31, no. 3 (2004): 77–98.

Takeuchi, Marcia Yumi. *O perigo amarelo: Imagens do mito, realidade do preconceito (1920–1945).* São Paulo: Humanitas, 2008.

Tarica, Estelle. *The Inner Life of Mestizo Nationalism.* Minneapolis: University of Minnesota Press, 2008.

Tauber, Eliezer. *The Arab Movements in World War I.* London: Frank Cass, 1993.

———. *The Emergence of the Arab Movements.* London: Frank Cass, 1993.

Taussig, Michael. *Shamanism, Colonialism and the Wild Man: A Study in Terror and Healing.* Chicago: University of Chicago Press, 1987.

Tejeiro, Guillermo. *Historia ilustrada de la colonia china en Cuba.* La Habana: Editorial Hercules, 1947.

———. "Vida agitada, pero ejemplar, del Dr. Sun Yat Sen," *Fraternidad* (March 1939): 4–6.

Tinker Salas, Miguel. *The Enduring Legacy: Oil, Culture, and Society in Venezuela.* Durham, NC: Duke University Press, 2009.

Tobler, Hans Werner, and Peter Waldmann. "German Colonies in South America: A New Germany in the *Cono Sur?*" *Journal of Interamerican Studies and World Affairs* 22 (1980): 227–44.

Tofik Karam, John. *Another Arabesque: Syrian-Lebanese Ethnicity in Neoliberal Brazil.* Philadelphia: Temple University Press, 2007.

Tölölyan, Khachig. "Rethinking Diaspora(s): Stateless Power in the Transnational Moment." *Diaspora* 5, no. 1 (1996): 3–36.

Tramontini, Marcos. *A organização social dos imigrantes: A colônia de São Leopoldo na fase pioneira (1824–1850).* São Leopoldo: Editora UNISINOS, 2000.

Trento, Angelo. "I fasci in Brasile." In *Il fascismo e gli emigrati: la parabola dei Fasci italiani all'estero (1920–1943),* edited by Emilio Franzina and Matteo Sanfilippo, 152–66. Rome: Laterza, 2003.

———. "L'identità dell'emigrato italiano in Brasile attraverso la stampa etnica: Il caso del

Fanfulla, 1893–1940." In *Europe, Its Borders and the Others*, edited by Luciano Tosi, 419–37. Naples: Edizioni Scientifiche Italiane, 2000.

Troconis de Veracoechea, Ermilia. *El proceso de la inmigración en Venezuela*. Caracas: Academia Nacional de la Historia, 1986.

T'sai, Shih-shan H. "Chinese Emigration through Communist Chinese Eyes: An Introduction to the Historiography." *Pacific Historical Review* 43, no. 3 (1974): 395–408.

Tschuida, Nabuya. "The Japanese in Brazil, 1908–1941." PhD diss., University of California Los Angeles, 1978.

Tsou, Jung, and John Lust, eds. *The Chinese Revolutionary Army: A Chinese Nationalist Tract of 1903*. The Hague: Mouton, 1968.

Tucci Carneiro, Maria Luiza, ed. *O anti-semitismo nas Américas*. São Paulo: EDUSP, 2007.

Turits, Richard Lee. "A World Destroyed, A Nation Imposed: The 1937 Haitian Massacre in the Dominican Republic." *Hispanic American Historical Review* 82, no. 3 (2002): 589–635.

U.S. Bureau of the Census. *Fifteenth Census of the United States, 1930, Outlying Territories and Possessions*. Washington, DC: Government Printing Office, 1932.

United States Department of State. *Slavery in Peru: Message from the President of the United States, transmitting report of the secretary of state, with accompanying papers, concerning the alleged existence of slavery in Peru* . . . Washington, DC: Government Printing Office, 1913.

University of the West Indies-Mona, Latin America-Caribbean Center. *The Haiti–Jamaica Connection*. Kingston: Latin American-Caribbean Centre, 2004.

Vallenilla Lanz, Laureano. "Disgregación e integración." In *Cesarismo democrático: Estudios sobre las bases sociológicas de la Constitución efectiva de Venezuela*, by Laureano Vallenilla Lanz and Nikita Harwich Vallenilla. Caracas: Empresa El Cojo, 1919.

Valverde, Estela. "Integration and Identity in Argentina: The Lebanese of Tucumán." In *The Lebanese in the World: A Century of Emigration*, edited by Albert Hourani, Albert Shehadi, and Nadim Shehadi, 313–38. London: I. B. Tauris, 1992.

Vanger, Milton. *The Model Country: José Batlle y Ordóñez or Uruguay, 1907–1915*. Hanover, NH: University Press of New England, 1980.

Vasconcelos, José. *La raza cósmica: Misión de la raza iberoamericana*. Paris: Agencia mundial de librería, 1925.

Velasco, Carlos de. "El problema negro." *Cuba Contemporánea* 1, no.2 (1913): 73–79.

Venezuela, Ministerio de Fomento, Dirección de Estadística. *Sexto Censo de Población, 1936*, vol. 3. Caracas: Tipografía Garrido, 1940.

Verrill, Alpheus Hyatt. *Book of the West Indies*. New York: E. P. Dutton, 1917.

Vila, Pablo. "Tango to Folk: Hegemony Construction and Popular Identities in Argentina." *Studies in Latin American Popular Culture* 10 (1991): 107–39.

Von Martius, Carl Friedrich Philipp. "Bemerkungen über die Verfassung einer Geschichte Brasiliens." *Martius-Staden-Jahrbuch* 50 (2003): 192–212.

Von Mentz, Brígida, Verena Radkau, Beatriz Scharrer, and Guillermo Turner. *Los pioneros del imperialismo alemán en México*. Mexico City: CIESAS, 1982.

Von Tirpitz, Alfred. *Erinnerungen*. Leipzig: Kohler, 1920.

Von zur Mühlen, Patrik. *Fluchtziel Lateinamerika: Die deutsche Emigration, 1933–1945;*

politische Aktivitäten und soziokulturelle Integration. Berlin: Verlag Neue Gesellschaft, 1988.

Wachholz, Wilhelm. *"Atravessem e ajudem-nos"*: A atuação da *"Sociedade Evangélica de Barmen"* e de seus obreiros e obreiras enviados ao Rio Grande do Sul (1864–1899). São Leopoldo: Sinodal, 2003.

Wachtel, Nathan. *The Faith of Remembrance: Marrano Labyrinths*. Philadelphia: University of Pennsylvania Press, 2013.

Wade, Peter. *Race and Ethnicity in Latin America*, 2nd ed. London: Pluto Press, 2010.

Wagner, Reinhardt W. *Deutsche als Ersatz für Sklaven: Arbeitsmigranten aus Deutschland in der brasilianischen Provinz São Paulo 1847–1914*. Frankfurt am Main: Vervuert, 1995.

Wanrooij, Bruno. "The Rise and Fall of Italian Fascism as a Generational Revolt." *Journal of Contemporary History* 22, no. 3 (1987): 401–18.

Ward, Robert DeC. "Our New Immigration Policy." *Foreign Affairs* 3, no. 1 (1924): 99–111.

Warner, W. Lloyd, and Leo Srole. *The Social Systems of American Ethnic Groups*. New Haven, CT: Yale University Press, 1945.

Wehr, Hans. *A Dictionary of Modern Written Arabic*. Ithaca, NY: Spoken Language Services, 1976.

Weidenfeller, Gerhard. *VDA—Verein für das Deutschtum im Ausland. Allgemeiner Deutscher Schulverein, 1881–1918. Ein Beitrag zur Geschichte des deutschen Nationalismus und Imperialismus im Kaiserreich*. Frankfurt: Lang, 1976.

Weinstein, Barbara. "Racializing Regional Difference: São Paulo vs. Brazil, 1932." In *Race and Nation in Modern Latin America*, edited by Nancy P. Appelbaum, Anne S. Macpherson, and Karin Alejandra Rosemblatt, 237–62. Chapel Hill: University of North Carolina Press, 2003.

Whitten, Norman. *Black Frontiersmen: A South American Case*. Cambridge, MA: Schenkman, 1974.

Wilfert, Max. *Die deutsche Auslandsschule in Südamerika und der Krieg*. Buenos Aires: Compañía Sud-Americana de Billetes de Banco, 1918.

Willems, Emilio. *A aculturação dos alemães no Brasil: Estudo antropológico dos imigrantes alemães e seus descendentes no Brasil*. São Paulo: Companhia Editora Nacional, 1946.

Williams, Brackette. *Stains on My Name, War in My Veins: Guyana and the Politics of Cultural Struggle*. Durham, NC: Duke University Press, 1991.

Williams, Glyn. "Welsh Settlers and Native Americans in Patagonia." *Journal of Latin American Studies* 11, no. 4 (1979): 41–66.

Wimmer, Andreas, and Nina Glick Schiller. "Methodological Nationalism and the Study of Migration." *Archives Européennes de Sociologie* 43, no. 2 (2002): 217–40.

Wirth, Louis. *The Ghetto*. Chicago: Chicago University Press, 1926.

Witt, Marcos. *Em busca de um lugar ao sol: Estratégias políticas: imigração alemã, Rio Grande do Sul, século XIX*. São Leopoldo: Oikos, 2008.

Womack, John. "The Mexican Economy during the Revolution, 1910–1920: Historiography and Analysis." *Marxist Perspectives* 1 (1978): 80–123.

Wood, Walter. *Venezuela; Or, Two Years on the Spanish Main*. Middlesbrough, UK: Jordison, 1896.

Wright, Winthrop. *Café con Leche: Race, Class, and National Image in Venezuela*. Austin: University of Texas Press, 1990.

Wynter, Cadence A. "Jamaican Labor Migration to Cuba, 1885–1930, in the Caribbean Context." PhD diss., University of Illinois–Chicago, 2001.

Yankelevich, Pablo. *Deseables o inconvenientes: Las fronteras de la extranjería en el México posrevolucionario*. Mexico City: Bonilla Artigas Editores, 2011.

———. "Hispanofobia y revolución: Españoles expulsados de México (1911–1940)." *Hispanic American Historical Review* 86, no. 1 (2006): 29–59.

———. "Mexico for the Mexicans: Immigration, Sovereignty, and the Promotion of Mestizaje." *Americas* 68, no. 3 (2012): 405–36.

Young, Elliott. *Alien Nation: Chinese Migration in the Americas from the Coolie Era through World War II*. Chapel Hill: University of North Carolina Press, 2014.

Young, George F. W. *Germans in Chile: Immigration and Colonization, 1849–1914*. New York: Center for Migration Studies, 1974.

Yun, Lisa. *The Coolie Speaks: Chinese Indentured Laborers and African Slaves in Cuba*. Philadelphia: Temple University Press, 2008.

Zanatta, Loris. *Del estado liberal a la nación católica: Iglesia y ejército en los orígenes del peronismo, 1930–1943*. Buenos Aires: Universidad Nacional de Quilmes, 1996.

Zanini, Maria Catalina. *Italianidade no Brasil meridional: A construçao da identidade étnica na região de Santa Maria, RS*. Santa Maria: Editora da Universidade Federal de Santa Maria, 2006.

Zanatta, Loris. "I fasci in Argentina negli anni trenta." In *Il fascismo e gli emigrati: La parabola dei Fasci italiani all'estero (1920–1943)*, edited by Emilio Franzina and Matteo Sanfilippo, 140–51. Rome: Laterza, 2003.

Zega, Fulvia. "'Italiani alta la testa!' La presenza del fascismo a São Paulo (1920–1940)." PhD diss., Università degli Studi di Roma Tre.

Zimmermann, Eduardo A. "Racial Ideas and Social Reform: Argentina, 1890–1916." *Hispanic American Historical Review* 72, no. 1 (1992): 23–46.

Zimmermann, Siegfried. *Theodor Wille, 1844–1969*. Hamburg: Hanseatischer Merkur, 1969.

Zolberg, Aristide. *A Nation by Design: Immigration Policy in the Fashioning of America*. New York: Russell Sage Foundation / Harvard University Press, 2006.

Zolov, Eric. *Refried Elvis: The Rise of the Mexican Counterculture*. Berkeley: University of California Press, 1999.

Zorrilla, Luis G. *Relaciones de México con la República de Centro América y con Guatemala*. Mexico: Editorial Porrúa, 1984.

Contributors

Jürgen Buchenau is professor of history and Latin American studies at the University of North Carolina at Charlotte, where he also serves as chair of the Department of History. His publications include *Plutarco Elías Calles and the Mexican Revolution*, the winner of the 2007 Alfred B. Thomas book award from the Southeastern Council of Latin American Studies.

Jeane DeLaney is associate professor of history at St. Olaf College in Northfield, Minnesota. Her articles on Argentine nationalism and national identity have appeared in *Comparative Studies in Society and History*, the *Journal of Latin American Studies*, and several edited volumes.

Nicola Foote is professor of Latin American and Caribbean history at Florida Gulf Coast University. She is the coeditor of *Military Struggle and Identity Formation in Latin America: Race, Nation and Community During the Liberal Period* (with René Harder Horst) and the editor of *The Caribbean History Reader*.

Michael Goebel is professor history at the Freie Universität Berlin. He is the author of *Argentina's Partisan Past: Nationalism and the Politics of History* and the editor of a special edition of *The Bulletin of Latin American Research* on "Nationalism and the Left in Latin America."

Steven Hyland Jr. is assistant professor of history and political science at Wingate University. He is the author of *More Argentine Than You: Syrians and Lebanese in Northwestern Argentina, 1880-1946*.

Jeffrey Lesser is Samuel Candler Dobbs Professor of Latin American History and chair of the History Department at Emory University. His newest book is *Immigration, Ethnicity, and National Identity in Brazil*. He is also the author of the prizewinning *A Discontented Diaspora: Japanese-Brazilians and the Meanings of Ethnic Militancy, 1960–1980* (published in both English and Portuguese).

Kathleen López is associate professor with a joint appointment in the Department of Latino and Caribbean Studies (LCS) and the Department of History at Rutgers, The State University of New Jersey. She is the author of *Chinese Cubans: A Transnational History*. She has also coedited with Evelyn Hu-DeHart a special issue on "Afro-Asia" of the journal *Afro-Hispanic Review* 27, no. 1.

Lara Putnam is professor of Latin American and Caribbean history at the University of Pittsburgh. Her publications include *Radical Moves: Caribbean Migrants and the Politics of Race in the Jazz Age* and *The Company They Kept: Migrants and the Politics of Gender in Caribbean Costa Rica, 1870–1960*.

Raanan Rein holds the Souraski Chair of Iberian and Latin American Studies and is the head of the S. Daniel Abraham Center for International and Regional Studies at Tel Aviv University. Rein is the author and/or editor of more than twenty-five books and several dozen articles in academic journals. He is also a coeditor of the journal *Estudios Interdisciplinarios de América Latina y el Caribe*.

Stefan Rinke is professor of Latin American history at the Institute of Latin American Studies, Freie Universität Berlin. Among his most recent publications is *Latin America and the First World War*.

Frederik Schulze is Wissenschaftlicher Mitarbeiter (assistant professor) of Latin American History at Westfälische Wilhelms-Universität Münster. He is the author of *Auswanderung als nationalistisches Projekt: "Deutschtum" und Kolonialdiskurse im südlichen Brasilien (1824–1941)* and the co-author of *Kleine Geschichte Brasiliens* (with Stefan Rinke).

Index

Africa, 17, 39, 50, 54, 55, 189, 234, 237

African: ancestry, 8, 32, 36, 49, 54, 60, 82, 93, 95, 115, 188, 197, 205, 216; descended populations, 141, 187, 192, 200, 219, 294; diaspora, 17, 18; migrants, 33, 93, 123, 150, 197, 282; religion, 217, 225; slaves, 2, 36, 68, 117, 133, 144, 182, 184, 185, 219

Afro-Caribbeans: communities, 47, 227; immigrants, 38, 40, 44, 48, 50, 189, 190, 206; nationalism, 55, 56; women, 217, 300. *See also* British Caribbean; West Indians

Afro-Latin Americans, 122, 219, 228, 294

Alberdi, Juan Bautista, 72, 94, 96, 112, 122, 136, 147, 285, 308

Amazon: Arab migration to, 146; Caribbean migration to, 206–7, 209–10, 214–15, 283; Jewish migration to, 25, 150–52; rubber boom in, 14, 207, 232, 285

Americans, 15, 68, 198, 220; African Americans, 68, 297; in Caribbean, 39, 46; in Ecuador, 211; in Mexico, 86, 191, 201; in Panama, 225; in Venezuela, 222

Anglo-Saxons, 124, 220–21, 249, 291, 296

Anti-Semitism, 8, 18, 108, 111, 149–50, 155, 289

Arabian nationalism, 16, 19, 22, 141, 256–76, 282

Arabs: in Argentina, 11, 158n16, 257, 259, 261–62, 264–68, 270–76; in Brazil, 11, 118, 142, 146–52, 257, 260–63, 265, 267, 269–70, 272, 275; in Caribbean, 43–44, 47, 57; in Central America, 11; in Ecuador, 11; and whitening, 297, 301. *See also* Arabian nationalism; Ottoman Empire

Argentina: Arabs in, 11, 44, 147–48, 158n16, 257, 259, 261–62, 264–68, 270–76, 292–93;

conflict with Brazil, 119, 121, 285; demographic transformation and immigration, 2, 10, 12–13, 66–67, 74, 76, 91, 93, 95–96, 104, 111, 148, 189, 285, 290, 302; ethnic violence in, 8, 150, 175–76, 289; French in, 12; Germans in, 11, 13, 22, 76, 160–64, 166, 168–69, 173, 175, 179nn22,36,37, 296; Irish in, 12; Italians in, 8, 22, 24n19, 234–53; Jewish migrants in, 11, 21, 110, 142–43, 146, 148–49, 154–55, 284, 292; national identity, 18–19, 24n10, 50, 93–94, 97–98, 100–111, 143, 148, 249–50, 257; Spanish in, 12, 102; women immigrants, 299–300

Armenians, 1–2, 11, 14, 16, 262, 264, 277n26, 297

Asia, 25n30, 38, 47, 57, 77, 128, 130, 153, 182–83, 189

Asians: assimilation of, 155, 186, 200, 296; in Brazil, 117, 128, 130–31, 133, 134; in the Caribbean, 41, 43–46, 49, 54, 59–60, 186, 190, 192, 197; discrimination against, 8, 32, 41, 44–45, 46, 49, 54, 59–60, 130, 152, 186, 190, 196, 198, 203n34, 284, 294, 298; indentured workers, 2, 14, 47, 154, 183, 201n4, 282–83; merchants, 55; in Mexico, 72, 77; in Peru, 186, 192

Assimilation: assimilationist policy, 7, 85, 87, 111, 115, 130–31, 133, 207–8, 224–25, 292; by immigrants, 99, 115, 161, 170, 235, 240, 289–90, 293–94, 297, 299; rejection of, 125, 128, 134, 167, 192, 291; theories of 3–6, 18, 26n60, 131, 227, 241, 253, 281, 284, 289, 291, 297, 301

Atlantic, 2, 10, 44, 49, 53, 74, 91, 146, 221

Australia, 32, 38, 45, 50, 55

Aztec, 74, 82, 146, 296